STORIES OF OUR LIVES

STORIES OF OUR LIVES

AN ARCHIVE OF KENYAN QUEER NARRATIVES

FROM AN ARCHIVE OF NARRATIVES COLLECTED FOR THE 'STORIES OF OUR LIVES' RESEARCH PROJECT (2013 - 2018)

THE NEST COLLECTIVE

THE NEST ARTS COMPANY LIMITED

The names and characteristics of individuals and places in this book have been changed and/or redacted for the sake of anonymity.

Warning: This book is not for sale to persons under 18 in Kenya.

www.thisisthenest.com

ISBN: 978-0-9967048-9-2 (First Edition)
ISBN: 978-0-9967048-0-9 (Ebook)
ISBN: 978-0-9967048-5-4 (Second Edition)

Design, production and editing by the Nest Collective.

First published in 2015 by the Nest Collective.
First printing August 2015.
Second edition printing August 2020.

For our love Solo, and our love Bethsheba;
we miss you, and we can't wait to see you again,

For all the wonderful people who
shared their stories with us,

And for you, who always thought you were alone

CONTENTS

PREFACE

DEAR READER:

THE BOOK YOU ARE HOLDING shouldn't exist, because the people in this book are said not to exist. If you believe what you've read, seen and heard in the news, homosexuality does not exist in Kenya, and the stories collected in this book must be some grand fiction.

If you do believe that queer people exist in Kenya, then the people in this book might disappoint you. They don't fit into the narrow African Homosexual Story that characterizes the African Homosexual as a creature of the night, promiscuous, diseased and abused-when-young, a corrupter of innocent children, and a godless, anti-family, anti-men, anti-society separatist.

Some of the people in this book were raised by single parents, and some came from 'traditional' nuclear families. Some of the people are deeply religious, and some are not. Some of the people in this book had traumatic experiences when they were young, and others can only count paper-cuts as their most traumatic childhood experience. Some of the people in this book are HIV positive, and some are not. Human beings rarely fit neatly into stereotypes, and that's why we wanted to work on this project.

We wanted to find out what being queer in Kenya is actually like. We found happy queers, sad ones, proud ones, broken ones, brave ones and silly ones. We found lovers, liars, dreamers and cynics.

We found parents who didn't kick their queer kids out, and we found pastors and imams who were open to the idea that being queer doesn't mean you don't know God. We found friends who became allies.

What we found were human beings. Of all kinds.

DEAR ANTI-GAY BRIGADE:

Be advised now that queer people have always been here, and will always be here. You cannot govern love and intimacy, bodies and skin, kisses and sex. Be advised that for all your misguided effort, some boys will continue to love other boys, and some girls will continue to love other girls. Some will even love both boys and girls. Some people will continue to not look or act like you expect them to, and love will always prevail in all its shapes and sizes.

And for the record, 'gayism' and 'lesbianism' are not real words. Stop it.

DEAR KENYAN HOMOSEXUAL:

You are not alone. Whether you're a man or a woman, whether you're somewhere in between or somewhere beyond; you exist. You might feel small and fragile in the face of Statutes, Laws, Caucuses, Stones, Insults, a Church-State and Family that tries to deny your existence, but you exist. You must never let them take that away.

Exist. Breathe. Love and Be Loved. Fuck. Thrive. Apologize to no one for your existence.

Even though we do not know you, and even though we didn't get to meet you and hear your story, understand what we mean when we say: you are not alone, and this is your story, too.

May you always walk in light and providence,

The Nest Collective
Dccember 2018

INTRODUCTION

The popular representations of persons identifying as Lesbian, Gay, Bisexual, Transgender and Intersex—in mainstream media spaces, policy conversations or religious thought in Kenya—are those of redacted parodies, which are too narrowly constructed to even begin to intelligently engage with the complexities of human sexuality and identity.

The caricature of the sexless, high-pitched male fashionista from a Latin American soap on television, the faceless, disease-spreading, HIV-infected gay male, the recruiting paedophile and the godless male prostitute targeting tourists at the Coast, only serve to deepen mistrust and justify violence against queer Kenyans. The consistent refusal to acknowledge that women do not have to belong to men is visited very dangerously on lesbian and bisexual women. This gives increased room for the deeper entrenchment of rape culture in an already self-actualised patriarchy. It also contributes to the even higher levels of violence, abuse and harassment faced by trans and gender non-conforming folk, who are punished severely by general society for refusing to conform to and behave according to cis gender socializations.

This problematized publicness imagines LGBTI persons as public subjects whose identities are formed, articulated and resisted in the public, and whose only social value is that of being a subject of conflict between the Right and the Left.

On June 30, 2013, we began collecting and archiving the stories of persons identifying as gay, lesbian, bisexual, transgender and intersex from Kenya. We called this project 'Stories of Our Lives'. Over a period of two years—with the help of large and small organizations across the country—we interviewed more than 250 individuals from towns all over the country. Armed with a short list of questions we developed as a guide, we asked respondents to talk to us about their growing up, love lives, their families and their plans for the future.

Interviews sometimes took the shape of cathartic confessionals. Some lasted a perfunctory twenty minutes, others stretched over hours. Accustomed to questions about their sexual habits from health researchers who were more interested in their public health contribution as disease vectors or 'key high-risk populations', most respondents told us, "No one has ever asked me that."

Somewhere in the middle of this process, we decided to make some short films based on the stories we were hearing. The resulting film—Stories of Our Lives—was released in September 2014, and went on to receive warm and conscientious engagement from film festivals and audiences in places as far-flung as Toronto, London, Rio de Janeiro and Berlin, but was subsequently banned from private or public screenings anywhere in Kenya, where the Kenya Film and Classification Board deemed it as 'promoting homosexuality' in Kenya. The film went on to win the Berlinale Teddy Jury Prize at the 2015 Berlin International Film Festival and has since screened at festivals in more than 80 countries around the world and won numerous awards, but is yet to screen in its home country. While only a few of the individual stories could lend themselves to the restricted film, we have committed a greater part of the archive to this book, now updated with new stories collected in 2018.

We could never have guessed, back in 2013, what it would mean for a film which had always been meant for small-scale LGBTQ community viewing, reflection and debate, to be released on a mainstream, public, global stage, and how that would disrupt every plan we had for our selves, and our personal, artistic and professional lives.

Few things can create bonds between a group of people like jumping off a cliff together, not knowing what lies at the bottom, not sure if you'll discover that you have wings, or crash and burn instead. That's pretty much what happened from the moment we released Stories Of Our Lives - our first feature film as the Nest Collective. Releasing a very queer film that unashamedly proclaims that God loves queer people and queer Africans deserve love is not something that you can retract or even hide from the public eye. We had done all we could to prepare, we'd gone home and (for those of us who are queer) talked to our families about this thing we had made, we put our affairs in order as Kenyans and as an institution, but nothing was enough to prepare us for what was to come.

Having to be queer, or queer-associated and affirming in public is a vastly different thing from doing it quietly, in direct messages and WhatsApp inboxes where nobody has to know. When Stories came out, we in the collective really learned belonging from each other, because we were the only people we could belong to at that time. Our families needed time to understand why any of us had done this thing. Our friends needed time to re-commit to our friendships and create a new normal with our publicly-out selves. The notoriety was catching, like an illness, and we could understand why people had to make their choices judiciously around how near they could come to us without noticeable proximity to those people who had made that film. Even the more visible people from the queer movement needed time to understand our politics and decide whether we were allies or oppression-tourists.

Ours is a society where a public moment for one queer person causes private ripples in the lives of many queer people. For instance, the very public coming out of Kenyan author Binyavanga Wainaina tangentially caused ripples in the lives of many other queer people, including coming-outs, public harassments, people being thrown out of rental housing and intense passive aggression from friends and family. Some of those ripples were mentioned by the people we spoke to for the first edition of this book. The buzz about the Stories of Our Lives film was no different.

Additionally, darker rumours began to swirl in Kenyan media: that we had made pornography—and not just any pornography, but fulminantly gay pornography. That we were seeking asylum abroad. That we had 'won the golden ticket'- we were being accused of weaponizing the controversies of queerness in Africa to gain fame and notoriety in the film and wider art world. We were not the first to have this accusation levelled at us, and neither would we be the last, but that did not stop the accusation from being hurtful, especially when we considered the deeply intimate story collecting sessions we had had with the many tender souls whose spirits and stories were the DNA of our little film. We had shared deep, true moments—laughter, philosophies, life hacks, tears, trauma and resurrections. The accusations came from both heterosexual and queer identifying people alike, in different contexts and ways.

While all of this was going on, there was still a significant contingent of people who had read about the film after its world premier at the Toronto International Film Festival, and appreciated its positive reviews in several publications, and were eager to watch the film back at home even as it continued its rounds at film festivals all over the world. That marked our first interaction with the Kenya Film Classification Board (KFCB), because in order to screen a film at a cinema you need one of 4 public ratings: General Exhibition, Parental Guidance, unsuitable for those under the age of 16, and unsuitable for those under the age of 18. Being unable to host thousands of small screenings at our office, which was quite small, we had to consider a public screening at a cinema, which necessitated the conversation with the KFCB.

After a dramatic back and forth with them, which should really be an essay all on its own, our film was summarily restricted, which was an effective ban on any public or private screenings anywhere within the borders of the country. A conversation with law enforcement then began, which on paper was about the criminality of shooting a film without approval or licensing, but actually about how unnamed people were displeased with the waves we were causing and about the kind of content we had made. This was another place where the word 'pornography' was used, but never written down because the Board knew there was no context in which the film we made could be considered pornographic. Collective member and executive producer George Gachara was arrested and put on trial for shooting a film without a licence. This case was eventually conditionally dropped after several court appearances (meaning that they reserved the right to take it up again at any time, should we violate the ban or cause further disturbance).

There are few things as frustrating as having a conversation about an absent thing. George often describes our film as being in exile, and as our in-house eternal optimist (every art collective needs one), declares with certainty that most exiles eventually find their way home. One way in which the stories from the project did remain with us was in the first edition of this book that we published some months afterwards, with which we were able to share many more from the over 250 direct stories we had collected during our tour. We were able to share diverse reflections with more nuance, and the first edition of this book became an underground favourite among many. We received many happy reports that some people had bought a second or third copy because the previous ones had been spirited away by eager readers. We also sent a few copies of the books out to the groups of people who had shared their hearts and lives with us, and they were so excited to see themselves, their friends and communities in the stories they had so kindly given to us.

We've learned many things since we released the film and this book, and been the custodians of the wider Stories of Our Lives project that aims to document queer lives qualitatively as the normal and unnecessarily interrupted existences that they are. We have learned to listen carefully to people who are framing the discourse of black and African queer people, Global South queers and queers of colour. The Western world tends to use these narratives, as it has with many other things, to label African queerness as primitive, Euro-inspired, and subject to violence - in the process erasing all the things that African queerness is. For us, this Eurocentric framing manifested in the many interviewers who asked us loaded, broad-stroke questions about homophobia in Africa, and expect us to respond with tales of bloodbaths and our own brave escapes. They were always disappointed to be told that we were not in immediate danger, and several would sulk at our reminders that there was still violence against non-heteronormative people within the Europe and the Americas. We always had our most constructive, mutual, healing conversations with black people and queer people of colour on the Continent and in the Diaspora, and with their allies who were conscious and aware of who they were in the world and what their histories meant in the present.

It is unavoidable that it has been the support and resources from the Global North that have been key in sustaining some very important conversations that have been crucial for the survival of queer people in continental Africa and in the diaspora. It is, however, also important to note the quiet, unending work being done by African LGBTQIA+ people to expand space for themselves, whether it is supported from outside or not. This work has been on activist frontlines, in small urban and rural community groups, by brave mothers and fathers in hostile neighbourhood residential associations or even church meetings, by open-minded employers in workplaces, by African academics, civil society workers, community health workers, sex workers, drag and gender play performers, relatives, friends and children of queer people, and many, many others. This has been in posters, in songs, in every phrase that has had the spirit and intention of inclusion, in every club bouncer who has seen a queer couple kiss and moved against their attackers and not against them, in every deep state maneuver that has moved the pointer away from direct violence on queer, trans, non-binary and gender non-conforming people towards something else for people to focus public outrage on. The work is done every time feminists intersect their struggle with that of queer people, and vice versa (and when we openly celebrate the queer and trans feminists who build bridges between these groups). The work is done in every personal conversation in which people can ask respectful questions, and do their own reading that cares more about lives than about, "how does it work when two men or two women...," or the even more irritating, "who is the man?".

The work is done every time people laugh out loud at the foolishness of 'Adam and Steve' as a church allegory against homosexuality (and perhaps gently pointing out that having exceptions makes the idea of God's love moot and conditional). The work is done by pastors and imams who know and still welcome, who may themselves be silently queer, and who know that tolerance is the necessary, morally exhausting, step before acceptance and active celebration. This work is woven thickly into the general silences of Kenyans and other Africans even around heterosexual sex, dating back to the theft of our voices and agency during colonialism, and which many have been working tirelessly to restore. The work is pan-African when it takes into account the similarities in struggles across borders, negotiates the nuances in different cultural expressions, recognises that we may have a long history of queerness in our ethnic and pre-colonial groupings, documented or not. This work seeks to see what new selves we can dream up as we redeem the redeemable in our old customs.

To diminish these and many other extensive engagements and reduce them to "Which country in Africa can have a Pride March" or "is Africa the most homophobic continent?" (as seen on CNN) is false and misleading. The deep and unseen work is actually where the activistic work can be rooted. Every story in the Stories of Our Lives book and film came directly from someone's life and existence, proving that real life is much stranger and more glorious than fiction, but also more palpable, more ordinary and thus much more resonant with truth. The truth being, for instance, that the idea of gay marriage as a goal that queer Africans can and should fight for is absolutely off the table. Nobody can care to fight for marriage when the fight to be alive has still not been won. Queer couples in Africa have been quietly finding ways to function, pass on property and negotiate lives without these state-formalised ways of engagement for decades. State recognition that goes beyond the illusory, fairy tale romance of marriage into the nitty-gritty of inclusive laws at every level to severely punish discrimination and harassment at all levels, and to value queer people, guardianship, parenting and partnership would be much more useful at this stage than any debate about state-sanctioned marriage.

Further, there are so many people who don't see themselves or the way they live and love described within the so-called LGBTQIA+ alphabet soup. In urban areas in Kenya, the question, "how do you identify" had some clear answers, but questions such as "who are you attracted to" and "who do you have sex with" proved much more useful. Many queer Kenyans are post-identity in that general sense, and while education about the different ways people express themselves and live has been useful to give some people context into their own lives and those of others, the wider question of belonging here has a completely different flavour. In this agrarian, pre-industrial contemporary (and even with the societal fractures brought about by urban migration within macroeconomic fragilities), people still have deep connections to family, clan, tribe and society. These could be as strong or even stronger than any affinity to a wider queer community. Thus, the idea of trading one set of belongings for another, especially when public queerness is continually fraught with violence, pain, heartache, tension, conflict and its own class hierarchies, is not a conversation people are ready to have.

We've had honest debates about how far respectability and 'proper presentation' can go towards keeping queer people safe. Some people have been open about the difficult compromises that come with changing one's appearance and mannerisms to become more accepted at home by parents or at work by employers, and the attendant problematic safeties that come with that. Some have discussed the increased willingness by religious leaders and other community influencers to speak up for them when they look 'normal'—for example when femme-identifying men cut off their long locks of hair and wipe off their makeup in order become junior elders who sit and negotiate the place of all queers in a community. This process has strong allegories to similar processes within our tribal contexts, and the queer people who have made these sacrifices have not done so in vain.

Their experiences and the data they have collected shows less violence against queer and trans people, and more anecdotes of acceptance and dialogue. Who is to say which methods are right or wrong? People are doing what works for them, and what gets the results they want, and making it up as they go along. Nobody has our blueprint ready—we are having to design our own. What is a Pride March, or what is gay marriage, when queer people can not yet walk on the streets unencumbered and unharassed? Give us the privilege of being usual, of defining normal. Give us the privilege of being invisible on our own terms. Give us the closets we choose, and the publicnesses we choose, where we can speak of our loves if we want, and where we can be private if we want. May our celibacies and activities have as little bearing on our characters, work and job outputs as they do on the lives and outcomes of heterosexual people. Queer people have never wanted what have been controversially called 'special laws' or even 'special treatment'. There is a deep betrayal when a society forces them over and over to fight to just get out of their homes without being asked more questions than any other person.

We just want to live.

Many other societies have had the luxury of being able to move from one step to the next. For African societies, time has been compressed, and everything is in fast forward. "Catch up, Africa," the world says to our 'developing nations'. We're having to do many things all at the same time. We are industrializing and developing a digital and knowledge economy at the same time. We are constructing massive metropolises and basic urbanisation projects within meters of each other. Women are struggling for evolved political representation and having reproductive rights rolled back at the same time. Nobody has a blueprint for African societies. We are having to design our own.

As the Nest Collective, we continue to ask ourselves many questions: why everything had to be so political, and whether we had really chosen this wild adventure. Whether the queer ones among us are going to be fine. Whether the straight and undeclared ones among us are going to be fine. We have continued to mix and meld works in film, fashion, literature and music, and we continue to ask our city and our country to allow us to make other things and start other conversations that also look for freedom, love and safety from other angles.

There is no blueprint, we design our own.

For a queer book, the contents of this book are ironically quite 'usual' or 'normal'. For all their subjective drama, there is a comfort in the normalcy of lovers' tiffs, earth-shattering breakups, tearful reunions, family squabbles, quiet meditations, playing truant from school, embarrassing moments around crushes, the tension in job interviews and the exhausting ritual of kitchen chores. There is nothing usual or normal, however, about the level of surveillance, harassment and violence faced by queer people in Kenya. This is far above any ordinary, especially when conflated with being women or of femme identity, being public, being trans, being darker-skinned, being less straight or cis passing, being poor and less influential, being less educated, having alternative beliefs etc.

In the second edition of this book, we are excited to include more stories from trans and gender non-conforming people, who have stepped both away from and towards conversations about gender and sexuality debates for infinite valid reasons, and who have challenged and been victorious over the idea of citizenship by documentation at its very root. We speak to older queer people who are reflecting on their lives, who let us know what has changed about being non-heteronormative in this current age versus when they were younger. And we look, as always, at the beautiful, the tragic, the funny, the basic and the glorious, because everything here is usual and normal, and everything but.

Here then, is the Stories Of Our Lives book—an attempt to explore the consciousness, ambition and expression of many queer Kenyans in their daily interactions with family, friends, schools, workplace, religion and ideas of the future, and in diverse social contexts in Kenya. his can be useful in expanding the imagination of and about queer people in Kenya.

Through these stories, the self-representing queer Kenyan grants the reader permission to explore private and intimate worlds—where the vagaries of queer publicness, silence, intimacy, militancy and love happen.

Other than redacting names and places to protect the identities of individuals, we have left these precious stories untouched, given to us in strength and power with full agency, BECAUSE IT IS IN THAT EXACT SAME SPIRIT THAT WE PASS THEM ALONG TO YOU.

STORIES OF OUR LIVES

MEMORIES

I HAD A CRISIS OF FAITH at some point. When I was in school, my friends in Christian Union used to encourage me and tell me, "There's a reason why you're queer and struggling with this. There's a reason for everything."

I couldn't understand it.

I graduated top of my class in law school, I got job offers from big law firms and turned them down for a Christian law firm, because I wanted 'the fellowship of brethren'. They found out I was queer and the work environment became very hostile. I had to quit, there was no love there. I wanted to go away from my life.

I spent two years travelling the world, and living simply. I went across Africa. I went to Kismayu[1] on a merchant ship. I slept in strangers' houses, churches and mosques. I was trying to find myself. I didn't know what to do with myself anymore.

On the first day, I went to Industrial Area[2]. I had a rucksack with carrots and water—I used to love carrots a lot those days—and a jacket. I waited for a cargo train, an empty one. I jumped in, and I slept until it reached Voi[3]. I woke up, and there were people doing morning devotions in churches nearby.

I went to one church and sat at the back. There was a woman there who looked very pious. I connected with her, for some reason. She looked like she was struggling with something. After the prayers, I introduced myself to her. She was a teacher, she told me her name was Sarah. She took me to her place, we had breakfast and I helped her prepare her kids for school. She told me to stay, and I refused. She gave me some money and some food, and I hitch-hiked on a truck, got to Changamwe[4] and walked all the way to Mombasa.

In the evening, I was trying to hitch a ride on Moi Avenue—the one with the tusks[5]. I came across a street family, and I joined them for a while. We sat down and ate all the food Sarah had

---

1. Also, Kismayo; port city in Somalia.
2. Industrial zone located in the south of Nairobi.
3. Market town approximately 327km from Nairobi.
4. Small industrial town that lies right next to Mombasa—Kenya's second largest city, and an important port and tourism centre.
5. Named after Kenya's second president, Moi Avenue is Mombasa city's main avenue, and known as the site of two pairs of giant aluminium elephant tusks.

given me. Then I wandered into the Old Town[6]. Some guy in a *tuk-tuk* told me I was walking in a dangerous area. He told me to get in with him. We drove around and he told me all kinds of stories.

He told me he had a gun, because of the insecurity. He told me about his life, he told me about homosexuality in Mombasa. We stopped at a coffee house by the port and drank coffee, and just stared at docking ships. He asked me to sleep at his place, I refused and decided to sleep on the street. The next morning, he passed by and took me to Nyali Bridge[7]. He told me I'd be fine there, that I looked like someone who could be picked up if I waved down cars.

Two hours later, some woman stopped. She looked Arab. I got into her car, and we talked a lot. She thought I was a beach boy, and she didn't understand what I was doing in Mombasa. We got to Watamu[8], and she asked me to accompany her to her place. I knew she wanted to have sex, so I refused. I left her, and spent two weeks on the beach. I slept there, and I sold my clothes in return for food. I met a guy called Hamisi, who was really cool. I really liked him, but he didn't know I was queer. Later on, he discovered I was sleeping on the beach and he took me to his place.

It was nasty. It was like a whorehouse. Many men would come and sleep there in the evenings. Sometimes we all had to leave when one of the men came home with a woman. We never talked about whether any of the men were sleeping with other men, but there were undertones of that. For them, it was purely business. Most of them preferred being on top, there was no romance. One day, Hamisi was accompanying a rich woman to Lamu[9], and he asked her if I could come along. I joined them. As soon as we got to Lamu, we split up. I went to Riadha mosque—it's a famous, old mosque next to the market square.

The imam there was nice. There were travellers from across East Africa in the mosque; Sudanese people, illegal immigrants,

6. The oldest settlement in Mombasa city.
7. Concrete girder bridge connecting the city of Mombasa on Mombasa Island to the mainland.
8. Small town approximately 105km from Mombasa.
9. Small town on Lamu island, one of the oldest Swahili settlements in East Africa.

people who wanted to learn Islam, people who wanted to reform their lives. They all slept in the mosque, so I joined them. I spent two weeks there, learning Islam, frolicking on the island. I told the imam that I wanted to go to Somalia. He thought I was disturbed, and he asked me why I wanted to go there. I told him I didn't know why, that I just wanted to go there and do some charity work in Kismayu, because I'd heard there was a war there.

I didn't have money, or any identification documents. He wrote me a note in Arabic and told me if I gave that note to whoever I met, I would be treated kindly. I got into a merchant ship and spent two days on board. I overcame my fear of large water bodies during that time. I got to Somalia, and I visited an orphanage that was run by Catholic sisters. They were taking care of children orphaned by war. I spent a week there, cleaning, teaching football with cans on the street.

There were Kenyan lorries at the market square in Kismayu—they used to bring supplies. I made friends with one of the drivers who was called Kamau. I hitched a ride back to Kenya with him. He dropped me in Garissa[10], but I wanted to go back to Mombasa. I hitched another ride and got back to Mombasa. I pawned a camera I'd been given for my graduation at a pawn shop in Nyali and got 1,500 shillings for it. I used that money to get myself a bus ticket back to Nairobi, because I was tired. By then my friends were looking for me, and I learned that my sister was pregnant. I wanted to be back by the time she was giving birth.

I came back to Nairobi, broke as fuck. But I didn't stay long. I went to the Democratic Republic of Congo (DRC) and fell in love with an ex-child soldier. We had an understanding. We couldn't use words to describe it. It wasn't love, there was no emotion. It was just sex. Unprotected sex. Violent sex, sometimes. I think I was just suicidal at the time.

I knew that he was part of a militia group, but we'd never talk about it because he was my way out of DRC and I was scared. That's when I started doing drugs, because I couldn't handle the things that were going on there. He would come back to camp, drunk as fuck, and brag about all these horrible things they did.

---

10. Small town located in the former North Eastern Province of Kenya.

It was dehumanizing, and that's when I decided I was going to go back home. I was done with finding myself.

I really, really wanted to go to the Nyiragongo Crater[11], and he took me there with his friends. That day I was certain that I wanted to disappear. The Nyiragongo Crater has a crater lake in the centre—a two-kilometre radius of boiling, red lava. You can walk to the edge of the lake, and you can jump in if you like. People do that. I wanted to do that.

I didn't do it, though. That night, I danced with my demons. I looked them in the eye, and told them, "Fuck you. I'm done running."

So I CAME BACK HOME.

–

I AM A MALE-TO-FEMALE TRANSGENDER. I've always felt different since I was young. I never identified as male, ever. Growing up, I never really knew real my parents. I've been in different foster homes—three of them so far. It has been tough.

The first foster family thought I was a girl. When I was eight or ten, I started exhibiting feminine characteristics; growing breasts and hips. My foster parents were afraid. They said, "This is an omen. *Hatumwezi*." We can't deal with her.

When I was in foster family two, I introduced myself as male, even though I didn't look male at all. The mother of that family was OK with me, but the father wasn't for the idea. They took me to Nairobi Hospital, where I was given some injections, and I started to develop masculine features. I broke my voice—I had such a soprano—and I used to have long hair. I had to shave it. I became very slim and I started doing heavy lifting work so that my muscles would develop.

After a while—as much as they wanted to change me into a man—I got tired of trying to be a man. I was still more drawn to being feminine. Finally they gave up and the father threw me out and I had to look for another family to live in. I couldn't tell

11. Mount Nyiragongo, an active volcano located inside Virunga National Park in the Democratic Republic of Congo.

anyone the truth, so I lied about myself until another family took me in.

The mother of the third foster family was nice, she understood and supported me. But the husband was against it. He said I'd spoil his children, and he didn't want me around. Mostly, it's the men in the foster families who were against my being transgender. The mothers don't mind. They listen, maybe because they give birth to children themselves. You never know what kind of child you'll get, so women are more understanding.

His wife continued to support me, she found me a sponsor who was willing to pay for my hormone therapy and counselling.

But after a while—I don't know whether the father filled her with gossip—the sponsor told me, "You're misbehaving, and you're disrespecting your parents. You're engaging in prostitution,"—which is something I'd never done in my life—"If you can't listen to your own parents, who am I to intervene? I'm going to stop sponsoring you."

Which is what she did.

Back then, the community used to see that I looked male but I was dressing feminine. I've never been physically assaulted, just verbal. They used to insult me and threaten to lynch me. I couldn't leave the house during the day. I'd leave at night, and even then I'd cover myself. If I walked openly, people would recognize me and follow me. After I started hormone therapy, I started presenting feminine characteristics and people were not able to identify my gender.

Now, the community treats me much better—except for those who knew me long ago. Those ones say, "*Ah! Yule ni mwanaume, kwenda kudungwa sindano. Anafanya mambo ya Kichina...*" Ah! That one is a man, he's got injections of these Chinese products...

Such gossip.

It's much less these days, but a while back, it was hard. My community is very religious, it's a very Muslim town. Yet they are the same ones—those sheikhs—at night, and in the dark, they call you and flirt with you. During the day, when you meet—he passes you like he doesn't know you and—if he's with his friends—he points you out and says, "*Ile ni shoga, ishikeni.*" That one is a fag, catch it.

These sheikhs, these pastors. All of them, these big people in Government. But they don't want people to know. So they attack those of us who present openly. At night, they're gay—but I don't know why they find the idea of accepting themselves so hard.

The challenges I have are just making ends meet. I can't get a job now. I don't have an ID because I don't know what to identify as. I've gone four times with my documents, but every time they send me back. They say, "You can't be male."

I've even tried to open a bank account, and they said, "If you come here, there's going to be a problem. You don't look male."

They even told me I could be a security risk because if I ever tried to use an ATM machine, I'd insert my card which identifies me as male, but the camera on the ATM would show that I'm female. That's what they told me. I don't know if it's true. I tried two banks, and they refused.

Even getting my birth certificates was so, so hard. For one, I was born in Mombasa—as far as I know—but every time I'd go there to search for my documents, they couldn't be found. So, it's been tough to trace my documents and my real identity. Who my parents are, and how come they left me or threw me away—whatever the case was. It's been tough.

Sometimes they even say I'm not Kenyan; that I'm Ethiopian and I should go back. Accessing services in the hospital. They tell me to sit down and wait. Then people arrive after me and are served and they leave me behind. When I ask what's wrong, they say, "Ah! You wait," and they don't explain. Then come closing time, you see them close up and go. You ask them what's wrong and they say, "You come back tomorrow."

That's what they did to me when I was looking for my ID. So, I can't come out at night. I can't get a job, I can't go to school—because in Kenya, once you turn eighteen you must get an ID card to identify yourself. Even simple things like getting a room in a hotel, they ask, "*Kitambulisho?*" ID?

I crammed a fake ID number which I use whenever I have to fill a form that asks for an ID number. Sometimes, I'm lucky when registering for a short job and they don't ask to actually see my ID card.

Many men are really curious about transgender women—I don't know why. When some of them find out I'm trans, they want to have sex with me. There's a big market for male-to-female trans in sex work. If they have money, I accept to have sex with them and get paid. I don't know whether to call that prostitution or what *[laughs]*. There's a ready market. I don't look for my clients, they look for me. In fact, I can't even walk around outside because they start to pester me. Those encounters help me with a little money to keep going; for food, clothes and hormones.

I don't have a specific religion. *Ukija 'bwana asifiwe', sijambo, ukija 'Allahu akbar' ni ndani, ukija kwa kihindi twende nalo.* If you come with 'praise God', I don't mind. If you come with 'Allahu akbar', it's fine. If you come as an Indian, go ahead. I don't care about the specifics. It's one God we worship, there's no need to divide Him up.

I was chased out of a club once because I walked in and all these married men came to fool around with me. They started fighting amongst themselves, "*Huyu ndio mimi nilimwona mwanzo!*" I saw her first!

"*Huyu twajuana kitambo!*" We've been friends for a long time!

Commotion! Eventually, the women gathered and said, "*Huyu ndio yuatuharibia soko.*" This is the one spoiling our market.

They chased me with broken bottles—wanting to cut me up. This is why I stopped going out. The only parties I feel comfortable going to are the queer parties. I went out to an annual queer get-together and this guy noticed me. He approached my friend and asked for my contacts. I'd given all my friends strict rules not to give out my contacts without my consent, so my friend came to me and said, "There's a guy here who really likes you."

"Which one?"

My friend pointed him out. He looked OK, so I allowed my friend to give him my contacts. She added, "But remember—don't fall in love."

My friend always warns me not to fall in love carelessly, because whenever I end up heartbroken I end up crying at her house. I'm a mess when I'm heartbroken, I can't eat, I can't sleep.

I promised, "OK. I won't love him. I'll only like him *[laughs]*."

He texted me soon after. I decided to give him a month to figure out whether I liked him. After the month ended, I still liked him. He didn't ever say he wanted us to have a relationship. He'd only ask, "Am I the only one you're dating?"

I'd tell him, "You're the only one. For now."

We kept meeting, and he was really cool. He'd even help me to buy hormones, and buy me clothes—he knew my size! This was a big change for me. My first boyfriend never gave me anything, I used to be the one boosting him—because at the time I had a few sponsors. He was married, but he used to come to me for money. "My child has been chased away for school fees."

Money.

"My wife doesn't have food to cook."

Money.

My current boyfriend is very different. He helps support me with rent and food. He works in a hotel, and there's not many tourists around—so it's up and down. When the tourists come, the hotel business is good and he's able to help me out. It's been like that since 2012. When he has a problem, we sit together and talk about it. He doesn't hide anything from me. Aren't those the right qualities for a man? When I decide to stick to someone, I'm very loyal. All these men come to me and I say, "I'm taken."

I'm very settled now. But you know men are shape-shifters. They can tell you're the only one, then they see another one and tell that one, "You're the only one."

I'm very happy with him, but I'm still cautious. Men are difficult. That's why my friend tells me not to fall in love. Fall 'in like'.

For my future, I want to complete my transition. We're saving money in a savings account for that, and once I transition completely I'll be able to get my documents, and for my correct gender. I want kids, and I want a nice job. I want to live freely. I don't live freely right now. The freedom to move and work. When I get that, I'll be happy.

–

I AM GAY. When I was in Form Two[12], I realized I had some queer behaviour. I was really aware that the way I looked at guys was very different from the way I looked at girls, and that I was more attracted to the guys. Nobody had told me anything about being this way—it had just come automatically. I always had my eye on the men.

In primary school I hung out with girls only. We were really good friends. We would talk, and I felt really free around them. Even when there were parties for the girls only, I would go, and never attend the ones with boys. Nobody ever talked badly about it to me. At the beginning of high school, I still had more friends who were girls. I think I was afraid to approach boys because they just made me feel something strange, and I didn't understand what it was. I acted like I didn't like to be with boys, and sat very far from them.

I think I took many genes from my mother, so I used to talk with my hands, with my head nodding. It reached a point where passing guys would greet me, "Look at the girl!"

But they had respect for me, even the teachers, because I never fought with anyone. Everyone was perplexed by my queer behaviour but never really reached any conclusions. In Form Two, I decided to start acting more masculine—to start walking around with my hands in my pockets, such things, and I managed.

In the first term of Form Three, I had a crush on a boy, and it really alarmed me. I started asking myself what was wrong. You know if you didn't have a girlfriend, your life was stressful. So I got a girlfriend like everyone else, but I couldn't stop looking at this boy.

He was light-skinned, medium height. Most other boys were very untidy and sloppy. But this one! His shoes were always perfect. His trousers were perfectly ironed.

I saw myself in him. We were the cleanest boys in our class. We started talking and getting close. We sat on opposite sides of the class. We were really good friends. Even during holidays

---

12. Between 1985 and 2019, the Kenyan school system followed the 8-4-4 curriculum, so named because it involves 8 years of primary education (Standard 1 to 8), 4 years of high school education (Form One to 4) and 4 years of university education (1st Year to 4th Year).

we would visit each other and talk for hours. But I never had the courage to tell him. I still felt a little mixed up and unsure.

So I finished school and started a job in a hotel. And then I became sure I was gay. This is what happened. I was just doing odd jobs—quick errands and such. Some lawyers came to the hotel, and one of them found me on the stairs and greeted me. He said he had looked at me and thought we could talk. I said OK, and he could say anything he wanted if he thought it would be helpful. So he asked, "What's the best place someone can go to around here? Like a pub, where I can go and relax?"

I gave him a list of places where I thought he would fit in. Then he said, "Thanks. Can I have your number?"

I gave it to him, without any problem. He was a customer, after all. Maybe he would look for a job for me elsewhere, or find me another opportunity—you never knew, with these things. That's how I was thinking. He also asked me how I was being paid, and such things, and I had been open about it.

That evening when I was leaving work, he called and asked where I was. I told him I was just leaving, but I was really tired and wanted to go home and rest. He pleaded with me to take a taxi and go where he was. I said I would go home and think about it. He called twice when I was home to convince me to go, and I went.

He asked me if I drink, and I said I didn't. So we had some snacks, and then he just put his hands on me. I was so shocked! I wasn't upset, just really confused about how strange this all was. We were still in the pub. So we left, and he asked if we could go back to his room. I said, "What? I can't, because that hotel is where I work!"

I told him if people saw me leaving his room, it would be crazy for me. So he took me all the way home and asked if he could come in. That night was the first time I was kissed by a man. It was amazing.

Then he went back to the hotel. We saw each other at the hotel a little here and there. I found myself wanting to call him all the time. So we started seeing each other, and then he left town.

Later on, I started working at an LGBT organization. That's when I really accepted that I was a *kuchu* [homosexual], you know? One day, I met a guy who had been my friend for more than five years in our office. I said hi, and he asked me what I was doing there. I said I worked there, and I didn't ask him what he was doing there because I figured he must be one of our clients, so I just left. I sent a friend a text and asked, "Is this guy gay, or…?"

There was no response. I asked again, and still there was no response. So I went to his house and asked, and I was told the guy was closeted because he worked with prominent people.

Later, I sent him a text asking, "How are you, my guy?"

Just being friendly. He responded, "Am I your guy or are you my guy?"

I decided to just ask him straight, "Don't lie to me. Are you gay?"

He replied, "Who told you?"

I said, "I just know."

He said, "Yes, but it's a secret."

From there we became really good friends. We did everything together, and we really understood each other. Even at home they knew we were friends. His family was exactly like mine. Both our dads were aimless guys who came home to make noise and disturb everything. He would call me and say his mother had no money for food, and I would send what I had. I could call and tell him I needed money. He would ask, "How much?", and then send it to me.

We were together for almost five years. Unfortunately, we had to stop seeing each other. I caught him with someone else. We were supposed to go somewhere together, and he told me he had someone to meet. We went to wait for the person, but he didn't come.

My boyfriend told me to go hang out with one of our other friends and said he would join us later. I went, and he texted later to tell me his friend had come and wanted to take him out. I was really irritated because I had left the house only to spend time with him, and he wasn't even there. So we fought, but I forgave him.

Another time when we were just having drinks, he saw another guy and went over to talk to him. He then came back and told me, "Sweetheart, just excuse me for a minute."

Then he went outside. Five minutes later, he told me he was going to another club and left. I was just adding all of it up in my head. By the time I got to the door, they had disappeared together. I was really angry.

I decided that even if I had to sell my phone that night to chase him all over town, I would, just so that he would see that I had seen him. That night, I went to all the clubs in town. I paid all the entry fees, and got stamped everywhere. This one club refused me to enter so I picked up another friend—a girl—so that she could enter and check for me. Finally, we entered another club and saw them. He came after me and grabbed me and dragged me to the gents so we could talk. When we got there I had no strength left, so I walked out. I was stressed for two weeks, then I forgave him; back on the drug.

We kept having incidents like these, and my head was just adding up all these facts. One day, I went out with some friends and someone asked, "Who knows this guy?", and showed a picture of my boyfriend.

They said, "He's really a whore these days."

I was finally fed up, and I told him, "You only get the chance to cheat on me once. You will never cheat on me again."

He then accused me of not trusting him, and we fought about it. He blocked me on Whatsapp, Facebook, his phone—everything. We didn't speak for a whole month. I went out with another bunch of friends and I met him on the road. I was almost not sure it was him. He had dressed really differently. All his clothes were new. He was really shocked to see me. I just said, "This is what you decided?"

He asked me if I was going home, and I said I was with friends. I added that he should enjoy himself, and I'd see him around. His message woke me up the next day. He said he was tired of this relationship and its drama. So I said as far as I knew it would be good to sit down and actually talk, not text back and forth. He said his mind was made up and he couldn't go on with me. So I said, "OK, as you wish."

He replied, "End of discussion, bye."

It just ended like that. Three months ago. That was a big hit, and the last relationship I have ever been in. There are people who are hitting on me but it's hard. There are cuter, hotter guys than him, but it was because of his heart, and the way we just used to sit and talk—I look at all these other guys and it just defeats me. A thing that really hurts is that even my aunts are asking where he is because they miss him. They got really used to having him around. All the people who knew we were sweethearts are still asking, "Where's your boyfriend?"

I'm really fucked up. I would enter the house and people would ask me where he was and I would just lock myself in my room and cry. I have never, ever loved anybody the way I loved that guy. I am completely unable to move on. Some days, I can't even go to work. I'll just sit in the house. I couldn't eat, or I was eating too much, everyone was asking me why I was gaining weight. Even my mother noticed I was falling apart. A song would play that used to be our song, and the tears would just begin to roll, even in the office.

To cover up, I have a girlfriend who is a lesbian, and she's very rich. She also has her own girlfriend. We used to go places, all four of us. I would sit with her in front, and my boyfriend would sit with her girlfriend at the back. But some people got really observant. She's a tomboy. But people at home know she is my girlfriend. On my phone, I had pictures of random girls from school. Me and my ex would go places together and walk far away from each other so nobody would know, but after a while he would call me 'baby'.

I MISS THAT, FEELING FREE.

–

I REALIZED I WAS BISEXUAL when I was ten. I was in a day school. One Saturday my friend invited me over, and said, "Let's kiss, like they kiss on the soaps on TV."

So we did. We made out. It was amazing, and I still liked boys. I was suspended in Standard 7 for kissing a girl. School ended at 3.30 pm, and there was prep afterwards. Right before prep, students would play football until the bell rang. There were some empty classes and my friend and I would make out in one of the empty classrooms. The story is that the teacher on duty caught us, but I always think that was fake. I think someone ratted us out, because we did that a lot and people knew. Boys and girls made out as well, it was one of those places.

The girl I was kissing had a boyfriend, and she was curious, but I'm the one who got suspended. Everyone said the other girl was good and that I was the rotten egg. The bad influence. That was my first run-in with the system, so to speak.

I was expelled three times in high school, because of 'lesbianism'. The first two schools were girls' schools, and the third was a mixed one. These expulsions were really annoying, because they always caught me after I'd done it for years. I was like, "Come on! You could have caught me last year!"

The first time was with this girl I was really in love with. It was the first time I was in love with a girl. It got so bad because when I'm in love with somebody I get possessed. Possessive. When a male teacher would show her hints that she was beautiful I got annoyed. We'd go for outings and boys would be all over her and I couldn't stand it. It was love in a twisted way, and so—we were caught at the dorm by the teacher on duty.

I got expelled, but she didn't. They expel the bad one—the one who is spoiling the other one. It didn't help that prior to that, I used to run away from school to go and strip dance at a club in town. There was a tunnel, and I would pass through the tunnel, go and do my stripping thing, and pass through the tunnel again in the night. The teachers knew, so they put a mesh in the hole. So one night when I was sneaking back in, the barbed wire caught my face. I was screaming and then the watchmen said, "*Tumekushika!*" We've caught you.

In primary school, I used to pass really well. My primary school marks were 546 out of 700 and that was good. I got into a nice school. I had dreams. I wanted to be a doctor, and my mother always said I had long fingers, and long fingers could make a good doctor.

So in Form One, I used to get straight As. I was really clever. Then my parents separated, and they did it in a weird way.

On closing day at my school everyone used to stand near the gate. And so my dad's car just came into the school, and he came out. Then my mum's car came in and she said, "Choose. Choose where you're going to go. Your dad's car or my car."

So I literally had to choose. And after that, every time I came back to school, I was the outcast because of that incident. I'd walk past people and there would be whispers. I never used to have friends out there because my dad was very strict. My dad used to make us stay in the house. I was so shy, I couldn't lift my head up.

We used to look like we had no life. He brought me up. My mum used to travel a lot. So when I chose, I got upset with them because the stigma that was at home was repeated in school. In school it was the same thing—there were whispers. So my education started going down, down, down. And that's when I met that girl that I fell in love with. She used to understand me, we used to sit together, and then that happened.

And then I got deep into drugs. My school was a really nice school, but it was located in the middle of a ghetto. We had Christian Union gatherings in the field at school, and there would be praying and people would break into tongues, and then you'd take a corner in the field and you'd be praying. One day when I was doing that, I saw this guy in the corner of the field smoking weed. I said, "Prayers, wait."

He told me, "*Nikikupatia, italeta shida.*" If I give you weed, there'll be trouble.

So we had this system where I'd dig a hole in the ground, he'd put the weed in there, then I'd get it, put money in the hole and cover it up and he'd come get his money. I was crazy. And then he told me about this strip dance thing where I could be sneaking to make some money 'because you're a pretty girl, and then just come back'.

The fact that he said I was a pretty girl, I thought, "Yeah, that's what's up."

He showed me how to sneak through the tunnel. The tunnel connected our school to the outside. We had cases where men from the slum nearby would come in the school and you'd find them in the dormitories. It was a school where you'd lose a textbook, then you'd walk out and find it being sold in that ghetto.

The first day, he told me he'd be waiting for me. I followed his instructions, and he was waiting for me. It was around 7pm. We went, I did my thing in the club and I got 2,000 bob—that was a long time ago and that was mega money. Super! So I kept going back. Then my grades started going down.

Ever since I was young, I had this thing where I'm a crowd puller. People want to hang out with me, I was cool. So if you want to hang out with me, you have to smoke weed. We were crazy. My parents found out about this, and my mum said, "We have to get her out of there."

I was expelled from the first school. The second school they took me to? Same thing; I was expelled, predominantly because of drugs. Then the third time, they took me to rehab. That's the first time I ever found somebody to speak to, you know, just like you right now, just listening, and asking questions and seeing where I'm from. I'd never had that before, it was my first experience.

The counsellor was a young, cute guy. I explained everything to him, and then he sort of explained it to my mum. And then I sort of fell in love with him, and then we started having sex during sessions instead of—yeah. After that I went back home, and I was told 'Go back to school, or we'll take you *ushago*.' Upcountry.

Go upcountry? No way. Me, I'm a cool kid. I told my mum: no more girls, no more drugs. So I went to my new school.

My new school was tricky because they knew about me and already they had branded me as a bad girl. They were not open to my new vision of no girls, and no drugs. Even if I was seen holding a girl the way girls hold each other, they'd come and say, "No, don't! This one is bad."

It was pointless. You think I'm bad. I'm going to show you. On the second day of school, I just took my weed and I lit it in the field. I said, "How many puffs will it take for you to catch me?"

Second puff, they took me in.

"Yes, Sir?"

"You're expelled."

"Thank you, Sir."

And I went home. My mum got tired. I only had one year left of school and nobody wanted me. At home, nobody used to talk to me. So I went back to my stripping. And then I met somebody—a boy. Back in the hood, I'd already gotten into this bad gang. They were really bad boys. They used to smoke weed, do drugs; even cocaine. This guy sort of 'broke' my virginity. I put it in quotes because my first incidence of breaking my virginity was rape. It was rape and it was done by a member of my family who I should not mention. He took away my virginity, and I think that sowed a seed of rebellion in my brain. That I think I have the option, who should be with me, and who should not be with me, and for even the longest time missionary position was a No for me. A dominating force on top of you? No. A friend of mine argued that as a woman you have more power because you decide whether to let this person in. I said, "Yes, but in cases of rape you don't."

I think for me, anything sexual is a power game. It's power. Because I want it when I want it. I don't want to be dominated. I want to enjoy it, and if you can't give me that I can't be with you.

Anyway I met the gang leader. I lost my virginity to him, and I chose that. I was hanging my clothes on my balcony when I first saw him and I said to myself, "*Huyo mrasta ndio atanivunja vajo.*" That Rasta guy is the one who will 'break open my vagina'.

I picked him out and I said he was going to do it, because he was the most popular guy. I was such a kid. So he did it. I actually gave myself to him. Then we used to smoke weed together. The gang used to beat up people and steal from them—they were just a bad gang.

Later, I met another boy in the club. All he did was order Fanta for me. He was a Muslim guy, and he would tell me things like, "*Nimekuletea buibui ujifunike.*" I've brought you a *buibui* so you can cover yourself.

He would tell me, "Do you know you're precious?"

And I'd say, "Whatever, man."

So, one day I told him, "You pretend to be so holy, I'd love to see your cum face."

He said, "No, I'm a virgin!"

Aha! So I found out where he lives, and one day I went to see him in a long dress.

He said, "*Umevaa nguo za heshima.*" You've worn respectable clothes.

I said, "*Nakuheshimu sana jamani.*" I respect you so much.

When I'm in trouble or I want something, I do a fake asthma routine. I did that, and he was scared, he suggested I rest in bed.

"*Jamani nitakulaza kwa kitanda.*" I will put you to bed.

"*Unaumwa wapi?*" Where does it hurt?

I said, "Just rub my chest."

And shit started going down, and in my head I was like BAM! In his moment of weakness, I asked him, "*Tamu?*" Sweet?

He said, "*Tamu sana.*" Very sweet.

Eventually, I fell in love with him. And then he started showing me that I'm worth something; streamlining me, not changing me.

Once, I was supposed to meet him and I went home and found him already at home with my mum, helping my mum cook. I was annoyed because he was intruding. What's he doing with my mum? Next, he'll be bringing camels.

I got mad. It was around 9pm and I told him to go away. I was high on weed, and my mum was scared of me, so he went. But now, the gang leader had gotten word of him and was jealous. So when he went out there, the gang beat him up, they sodomised him, and they warned him, "We don't want to see you with our First Lady again."

That was my turning point, because the next day when I found out that I had put someone's life in danger, that was a wake up call. I realized I was actually in a dark cloud and this was crazy. I realized that the gang could even beat up my family members and—I hadn't noticed till then—that my family members were scared of me.

So we moved out and I went to my next school, where the principal said, "I've heard your stories and I will never expel you. I will punish you until you finish. I am powerful. I'll never suspend you, I'll never expel you."

At my first parade there she announced, "We are here with a very truant student. Beware of this girl. She's very bad. And

I have promised her that I will never suspend her or expel her. I'll punish her till she finishes." So everybody was avoiding me. Which worked wonders because I actually finished school with no friend—except the workers—and many punishments.

So I finished school. I got out, and I joined the theatre, started acting. Then I fell in love, and then I got married at the age of eighteen. I'm a spontaneous person and when I believe in something I go for it. When I got married, I'd have sleepovers with my girlfriends. I'd be in the bedroom with my husband, but I'd have the urge to go to the other room where my girlfriends were sleeping. Then I'd tell him, "Let me go check on them."

I'd go and make out with my friend, have sex, and then come back. We were married two years, and this went on the whole time. I guess I got married because he was the first person to propose. I felt like everybody judged me, so having this nice guy propose to me was something I could show off. He was a really nice guy. So I got my baby and then I got separated, because he became violent and possessive. I sure know how to pick them.

Then that ended, and from then I was now open. I believe I can't stay in a relationship for long. I'm not judgemental—I date whoever I feel I like, I don't care. Even if all my friends say, "Don't date that one."

Girl, boy, I don't care.

I don't believe I want to settle down. I don't believe anybody can understand me, or handle me. Fathom me the way I want to be understood. I'm a creative mind, I'm a free spirit, I'm dynamic, and one thing I value is my space. Relationships crowd that. I'm the type of person who immerses herself into something totally and when I'm let down, I'm crushed totally because I'm the kind of person who loves 100%. I'm there. So I made a vow to myself to just stay alone till I'm really old, but have many friends.

I have a daughter. She's amazing. She's beautiful, and she's turning six next year. She's sweet and open-minded. I'm trying to force her to be an artist and she's not interested. She's always passing her Maths. It's her grandma's influence and I guess it's cool. So when I get fake boobs and they explode she'll be the doctor who'll deal with that. Me and her are in a relationship, whether I like it or not.

I don't talk badly about her dad. I tend to be positive about him because that's her dad, man. We had our problems, but that's her dad.

My relationship with my mum now is much better. She's my best friend. Me, I'm fun. I bring the party. I'm her roommate—you know we're living together now? I think my mum's problem with me was when I did not have focus. But once she saw that I was serious with this art thing, then she brought her energies there. Now that I have focus, she's happy. Because any parent wants that for their child. I would like my kid to know where she's going.

I was such a loss to my mother when I was young; wasting her school fees money, wasting her time, tarnishing her name with all my drugs things. But now I have focus. I know what I want in life. I know that I am music and that is me. And I'm going to be the best. I AM the best. I don't even smoke weed any more. I just don't want to. Right now I'm so in love with what I'm doing, that I want to be in the moment. I still like weed—don't get me wrong—but I want to be in the moment, I DON'T WANT ANY HIGH.

–

I'VE NEVER REALLY BEEN the normal kid. I always knew I was different. I just didn't know how. There was a guy called David. He switched, so now he's a girl. He lives in Tanzania nowadays. We used to fool around in the dorms. After we finished high school, we went our separate ways. He went to the coast, then I heard on Facebook that he transformed and became a girl. I heard that there is a lot of that going on in Tanzania.

The first time I had sex with a girl, I was in Form Two. I did it because everyone was doing it, and I wondered what that's like so I tried it out. She was a house help called Angela, at home. I came back home from school and found her. Then we started talking. Then it just happened like after thirty minutes. It was different. She was not like David, she was so different. I didn't think it was all that. That's what I realized, because guys in school were so hyped up about it.

I have always been a believer in individuality. My style is not your style, and that's what makes people different.

Our high schools are very homophobic. Once when I was in high school, two guys were caught making out in the middle of the night in a block of bathrooms. Because it was at night, they thought they wouldn't get caught, but then someone found them, and sounded the alarm. Everyone woke up.

The two guys were told, "Show us your girlfriends."

They brought out ten other guys. All twelve of them were beaten by other students in front of the school principal and other teachers. Physical violence. I was wondering how the principal could not stand up for them. He expelled all of them afterwards. All twelve of them.

It was very sad for me personally, but I couldn't speak up. I had been expelled twice before and this was my third school. I couldn't do shit. I couldn't get expelled again because then I wouldn't finish high school. I just had to sneak back into the shadows and watch from the sidelines. It was not pretty though, because those guys were really beaten up.

I love gay people, partly because I know I will never get to be very out because of family. I don't think I'll be able to be fully fledged. I live through my gay friends. For me, I don't think it's ever going to happen, being fully out. I've never really done the whole nine yards, only second base.

Because of the people I live around, I've always had a girl around so that people don't ask questions. I know it is a lie, and that I am not into it. I have gone all the way with a girl. The house help and some other girl. It's very hard.

Culture is a bitch. We have married men who live lies, and married women who are also doing the same. I love Uganda. Although they have stringent laws for gay people, there's a very big gay community and they are so meshed together. I've been to a few parties there. The community there is very vibrant. They have lots of get-togethers and they check up on each other. That is something people in Kenya lack.

The first time I fell in love was with Willis. Willis is the one guy who just does it for me. He is one of those spoilt rich kids who travels whenever he wants. You can never pin him down.

When he's around, he's around. When he's not, he's not. He's so real. The realest person I know. He is in touch with himself, he knows what he wants. He doesn't mess around, it's either you're in or you're out. He is very cute too, very easy on the eyes. He lives in ██████, he doesn't have to study like us. He's younger than I am. They own businesses so once in a while he makes appearances here. He's one of those guys, if you put water on him it turns to ice, you know? He's so cool. He's one of those guys you just want to know about. He has that vibe. He's like a Jamaican. The weird thing is that he's not on social media at all, but he's on Google+. He's that cool, you see? He does shit me and you don't get.

I met him at some party in ██████. We were tipsy, and he was leaning in and I was thinking, "What the hell is happening?" I didn't stop him, he just went in. It was very different. These tiny hairs of mine stood up, that feeling you can't explain. It's kinda sweet but different. I slapped him afterwards. I was confused, a thousand things running through my mind like, "What the hell am I doing? Oh my God!"

A lot of things.

He looked at me and stormed off, and I thought to myself, "Fuck, what have I done?"

I went back and started talking to him, and he said, "I know you like me, and you don't want to admit it."

I didn't have words for almost two minutes. It was true. I didn't want to show him that he knows me. We went to his car and made out. There was no tongue, but it was nice.

I want Willis. He's a party boy and a player. Pinning him down is hard, I know that. When you like someone you like them with their faults. I'll probably meet someone better but for now, I just want Willis.

–

I identify as a queer woman. I think that's as far as I've thought it through. I've never really been able to answer the question: 'When did you first realize you were queer?'

Even when I was a kid I would have all these feelings for girls that were my friends and I didn't know what to do with them. I remember being three and really being attracted to my friends. Really liking them and wanting to spend a lot of time with them and wanting to kiss them. That's my earliest memory.

I think when I really knew—or started to realize—was when I was seventeen, when I met this one girl. She is the love of my life. She changed everything for me. She changed how I saw everything in the world. She taught me stuff about myself that I had no idea about. She was so hot. She played basketball and she was just cool and had swag and I was just really attracted to her.

But I was really in denial at that point. I considered myself to be a Holy Joe. There was no way I could be gay. So I went to church a lot, I prayed about it and I said, "God, I cannot be gay, remove these feelings because this is not me, this is not who I'm meant to be. My family will literally kill me if they ever find out. This cannot happen."

So I was in a lot of denial and I think that's what led to our demise. We weren't in a relationship but she knew that I liked her and I knew that she liked me. Nothing ever happened. We never really talked about it but we were very close and everyone could see it as well and I think everyone else suspected there was something going on.

Later on, I came to my senses and realized, "OK, this is who I am."

I tried reaching out to her but it was too late. We're not friends now. I know where she is because I'm still friends with her sisters, and I know what she's up to. But now she is the one who's in denial. Every time I try to reach out to her, she says, "I'm straight. I don't know what you're talking about. Leave me the hell alone."

I studied abroad. High school was amazing. High school was the best experience ever. Middle school—not so much. I was still struggling with depression at the time but I didn't realize it was depression. I thought it was normal. When I look back, I remember being sad a lot, experiencing profound loneliness. I couldn't explain it. I wondered, "Why am I feeling so lonely when I'm surrounded by all these people? I know I'm loved. So, why?"

It was only in Year 12 that I started to realize that I might be depressed because I think that's when it got really bad and other people actually started asking, "Why are you always by yourself, in the dorms?"

I started having a lot of feelings of wanting to commit suicide. I think that's when I realized that something was wrong.

I was able to come to terms with my identity when I was in my third year in university. First of all, I purposely moved to the Gay Village in ████████, even though I was still very much in denial at the time. I thought to myself, "It's OK, straight people can live in the Gay Village too. That's fine. It doesn't mean that I'm gay just because I want to live here and just because it looks like so much fun. I can still be straight."

Then one summer, I started talking about it with one of my friends. She started talking about how she might be bisexual and I was thinking, "I don't know what I am."

Finally—by the end of the summer—I realized that I was not straight. I confided in another close friend of mine, and that was the scariest thing ever because that was the first time that I had actually said the words. She took it so well, way better than I had expected.

Obviously, she was shocked because I don't think she expected it, but she said, "That's awesome! I'm really happy for you if that's how you feel."

After that I was more comfortable with myself. That's the first time I acknowledged it to myself—by acknowledging it to her. Later on, I got more and more confident about acknowledging it to other people and being myself.

I'm out to my family. Not by choice, though. My sister outed me to my family. There was one time I was visiting her, and my girlfriend at the time lived nearby. I was really sick at the time so my girlfriend was visiting a lot and staying over and by watching our interaction my sister sort of just figured it out. She asked me, straight out, "So, are you guys together?"

Because of the way she asked—really matter-of-factly—I said yes. I wasn't scared to tell her. That particular sister of mine was considered to be the rebel of the family for a long time. She was the most liberal one in our family. So to me, coming out to her wasn't a big deal. I said, "Yeah. Yeah, we're together. Whatever."

She said, "OK. Fine."

Later on after I left, I got an email from my mother asking, "What is going on?"

It was a 2–3 page email talking about how she will not have any homosexual children in her family, and how I have turned away from God and how I need to repent my sins before His wrath is unleashed upon me. It was a really, really long email. She said that my sister had told her and everyone else in the family. That's how my family came to know about me.

My relationship with my mum up until I was eighteen was awesome. It was pretty amazing. Especially since I was about twelve, I worshipped her and I thought she was the greatest woman on this planet. I thought she could do no wrong and I thought she was a saint and I thought the world of her. Then I moved to █████ and went to university and our relationship became a little strange. Especially because she started to realize that I wasn't her perfect little daughter. She realized that I enjoyed drinking, for instance. And it was fine. We could still talk and everything.

After she found out I was gay, we didn't talk for about four years. We spoke really rarely and when we did, it was about logistics and stuff. When we started talking again, it's like that never happened. It's like she just decided to ignore that part of me and when she does bring it up, she makes it clear in that it's not something that she will ever be OK with. She says that I need to repent, that I'm losing my way, that if I want to get married to a man or if I find a man to marry then she'll be able to talk to me about that. She told me, "If you can bring a man here, to the house, then we can talk. Then I'll be fine. But until then, we're not talking about that."

I do identify as queer. I don't identify as lesbian or bisexual. For me, queer is a wider spectrum, which to me means that I would be comfortable dating anyone of any gender or sexuality. It's not impossible for me to get married to a man. I think it would be near impossible, but I don't think it is impossible. And if that were ever to happen, I definitely don't think that would be something I'd be comfortable to share with my mother because I feel like if she can't accept me as I am now, then why would it be OK if I was getting married to a man?

I still have a problem with the word queer because it's a label and I really don't like labels. But I feel like the word queer kind of encompasses everything for me and that's the word that I've found so far that I'm most comfortable with. I feel that it's not about who you're having sex with or who you're attracted to. It's about who you connect with. On a personal, spiritual level. It's about whose soul your soul connects with. It's not about what's in your pants, it's not about any of that. It's just about being able to really connect with someone and love them for who they really are. And not just because of a label they have or a box that someone's put them in.

I don't talk to any of my family anymore. We haven't spoken for two years now.

The people I consider my family are my friends. Because I really believe in chosen family. For me, my family are my closest friends, my two cousins that I absolutely love and adore. To me that's real family.

I want to get married. I'm not crazy about kids so if I never had kids I would be perfectly OK with that, but if I ever met someone who really wanted to have kids then that is something I would definitely consider. I also see my family including lots and lots of animals. I just see my house being a zoo. Dogs, cats, monkeys, lions—tamed ones, tigers—little ones, fish, birds, reptiles. I want all kinds of animals in my house.

I considered myself to be a pretty good Christian. I would go to church, I prayed every day, I would read my Bible every day, I loved God, and I still love God. I was saved, born again—whatever that means. And even when I moved to ████████, I found a really good church that was a really good experience for me. But then once I started coming to terms with my queer identity, it was weird to go to church and hear that it was a sin.

I remember one day being in church and there was a Pride parade going on nearby. At the time I still really wasn't comfortable so I hadn't gone to Pride. I just went to church and I remember the pastor saying, "All those people out there are an abomination and we need to pray so all of them one day will come in here instead of going out there on the streets."

I remember having such an issue with that statement.

I think that's when my relationship with the church and with the Bible really started to change. Because I felt that God loved me no matter what, no matter who I was but I didn't feel the same from the church. After a while I stopped attending. I stopped reading the Bible because I just couldn't reconcile how I was feeling and what I had grown up being taught. I felt that I still believed in God and I still loved God. It felt like God loved me no matter what. My relationship with the church and with the Bible definitely changed, but I don't think my relationship with God changed. Or maybe it did. I don't know.

I have worked in places that were really homophobic and I remember my co-workers having serious issues with it. I had to leave in the end because it was too much. It taught me not to mix work and my personal life. So I stopped mentioning that I was queer. Some people would suspect I was, but I wouldn't come out and say it straight out. After that, it was pretty much a non-issue.

My first real relationship taught me a lot about myself. Up until that point, I had considered myself a pretty good person. The relationship actually taught me that I wasn't a good person. There were a lot of things I needed to work on; deep-seated issues that were coming out in the relationship. It was an amazing relationship. Obviously, it wasn't all perfect but it did teach me a lot about treating people with respect, being kind and being honest with the people you care about, and being A LITTLE LESS SELFISH.

–

I WENT OUT FOR A DRINK with my classmates one night at a local bar. We were seven, and I was the only guy. There was a table close by with guys who were looking at me. I think they could tell I was gay. They left at some point. At around 10pm, I left the girls at the bar because I needed to wake up early the next day and study.

The street-lights—for some strange reason—were off that night. I didn't think much of it, because I'd walked on that road many times in the past. I was walking one minute, and there was this thud on my face. I found myself on the ground, being kicked repeatedly by a few individuals. It was so dark, I couldn't see their faces. The worst thing is that there were all these parked cars around us and no one came out to help. These guys were kicking me, and kicking me.

It took two seconds to realize, "Oh, shit. This is happening."

At some point, someone was punching my face and the sounds had started to register. They were calling me *shoga* [fag] and one of them said they were going to shove a pipe up my ass. Something told me, "Just get up and run."

I got up and ran, and ran. I didn't run towards home, I just ran to get as far away from them as possible.

I ran, and I ran and I ran. I lost track of time, I didn't know where I was running to. I fell several times, but I didn't care. I picked myself up and continued running.

When I stopped, it was raining and I was in an alley somewhere. I couldn't believe that had happened. I couldn't feel the pain on my face, I was just in shock that it had happened. I had no idea where I was. You hear of these stories, and it happened to me. I looked around, I didn't know where I was and it was quite late. I didn't have my watch, and my phone was broken. I crouched myself into a ball and I stayed in the alley till morning.

In the morning, I woke up and I could hear people. I saw people walking around, and I realized that I was in Kibera. I had run so far and so fast. That's when the pain started to register. I looked around and decided to follow the people who were walking. I eventually got myself to a bus stop, I told myself that I wasn't going to cry.

Some man asked me if I was OK, and I couldn't answer him. I just stared at him, then the bus arrived and I got in. I got home, and my mum and sisters were waiting for me. They had tried to find me, because I didn't go home and my phone was off. I told my mum what had happened, and started crying. I had told my mother once before that I was gay, but she took it lightly, like a joke. This time, I told her the names the attackers had called me, and THIS TIME SHE UNDERSTOOD.

–

I'M A LESBIAN. I knew in Form Three. I had a desk-mate who had a crush on me. She was scared of approaching me, then one night she came to my bed and she just kissed me out of the blue and ran away. She just kissed me, and she didn't say anything! Then we talked about it the next day—she asked me if I liked the kiss and I said I didn't mind it. Then she asked if I had ever noticed she liked me, and I said I hadn't. So she asked what I thought about all that. I said I didn't mind, and I thought it was OK.

I actually knew that she was into me, because she would look for me when I was alone in class and come to give me stories, and she would dress like she was seducing me. She would unbutton her top halfway down, and wear these really short skirts. And she was tall and looked like a model, so it was really something.

I used to really admire women from afar. I thought it was a bit abnormal, but I used to admire women a lot. I didn't like guys that way—I saw them as just friends. Some of them would try for more, but it didn't make sense. I didn't feel it.

So I told my desk-mate we couldn't have a relationship in school. At that time, I didn't know she was also dating my classmate. Then this classmate also started seducing me, and I think they were trying to get back at each other. They were the bad girls in the school, and I was unsure about relating with such girls. So I told them to keep off me and deal with their own issues, so they left me alone. But we remained friends, and we are still friends even now.

I didn't have any other relationships in high school. After high school, I met someone on Facebook. This chick from Tanzania just sent me a message. She had read a little about what I liked and saw the people I was following. She asked if I liked girls and I said I did. She asked, "How?"

I said, "Sexually."

So then she said, "In short, you are a lesbian."

I said, "Yes, I am."

Then she said, "Me too, and I like you."

We were together for three months in a long distance relationship. She came to Kenya and we saw each other for two weeks, but she turned out to be a player.

I already have one child now; a daughter. She is three years old, and already in school. I met her father when I was in high school. I had a problem with how I was attracted to women, so

I tried dating men on the side. It never really went too far. Some time in Form Four, I happened to go out with some friends who were boys, and they introduced me to this guy.

He confessed that he liked me after we had gone out many times. One night I got drunk and we went to his place and stuff happened, and I got pregnant. I decided to have the baby. He said he would take care of everything and marry me, but I told him I was attracted to women. He said he was OK with it. We lived together for a year, then he travelled abroad. When I was sexual with him, it was always 'do your thing and let me be'. Not like it was with women. He came back from overseas and told me he had a new girlfriend. I told him I understood, because I was also dating someone else. WE ARE STILL GOOD FRIENDS.

–

I IDENTIFY AS CONFUSED, in that phase of experimenting. I would say I am bi-curious, I just don't know. I am just experimenting. It is hectic.

I hated boarding. I went to a rural school, and I had this girlish character. During the drama festivals, there was this play where a guy talks to a lady called Suzie, and I was the only person who could pull off the lady role. I did it and did it well, all the way up to the national level. So everyone at school started calling me 'Suzie'.

I hated it.

Teachers also started calling me Suzie.

"Suzie, come here!"

"Suzie, go there!"

Hectic.

In Form Three, I had a crush on this guy, he was so hot. Because I was dorm captain, I had him move to my dorm. Being in power is nice. As prefects, we'd get the best food. So I'd get the best and give him some of mine. I even had the Form 1s wash his clothes for him.

One day as we were watching a film, on a Friday—we used to have entertainment[13] on Fridays—our entertainment captain put on some porn. Everyone was horny. So as we walked back to the dorm, my guy told me, "Come, let me take you somewhere."

We went to the showers outside, and I closed the door. Then he said, "I like you", and he kissed me. The world ended. I was in love. It was my first time, I was so naïve.

So it became a thing. Whenever there was a power blackout, or when everyone else was at preps[14], I'd have the keys for the dorm. I'd make sure everyone was upstairs reading, then I'd take him, and we'd go to the dorm.

After that one incident, I had to have him in my room. We used to hang out in the evening. We used to have fights, and we used to get jealous when we'd see each other with other guys. This went on until I finished school, and I left. Before I left, I made sure he was made a prefect. We're still tight buddies. We've not done anything since we finished school in 2010. We're just friends, he tells me stories about his crushes, and his boyfriend.

People in ██████ are very discreet. Guys know how to pretend. During the day guys are straight, with girlfriends. At night, you see them in the club, you get shocked. Most of my friends sleep with guys for cash. Luckily for me, I was born with money so I don't do that. I hate it when a guy wants to buy you. I tell them that I have my own money, so if they come to buy me a drink, I tell them I can also buy one for them.

When I left high school, I got a girlfriend. She was hot. I loved her, funny enough. I could have done anything for her. But lately I've been sleeping with a lot of other girls—that's why I'm telling her I'm confused. I don't know. I still have crushes on guys. I'll see a hot guy and say, "God, he is hot," but I won't do anything about it. I'm one of those dogs that bark, but never bite.

With girls, it's different. I will follow the girl until she gives.

I have a close friend who I've been friends with from way back. On New Year's Eve of 2012, we went out, and then back to his place, then we slept together on his bed. He was all over

---

13. Common in boarding high schools, 'entertainment' refers to an evening—usually Fridays—when students are allowed to take a break and watch a movie instead of studying.
14. Preps refers to mandatory evening studies, another common feature in high school.

me, touching me, making out with me. I asked him what he was doing. He said he had had a crush on me for a long time. He was so hot, I had a crush on him but I never told him. Apparently, he also felt the same way about me.

I don't know what he and I are doing, because he has a chick, for crying out loud. He's in University in Nairobi. When he's in Nairobi he's with his chick, then when he comes to ██████ he's with me. I've learned to compromise. I just have to survive. Whenever I see him with a lady I always get so jealous.

I tell him, "Fuck you, I want to kill you."

And he says, "Oh, you know I love you."

The first time I fell in love with a girl, I was in Standard 6. This new chick transferred to our school, she was hot. She became my desk-mate, and I used to have a crush on her. I never told her how I felt. She transferred again in Standard 7, and we never saw each other again.

When I joined Facebook years later, I saw her and I sent her a message. She said, "I used to like you in primary school but I never had the courage to tell you."

I said, "Fuck, you should have told me. I also used to like you."

I never tell people that I have a crush on them. I cannot, unless I am drunk. Then I will blame it on the alcohol. I fear the rejection part, because I have never been rejected in my life. Even heartbroken. I have never experienced heart break. That's why I am afraid of relationships, because they have a lot of drama. I have seen my parents, they have drama. That's why I don't want it.

No one in my family knows I'm gay. Hell no. No one at all. I have two brothers and one sister. I remember there was a day I was angry with my mum, so I wrote this letter to her saying I was gay, and that I wanted to be a Muslim. I think I was rebelling. Then my mum called a meeting at home. My grandma and my uncles came and talked to me about being gay. I told them that was just a phase, nothing to worry about. Then they told me to forget about being a Muslim in our house. My dad never talked to me about the letter, it was just my mum and aunts. I don't like lectures, I'd rather be hit. I hate emotional stuff. So I told them that IT WAS JUST A PHASE.

–

I'M A LESBIAN. For me the title doesn't matter—I just know I love girls. I was around twelve years old when I knew. I'm always in cliques of girls, and I love talking to them. I feel like I have more freedom around women. I realized it was sexual when I was in Form One. I used to dress kind of queer even then, because everyone was in skimpy skirts, but I would wear it my own way, you know?

One night the lights went off in the library, and this girl came up to me in the dark and told me she really liked me. I asked her, "Why are you telling me this in the dark?"

She told me she just had to, and then she kissed me. I really, really liked it. It was my first kiss.

I approached this other girl once, and she made life really difficult for me. She told all my friends and everyone else about it. It was terrible because everyone now knew. But this other girl, the one who kissed me the very first time, she was really there for me. She made my life in that school worth living. It was so bad that I really wanted to kill myself.

Even at home there was stress—I was so uncomfortable. I was staying with my step-father, and he had been abusing me. When my mum found out, she blamed it on me. She said it was my fault he had done it to me. I had to run away at some point for a while. I had to protect myself from him and his family all the time. When we would go upcountry, they knew I was just his stepdaughter, so they would all harass me.

I tried to commit suicide once. I drank tick-killing medicine, the one they use for cows. I blacked out and found myself at a clinic. My relationship with my mother broke completely then, so I ran away and went to stay with my grandma.

I even tried to date guys when I was in Form Three and it was such a disaster. The guy would want to be intimate and my body would refuse. I couldn't explain when he asked what was wrong. It was just not working. In school, girls would tell me that they had a bad kiss the day before, and I would say, "You don't know how to kiss? I can teach you!" Yeah, I was that girl! So I would teach them how to kiss. It was tough, but I finally finished school. Then I hooked up with this girl from Nairobi, and I knew for sure then that I was a lesbian. If a woman even touched my arm I just used to feel SO AT HOME AND SO GOOD.

–

GROWING UP, I NEVER LIKED playing with boys, I used to play with the girls. Sometimes I'd wear my sister's shoes or apply make up.

When I finished Standard 8, my twin brother, my cousin and I went for circumcision. We stayed in the village for two and half months. After we started healing in the first month, we were separated. My twin brother got a separate room—because he is older than I—and I had to sleep in one bedroom with my cousin.

That is when I realized that I'm gay. It started with touching and holding each other in the bed, and telling each other stories. We ended up shagging. The best kiss I've ever had was with him. He's the kinda person who kisses so in-depth until you feel your mouth is dry. It is so intense. After that, he went back to Nairobi, and I came back to ██████. We kept in touch for a while, then after that I went to high school, and he got over it.

I fell in love with another cousin of mine; it was mutual. I loved him so much because he was humble, he didn't talk much. That was my second sexual cousin. A different cousin from Nairobi. When I went to Nairobi, I stayed at their place, and I slept in his room with him because I'm his age. He proposed that we sleep together. That's how it happened. We fell in love, it was awesome, I loved it. He left the country in 2010. That's when we called it quits.

I believe that God loves everyone, so I don't think it's a big deal to be gay and serve God at the same time. I think I love God, nothing will change that. I'm gay, nothing will change that.

I am not out to my family, and I wouldn't want to come out to them. They don't ask. Why would they? They don't bother. My parents are conservative, so they don't ask such questions. I am only out to two of my cousins.

Living as a gay man in ██████ is OK. Not the best, not the worst. There's a big community here, and my closest friends are gay. There are spaces that are specific for gay people, but then we normally meet at ██████ and ██████. I feel good about being gay. I'm more at home with guys than when I'm with a lady.

I will definitely have to get married. I love kids; my own, my blood. I'd love to get married to a woman. With a man, there won't be blood children. I slept with a woman two years ago. It was awesome. I had to because the girl was following me and was very much into me. I said to myself that if I slept with her, maybe she might get bored and go away. That is what happened. After I had sex with her, she got bored.

My most memorable moments of being queer, was being in a foursome. I found it gross, but I enjoyed it. It was very random, I had a friend who asked if I had ever participated in a threesome. I said no. A foursome? I said never. Then he said he had two friends who wanted something like that. I agreed, and we went to my place. I found it weird, but I enjoyed it. It was weird because you're doing stuff with one guy, then another appears behind you. I don't think I'll do it ever again, it was my FIRST AND LAST ONE.

–

I'M TWENTY-TWO YEARS OLD, and I'm bisexual. I've known for two years now. I just found myself getting feelings for my fellow men. In high school, I had such a crush on a certain guy, so I just realized like that. Actually, I'm not really bisexual because I'm not interested in girls that much. I just socialize with them. I've had sex with only two girls but guys...I like it. I enjoy it more.

Before I realized this, I had suspicions about myself because I was very effeminate. I never liked playing football. I preferred socializing with girls. I liked *kujipodoa-podoa* [beautifying myself]. I had that girlish behaviour since I was a small kid.

In Form Three, there was this guy I had a crush on. The first time I met him, he called me 'Baby'. I wondered if he was gay so I dared him to have sex with me. He did. I really enjoyed it. We went on having sex for one and a half years until we were caught. Both of us were suspended and transferred to different schools. He stayed in [redacted], and I had to come back home.

After high school, I attended a meeting for gay people. It was very educative for me. I learned how to have safe sex. When I was in high school I was in danger because we never used condoms. When I arrived at the meeting, I was suddenly surrounded by so many gay people, I was flattered. No, I was scared—because every guy wanted to be with me. They were even pushing each other and offering me seats.

The peer educator training lasted for three days, and because of this, my parents almost found out about me. I never told them that I was going for the meetings. I used to tell them that I was going to see my friends. But because all my friends were gay, and because of my behaviour, people started asking my parents if I was straight or gay.

I used to share a room with my small brother but my parents separated us when they heard that I was gay for fear that I would spoil him.

I used to fear that one day my parents would chase me away because of my behaviour. But when I got into the gay crowd and started mingling with other people like me, I got courage. Here in ███████, people used to use the term *shoga*. Fag. These days when they call me that, I tell them, "*Eeh, mimi ni shoga, nadate baba yako.*" Yes, I'm a fag and I'm dating your dad.

Now, I don't live in fear. I'm so proud of what I am. The taxi guys outside of clubs are so provocative. When I come out of a club with my friend, for example, they say, "*Unajua huyo jamaa ni shoga?*" Do you know that guy is a fag?"

I respond, "Yeah, and I'm going to fuck him. He's so sweet, unlike you stupid straights."

NOWADAYS I DON'T FEAR ANYTHING.

–

I KNEW I WAS GAY when I was very young, in Standard 4. I used to like boys' company. Then I realized I was bisexual when I was in high school; I tried to have sex with a woman and realized, "Oh, it can work."

My first sexual encounter happened in Form Two. There used to be this dude, he was actually my best friend. We would hang out together after preps. One day we were in our dormitory and there was a blackout. He had some chocolate, so I asked him, "Aren't you going to give me any chocolate?"

He said, "Come and get it."

I asked him where it was and he replied, "On my lips."

I didn't think twice. I just went for it and he snogged me. It was awesome. We used to kiss daily, but we never fucked. Just kissing, and he would wank and that was it. This went on until he finished school. He was a class ahead of me.

When I was in Form Four, I met another guy. He wasn't a student. We met in a *matatu*[15]. He approached me, and we talked. He asked me if there were any gay people in my school and I said, "Oh no, I've never heard of that."

He offered to buy me coffee when we alighted. He told me he was about to get married, and his wedding was two weeks away. He gave me his number and told me to call him when I'd be going back to school. I called him a day before I went back to school, we arranged a meeting and I went over to his place. He showed me gay porn. I had never seen those things before. Then things happened. So I can maybe say, he was my first boyfriend.

We continued after that. I finished school and we would meet, even after he got married. We wouldn't go to his place though. Maybe his friend's place. This went on for two years. I wouldn't say I dated him. It was just sex, nothing serious. It wasn't really a relationship because he would meet with other guys and arrange for me to go watch him having sex. It was my idea initially, to watch him having sex. He had that power. Just approaching someone and *wanaingia box*. He would successfully seduce them.

I used to love watching him having sex and he would organize lots of sessions like that. He wanted us to have a threesome but I would never agree. I'd just do the kissing part and they'd do the fucking part. I was the cheering squad. I used to cheer, "Whoooo, slowly baby, slowly baby, you'll kill him!"

Now, we rarely talk with him but he is still in this town. He was involved in some scandals so we cut off communication. Sexual scandals. Robbery. It was through him that my family knew I was gay. We were down the streets one day, holding hands, and

---

15. Slang for privately owned mini-buses that function as public transport in Kenya.

we just bumped into my aunts. I didn't panic. I just greeted them and they went away. Later on, we had a family meeting which I was told was about my cousins who had some problems. At the meeting we didn't even discuss my cousin's problems—they had come for my issue. My aunts told everyone in my family that they had met me with a guy who was know to be gay. I told them, "Yeah, it happened."

So the guy and I were taken to the Chief's Camp. He came with his mother, I was there with my aunts and uncle and he was fined 5,000 shillings and then we went home together. Our parents walked ahead, and I walked with him. I don't know what he was fined for. *Ati anaharibu mtoto wa shule.* Corrupting a minor. I was still in Form Four then.

When I used to go back to school, my cousins would tease me, "*Eh! Enda ukasome. Usiangalie akina Kamau, akina Njoroge ukawanoki.*" Alex, go and study. Don't look at Kamau and Njoroge and fall for them.

It didn't stress me. I just accepted myself. My family has never asked me about it again. They just know that I am. They just see me with boys, with boys, with boys, with boys. One day my aunt told me, "Eh, you just have one password."

I just laughed it away. I didn't respond.

The first time I was with a woman was three years ago. It was an arranged thing. My neighbour used to tell me, "Oh, I have a niece who is beautiful."

I told her, "When she comes to ██████, you can arrange a meeting."

She called me one day and when I went there, this beautiful woman was there. I talked with her. When it was time for me to leave, I told her that she could escort me home. While on our way home, I kissed her.

She decided to come to my place one day. I was nervous. I kept asking myself, "Will I make it?", but it happened. We had sex. I was surprised. Really. I definitely knew I wasn't going to get a hard on. How the hell it happened, I don't know. We had sex four times that year and then it was over. We broke up indefinitely and we never talk about it. That was two years ago.

I have been in love, with a man. The first time I fell in love with a man, it was with my best friend's boyfriend. He had come to █████. He liked me, so we got to talking. Whenever I'd visit Nairobi, I'd stay at his place. We had some romantic times with him, though he was a taken man. They eventually broke up, but not because of me. They had some issues. My friend has never known that his boyfriend and I used to fuck. I never told him, but he used to suspect it. My first memorable kiss was with him too. My friend's boyfriend. He used to kiss me the way I love to be kissed.

I'm currently in a relationship that's been going on for a year and two months now. It's my longest one. We stay in the same house. We used to chat over the internet and one day, we decided to meet up at a hotel. We became friends and I found out that I liked him. So every time I would go to town to look for him and then he would come to my place. I used to live in a big house alone and he would ask, "You don't get bored in this whole house, alone?"

So he asked me to stay with him. I didn't think twice. I moved in a year ago. My family know I live with him because WE GO HOME TOGETHER.

–

I'M TWENTY YEARS OLD, and I'm gay. When I was pretty young, I apparently used to love playing with my dolls. I never liked doing the boy stuff. I was always attracted to boys. When we used to play little games, like *Cha Mama, Cha Baba* [playing house], I was mostly the mother of the house. All through primary and high school, I was never attracted to a girl, not for a single moment. It was always boys.

In primary school, it was just kissing and stuff but nothing sexual. Just a little bit of kissing and touching.

I went to a mixed boarding high school and I was still attracted to boys. When it came to school drama, I was always given the female role. Never a male role. And I was very comfortable with it. I was happy, and I used to own it. I have pictures to prove it.

Most students used to say I'm gay. Some actually asked me the question. I'd tell my closest friends, "Yes I am," and they would support me because they knew me as a fun person, good to hang out with and very honest. Some would tell me it's OK. But some hated me, as you know there are always haters around. I was comfortable with those that were comfortable around me.

I had three relationships while in high school. The first, during Form One was with a prefect in Form Four. Form 1s used to go for a line up every evening for garbage collection around the compound. One day, when we were almost breaking for mid-term, he called me and told me to remain behind and go to his office. Then he said, "Today, sit here and keep me company."

We chatted for a while and we actually became good friends. Instead of doing my duties, I used to go to his office and we would chat all through. On weekends we used to hang around together and do fun stuff.

One day we were talking about relationships and he asked me if I had a girlfriend. I told him I didn't. Jokingly, he also asked if I had a boyfriend. I told him I did not but I wished to have one. He said, "Wow. Can I be your boyfriend?"

I said, "Well, time will tell."

And time told.

He made the first move. He asked me out and used to profess his love for me and write me cute letters. You know, the cute high school letters, the little notes that you find in your locker. He used to do that. He'd also give me favours. I never had to do any cleaning chores and that was very, very nice! I enjoyed that. I used to get free trips since he was a prefect so when there was going to be a trip, I'd go. It ended when he left school. We used to talk but then he was insecure. He thought I'd get a boyfriend after he left. So we both thought it was wise to break up.

I started drinking at twelve because of influence from friends and my brother—but mostly friends. By the time I was fourteen I used to drink, go out and party like hell. I used to sneak out of school. I won't lie, I was a bad boy. These days I'm focused.

Then I fell in love with another guy. We met at a music festival. He spotted me while I was watching a choral verse competition, holding my certificate. He came over and said hi then asked a few questions. After a while I told him I was gay and he told me, "Wow, me too. I thought you were. That's why I came to say hi."

So we chatted for the whole time till our school bus was almost leaving. I gave him my number. During mid-term, he called me. We used to talk for hours and hours till my dad confiscated my phone. And we met again in Nairobi and we chatted. We grew very fond of each other. I love him, up to today.

My first real kiss? I actually know the date. Don't be freaked out by this. It was March the 12th at 11pm, in the middle of the field, in the moonlight. I had in my hand a bottle of Krest and my very, very cute boyfriend was standing next to me. That was in Form One. 12th March, 2008. It was magical. The moonlight was there. That's all I needed.

I want to get married to a man. I want children. Badly. Like five of them. I love children. It's one of the things that made me love medicine. I'm actually specializing in paediatrics. Five children are not many. Five are normal. I want three cute little girls and two boys.

I was born Catholic, but as I grew up and started to learn more about religion, I've come to believe religion is a big enemy to the world. World War III will be caused by religion. And it is starting; Christian Army versus Muslim Army. Why? Religion. You worship the same God. Why are you fighting? I'm more of a deist. I believe there is a God but I don't believe in religion. I've been a deist since 2012.

I have not come out to anyone in my family. No one knows but my friends. I would tell them but I know they suspect I am. I'm pretty sure they know, because my mum freaks out when I hang out with boys.

When I came out to my friends, some were very supportive. One of my girl friends told me, "Ooh, let's go look for boys for you," and I asked, "Are you for real?", because I knew she was such a staunch Christian. I haven't lost any friends because of my sexuality. Most of them have been very, very supportive. I was afraid to come out to them because of the things they used to say about gay people. And I came to learn that they are quite supportive if you prove to them that sexuality is not something that a person chooses, it's something you're born with, and YOUR SEXUALITY DOES NOT DEFINE YOU.

–

SEXUALLY, I AM A very, very, very, very, very, very closeted lesbian, because of my line of work. I am a business person, and my business would be affected if the people I deal with knew my sexual orientation, so I am very closeted.

I found out I was a lesbian in primary school, around Standard 6. I would get attracted to girls. I joined high school, and it became more intense. I don't know if the other students knew or suspected I was gay, but we would write small love notes to each other. We were suspended from school for doing that many times. In primary school, the teachers assume that 'lesbianism' doesn't happen, but in high school they know that the girls are now mature, so teachers are aware that this thing is happening. So, high school was tough. There was suspicion and reporting, and the notes we would write were used as evidence.

In my final years in the school, I became a prefect. This other girl was also a prefect. Because I was a prefect, I had the privilege of having my own room. So we became close, and I started having a crush on her. I was interested in her, and she became interested in me, history happened. We had had sex many times, because she had her own room, and I had my own room. One Sunday I was coming back to school from Catholic Mass, and I found my friends waiting for me at the gate. They told me, "We need to talk. Let's go to your room."

When we were walking from the gate, everyone was staring at me. People were whispering and jeering at me, and I was wondering what was wrong with them. We went to my room and they asked, "What is your relationship with this girl?"

I said we were just friends.

They kept insisting, saying, "We are your friends. You have to tell us what's going on with you two."

I insisted that we were just friends. So they explained that on that day—during the Protestant church service—my girlfriend gave a testimony about us. She talked about how she was living in sin, and she was having a relationship with a girl, and she named me. Everyone knew me because I was a prefect at the time. That was my worst experience ever, because some years before I had been suspended for 'lesbianism' but they did not have concrete evidence. They accused me but did not know who my partner was. For some reason, my dad defended me. He insisted that they would have to show him my partner, because I could not be a lesbian without a partner.

So there I was, my partner had come out and confessed to the whole school. The teachers knew, the headmistress knew, and if I was suspended from school, my dad would kill me. But I got out of it without getting suspended. My guidance and counselling teacher and I were very good friends. She understood me, and I understood her. Also, I performed well in school. My teacher defended me, saying that if the school suspended me and I was one of the best students, the mean grade of the school would drop. So they agreed that what I did was bad. It was against the school beliefs, but were they willing to affect the performance of the school just because of my sexuality? No. So I was saved.

After that, my former girlfriend was kept away from me. I was not supposed to talk to her—not that I wanted to, because I was so mad. The last thing I told her was, "You're the one who made the first move on me. Why did you go and say that I 'introduced' you to this?"

Her story was that I tempted her and she fell into sin, or something of the sort. It really affected our relationship. We ended up going to the same university, and she tried talking to me about what happened in high school, but I told her, "Don't even… I don't want to see you. Please just leave me alone."

She said, "Please, I was just a kid," and I said, "No, you made high school a nightmare. I don't want to see you."

She made my high school life so bad—I couldn't even shake hands with anyone, because they would say, "*Wewe, utaniconvert.*" You'll convert me.

Even one of my very good friends told me, "I've always said if I find out any of my friends is a lesbian, that's the end of that friendship, because I don't want to be converted."

I looked at her and said, "Aren't we supposed to be friends?"

She said, "Not any more, sorry."

I said, "OK, this is crazy. We know each other. We are friends."

But she didn't talk to me again and she stopped being my friend. Not a word, because she 'doesn't want to be converted'. That's why I am so closeted, because of my past experiences. Only one of my high school friends remained my very good friend, up to today. Her father is a bishop in a church. She said, "I'm not judging you because of how people see you, I judge you on how productive you are in the society. That's it."

You know, kids can be ruthless. After the story came out, I remained a parade prefect. Part of my duty was to stand with teachers during parade and make student announcements. Every time I'd talk, there would be murmurs in the crowd, "Oooooh, lesbian!"

Then the teachers would defend me, saying, "Can you stop? She is a prefect. You are students. Have some respect."

But kids can be ruthless, they'd say it to my face. My friends would not. If they were talking behind my back, I didn't know. Even when I went to university, the rumours continued, because there were all these people I came with from my high school who knew about my sexuality. So in university, people were pointing fingers at me but it was better—because it was not like high school. You're not going to suspend me in university because of my sexuality. It's my sexuality. I'm not staying on campus. I have my own house. Whatever I do in my house is my business. Whatever I do outside campus is my business. My business in campus is to attend classes, perform well and pass my exams; that is it. So you people can talk, and I don't care.

I had one girlfriend from 1st Year to 4th Year. We were in the same class, and I noticed her because she came to class with a black eye. I looked at her, and she looked so sad. She used to be our best performing girl in campus. I asked her, "What's wrong?"

She said, "Nothing."

I said, "You have a problem. You come here putting on sunglasses, and it's evening. There is a problem."

Then she told me, "I'm in an abusive relationship. I'm living with my boyfriend, and he's abusing me. We fight all the time."

My heart went out to her, so I told her, "You're a woman. You're beautiful. No one is supposed to abuse you. So, if you want to run, my place is your place. If ever he beats you again, get out of that relationship. My house is your house. I'll stay with you."

A few days later, it got really rough. She was beaten and he tried to strangle her, so she called me. I said, "I'm coming to get you."

So I went to get her. She came and stayed at my place. She stayed with me for a while, and I was worried because I hadn't told her about my sexuality. I thought if I told her about my sexuality, she would feel uncomfortable because we were sleeping in the same bed. So I kept quiet and didn't talk to her about sexuality. But I really liked her. I thought with where our friendship had reached, we could sustain a relationship. If she was uncomfortable, I hoped at least our friendship would still stand. So, one day after dinner—she liked cooking, so she had prepared a good meal—I told her, "There's something I have never told you about me. I'm gay."

She said, "What?"

I repeated, "I'm gay. No one knows about it in campus, apart from the rumours from high school, but now you know."

She said, "I don't mind. We are friends."

A few days after I had confessed, I made a move while we were sleeping. She didn't push me away. What happened that night happened, and we continued for four years until we got out of campus. We don't live together any more, but we are very good friends. Now she's in a relationship with a guy, I guess she's bisexual. We still hang out, she comes to my place, I go to her place.

I guess we drifted apart because of distance. Also, we are both so ambitious. She wants to be this very great lawyer, and I want to be this very great businesswoman. Our ambitions are too much for us. She can't move from Nairobi, she can't leave her career in Nairobi. I can't leave what I've started here in ██████.

Her boyfriend kinda knows about us, because once we met him and she accidentally introduced me as her girlfriend. He said, "Oh! OK."

When they met years later in Nairobi, he asked her, "Where is your girlfriend?"

She said, "Huh?"

He said, "Your girlfriend, the one I met you with in campus."

She denied it and said, "No, no, no. She's not my girlfriend like that, I meant girl friend, like friend."

So, the guy doesn't really know, but he understands that we have history that he can't come between. It's something that you cannot erase, and he respects that. But he doesn't know what was really going on between us.

My dad wanted me to be a lawyer, but I wanted to do business. So I had to fulfil my dad's dream for me to study law, then I went ahead to fulfil my dream of doing business after that. I didn't want to study law. It wasn't my passion. My passion was in business. Right now, I am running a farm. I also have a shop and—hopefully by next year—my ultimate dream is to go into real estate. But for now, baby steps.

I share the shop with two other girls. It's in a mall where we get walk-in customers. Everyone there knows I'm gay, because I once had a fight with a girl I was seeing, and she came to the shop, shouting and causing drama one morning. I heard her and came out to calm her down, and she was shouting, "Do you want me to tell people what you do? You want me to tell people what you do in the dark?"

There was a crowd around us, and the mall was full of customers and they all heard her. So we ended up outing each other. It was horrible. Everyone now knows, but they cannot come and ask me about it. The bad thing with ████████ is that it is a small town. Everyone knows everyone, you see? The only thing that keeps us safe is that people can't come and ask you, "Hey, are you a lesbian?"

They'll just talk, and that's it. I'm so closeted. I cannot date a butch girl. I cannot. If you're not femme, no. But people talk, you know? My dad knows I'm a lesbian. My brother, too. But he's my small brother, and he doesn't have the guts to ask me about it. Before he got a job, I used to stay with him, and the girls who would come to see me were so butch! They were wearing Timberlands[16]. I kept telling them, "Don't wear Timberlands when you come to see me. Don't wear Timberlands, please."

---

16 Timberland boots, usually associated with hyper-masculine men.

Once, my friends came over for dinner, and one of them was so butch, you couldn't even see her boobs. My brother looked at them like, huh? Then when we were in the kitchen, *haskii sauti ya chali*. He couldn't hear the voice of a man. Just girls. He was like, huh? So he'd pretend to come into the kitchen to get some water, and really look at the butch girl.

Later, he told me, "I thought that girl was a guy."

I deflected the issue by telling him the butch girl had fought with her boyfriend, and that we were trying to console her. So, I don't know what he thinks.

I'm in a long-distance relationship with a German man. My mum asks me when I'm getting married, and I tell her, "Mum, I'm dating this person, he's in another country, I'm in Kenya, what do you want us to do?"

If he actually says he's coming, I'll break up with him. I'm hoping he will never come to Kenya, or even near East Africa. So my parents don't know what to say. They say, "That girl *na wazungu wake, na wa-Chinese, na wa-Hindi…*" That girl, with her white men and Chinese and Indians…

I have an Indian friend. He's gay, and I think he's under pressure to get married too. He was telling me we should pretend to be together. I told him, "No. That's weird, I can't pretend with you. It's not going to be easy, because an Indian dating a black person is a whole other problem, it won't work."

I usually joke that if my parents insist on me getting married, I will get married, and I will break up within the first year of my marriage, and I will be single for the rest of my life. I will have an official reason to hate men. I'll say, "You see what that guy put me through? I'm not doing that again."

That's my plan.

I have five sisters, and two of them have gay male friends. I always wonder, "If they can have gay friends, can they accommodate me? Can they have a gay sister?"

But I've never had the guts to tell them. In fact, once I was with my guy friends—who were all gay—at the shop, and my sisters called to say they were coming. So I told my friends, "OK, here is the deal. My sisters are coming, so please try and behave like men. Please. For my sake."

I don't know, but they behaved the opposite to my advice. In fact, they became extra-girly.

I asked them, "Guys, what had we agreed on? Why are you doing this?"

My sisters watched my guy friends behaving like women and asked me, "*Ai? Kwani* how are these guys behaving? They are gay."

I said, "No, they are not gay."

My sister said, "We have friends who are gay and your friends are behaving just like them. Those guys are definitely gay."

I denied it again. Then my sister told me, "You are in denial. You're not seeing that they are gay, but they are gay. Be a good friend. The day they decide to come out to you, be their friend. Maybe they haven't recognized that they are gay, but they are. So when they decide to come out, just be there for them, because they are gay. We know."

Another time, when I used to live in my parents' house, we used to rent out the servants' quarters. One of the tenants at a point was this man with a wife and a kid, they were married. They moved out after a while, but years later, I was at a gay get-together and I saw him there. I saw him and I practically started running from the room. One of my friends asked me, "Where are you going?"

I said, "Oh my God, my former neighbour is in this meeting. I don't want to be outed."

My friends told me, "No one is outing you. If he outs you, he outs himself."

I thought, "What? Oh. OK, yeah."

I still wasn't comfortable, though. I thought, "If this guy is not gay, he's coming to *chunguza* [investigate], I'm still at risk."

That day, I didn't introduce myself as a lesbian, because I wasn't going to take that risk that he wasn't one of us. We didn't say a word to one another. Just a quick hello. I think he was also wondering, "Will she out me?"

That's how hard it is to be in the closet in this small town. You always run the risk of being outed. I'll tell you another story. Once we had a group of gay friends from Nairobi come here for the weekend; gays and lesbians, girls and boys. But among them was this one straight girl who didn't know we were all gay. The group was full of men who were behaving like women, and women who were behaving like men, but somehow she didn't know. It was her birthday, so her cousin—who is a lesbian—brought her over.

So we went to a bar, and this really, really rich guy was interested in this straight girl. He found out it was her birthday, so he said—to impress her, I guess—"I'm going to take all of you guys out for dinner, and after that we can go clubbing. All of you."

So we were happy; sorted. We didn't need to pay for anything. We went for dinner, and we were sitting at a round table. Our 'host' called his other straight guy friends and told them, "*Kuna bash, na kuna ma-dame, so kujeni mkatie.*" There's a party, and there are girls, so come and get some.

So they came, and there we were sitting on this round table. We sat all mixed up so that everyone could mingle. One of the straight guys started hitting on one of our lesbian friends, and—I think she had smoked weed, and I think it was her first time so it really had hit her—she said to him, "Boss, I don't do guys."

I was looking at her sternly, wiling her to shut up.

She continued, "*Boss*, I don't do guys. I do girls."

The guy was confused, "What?"

She went on and told him, "What's wrong with you? Don't you see something unique about everyone who is here?"

So this guy was now looking at all of us, like huh? Then he realized we were all gay, and he tells our host, "Stop spending."

We had all eaten and drank by that time, so our bill had already reached some twenty-something thousand. This guy told our host, "Stop wasting money on these people. They're all gay."

One of the other straight guys even looked at me and said, "In fact, I know this one. She's been a lesbian all her life."

I looked at him and asked him, "Do I even know you? I don't know you, you don't know me."

He stood his ground and told the host, "I am not going to allow you to continue paying the bill for these gay people."

They were so annoyed, but our host didn't care about it. He paid the bill anyway and insisted that we all go clubbing. Somehow, we ended up in the club. Our host told us, "I've been told not to buy drinks for you, but I'll buy you drinks. Just don't say I'm the one who bought the drinks."

But even there, these straight guys went around telling people in the club, "You see that clique? They are all gay."

So people in the club came to us and said, "*Unajua tutawachapa?*" Do you know we're going to beat you?

So we got out. We had to get out quickly, because the situation was becoming tense. So we jumped into the taxi because people were following us, and we escaped.

But we're surviving. The guys are more out than the girls here in ██████. Maybe it's because they're tough. I don't know.

Sometimes I wonder, "Does my faith allow this?"

As a Christian, when I go to church on Sundays, I wonder whether I should stop going to church altogether. Because after I come home from church, then my girlfriend says she's coming for Sunday lunch, and I think, "Oh my God, did it have to be on Sunday? I just came from church."

So sometimes, that thinking really affects me. Sometimes when something goes wrong in my business, I wonder, "Is God punishing me? Should I just stop being a lesbian?"

I really can't, because I love girls. That's why when it comes to things like religion and homosexuality, I really don't like talking about it, because my religion tells me it's wrong but in my heart I know I'm happiest when I'm with girls. I can't change that. I've gone to Catholic schools all my life, and they've said it's wrong, but here I am with my feelings. I can't control them. I've tried dating guys, and I look at them and think, "I'm not doing this."

I've tried. You can't say that I haven't tried. I've tried dating guys, and it hasn't worked. I tried dating guys, and we'd be walking together—talking—and a hot girl would pass by and I'd think, "Wow! I like what I'm seeing."

And then I'd turn back to the guy and he says something like, "OK, wow. You're not supposed to look at girls like that. You're supposed to concentrate on me. I'm your man."

One day, if I get a girl who is serious about her future, definitely I might settle down with her. Right now, I haven't found that girl. I want someone who knows what she wants with her future. If I get that girl, I might consider settling down. I usually say, when my parents die—God forbid—I will be able to come out.

I remember one day my girlfriend and I went to Nairobi to see another lesbian couple. While we were in their house, the mother of one of the girls decided to visit without calling to say she was coming over. She just knocked on the door and there she was. In the sitting room, these girls had put up pictures of themselves holding each other. Now, when the mother went to their bathroom to help herself, they started harvesting the photos off the walls. Her little brother—who had come with the mum—was asking them, "*Mbona mnatoa? Si muache tu? Mum ashaziona.*" Why are you taking them off? Leave them, Mum has already seen them.

My dad is a very staunch Catholic. That's why I've never envisioned myself with a partner. When I look at my parents and imagine taking off pictures of my girlfriend and I from my wall so that my parents don't start suspecting, it makes me hesitate to settle down.

I really want twins, though. Actually, I've already talked to my gynaecologist. She told me it's possible if I get sperm donors. I can get my twins if I want. Most probably by the end of next year, because my parents are looking at me, and they're saying, "*Huyu anachelewa.*" This one is getting late.

Being a lesbian is hard, but there are times when it's good. I love being a lesbian when I'm in the privacy of my place. Like yesterday was Valentine's Day, so I took my girlfriend out for pizza. We had our pizza and that was great, but as we were leaving to come back home, someone said, "*Hao wanaenda kuingizana vidole.*" Those ones are going to finger one another.

So manner-less. I was so annoyed. My girlfriend—people fear her—told them, "*Si vidole zenyu tumechukua. Ni zetu tunatumia. Kama tulikuwa tunatumia zenyu ingekuwa* issue, but they're not yours, so relax, guys." We're not using your fingers. We're using our own fingers. If we were using your fingers, that would be an issue.

Everyone laughed and it ended there. They kept quiet. She doesn't care. She's out, and she says she's not going to compromise her life. She doesn't care if people talk. But I am afraid. But you have to live. I know I didn't choose to be a lesbian. Someone once told me she believed gay men were taught how to become gay. I told her, "Seriously? Who teaches someone how to become straight or gay? Who teaches them?"

And she said, "I was just told."

So I told her, "Don't be silly. Nobody taught you how to start loving boys. You didn't go to school and study how to like boys, you just woke up and you were like wow! Every time you see boys you tremble. No one told you to start trembling. When you want to meet a boy, you start putting on make up. You want to impress the guy. Who taught you that? You just felt like you have to impress this guy. So in the same way, this boy just woke up and felt that way for other boys. It's AS SIMPLE AS THAT."

–

I AM GAY. I realized when I was thirteen years old and in Standard 8. I had a huge crush on this boy who transferred to our school from a different school. Aww, he had very beautiful eyes and he was tall. He was fifteen and puberty had set in. He had broad shoulders but he didn't have masculine legs. He had chicken legs, but they were cute. He came to our class—we were in the middle of an exam—and he just showed up with a desk on his head. He was a new student and everyone was staring at him. I immediately thought he was hot. I even stopped concentrating on the exam to stare at him. At break time, he came and talked to me. I was the most popular guy in school and I was in with the girls, so he had to talk to me. It was very interesting.

He is still my Facebook friend, I looked him up on Facebook when I was eighteen but now he lives in Europe. He is cute as ever.

In high school, I was interested in a guy—let's call him Andrew. He was older—I have a thing for older people. He was as rugged as they come, and he was the captain of the rugby team. He had a nice face, and his eyes were very interesting—brown but almost orange. He was a bad boy, the kind that you just stare at. He was mysterious. He was firm in the right places. He had abs and biceps, and he would wear those tiny rugby shorts. I started watching rugby just because of him.

In our school, we had a weird custom where Form 3s would get Form 1s as bed-mates. So, my bed-mate was a Form Three who was friends with Andrew. Andrew would constantly come to see my bed-mate and I used to wonder why he would visit him every other day. When my bed-mate wasn't there, Andrew would try to make conversation with me and he would hold my hand.

In Form One, I was shy and awkward. I was tiny. He would hold my hand and I would wonder what he was doing. He would start telling me stories like how he thought I was handsome. I would always ask him to stop it. I didn't act on my feelings because I didn't want to confirm that I was gay. Being intimate with a guy would mean that I was gay, and at that time my father was a Christian pastor. My parents were like church elders; he was a pastor, and very close to becoming a bishop. My mother was on every church committee. I didn't want to embarrass our family.

The thing with Andrew, though, is he wasn't my type. He had such a perfect body but he was not very bright. Oh my God, how could you have a conversation with him? He was so dumb. But he was a man's man, the captain of the rugby team. He was masculine. And here I was, a tiny Form One who was in the praise and worship team in the Christian Union.

In February, the school closed for a mid-term break, and before I left for home, he invited me to his cubicle after everyone had gone. The rugby team were remaining in school because they were going for provincial competitions. I went to his cubicle, and he started to tell me stories about how hung he was. He started undressing in front of me. I was seated on his bed, and I tried to cross my legs, trying to act like I was not affected. He said, "I like you."

I said, "You like everyone."

"Not in that way. I mean I like, like you," he responded.

He began talking about his sex life, and about how good he was in bed. He said, "I am so big."

I decided to rock the boat. I told him I wanted to see. I teased him that I thought he was small, the size of my little finger. I stood up and said I was leaving. He took my hand and put it on his crotch. It was the first penis I had ever been in contact with, other than mine. I had never watched porn, but I had fantasies.

I used to write vivid stories in my notebooks and all my story characters were boys. Anyway, after I touched him I was just mesmerized. He pulled me to him and leaned in for a kiss. I refused because of his lips. I had a problem with his lips. They were chapped. I also thought that kissing was too intimate.

These days I like kissing, but he was the only person I could do everything with except kiss. He was really good with his hands and after two minutes I climaxed. I was embarrassed. It wasn't a hand job, it was just him being close. It was the most amazing five minutes of my life.

He wasn't a bully. He did not force me into having sex. When he realized that I had come, he suggested that I should clean up and asked whether I wanted to continue. I said no. I left quickly and all the way home I was feeling guilty. I kept telling myself that I was a sinner. After the mid-term break I started avoiding him. He was a prefect and he kept trying to meet me. He would come and signal me after assembly, and everyone would think I was in trouble. Even when other students were running for sports, he would ask me to stay behind. Other students realized something was going on, and I told him that other students knew that he was always picking on me.

We kept fooling around from that February until he sat his last paper. We were together for ten months and we would do all kinds of things. Every Saturday—while all other students were not yet awake—I would go and wake him up at four or five in the morning. It was a very clandestine affair. I felt like I was sleeping with the President. I never thought about the consequences if we were caught, but I always felt bad that instead of going for morning devotion I would go and do this. He had the most amazing body. I haven't found anyone ever since with that kind of body.

He was rough and sometimes he would joke about raping me. It wasn't cute. I would tell him that that was not right and that he should never say that. He would apologize and say, "I like you."

He never told me that he loved me. I didn't know whether we were exclusive, so I didn't want to go down that road. I was never comfortable with having sex in a cubicle with other people around. I had romantic ideas about how my first time would be—that's why I never did anything penetrative with him. Also, students in our school used to say very homophobic things. If you were close with someone they would assume that you were shagging and they would say mean things about you. There was an alleged list of homosexuals in school and I didn't want to appear on it. He had to keep up appearances and I had to do that as well. Sadly after high school we never saw each other again. I heard that he is now in ███████.

After he left there was a vacuum, I didn't think that I would meet anyone else. In Form Two, I came out to my desk-mate, Eric. He was the first person I ever came out to. Every time we talked, he would bring up a story about girls. At some point it was uncomfortable. I told him that I was not into girls, that I was into guys. Funnily, he was accepting. He was very open-minded. He was the best desk-mate I had. This was in the early 2000s and he didn't ever use it against me. We were desk-mates throughout Form Two to Form Four. In Form Three, his brother—Fred—started hitting on me. It was awkward because he took the romantic angle. He wrote me cute poems—except for one weird one he wrote about his penis. He would pick me from class, and we would go for walks together in the school.

He was the first person I loved. He was into rugby and was a bit older. He had a nice physique. He was romantic. He had a way with words. Once, we met and made out in the CU patron's office. But he was very preachy and I didn't like it when he talked. Sadly we never got to consummate the union. I liked him, but I am glad that we never did it because a month later I started to realize he was a douche-bag.

After that, our CU meetings became icy. We stopped talking. He was such a douche-bag. I was an idiot for falling for him. Thankfully, I have never fallen for anyone else since then. I have been with people, but I keep my emotions to myself. It made wary of men. I treat them as food.

Later, my desk-mate decided that he wanted to cure my queerness. It was an interesting approach. He thought if he told me that he loved me I would freak out. I did. He kept on persisting that we could date, and I kept rejecting his advances. We fought, and did not speak for five months. Eventually, I did make out with him. It was amazing. He was good with his hands, and he had good lips. He was the first person I ever kissed.

He wanted to date me, but I told him he was my best friend. I thought he was trying to annoy me so that I would abandon being gay. I don't know. Until I cleared high school, I had fantasies about him, but I never acted on my feelings. My mother fell sick and I blamed myself for it. After high school, my mum died. In an act of rebellion, I watched my first gay porn.

Now that I was done with high school, I joined my first dating site. I don't like dating sites but I thought I could meet someone. It did not yield much. The first person I met threw me off. He was balding and very fat. I closed my profile on that site. A few years later, I joined another dating site and met someone. He was Somali. He was interesting. We had a long distance relationship. It was the weirdest, most short-lived relationship. We never met, but he used to call me every day. He never pressured me to have sex, at least.

I asked him whether we could meet, and he said he was willing to come to ████████, but then I realized we would have to hire a hotel room, and I was not sure about two men sharing a hotel room. He was also excited about an oral experience he had had in high school and wanted to relive it. He was also very closeted. I couldn't keep up with him. The relationship died like that. I felt bad that we did not get a chance to meet. He tried to call me once, many months later. I could not remember him and he was offended.

My aunt took me to a college that was in a very remote area because she thought being in a town set-up would spoil me. Her own son was there—my cousin. It was a Catholic college with a high population of girls. I joined the college, and even there I never dated.

In my second year, I met a guy called Hamisi. I noticed him because he looked like he had no eyebrows. Not that he had tweezed them, it was natural. I didn't know of any straight man who tweezes or shaves their eyebrows. I began talking to him, and we established a rapport. He was in the military and was staying at the chief's place. He had been transferred from Nairobi and he didn't like the village. He was bored. He invited me for dinner and we bonded. Dinner took five hours and I slept there. It became a habit, I would always go and visit him and have dinner. I then started playing housewife. Initially I would cook him *chapatis*. I then started noticing the dirt in his house, so I cleaned the house and bought him pillows and bedsheets.

It was not sexual. He used to tell me that he respected me as a young brother. We never shared a bed. He had two beds, and he would let me sleep on the bigger one. We would eat together and other times I would stay at his place for three days. Over the holidays I would stay with him for a week. I made the house homely. In the beginning his house looked like a pastoralist stayed there. By the time we were parting he had a carpet, a stereo and a home theatre system. He had nice things and I would cook him nice food, too. It was not that I was in love with him. I just did it. He began talking about how I could be a good Muslim, but I told him no. I just loved being away from school. School was boring. He was a welcome relief.

My classmates began talking about how I was never in school. Hamisi would drop me back to school in a government vehicle—usually at midnight. One of my girl friends remarked that I was spending a lot of time with Hamisi. Another girl who used to have a crush on Hamisi asked me why he would leave her to spend time with a skinny boy like me. She had tried dating him but it never worked between them. Someone made an anonymous call to my aunt and said they thought I was gay. She was furious, she asked my cousin—who was my room-mate—about it, he said that it was not true. He lied that we spend all nights together.

Hamisi was very sweet. I don't know if he was a high-ranking officer, but he would always make time for me and if he could not he would send someone to see me on his behalf.

Once, I went to visit my small brother in school which was very far—somewhere in ███████. I got stranded on the way back, and I called Hamisi to ask him for some cash as my fare was not enough. He drove all the way to come and pick me! That was the sweetest thing. He did not ask for anything in return. He got transferred to ███████ and we didn't get to talk again. I lost my phone and lost touch with him.

Romantic attraction that leads to sex scares me. But with him I felt safe, he wasn't explicit. I could be myself around him and he did not judge me. He didn't make me change; his friends would come and find me on the bed and they would wonder what was going on between us, but he never told me whether there was any problem.

I met someone interesting last year. He is way older, and he is not Kenyan. We were friends before and so we decided to start dating and see if it works. He is amazing, and if things work out I would see myself growing old with him. Growing old with someone is challenging in the African context because you have to eventually come out. I used to be afraid of coming out to people because I did not know how they would react. But I have come out to my younger brother and he was very supportive. He is actually my number one fan—I tell him everything I am involved with. He says he wouldn't want me to get hurt because it would hurt the family. So I would not go protesting on the streets for the rights of gay people, for instance. He is OK with anything that will not hurt them as a family or me.

My sister might know but she never asks me. They knew my ex-boyfriend and they kept on asking about him but I told them it couldn't work. They say he was nice. If I get serious with someone I will introducc them to my family because it is important for them to know. I wouldn't want to come out to the extended family because I think it is none of their business.

I wouldn't want to come out in public because of my aunt. She once saw my hairstyle—I was going through phases with my hair at the time—and I was also wearing very short shorts. My hair was shorter than usual, so she told my sister that I was either in a cult or I was gay. I think she knows that I am gay. Whenever I go to visit her I am always in tight pants. She once sent me a friend request on Facebook, I accepted it then I blocked her. She will realize slowly that I will not have that conversation with her because the shock WILL JUST KILL HER.

–

THE QUESTION OF WHAT I IDENTIFY AS has never been easy for me to answer. I identify as a person. I find myself attracted to men, but I also find myself attracted to women. However, I find myself more attracted to women, especially over the last five years. Over the last couple of years I've been living as a lesbian. Before that I was living as a bisexual.

I met the love of my life, and we ended up breaking up. I think the reason why we broke up is because I kept trying to get her to identify as a lesbian, even though she was also attracted to men. Let's call her Jane.

Our relationship was very good at the beginning, but then it turned into this thing where I craved attention from her, because I felt I wasn't getting any attention from her. I felt like she wasn't fully committed. This was my first actual lesbian relationship. I had been with really idiotic men until that point. I'd never dated a woman, and at that point if you had asked me if I would ever date a woman, my answer would have been no. I'd been attracted to women, but I was never going to make that leap to actually dating them. It's very easy to fantasize. It's easy to objectify a woman. That line between 'I could tap that' and actually doing it—I would have never crossed that line. I didn't feel safe enough with most women.

With her, it was different. I felt very safe around her. You know how you're constantly trying to impress people, especially the ones you're attracted to? With her, I didn't have to do all those things. I didn't have to prove anything to her.

I was hungry for her. I used to want to be with her all the time. I used to go to school, then as soon as class was over, I would get into a *matatu* going to her place. I would spend ten, fifteen minutes just holding her. She's small. That kind of skewed my attraction to women. Now I like them small.

I'm still hungry for that woman, until today. That's what happens with the love of your life. She was everything. Eventually, her being attracted to men became a problem. To some extent, I blame myself that we ended. If I had asked for things that mattered as opposed to stupid identity issues… I should have asked for honesty and openness. I should have asked for her commitment to our relationship, not to her sexual orientation.

When we met, I was just starting to come into my own. I had just figured out that the fact that I liked women wasn't just fun and games for me. It was a little more serious than that. Up until that point, I'd go out and my boys would use me as wingman. A lot of women saw me not as a predator, they'd see this cute little boyish-looking girl and say, "Aaaw, that's so cute! I want to dance with her, because she doesn't have a penis that will stab me in the back."

You know? I became a toy, and at that time I was fine being a toy, because hey—fringe benefits; a loose make-out session here and there. At the time that was enough for me. Then I met Jane, and that had to stop, and I wasn't ready. I would still go out with my boys and I'd have to reconcile with the fact that I was now seeing someone… Or was I? We hadn't really talked about it… She still had her boyfriend. We hadn't really made anything clear.

I remember the first time we had sex, though. I didn't know anything about women—I didn't know how to please them. I didn't know how to be with them. She was the first woman I had sex with. I remember she came over to my house for New Year's, and I was at home alone with my dad. My mum had gone to church, and my dad was downstairs watching TV. We ate and prayed and then we went to bed. I got into my pyjamas, she got into hers, and we started making out in the dark. She took off her shirt, and I freaked out! "Whaaaaaaaaat!? There's a topless woman on top of me."

I was very… I didn't know anything. But she taught me, and I'm forever indebted.

One night, I went out with my friends to find a place to smoke *shisha*, and we found a nice place with a little couch-bed-thing to snuggle on, and we had a good night. I got home much later in the night and went straight to bed. The next morning, at 7am, I was strung out on the couch and my phone rang.

I picked it up and this guy said, "Hello. It's Andrew."

Andrew was Jane's boyfriend. I wondered, "Why the fuck is this guy calling me, and how did he get my number?"

Andrew proceeded to tell me that Jane's mum had died that night. I was so confused. I looked at my phone and found a missed call from her. Apparently she had called me that night and we had had a conversation. She had told me that her mum had died, but I was so drunk that I said, "Cool. I'll call you back," and I had passed out on the couch.

I have never been more ashamed of myself than in that moment. I tried calling her, and she wasn't picking up her phone. I tried to call Andrew back, but he couldn't talk because he was at her house, busy with the family prayers and all that. I didn't know what to do. Should I go? Should I wait?

I didn't understand how this was happening. You always think of yourself as a good person, and you always think that if you care about someone, you'll be there for them. I wasn't there at the moment that she needed me the most. My friends drove me to her place. Jane wasn't there when we arrived. I stood there wondering what to do. I didn't want to leave because it'd be like I hadn't been there. My mum was calling me to ask where I was because it was getting late.

Eventually, Jane came back. She had taken a walk. We talked and she said, "I can't believe you did that to me."

I told her I was really sorry. That was the one moment I really failed her. We dated for two years and remained in that place where we couldn't tell our parents. She got a really great job working with a big financial institution. This company was super strict about employees 'carrying the brand', so anything she did had to positively shed light on the brand. That meant we couldn't be seen holding hands in public. Even in the club, I couldn't lean in to ask her if she wanted a drink. I couldn't dance with her. Our relationship had to be hidden.

She changed. She was constantly being reminded; you are a brand, you are a brand, YOU ARE A BRAND. She had to act like a brand, she had to dress like a brand; she had to make friends who fit within the brand. Of course, I never fit into that idea of this fucking brand. All I wanted was just one day where I could just be with my girlfriend, and even that became an issue. She'd get invited for events, and she had to show up with a date, and—as great as I look in a suit—I wasn't a man.

So I proposed to her.

All that was clear to me was that I loved her. I was in love with her and I wanted to spend the rest of my life with her. They were my truths, and they made absolute sense to me.

Of course she said no.

She said no, because she's far more pragmatic than I am, which is good. But you can only suffer so much rejection in a relationship. I was not a person she could be seen with, I was not the person she could spend the rest of her life with, which all boils down to one thing: I am not a man.

My insecurities started showing. I compensated and became an asshole. So, after two years she broke up with me.

We broke up while we were on vacation. It was New Year's Eve, and we were on a bus to Malindi. After several hours on the bus, I got tired of talking to her—because there's only so much time you can spend with one person, especially in a bus. I went to the front of the bus and started talking to another girl called Annie. Jane had always had a problem with Annie, because she always thought I had feelings for her.

I talked to Annie for a while, then I went back to sit with Jane. Jane said, "Go back to her. I don't mind."

I hated that passive-aggressive nonsense, so I went back to continue talking to Annie. I sat with Annie for about forty-five minutes. I remember I didn't even look back to see if Jane was fine, because we were having a nice conversation. We finally got to Malindi, and we went in for this huge New Year's Ever party. I didn't see Jane the whole night. But I figured that regardless of whatever fight we were having, I'd find her before the countdown to midnight. I didn't find her, and I didn't see her until 6am the next morning.

We got back in the bus, and she fell asleep on my lap. We drove back to the hotel, I woke her up, took her back to her room, covered her, and fell asleep next to her. That day, she broke up with me.

She said I was smothering her.

I told her, "I don't know what that means, because I love you and everything else figures itself out. As long as we're coming from a point of love, we'll be fine."

But I think she had become tired of our relationship. We got back to Nairobi, and we broke up.

After a while, she moved out of her parents' house, and she needed a place to stay. I lived in a big house and there was lots of space. I told her she could move into my guest room. She agreed.

She started dating some new guy, and I was so angry. I didn't understand how she could go from being with a woman to being with a man in one stride. I thought, "Date another woman first, then ease out a bit! Don't just quit me cold turkey!"

It didn't make sense to me. To make it worse, I knew this guy. He was a serial dater; every week he had a new girlfriend. I asked Jane, "What makes you think you're not 'girl of the week'? If you expect a guy like that to give you more, he's going to break your heart many times."

I told myself I was protecting her, but I don't know if that's what it was. I was being very selfish about the whole thing. It turned out that she was just another 'girl of the week', and of course she wanted more.

We fought about her dating experiments with men, and I'd constantly use the fact that she had horrible taste in men against her, especially in an argument. Eventually it got to the point where I'd say really mean things to her. She would cough and I'd say, "That's from kissing all those random people, isn't it?"

At some point in time, that toxicity between us—all these verbal arguments we were having—turned physical.

She'd been a little depressed from arguing with her dad, and arguing with a friend. I convinced her to come with me for a music event. She said, "The only way I'll go for this is if you promise to sit with me the whole night."

I said, "Not a problem," because she's decent company. We went, and then I met a friend of mine. I walked away for two seconds to talk to her. When I came back, I found Jane wasn't sitting there; she was gone. I looked outside and she was there, having a cigarette with some other chick.

I went out to stand with them. Jane said, "It's time to go home."

I said, "OK."

Then she said, "I'm going to ride with this chick."

In my head I thought, "To whose house? Because it's my house. It's my motherfucking house and I'm letting you stay there, understand."

Jane saw my expression and said, "She's just coming over for a little bit. Don't worry about it."

In my head, "It's midnight. What is she coming to do? It's my house. I don't see why she should be coming to my house."

I got into my car, and Jane got into the other girl's car. I started to drive home, and I remember looking at my keys and thinking, "I don't have to go home."

I looked at my wallet and I had some money; I could go out. I called some friends who said they were going out. So there was a plan, and there was money.

But I knew Jane hadn't carried her keys, so she'd be locked out of the house. Because I'm a good person, I went home. I walked up to the door, and the whole time I was battling with myself. I was thinking, "This is a bad idea. Whatever is going to happen in this house tonight is a bad idea."

I went to the kitchen, grabbed some whiskey and lay on the couch. We left the event at the same time, so they should have been right behind me. Nothing. I sat there, watching TV and sipping my whiskey really slowly and carefully. I finally heard a car pull in. I opened the door, and I saw Jane and the other girl.

I stood there, waiting for them to say good-bye to each other, but they walked in. I locked the door, and went back to sit down. Jane sat on the couch with her friend. They started to cosy up, and I lay on the couch thinking, "There's no way that this is happening as I'm sitting right here. These people are crazy if they think that this shit can happen while I'm watching."

I grabbed a cigarette, went outside and tried to calm down; nothing. I decided to go to bed, because I figured the moment I closed my eyes, I would sleep and morning would come; because it had to. I went to bed but—of course—I couldn't sleep. I woke up about an hour later, and there was no one downstairs. I checked outside and this chick's car was still outside. I thought, "No, no, no. There's no way… Maybe they took a walk."

I went to her room and opened the door, and I found her on top of this girl. The girl's pants were on their way off her body.

I flipped—I was done. I put the lights on, and Jane shouted, "What the fuck?"

I stood at the door, pointed at the girl and said, "You. Get the fuck out of my house."

She looked at me like I was crazy.

I repeated, "Please get the fuck out of my house."

I stood aside from the door, because I felt like if this girl had to squeeze past me to get out, I would kill her. I moved aside to the window, and Jane tells me, "She doesn't have to go anywhere."

I pulled my hand back and I swung it, and it hit the window. I heard glass breaking, and I couldn't stop. It was either I hit someone, or I hit the window. I kept punching at the window; eventually I had no more panes to break because all the panes were broken. I ran out of window to punch, so I turned to them and said, "You two need to get the fuck out."

The other girl had freaked out, ran downstairs while I was hitting the glass. I heard her tires screeching away. I turned to Jane and said, "I need you to get out of my house."

She said, "Where am I going to go?"

I said, "I don't care if you sleep on the fucking side of the street. I need you to get out of my fucking house."

She said, "No."

No? I picked her up, put her on the ground and said, "Get the fuck out of my house."

We started fighting. We fought for the first time ever. She was biting my neck. We fought so much. We somehow ended up downstairs and I'd had enough. I couldn't fight any more, and I was in pain. I was tired. I didn't want her in my house. But Jane gets convulsion attacks. Her body tightens up. She got one of the attacks. I stood there, watching her in pain. I got down and held her to make sure she comes out of it OK.

And that's the first night I carried her upstairs, put her to bed, covered her, and went and slept in my room. But I couldn't sleep because… Where had I go wrong? How could she just turn around and do that to me? How was it that she could almost fuck someone in my house when I was asleep in the next room? How?

That was the beginning of me trying to get over her. That was a year ago. Now we're friends. I know for a fact that I still love her. I do want to spend my life with her—I know that. That's not changing. It's unwavering. She's the person I fell in love with. This other person that she became is just a weird derivative of her. She's started dating this new guy, and they've got issues.

There's still the occasional rolling around in the sheets together, which has never been a bad thing. My mum loves her, and my dad loves her, my sister loves her, my nephew loves her; she's part of my family. I'm even worried sometimes. I don't know how my mother hasn't figured us out. They don't know. They really love her.

I want to salvage what little friendship we have left. It's a good thing that we're still talking, and hopefully something good comes of it. I really don't see myself with anyone else. I've tried going on dates with other women, but I get bored with them so quickly. I'm doing everything I possibly can to think of her as a friend, but I just want her TO BE PART OF MY LIFE.

–

I IDENTIFY AS GAY. I realized this when I was in Standard 4. My mum must have noticed early on, she always used to ask me what was wrong with me. I guess it was because I always preferred spending time with my sisters and not brothers. I always used to play with dolls, and I never hung out with boys.

When I was in Standard 8, there was a boy called Hassan. He noticed I curried favour with the girls; and that's the angle he used to get to me. He would give me letters to give to girls in school, but it was all a façade. In due time he made his intentions known. He wanted me. He invited me over to his house, and that's where I had my first kiss. It was wonderful!

Life in high school was wonderful for me. Being gay in high school was a really pleasant experience for me. Boys wanted to do things for me, they always got me what I want; money, food, you name it! I was made to feel special. I loved the attention. That's how I met my first boyfriend; he was in Form Three at the time, and I was in Form One. He seduced me. That was my first sexual experience with a man. We dated for two years until he got expelled from school for being gay.

My mum questioned my sexuality even more after I got home for the holidays. She kept going on and on about how I was particularly inclined to doing chores that were considered feminine, like cooking and cleaning. She commented on how reclusive I had become and wondered what had happened to me in school. I brushed it off. This persisted all through high school.

I finished high school and got into beauty school. One Sunday a friend of mine came over to visit me at my parents' home. My mum walked in on us, I had no idea she would come home early from church. I think she must have forgotten something; I don't know. She was extremely angry and kicked me out of the house.

I had nowhere to go and nothing to do. A friend of mine told me to go visit him in Nairobi. When he realized the situation I was in, he suggested I should try being a sex worker. I needed the money and I had run out of choices, so it made sense. It was OK—men in Nairobi know how to pay. The men here in Mombasa are not as generous, I found that out when I moved back. Here, they think I am doing it for fun. Also, some clients can be mean over here; I have the scars to prove it. Once, I was picked up by a client, we got to his place, he fucked me, paid me and then decided he wanted his money back. I declined. That's when he started to assault me. He beat me so much, I can't remember how I escaped, but I am glad I got out alive.

I tried relationships. They were not good experiences, either. I had a boyfriend for a year, he was from Uganda. He was a lazy man. I was the breadwinner in our relationship. He knew I was a sex worker and he encouraged it because it meant I would bring him money. He was also very jealous at the same time. I felt like I had no freedom. I could not be seen with another man without it being a major issue. It ended in a sad way. I had gone to see a client in Nairobi, and when I came back home I found he had cleaned out our house and left. It hurt because I really loved him; there was nothing I didn't do for him. It hurt even more because he was the first man I ever truly loved.

My relationship with my family is sort of in a good place now. We talk with my mum once in a while. Things are not fine between us, but they are OK. Me and my dad are not OK, though. When I was young he would beat me and say, "*Wewe si mtoto wangu. Hizo tabia uko nazo umetoa kwa mama yako.*" You are not my son. You got those habits from your mother.

I guess that makes sense to me because I always felt like I was not his child. I don't resemble anyone at home, physically. My brother is OK with me being out. He just insists that I don't carry on with any of the neighbourhood boys. I used to fool around with boys in our neighbourhood, until I realized word always got back to him and it affected him in a bad way. So I avoid it nowadays.

I go to church once in a while. I am not a Catholic, but I go to a Catholic church. I prefer them to Protestant ones. At least Catholics don't ask newcomers to stand up and be seen. So I don't have to suffer through those awkward moments. Where I go, you get in, you pray, worship and leave. That's it. I want to get married to a man, and I want kids. I love kids. I want two kids. I don't want to adopt them, though. I WANT MY OWN.

–

I'M VERY, VERY GAY. Men just do it for me. I tried and tried women. I used to be 'bisexual'. I think everyone goes through that phase of trying to be bisexual and saying to yourself, "I'm not really gay."

I wasn't really happy calling myself queer. I used to say I was bisexual but more on the queer side. I'd get really offended when someone called me gay; throwing tantrums, starting fights because of that—but at the back of you mind I knew, "Definitely, I'm gay."

I think it's the denial. Society doesn't expect you to be like that. Many of us try to be bisexual because you're expected to have girlfriends—peer pressure and all that. Then you meet a man and he gets into your head and you really understand that you don't really feel women. You say to yourself, "Now I'm going to look for a chick, get serious, and focus."

But two or three days later you meet a man and things are going crazy and you're like, "Ah! Screw that shit."

I remember realizing I was attracted to men in primary school—maybe about Standard 2 or 3. I grew up with three sisters. My dad used to travel a lot and was based in another town.

He used to drink a lot and come back home really late—so we didn't hang out too much. It was just me, my mother and my sisters. I was very feminine and girly at that time. Girl stuff, you name it. Dolls, plaiting hair—I still plait hair by the way, even now. People are usually surprised to hear that! My friend has a salon and I usually just go and help them finish braids. Everyone is always so shocked!

When I was a kid, I even dressed like a girl. People used to call me 'that other sister'. You wouldn't believe it, looking at me right now. I think high school changed me a lot. I went to a crazy school. There was a push to be manly. I started playing rugby and did manly stuff. I even had two girlfriends, but after high school those relationships just died a natural death.

My first boyfriend, though, was in Form Three. In Form One, I had heard stories. Personally, I'd never even heard the word 'homosexual' until I got to high school. I'd never even really thought about it. Before high school, it was just a physical thing—playing with guys, you'd touch each other and stuff. But for me it never really clicked in my mind that this is what did it for me.

One night, the lights went off in the dorms. This guy just slipped into bed next to me and started touching me. The guy had such balls! It felt so right. I never once felt like it was wrong, you know? I just felt like it was right for me and I needed to do more of this. So we left the dorm and went behind the toilets and stripped and played around. The first guy I really, really made out with was in Form Two. There was a lot of touching. At that time I was still young, and I couldn't really ejaculate. So we'd strip half-naked, slip our dicks between each others' thighs—they call it frottage, I think?—touching each others' balls, wrestling. I think at the back of our minds, subconsciously we wanted to fuck. You'd always be very selective about who you were wrestling with, and some guys would somehow always end up wrestling with the same person every time.

There was all this physical attraction, but in such a male society and context you never quite knew how to interpret it. You just knew you needed to get physical with this person. At one point I almost fought with a guy. We were there grabbing each other shirts, and suddenly we had each other up against a wall, kissing.

Those four years were some of my best years—so much happening, nothing ever in black and white, people just being themselves without explanation. Nobody really had a name for what was going on. We did know that homosexuality existed, but most people thought that it was just the extra feminine ones who were actually gay. All the rest was just stuff that guys did. We didn't fight with clothes on—we fought in our vests and boxers. Someone would have to hold your balls to win. In the process of trying to hold your opponent's balls, you'd realize the guy you were fighting with was hard. It was weird.

So there I was fighting with this guy, and I didn't realize it was the physical attraction I had towards him. We were there pushing and shoving, and I bumped into his hard-on and got a hard-on instantly as well, and we just started making out right there. High school! High school was crazy.

My first boyfriend and I got together because we used to talk to each other a lot. With all the other guys, we'd meet and fool around without talking about it because nothing should be said or discussed with these things. But with him, it was different. One day we were in the cube alone, and we started talking about chicks. We talked about shagging chicks and then I got a hard-on and told him, "By the way, I'm very hard."

"I can calm you down," he said.

"How?"

"I can suck it."

"What? You can do that?"

"Why not?"

So, he did. We used to talk about everything. If I made out with someone else I would come and tell him, and he would tell me about his own adventures. It was an open thing, with no jealousy. We used to talk—we bonded and shared a lot and became really tight. He was one year behind me, and we used to hook up after classes. But we also shared the same cube. We used to sneak into each others' beds, and shower together. When I was in Form Four, I was a very bad boy, so no one would bother me. We'd be in the dining hall eating, and then I'd pass his table and look at him and wink or something, and he would know, "Today, it's on."

So when he went back to the dorm he would drag his feet, not leaving, and I would show up later and pretend we were discussing something, and then when everyone else would finally leave for preps, we would be left to our own devices. THEN we would go shower or whatever. It was really nice.

The last weekend when I was just finishing school, we were busted making out behind the mosque by three Muslim kids. But since I was a bad boy, they couldn't tell everyone. They only told one guy, who told someone else and another person and that was how the story went round. Some people couldn't believe it. Others said, "That guy? We always knew he was queer."

Others said there was no way I was gay. I was the bad boy, rugby player, even a rapper, always getting caught up in school drama. So some folks would say, "That guy can't be gay. It's a lie."

I left high school soon after that scandal, but we kept in touch. Facebook had just started, so he and I continued talking every now and then. We also used to send emails to one another. A couple of months after high school, my dad gave me a phone as well, so we would talk and try to meet up for coffee. We used to have the same friends, and some were jealous because of what had happened between us in high school.

He got a girlfriend, and once I told his girlfriend what happened, and she started asking for his Facebook passwords and attacking me. She would call and text and tell me to leave her man alone. One day I just snapped. I told her that what he and I had was special and there was nothing she could do about it. I told her, "The day you grow a dick is the day you'll be my competition."

That shut her up for good.

But my friend freaked out and went into the closet, because he was still in school and people used to talk about what had happened between us. He kept a very low profile and in a way that really killed it for us.

We still talk till today, though he says he's 'straight'. I don't understand that. He went to the extent of having sex with me, being the receiving partner—and for me I think receiving is actually the epitome of being queer. If you are turned on by the thought of someone else dominating you in that way, I don't really understand how you can turn around and say you're now an alpha male and straight. I've not really wrapped my head around that. Anyway, that's not my problem. If he wants to live in denial, that's his problem. But we are still friends, we still talk—and I'm sure if we end up in one room, stuff is bound to go down, no matter how 'straight' he says he is.

His girlfriend trapped him with a child. She told him, "If you don't shag me, and if you leave me for that guy, I'll tell everyone. I will tell your mother and all your friends why you left me. I will tell them the truth."

There is nothing as bad as telling a woman who loves you that you are not really into her. She can do crazy shit and tell everyone out of spite and mess things up for you. So that's what she did. I told him it's OK. If it was not meant to happen, it wasn't meant to. It was high school and we had fun, and maybe we just had to leave it at that. So apparently now he's 'straight', but he still watches queer porn. He's always asking me to send him some on Whatsapp. I doubt it's possible for someone to be straight and enjoy queer porn. How? What would turn you on? If I watch straight porn I'd be checking out the guy's butt and his body, not the girl. I think it's really weird for him to want to watch men fucking and claim to be straight. I think it's just denial.

After high school, I kept some contacts and lost some. The year after, I broke up with my girlfriend—our relationship died a quiet natural death. She never suspected I was gay. Also, we had never really done anything—the furthest we ever went was kissing. I really wanted to shag her, but out of the respect and love I had for her I didn't. I'm the kind of guy who wouldn't want to jeopardize the connection I have with someone because of sex. I still have that same conflict with guys. If I really like a guy I let him decide if he wants us to have sex. If he's drunk I will say no, because I'd want us to both be sober when we do it. I wouldn't want him to say I used him or I got him drunk, even if he is getting drunk to work up the nerve to tell me he wants to have sex. Some people are very shy and only open up when drunk and you're alone together. You can really bond with someone that way. But you want it to be special, you know?

I was single for a while. I went online and checked out some profiles. I think three or four guys took my number or my email. I met up with someone once—oh my God! That was DRAMA. He was very feminine, really tall. I was just this *kawaida* [ordinary] guy, very straight-looking. My fashion sense was more hip-hop; Timberlands, sneakers, shorts, jeans, t-shirts and hoodies. I meet this guy in town and he is in tights, walking like life is a catwalk, touching himself and being really suggestive—it totally freaked me out. I was sure he was going to out me. At that time I was really sensitive and conservative. I didn't want anyone to know—it was still a big secret. I really tried to hide it but then that guy was SO out, and I felt like he was spoiling everything for me. Everyone was looking at us and I didn't need that extra attention. I really freaked out. We had drinks and chatted a bit, then we left. So I went back home and deactivated all those accounts.

I dated another guy I met online for eight months. Back then, I just wanted the emotional connection. I didn't really want the shagging, so much. The connection for me is about being able to talk about anything and everything under the sun, and be making out and just feeling deeply, crazily together. That's when you get to know someone intellectually, know what he's thinking. Someone who's sharp and focused would be a turn-on, definitely. The most physical thing we did was hold hands in town. What would make me really happy was him coming home, and we'd have drinks, play music and talk, take walks—I'm such a hopeless romantic. Then he broke up with me, saying I was going to cheat on him. I think he was just looking for an excuse, because I'd never really felt the urge to have sex with him.

A few months later another pal of mine gave a guy my number. We met in town. I saw him and we just clicked. We were together for a while. He was the first guy I ever tried to shag—but it never really worked. It was painful, so we just stopped. Both of us were new to it, and we really didn't know what to do. It was going to be the first time for him to be a bottom. I was curious about how it felt to be a bottom, but even the idea never really got me off. Whenever I thought about sex with a man, my focus was usually on topping him. Even in any relationship I am just the man, in the straight way of defining it. You know, I pay the bills, make the first move, and push things in a certain direction for the relationship.

If you ask most bottoms, when they're horny they want to be penetrated. They see a dick, and they go crazy and they want it in them. When I am walking on the street and I see a guy in tight pants, I see his thighs and his ass, and I think, "Whoa. I want to take those pants off and stick something in there."

It just came naturally. I tried bottoming with two of my friends, out of curiosity, to know what it feels like to be bottomed. It never went further than the head. Like, they were tiny—in terms of dick size—but I was not really into it. If you're really into someone, maybe it could work. We have people who are strict tops—like me—and strict bottoms, and others who are versatile and can swing either way. You can ask some bottoms to shag someone and they won't even get a hard on. They just can't. Everyone is different.

So we hung out for a couple of months, and then started growing apart. He was too busy, and it just sort of ended there. I think that was the beginning of my many interactions with gay people.

After high school I went to college. There, I had a crush on guy who was driving me CRA-ZY. I would see him in the library and I could not even read. He was slim, he used to wear tights, and wore bracelets. He was a bit feminine. I was now very attracted to feminine guys. He used to wear white boxers, and the way he used to stand and lift his shirt you would see them. I was just going MAD. We had the same circle of friends, so we'd be in the cafeteria and he'd just talk to me and sometimes sit near me. When someone sits next to you so close to the point you see the veins on their neck and you want to grab him and just make out right there! I'd be like, "Fuck everybody else, I really don't care. We're doing it and we're doing it here NOW."

We'd touch each other under the tables and do crazy shit. This guy drove me nuts, but I never told him anything. I'm not that brave. When it comes to other things I can be brave, but when it comes to approaching someone with my feelings I'm not really that bold. Maybe on Facebook or on the phone or something. But in person I will blush and become something else. I lose words and end up just saying nothing. So I never did anything. Just had all these feelings, for a while.

The first time I ever shagged a guy, he wanted a one-night stand and I was really into him. After that we just cut off communication and I was really depressed. It was the best experience ever. I thought, "I should have done this sooner! Why didn't I do this all this time?"

That's when I actually started being serious about hooking up with guys. I got a job when college was done. I used to work at ██████ somewhere on Mombasa Road. It was another eye opener. That year, also, my family started suspecting I was gay. There was a time I used to share a handset with my sister because my own phone was faulty. I had explicit texts in there, and my sister confronted me and asked, "So this is what you do?"

I had been texting some guy I was dating. I'd heard rumours that he was shagging someone else. I had a tiny circle of five or six friends, and my family knew them all because they used to come over and hang out. So she said, "Oh my God, are all these people you've been bringing home like that? This is what you do, sleep with men?"

All my siblings were there; I freaked out! I felt like my stomach was going to pop out. I grabbed the phone from her and deleted the texts but the cat was out of the bag. I actually had to come out then. It was more like I was plucked out of the closet. After that I came out properly to my small sister. It felt like this was the time to get past it. We were in the kitchen and she told me how she had lost her virginity, and we just started talking. So I told her I was bisexual. She said, "Really? You're really bi? You're not gay?"

So I admitted I was gay, not bi. I think from that day we have really been tight. We hang out and party together. People even think I am dating her! She knows all my gay friends. Her best friends are mostly gay guys, now. Once my dad asked me if I was gay. I was nineteen and still in college. We were having dinner, and everyone was there. He just said my name, then, "Are you gay?"

It was the first time he had ever brought it up. I almost fainted. I froze for almost ten minutes. Then he asked my siblings, "Do you know what gay is?"

My sister said, "Yes! Just men who are in love with other men."

I never said no or yes. I just kept quiet. So I think they know. There is even a time my mother told me, "I think you have too many female hormones."

I think they hoped it was a phase I would get over. I've never had scandals with chicks. If I was straight, by now I should have impregnated someone, or gotten into a serious relationship with a girl. Obviously, I am not, so I think by now they know. I have been forced to come out to most of my friends, and they are OK with it. There is one I told, "This whole time you have known me, I've been gay."

He said, "What? All this time?"

I said, "Yes, and I've never been any different. And you knew me way before high school."

In a weird way I think my faith has grown stronger because of my sexuality. I started this journey a while back. I grew up in a Christian family, and my mother used to take us to church every Saturday. There is a group for gay Adventists that I am a member of. They usually have meetings but I've never gone; I get really busy with work.

Before I really accepted who I was, I used to feel like I was really sinning. So I would drink and party a lot. Then I stopped, and said to myself, "Let me at least do this one sin that I cannot do without." Booze I can do without. I went for a Christian camp and prayed. I deleted numbers of all the gay people I knew. It was really a struggle for me. After that camp, things really changed. I fasted and prayed about it, and I told God if He wanted me to be straight then He should take the feelings away from me, and that I didn't want to meet anyone who was queer.

Then I'd bump into nice men, bond, fall in love... If He didn't want me to be gay, then I wouldn't be this way. You are born this way, you cannot be made into anything else. You can't help who you are attracted to. I guess it's God's will. If it wasn't for that, I wouldn't have met the wonderful people I have met because of being gay. I think it's an opportunity I was given to get to meet these people, and would I have it if He was so against it? So I reconciled with it and I am happy. I pray to God, and I love Him very much. I think He loves us just as we are.

Last year I was married to a man. We were together for nine months and we lived together for most of it. The longest we had ever been apart was about two weeks. I don't think there was anything I didn't do for him. I bought him clothes, a phone—all the things a man does for his wife. I'd go home to him every night. His friends were the ones I had questions about. His folks had kicked him out because he was queer, so he used to live with his friend who was like a big brother. This friend of his, though, had a thing for under-age boys. That got on my nerves. I have a small brother and I wouldn't want to have anyone take advantage of him. When he is legal, he can date someone closer to his age—and there is no issue. This man would date sixteen year old guys, and it really bothered me.

There was another friend who used to live with them who was such a slut. And another guy was a pimp who used to live in Mombasa. These were the kind of guys my man used to call his friends. When he wanted something and I was broke, he would say, "It's OK baby, I'll wait till the money comes."

His friends would hear about it and tell him that I was broke, and that he should leave me alone. I got really angry one time when I bought him a phone and his friends thought it wasn't good enough. They kept trying to introduce him to rich, old guys. They'd tell him, "Come and have fun with this old man. He'll buy you a good phone. Leave this broke guy alone."

I was so angry with them for saying that. What had they done with their lives? That pimp guy was almost eight years older than us, and he quit his job to be a pimp. Is that someone who is in a position to judge me? The other guy would spend his money on boys. He had nothing to his name and nothing to show, and I would go to his house and feel like in comparison, I had done so much more. They used to say I was young and broke, but I know I am focused and I have a plan for my life. I have so many responsibilities. I am a first-born son, with siblings who look up to me. I cannot ask my mother to do things for me. I have friends who lost their parents, and their small brothers look up to me as well. It's all very messed up. But I thank God that he has given me resources to help others. I am OK where I am.

Anyway, this fighting with his friends really got to me and I just got tired. That's when things really went south. I didn't know if he was truly into me because of me, or because of all the things I would give him. You know? Someone can be in love with you just because you can house them. So you're perfect for them at that point, but you never really know. It ended up being one of my biggest headaches. There was war in my house, before we broke up.

I love commitment. I love being in relationships. You're less at risk when you have a steady partner. Your focus is just him. The more you go sticking your dick everywhere, the higher your chances are of contracting something. And it's not just about sex. If you keep shagging everyone you lose a bit of yourself. Sometimes you shag so many people you feel empty. It becomes meaningless and boring. But when you are with someone you love and you spend time together, it's like an investment. I think at my age, I want to be in a serious relationship.

When it comes to things like marriage, I'm thinking about investing together with my partner just in case I die and then someone tries to make him suffer. Because I'm here, they may not have the guts to come and kick him out of my house. But when I die, things might change. Even in my death, I want him to be cared for. You have to build each other; what is his career, what is his business, does he need help? When you have a bad day, there's someone there to cheer you up. When you have a difficult situation they can tell you, "That's not a smart move. Do this instead."

That's what I need at this point. Someone I can discuss intellectual, serious things with. Someone I can sit down and debate things with, hear each others' different views. At this age, I need someone who's focused. Getting that person, though, is a problem. It's really difficult. I'd love to be with one person, and I want something that leads into marriage. I want to be so in love with them that I can just go to my parents and say, "I love him, and if you don't want me to be with him, then I have no business being with you. You either accept me with him or you let me be."

Same with your friends, straight or not. You can just tell them, "This is the man in my life."

Being queer is challenging. I think it's more challenging now. I don't know how we're going to hack it. When you're young, people want to take advantage of you. When you establish yourself, people want to take advantage of you for different reasons. When you are older, people are not interested in you because of your age. So I don't know.

Sometimes I just say to myself, "I'm single. Let me just stay the way I am. At least I can manage being single."

Then there's the issue of kids. I want to have my own kids. Two of them. I want to raise them full of love. After all, what are we doing all this for—all the investing and things—if it's not for our kids? I'll probably hook up with a lesbian and have kids. I want both my children to be related on both sides; me as the father, and her being the mother, and then we can co-parent regardless of being queer, and just be there for our kids. If I found someone open-minded, it could really work. When you get kids, I think your way of thinking changes, because your interest is in your children. I've thought about finding a girl—I can shag a woman, anyway—and having kids, then the focus of my life would be them. I think I would be happy then, because I would love them unconditionally, and they would love me unconditionally as their father, and I think that love would be enough for me. They would be my reason for living and maybe I could kill my queer side. But how long can you do that? You can't do that for long.

As a parent you need to be wholesome in your way of thinking, with your head being right. Most of the problems kids are having out here—especially teenagers—is because their parents are not functioning properly. In order to direct someone else and give love unconditionally, you need to function properly. If there are two fucked up parents, kids see through all the fucked-upness. When they get to age nine or ten they become sharper, and they can read your face, your moods.

You can stay in a bad marriage, and say to yourself that you're in it for the kids, but you're messing up the foundations that the kids will have—the basic things that build how they relate with the opposite sex or HOW THEY MAKE FRIENDS.

–

I AM A LESBIAN. I realized this about two years ago. The person I am with now is my first girlfriend. I always knew I had a thing for women, especially in high school. Back then, I would make out with girls but I never thought I would actually date a woman. Before that, I had tried dating men but none of those situations lasted longer than a week. It was not my thing.

In Form One, I had a 'partner', but it was hard being gay in high school. There was a lot of sneaking around involved, and it was risky. Getting caught would have meant expulsion. But there were always notes being exchanged—love notes—between girls. Very many girls in my school were lesbians; some were just experimenting, others were doing it because I guess there were no boys around—it was an all-girls school.

I knew I could not date in high school or be seen as 'being' with someone over a period of time because I was afraid. There are things you can't hide when you are dating someone. If I got caught, what would people say about me? What would I tell my parents? I couldn't risk it, so I stayed away from relationships.

I met my current girlfriend on Facebook, I lived in Nairobi at the time. We started chatting online, exchanged numbers and I moved to ██████ to be with her. Only my friends and cousins know about us, no one in my family knows. My brother suspects the two of us, though. One time we were talking on the phone about my job situation and he asked, "*Mbona usirudi Nairobi kama kupata kazi huko ni ngumu? Mbona una-insist kukaa huko...wewe na huyo msichana unaishi naye?*" Why don't you just come back to Nairobi if you're having difficulty finding work there? Why do you insist on staying there...you and that girl you live with?

I guess he found out about us from his ex-girlfriend. We were pretty close and I came out to her, so maybe she told him about us. No one else suspects a thing. My girlfriend has even met my parents, but they don't know anything. I would like to tell them but not now, maybe later.

I am a Christian, a God-fearing Christian. Before I met my girlfriend, I prayed to God. I told Him, "I have found out that I am a lesbian, and all I want is someone to settle down with.

Someone good. Someone who I can get along with. Someone who will love me."

And that's what He did. I always pray about us; I pray about our relationship, even our arguments. I want to get married to her in the future. I want to have kids too. She already has a child, and she is against artificial insemination. She thinks it's not safe, so we have been going back and forth about it. Maybe I will settle for the more traditional method of getting pregnant. We have plans for our future, when I get a job we talked about getting kids and buying land together, where WE WILL SETTLE.

–

I AM AN INTERSEX PERSON. I was born a man, but I had a fallopian tube. Everything else was male, but the tube was just hanging there randomly. It was supposed to be corrected, and they did it when I turned fourteen. I'm sexually attracted to men, and I have never been attracted to women. I was in Standard 7 when I knew I liked men.

I remember watching a TV soap called *Soul Food*[17], and it had such cute men. I was watching that program purely because of the men.

My childhood was OK, but being intersex made things a little hard for me. I didn't understand much about it. I knew that being a 'hermaphrodite' was a thing for animals. I used to have really bad cramps from when I was about twelve or thirteen. So I went and had a scan, and they found the tube. Finding that out wasn't as stigmatizing as it could have been because it was not visible on my genitalia. It was just me and my parents who knew. The doctor gave us advice, and my parents decided that I should be the one to decide what to do. I decided it should be removed. My hormones by that time were really complicated. I also had to have hormonal therapy because I started ovulating. I was put on testosterone. I now identify more as a man, and it's what I feel.

I met my first boyfriend after high school. We met at a club. I really found him cute. I bought him some drinks, and we started

---

17. Soul Food: The Series—an American TV drama that aired on Kenyan TV in the early 2000s.

chatting and exchanged numbers. The next day, I texted him and said, "You're really attractive."

Straight to the point, no beating around the bush. He replied, "I also think you're attractive!"

So we started texting back and forth, and falling in love that way. I'm the one who eventually asked him out—to make it official—and we dated for almost two years after high school. We used to go out a lot, have a lot of sex and dream about the future. We wanted to get married and stay together. We even lived together for a while. Marriage would have been hard, because it would be unconstitutional in Kenya for two men. Maybe we could get married in South Africa and then come back here.

We're still together, even though he moved abroad—it's been four years now with ups and downs. We break up and get back together, I get tired of the relationship and feel like I can't do it any more, I go test the waters elsewhere—but him, he's so polite and very lenient and patient. I'm the one who is rude sometimes, and I say how bored I am with everything and how I want to try other things and people. We're used to each other like that. He's studying medicine.

I also work in a hospital as a clinical officer. We work on the ground—we are there with the patients directly, more than the doctors who just come for ward rounds and leave. It's a passion. It's not like being a doctor—sometimes doctors can take so long to get some things done. I really enjoy being with patients, and bringing them back to health. I also love to help people who are in need, who can't afford good care. I'm interested in questions about how we can do better by influencing hospital policies. As a young practitioner, how can I connect to professional bodies and see how they can really reach the community level rather than just the hospital? How can we work at the local level, and at the level of the people?

I really love my job, and I give people a lot of advice even outside my job and practice, rather than having them come to the hospital. Some things are simple, like with psychiatric drugs—anti-psychotics—some of these drugs are the same colour, and over the counter people can assume they are getting a Valium pill, for instance, and it turns out to be something else, like a

Haloperidol. The treatment implications of either of those are very different. So we're trying to argue that these things need to have different colours, and the people need to know what they are and how they are different. People need to be sure of what drugs they are taking.

The other thing is how people stigmatise mental health issues in Kenya. I heard once about this woman who had a daughter who was lesbian. The mother took her daughter to see an emergency psychiatrist. The doctor decided that the girl had a mood disorder, like depression. They decided to give her electro-convulsive therapy—shock therapy. You see what a long journey we have ahead of us? A lot of people think LGBTI issues are 'psycho-sexual disorders'. But all the books these days say that being LGBTI is not a disease. I work with an organization that is really trying to work closely with the Ministry of Health to influence curricula that teaches medical students such outdated things. Students need to be made aware of these things before they graduate. How can we change the current literature in university psychiatry departments?

The members of the LGBTI community face some specific health challenges, especially with matters to do with STIs. Some of these things are too stigmatizing to present to any medical practitioner in a casualty, for example. If I presented these conditions, the nurse can even go and call other nurses to come and see the case. They know you didn't get it from having straight sex, you know? It's anal sex you got it from, so it means you are a *shoga* [homosexual]. These things really hinder community members from accessing health services because we do not have friendly services in the governmental hospitals, and we don't have friendly practitioners who have been sensitized regarding LGBTI issues. Most of them are really ignorant—they don't even believe such people exist. And then this stigma around anal sex—even straight people have it, but even they can't be seen to be having it. Sometimes lesbians want to go for pap smears and cervical screenings, and then issues come up when they are asked about their partners. We are supposed to treat all women equally, but not lesbians? What's that about? Lesbians need to be treated like any other women. Pap smears are for any woman.

Maybe in Nairobi people know their rights a little better but in the regional level—like ███████, the stigma is everywhere.

Concerning trans and intersex persons, the literature isn't very focused. People may know of the conditions, but they don't know how to manage them well. My organization is trying to figure out how to get these people taken care of by the hospital, rather than managed by the community. Trans and intersex issues are more about the medical condition than the sexual orientation. You can't decide for a trans person, "You are a man. Be a man."

Also, for trans people—it's a medical condition but people group it under psychiatry as a psycho-sexual condition—and that is a very big problem. People call them cross-dressers, or people that want to remove their genders—and that's really not what's going on.

The other issue that comes up especially with LGBTI-support organizations is sustainability. These issues can be donor-driven and they are not permanent—we really need the government to step in for sustainability. We are there for two-year, five-year projects that are funded by donors, but a donor cannot fund you for 100 years and the issue remains. The government is here to stay, and these people are Kenyans. So working closely with them and policy makers is necessary to ensure sustainability, so that the community can be sure they will be treated regardless of which organization is there and after they have gone.

When our organization started, we started meeting in hotels. We were just five—and we didn't know any other queer people in ███████. Even these five people? It is so odd how we met. I had just come from South Africa and had gone out to a pub. I was talking to someone on the phone. This lady nearby happened to overhear the conversation and asked me, "You mean you're queer?"

I said, "Yes, I am."

She said, "I'm also a lesbian, and I have two other friends here!"

So we started hanging out and they brought another friend. That's how we became five.

We thought that maybe there were more queer people out there in this town, just suffering—wanting to come out and find others, but not knowing how. Just talking about being queer in ██████ back then could get you burned in the streets. It was such a small conservative town. It was really hectic because even photos could not be taken. Remember those days when we didn't have Facebook? Straight people would send pictures outing gay people via MMS. "Look at this gay person."

One day, all five of us went out, and we were feeling happy and full of dreams about the kind of community we wanted to be. People were dancing and kissing, and looking for opportunities to be intimate—you didn't want to lose a chance with someone because if you did, you might not see them again until next year! Someone took photos in the club that night and circulated them to the whole town. Until then, I was used to hanging out with straight people, and I was really friendly and people knew me. I was pointed out in the pictures, and it was hectic. I would enter a club and people would say, "*Achana na yule shoga.*" Leave that fag alone.

Even going to class was hard. After that, we didn't have anything to lose, so we decided to meet in a hotel and make our group official—to form a movement. We needed to find people like us. Everyone was told to come with one new person, and so we became ten. At the second meeting we were twenty. We even got to fifty. I realized that with the things I have studied, I could develop partnership agreements, policies, a structure and a constitution for the group—but members would have to discuss all these things and elect officials—a chair, a vice-chair, secretary and treasurer before we even had any conversations.

They chose me as the chairman, because I was that guy who would fight with people at the bar for them. There were times we would want to host a queer party, but none of the bars were willing to host us. I had to go to these clubs and tell them we were here to stay. I would ask to speak to the supervisor or manager when we wanted to host a queer party, and I would explain things to the management for them to understand that being gay or lesbian is not a psychiatric disorder. I would tell them that I had studied, and I had clear definitions about homosexuality. I also added that stigma from people is the thing that now brings about personality disorders and even real psychiatric disorders like suicidal thoughts.

At one of these bars, the bar supervisor and manager said they knew me as a customer and appreciated my medical work, that I had treated many people they knew. So they said they would accept my people, as long as we didn't misbehave and try to 'promote homosexuality'. I asked, "When straight people misbehave, why is that not a problem?"

They replied that for the security of the business, they needed to allow straight people to do what they wanted, but not gays. They said they could allow lesbians to dance together because there's not so much stigma with women being together, but men couldn't do anything physical.

They agreed to allocate a space for us, but then we realised we might be too segregated and easily identifiable—any violations and violence that arose would be easy to start, because people would know they could find us there. We wanted to create a place where we could be free, where we could sit anywhere and have freedom of association. They said, "Yes, it's in the Constitution and it's your fundamental right. So if you enter and have fun without bringing problems, it'll be OK."

That's how that club started allowing *kuchus* [homosexuals] in. The problem was that this club was also a favourite for a whole bunch of rugby people—and you know how violent those ones can be. The rugby people would come, buy one drink and then create so much chaos. But us queer people would buy our drinks, and just do our thing—no chaos. So we told the owner of the bar, "Either we move to another club because of this violence, or we stay and your business continues."

Eventually, he chose us and kicked the rugby crowd out. It's been two years and his business is still strong. We put his pub on our website and told EVERYONE about it. That queer people could go to that pub and feel safe, and it's such a friendly place because nobody cares if you are queer or whatever. You can dance how you want with each other, and there's no problem. At this club, you could really be yourself.

So the original five of us did all this work over a year—these things can't be done in one day. You write a letter and it is rejected, you visit a place and they refuse to give you an appointment, and you persist until they are so bored they are the ones who will call you. We struggled that whole year, and made that our business.

When we got to fifty members, we decided that we needed to make things formal. We needed a safe space where we could meet and put the money we were using in hotel meetings to better use. We had to become more and more formal, because we wanted to build something that could take us to the future. People were used to stepping down and changing responsibilities just because they wanted, until it became formal. Some people got annoyed at that point because they had been founding members but had to step down because they didn't meet the new criteria. To be a proper member, you had to be willing to work. We graduated past needing people to be members just because they exist. We all went back on the drawing board—even me, who had done all that struggling from the beginning.

We started developing policies, writing partnership agreements, introduction letters to various partners, and fortunately we got a few new partners. We applied for all kinds of training—remember, we were just friends who used to meet in a hotel! My profession was completely different from any of the things that were needed to build an organisation. Now we have all these things in order. We were better able to ask ourselves if our partners were helping us meet our objectives, not just taking on partners for the sake of having them. We say, 'nothing for us without us'. You cannot program for MSM members without involving them, for instance. Some of these projects will just train anyone they can find just so they can meet their numbers.

We got an office, and got down to really work for our community. We work closely with several government agencies now, and we are pushing to make the government more sensitized. We are asking them what their plan is to ensure services keep being provided even when the donors move on to the next sexy thing. We also took part in surveys they did on PrEP and microbicide use. How sure would we be that these drugs would work if we introduced them for eighteen months to a certain population who are also using condoms? Are we sure that people are correctly taking

PrEP and using condoms? When we demonstrate these things to the general public, what will we be telling them? PrEP is really new. If for those eighteen months we focus on this population, and they use condoms correctly, we can't know for sure if it's the PrEP that is working or the condoms. Yet, you can't ask people to stop using condoms and test the efficiency of PrEP on its own, because what happens when the study participants get infected with HIV or other STIs in the course of the trial? These things are yet to be discussed.

I really wonder about that efficacy study, because if I am using my condom correctly, I won't need PrEP. I honestly don't see the study working. If I had unsafe sex and took PrEP, I could still get an STI like gonorrhoea, or whatever. They did this study elsewhere and it was successful, and they figured it would work here in Kenya, but people here are really afraid of using PrEP. The girls, for instance, are finding that the microbicidal antiviral gel isn't working—girls are being tested and found to be positive. Also, stigma applies. If someone sees me taking a blue pill—everyone knows Truvada is blue—stories start flying. If I am seen coming from 'that place' where people get ARVs from, everyone ends up knowing my business.

In ████████, most sex workers register in ████████—twenty kilometres away—because nobody knows you in that town, and the ones from there come here. That way, nobody knows you. Some people even go to the provincial hospital, where people are so many that no one can identify you from one visit to another.

The government also has to introduce better ways of testing people for HIV before treatment. The test itself can fill people with such fear that they will wait until they are terminal, or infected with tuberculosis and other opportunistic infections, or with CD4 counts of 33[18]—just at home; afraid. Sometimes people will assume that it's just a random infection.

People are signing up to become research subjects because there's some money available for it, but are they then subjecting

18. A CD4 cell count of below 200 indicates that a HIV-positive individual is at risk of becoming ill with an HIV-related illness.

themselves to risky behaviour? There is no compensation in the event that you take part in the study and you become HIV positive. It's just you with your positivity. How are you going to get people to sign up for a study like that? Who's going to allow their body to be used like that? We're having to think through these things.

We're also trying to make documentation about intersex people to educate people on what being intersex is. People think it's being possessed by a demon, even government and church officials.

My personal challenge with this work has been feeling burned out. Sometimes I feel like we work and work and nothing is changing. Also, people really gossip about me. They put bad stories about me on Facebook, they talk badly about me on their blogs. My parents are also always on my case, asking who I am working for, saying it's ungodly, outside of the church. I have a lot of family pressure. But I cannot, cannot stop.

Even at the hospital, those guys are the worst. When my co-workers at the hospital found out about the work I do, they went to talk about me to tell everyone that I am queer—the entire HOSPITAL! I used to go to the hospital, do my work and leave because everything had become so tense.

South Africa is easy—they don't have homophobia. But they have issues with xenophobia and with racism. Studying there was really good, though.

My family knows that I am gay, but my mother can't ask me about it directly. She just knows, quietly. My sister is the one who can talk about it. Maybe it's just that my mum respects me—I have studied, so it looks like I am adding value to our family. My brothers have studied as well, but I am the one they look up to because I am really of help to them. I dissolve disasters, ha! I'm usually the one at the centre, helping out when there is conflict. I'm also kind of the breadwinner. Once, I tried to bring up an issue about homosexuality in the sitting room. There was one of those silly 'exposes' on the gay guys in Mombasa who wanted to get married showing on TV. My sister was all over the place with her opinions, "This is ungodly! I would never let my children be like this!"

My mother said that rather than deciding who these people are for herself, she wanted to understand more. My mother used to be a nurse, so she tends to be really understanding regarding many issues. My family has many nurses, so they have come across homosexuals, but they don't understand the issues as well as they could.

My sexual orientation doesn't bother my God. I normally pray and God hears me. I know I am a Christian, and all of that doesn't bother me. I just pray for God to show me the light. Is it possible for someone to be gay and be in the church, and pray, all these things? Of course. So when people point at me and say that I have a disorder because I am gay, I point back and say, "I sweat. My body metabolism is OK. I am not agitated. My speech is OK. I can remember five things in five minutes. I ejaculate. I can minus seven from 100. My judgement is OK. So, where is my disorder? Is my disorder my dick, or where it is going, or what?"

That's the question. They feel so bad when they find someone who has studied psychiatry, because you really, really know what you're saying. If I can pass a mental state exam now, what is my disorder?

In future, I want to be a very rich person. I want to own a very big, safe space for LGBTI persons, so that if they are chased from home they can come and stay there. I want to own a children's home, and a home for the aged. I want to help the needy, the poor—people who can't help or shout for themselves, and empower these young, young *kuchus* [homosexuals] who want to study hard and be whatever they want to be. I'll tell them, "You deserve this."

I don't want a wife, for sure. I just want a child, one of my own. That's all. I'd want to raise the child with my partner or husband. I'd want the child to grow up knowing all they needed to know—where we don't have to hide things, and we can discuss things and he or she can understand and be very mature. I want just one child, and I'd love a daughter. I'll really raise her well. You feel good when you are raising your own baby, and you have the capacity to have your own child. You know the kind of child who will bring her problems to her parents to discuss? That's THE KIND OF CHILD I WANT.

–

I'M A MALE SEX WORKER, and I'm gay. I realized I was gay when I was eight.

I was raped by a neighbour. He was an old man, with a wife and kids. This went on for a long time, and it only stopped because we moved house. I ran away from home when I was fourteen and started working as a sex worker. I ran away because of my father, he used to beat me. He beat me because he could see that I was different, I was quite effeminate and sometimes he'd see me applying make up. After some time, my brother also started beating me. My mother and sisters didn't have an issue. My mum would try and speak up for me when my dad would beat me but that didn't stop him.

I didn't go to high school. I left home because I couldn't take the beatings anymore. I wanted to start my own life, away from home. The streets were very hard; hunger, cops and thieves. You can see my neck is full of knife marks. It was very hard. I didn't have anyone to look out for me. At the time, I would charge between 100 and 200 shillings for sex, and my clients were mostly older men. I'm thirty-eight, I've been a sex worker for 24 years now.

I've been attacked, raped and jailed many times. There isn't a jail I haven't been in. Jail is terrible. As soon as I enter, everyone can tell I am gay. Some of the prisoners like me, but the wardens always beat me. However, when I went back recently, the wardens treated me very well. I think they now know about gay people, so they are much kinder. I've never really had any issues with the inmates, whenever they see you *wanajua wamepata chakula*. They know they've got something to eat.

They're very happy. Very quickly, they start approaching me. It becomes a competition. They try to outdo one another, So one guy says he can get you cigarettes, another says he can get you weed, another says he can get you good food. Everyone is trying to prove they can provide for you more than the other. We're treated like queens in prison, us gay guys.

Because I'm a sex worker, I always have more than one partner in prison. When they find out, they always fight amongst each other; never with me. The wardens are the ones who come to put me in solitary for causing fights. But even then, the big pin inmate will bribe the wardens and I'll be released and taken to his side of the prison.

When I ran away from home, I hitched a ride on a truck to get from Nairobi to Mombasa. On the way, the driver propositioned me, so I had sex with him, then with the conductor as well. When I was getting off the truck, they paid me. So I realised there was a business opportunity there. I got a free ride, I was fed and I was paid for sex. So after a short time in Mombasa, I went back on the road with the truck drivers. I would go to a stage, get onto a truck then get off at the next stage and wait for another truck. I think that's the time I contracted HIV, because I wasn't using any protection. Who knows?

I never had any bad experiences with the truck guys, they were nice guys, and they were good to me. I worked in Nairobi as a sex worker for six years. In Nairobi I used to operate mostly around Koinange Street, Simmers and Mad House. I left Nairobi because of the environment and in search of greener pastures. I kept hearing Mombasa was the better environment for gays. I heard gays there were treated well, so I moved to Mombasa. I went to Watamu and Malindi. Mombasa is a nice place for sex work, because of the tourists. There's good money, and it's a lot easier to get a client in Mombasa.

When I started dressing well and grooming myself, I revised my rates. I was also older so that meant I had a better sense of how much to charge for what. Because of dealing with tourists, I learned how to get a lot more money. Also, different 'hot spots' have different prices. We charge differently for different clients. With *mzungus* [white people], you don't have ask for money, they just give it to you. Sometimes 200 dollars, sometimes even 500 dollars. Some even pay you and still send you money via Western Union when they get back home. For the rest, you look at the way he's dressed, the cologne he's wearing, the car he's driving. If you're a sex worker, you can see these things, then you see he has money so you tell him anything from 5,000 shillings and above. *Mzungus* are really good, they pay very well but they are seasonal.

It turns out Mombasa isn't that great either, I've been beaten and arrested several times. A lot of my clients in Mombasa are Indians. I don't like Swahili men. Sometimes they take you, and you think it's just one client then you get to the house and you find there's a whole group of them waiting for you. They beat you, and they do all manner of things to you. The Indians are very nice, even the Africans, but the Swahilis; no.

My friend and I were once picked up by these two Swahili guys. We thought it was just the two of them, but when we got to the house, there were almost 30 guys. They raped us in turns then they started beating us. My friend died. They beat him until he died. I got away, I don't even know how, but I did. I had to scale a wall that had glass shards at the top. Look at my hands. I just scaled the walls, grabbed the shards and jumped.

I've been in love once, he was a Meru guy. He was the first and last. Whenever I got paid for sex, I'd give him the money. I wanted him to dress nicely, to eat well and I rented him a small room. He knew I was a sex worker, and he didn't have an issue with it. I was also his first love. He loved me, and even wanted to introduce me to his parents. After a year, I asked myself, "What am I doing?"

I was losing weight, I wasn't eating, I loved him too much. So I asked myself why I loved him and yet *hizo mboro ndio napata kila siku? Si napata kila siku hizo mboro? Wacha niendeleee kuuza ngono.* I still get dick every day. What's the difference? Let me continue selling sex.

So I left him.

Nowadays, the cops don't arrest me anymore; they've gotten tired of arresting me. Sometimes when I see them around, I call them, "Come! Come! Come! Come and arrest me!"

They say, "*Kwenda, malaya wewe! Shoga!*" Go away, you whore! You fag!

They chase me, but they don't want stress. I always tell them, "Take me back to prison! You want to feed me for free don't you? So take me back!"

They tell me, "*Kwenda, wewe tushakuzoea.*" Get lost. We're used to you.

Before, I was afraid of them. I used to run. Nowadays, I'm not afraid of them, in fact I call them, "*Njoo! Njoo, afande nifanye na wewe short-time!*" Come! Come, Officer, let me give you a quickie!

I'm not scared of anyone anymore. I can wear whatever I want, I walk wherever I want, I don't want anyone to ask me anything. Who are you to ask me? You don't feed me. I'm not scared of anyone anymore.

The community in [redacted] has grown quite a bit now, nowadays I'm always so surprised when I see people walking around openly, they used to hide. They have become a very large and caring community. Whenever one is unwell, all the rest will go and visit him. It's very nice, it's not like my time.

I like to wear sexy dresses; short sexy dresses. Sometimes I wear saris, the Indian sari. Whenever I wear saris I get Indian clients. Sometimes I wear minis, sometimes I wear jeans and sometimes I wear tights. It just depends on the occasion and my mood. If I had money, I would have changed my gender a long time ago. I would go all the way, and I'd have boobs; a complete overhaul.

I use protection with my clients because I'm afraid of re-infection and STIs. Sometimes the clients don't want to use condoms and sometimes I agree, but the money has to be worth it. There are some clients I tell I'm HIV positive but they don't believe me. They tell me I wouldn't tell them if I was HIV positive.

I've never met my family again, I hear they're all in Europe. It would be nice to talk to them but I don't have the means to talk to them. I don't know if they're alive, they don't know if I'm alive. But it's fine, I thank God for everything.

I believe in God because He's the creator. He's the provider. If you get something, you thank God, if you don't get anything, you still thank God. God is everything. He doesn't care if you're Muslim, Hindu or Christian. Even if you're a sex worker, you just know God is looking at you and providing for you. My mother was Muslim and my father was Christian, I never been to a church nor a mosque, but I believe in God. Whenever I get good money, I give to the needy and I know God will reward me for that.

I want to get married. I wish a man would come and ask me to marry him, and take me to Europe, I'm tired of Africa now. I want to go to Holland, I know all the crazy things happen there. I want to go and be a stripper there. I don't want to be a housewife or whatever, I want to continue sex-working until I die. If the man who wants to marry me wants me to stop, I'll pretend, but when I reach there, I'll just continue.

I think I want to adopt two children, two of them. Two girls, not boys. Boys might grow up and say, "You're a man, you're not my mama," then start beating me POW! POW! POW! AFTER SMOKING MARIJUANA.

–

I'M A PURE LESBIAN. I realized it when I was in secondary school. I used to receive letters from chicks in my school. I'd read the letters and see that the letters were written well, just like a guy would write to a girl. They would sign at the bottom something like, 'Meet me in Form 4A' or 'Form 2B', but I never went.

I found them weird at first. There was this particular girl who used to write me over and over and I wondered who it was. One night—during entertainment—I was walking back to the dorms when she grabbed me and kissed me. That's how it started. She was a Form Four and I was a Form Two. She didn't say 'hi' or 'bye', or anything. She just kissed me and walked away. She wrote me a letter the next day explaining how she felt about me. The thing is, I liked her kiss, because it caught me unaware. I liked it.

So I met her after I received that letter. We became friends. She told me she was a lesbian and that she was attracted to me. I told her that it would take some time for me to like her too, or for us to like each other. She said she was in no rush. It took me a month till I became intimate with her. We kissed and made out. It was at her place and the first time I had sex with a woman. It was very good. All this happened when she was in Form Four. When she left, I became lonely. I was so used to her.

After high school, we continued dating for two years, and then we left each other due to too many issues. She thought I was cheating on her and she changed. She used to be a tomboy, then she got a job as an air hostess. That changed her.

Life after high school was hard, but sweet too. I thought that after high school, those feelings would be over. I went to a party one day that had both boys and girls. Some of those girls were lesbians. We mingled and I found one with whom I'm still with till now. It's been three years. The relationship has been good but not without ups and downs.

Sometimes if look at a beautiful girl, we fight about it with my girlfriend. If we go for a party and I appear to be close to some girl, we fight about it. There are girls who don't care whether you're with someone or not, they just pursue you. That affects my relationship. I try to tell my girlfriend that there's nothing going on but because the pursuant girl continues to show interest in me, it looks like I'm cheating. That's the biggest challenge I face.

I've told my mum about me because she used to suspect I was gay. She said, "No, nothing like that is in our family, so *isianze na wewe*." So don't let it start with you.

That scared me, so I shut up. She sees that many of my friends are tomboys but she's never asked me about it. She just says things like, "*Ah! Huyu rafiki yako anakaa homo!*" This friend of yours looks like a homo. I play it down.

All my friends know I'm gay and they are cool with it. Since I realized I was a lesbian, I haven't been so religious. I even rarely go to church. I sometimes feel guilty and I tell my friends, "I only have one sin—being a lesbian—and I can not control it."

But I pray.

–

I identify as gay. I think I realized that when I was six years old. I used to like men. In Standard 5, I went to boarding school. There, it was like a free world. It was the equivalent of a national school—many politicians had children who were there, and we had people from all parts of Kenya. There was a lot of playing around happening. Nothing penetrative, just holding each other, playing with each other, and telling stories with older boys or classmates. Every now and then, I'd hear rumours that someone was a 'homo', and I'd always approach that one, wanting to know more.

That way, I would get to know others like me. In our school, people were using Blue Band[19] as lube. It was the best. Never runs dry. I never had the guts for penetration, though.

When I went to high school—oh my God. I had a field day. There were many people like me there. You'd go to the toilet and people would write crazy things on the wall, you know? So I started listening and watching. In Form Two, I joined the Drama Club. I was always cast to play female roles. At night, people used to approach me, whispering sweet things to me. There was one guy I really used to like. I saw him showering once, and I liked the package. He came to me and kissed me in my sleep. When I woke up he ran away, and I saw his silhouette disappearing. I wondered, "What do I do now?"

The house captain was my friend. I spoke to him about it, but he was really furious about it. He really beat up the guy that night, from 2:30 in the morning to 5am. I really felt sorry for him, pleaded for him to be forgiven and for him not to be reported to the principal.

I think the fact that I didn't proceed with the case showed the guy who kissed me that I was not against what he had done. So he came back to me and asked, "Why don't we explore this?"

My cubicle was on one side of an aisle, and his was on another. It was really easy for us to have a relationship. I didn't need much convincing. I already knew what I wanted. By the time I was in Form Three, I was a professional *[laughs]*. The dormitory next to ours had a common shower area with concrete sinks and taps, unlike ours which had private shower cubicles. I preferred the open one—it was a marketplace! I'd shower there in the afternoons after games practice, and look around and identify four or so interesting people and start hitting on them. It always worked.

We used to study daily at the library. The library tables were small, so we would all be really close together. I used to work with my legs. Someone had done that to me once before in the library and played with me until I came. The Drama Club captain was a good friend of mine, and our mothers were friends so we had known each other a long time. He's the one who taught me

---

19. A popular margarine brand in Kenya.

how to use my legs like that. I used to give him such 'foot jobs' every now and then.

My father was a school principal, so I had a lot of goodies and money at the time. I used them to bribe the boys. When we were supposed to be eating *githeri*[20] or beans, or other yucky foods, I would buy chapati or chips. I used to have it all.

There was one guy I was really interested in. He was a footballer, and he was really cute. Oh my God! I used to watch football just to see him play. I never gave up. I'm very patient, by the way. During preps, I'd leave my class and go to his, to sit behind him during studies. It took two years, but one day after preps, I went back to the house to pick up my sweater. I found him there. Suddenly he switched off the lights and pulled me close to him. The rest is history. He's the guy I used to periodically give 'foot jobs' with my feet in the library.

Our school was huge. It didn't have a fence and it was almost 100 acres. There was a lot of space. So you would never run out of ideas and corners to try them in. I fooled around with so many boys, oh my God, I'm losing count! There was one in my agriculture class that used to stand behind me and press his dick on my ass. Oh! Should I call myself a slut? I really was.

Me and the football guy are friends to date, thirteen years later. We met once in Nairobi and we went for drinks and then I took him home. Oh! We revisited our past. He wanted us to go unprotected like we used to in high school, and I told him, "That's not possible. We've not seen each other in over eight years."

We still see each other once in a while.

After high school I went to university, and I had a field day there too. I was really out by the end of my first year. Once, we went out to a club and some guy found me outside taking a call. He started calling me loudly, "*Wewe shoga!*" You fag!

I think he was drunk. Two days later I saw him at the student canteen. When he was shouting at me outside the bar he had wanted to embarrass me, so I wanted to do the same to him. I

20. Staple dish of maize and beans stewed together. Githeri is a dish commonly served in Kenyan schools.

asked him loudly, in front of everyone, "What is your problem? How does my gayness affect you? Do you want to be gay, too?"

He was really embarrassed. I noticed then that he had very low self-esteem without the alcohol. Since that day, he became really afraid of me because he knew I was proud of who I am. Every time I'd meet him on campus he would take a different route.

I've spent some time abroad. I went to Dubai to visit once. I spent a month there, and I met quite a number of people. Arabs really like sex! When I'd cross the road, they'd stop their Jeeps and say, "Oh, *habibi*! Come!"

And they'd even lift their *kanzus*[21] to show me their cocks. It's very open in Dubai. I learned that Africans are a fetish for them. But you have to be careful not to be caught, because the police also go undercover to catch homosexuals.

Thailand was also marvellous. I was there for three weeks. It was the first time I have ever paid for sex. In Bangkok, there were these go-go bars with some really cute Asian boys, and some who were mixed-race; European and Indian. They were dancing in little white boxers that each had a number on them. It was very nice, and it was really cheap at that time. You buy them a beer at the bar for 400 bhat, and then you agree with them how it goes. Since I was staying with someone in the hotel, I couldn't bring the guy back with me, but they had their own rooms there. So I slept with him. It was his first time with a black man. They don't talk much—because most of the time they are intoxicated—but he was really sweet. It was due to his demeanour that I chose him. There were others there who were very mouthy, but he was very quiet. I'd talk to him and he'd look down. I said, "Correct. That one."

I found paying for sex challenging. I couldn't believe that I could do it at my age. I was just 24, then. But after talking to them, I thought they were really nice. We could relate to each other because we were in the same age group. I think I was a year or two older than the one I chose. This way I also learned a little

---

21. White or cream coloured robe worn by men in the African Great Lakes region. It is referred to as a tunic in English, and as the thawb in Arab countries.

about the city. The next day, I met him again and he showed me around. It was interesting because he had never seen someone black.

At the time, I used to date an old white man. The Asian boys looked at him and asked me, "Your boyfriend?"

I said, "Yes!"

Then they said, "OOOOOOH! So you're a slut like us!"

I had blue contact lenses on then, and the people would say, "Hey! You are black and you have blue eyes?"

Then they'd rub my skin to see if the colour would come off. They were doing it genuinely—you can tell when someone does it to mock you. Then they would say, "This one has come all the way from Africa!"

All the Africa they see on TV is hungry children and machetes, and here I was, having flown all the way from Africa. They then said, "I can't fly to Africa. It's too expensive."

So I was received well.

I went to Europe after that to study. Amsterdam was really shocking for me. I went to the red light district with my friend, and people were selling sex from the windows. The girls would get a client and close the display window. Another Kenyan friend took me to a gay club and it was the first time I had ever seen anything like that. Upstairs there was drinks and dancing, and people would then disappear downstairs. I gathered courage and went down to see what was happening. They had red lights on, and I could hear people fucking. I peeped and saw skinheads! I got a terrible headache because I was so overwhelmed, and I went quickly back upstairs. The same people I had seen down there came back calmly upstairs to continue having their drinks.

One notable experience I had was in Rome, about three years ago. I went with a friend, who is transgender. When we arrived, we needed to take a cab. We got into one and negotiated a rate. The driver said he would charge us a maximum of 50 Euro. When we got to where we were going, the meter read 47 Euro, but the driver wrote a receipt for 72 Euro. I asked, "Why are you writing 72 when the meter says 47?"

He said, "There is extra tax, and also you have a bag."

I said, "How can you charge us for a bag? Are you an airline?"

We didn't have time to argue, so we just paid. We spent the day roaming around, we had our lunch, some wine and walked around. We got into a bar around the corner and the barman was Nigerian! So—African style—he gave us a whole bottle of champagne! We drank and drank.

Then we discovered another bar called 'Trastevere'. It sounded like 'transvestite'. We went in and bought a bottle of champagne each. There were these beautiful girls dancing on the table as well, and we bought them a bottle too. We were feeling bitchy, getting drunk and swiping our cards. We realized we were drunk and decided to go back to the hotel. We took a taxi outside. The taxi fare back was supposed to be 8 Euro, but the man told us to pay him 15. I asked myself, "What's wrong with Rome?"

It was the same thing as in the morning when we landed. We asked, "Why are you charging us 15 and the meter says 8 Euro?"

He said, "Taxi don't pay, will take you to police!"

We said, "Let's go, then!"

When we got to the station, he changed the story and said we owed him 50 Euro. As much as I don't really know Italian, at least I can count in Italian. So I told him—in rough Italian—that he was lying, and that we owed him 8. He was very shocked. Then he said OK. I paid him, and that case closed. But he drove off and left us outside the police station.

The police saw us outside and they started bothering us. We were drunk, so we started bitching. Before we knew it we were arrested. When we were handcuffed, they took my watch. I asked, "Why are you taking my watch?"

They slapped me. They put us into the holding cell at about 2 or 3am. The next morning we were taken to court. The charges were that we had assaulted the police and destroyed state property by denting police cars and breaking their windows. Two policemen had pressed the charges against us. They came to court in plaster casts! We couldn't believe the lengths they had gone to!

The translator was half-Indian, half-Romanian. He told us what was happening because everyone was speaking in Italian. He told us that in the Italian system, when there is drama, nobody ever contests what the police say. You are just supposed to accept the charges. So we accepted the charges of having destroyed state property and having beaten the policemen up. The judge looked at how small we looked, then he looked at the size of the men alleging we beat them up, and the damage we were supposed to have done, and it wasn't adding up to him. In the end, we were released.

They had to give us back our passports, papers and everything. I was chatting with my friend in Swahili, then she made a mistake and said in English, "Police are so stupid."

They heard what she said. We went to the bus stop to catch the bus to our hotel, but before we could leave, we were re-arrested at the bus stop for saying the police were stupid. We were taken to another county outside central Rome, because there was no way we could be taken back to the same station. There, we were beaten by eight policemen. They even stepped on us with their boots. What saved us is that my friend faked an epileptic fit. They called their paramedics, who did a check-up and said, "These ones are OK. Book them."

We were taken to court again, and the minute I saw the judge I told my friend, "This one will put us in."

We were remanded pending a second hearing. We stayed in there for another six days. We were supposed to be leaving for Zurich on Friday. We stayed in the whole week. We were scheduled for court on Monday but it was a national holiday, so we went to court on Tuesday. By Tuesday we looked better, not like we had been beaten. Luckily, we got a different judge. He released us, but he said we would still need to go back to the cell for him to send a fax authorizing our time of release. He sent the fax at 4.30pm. The police released us at 7pm just to fuck with us. While we were waiting, they were making fun of us being gay. They asked, "What is your reason for visiting Italy?"

We said, "Tourism!"

They said, "No! Prostitution!"

They don't believe black people can go on holiday, and they are also not used to dealing with Africans with valid papers. They are used to illegal immigrants from Libya and Morocco. So every black person is treated that way. They said we had to come back the next day for immigration checks. We said, "But here are our visas," so they let us go.

We took the last train to Rome. It was a minute to midnight. Immediately after, we took the next train to Zurich and got out of there. When we got to the border we said, "Thank God."

Italian police are worse than Kenyan police. Kenyan police will collect your things when they arrest you, but they give them back to you when you are released. In Italy, THEY STOLE MY WATCH.

–

IF SOMEONE ASKED ME directly if I was gay, I'd say no. I'd even beat them up, because I'd not be sure what they wanted by asking me that. There's no day I've gone to the club and someone has failed to approach me. Sometimes I wonder, "Do I look gay? Is it the way I dress?"

I wear official clothes a lot, so it would be hard to look at me and say that I'm gay. But I still wonder, "Does this person like what I'm wearing, or is it something else they can see?"

I love men, even though I have a girlfriend. I spend most of my time with the men I date. Sometimes my girlfriend asks me, "Where are you?"

Obviously, I spin some story. When a man asks me where I am, I tell the truth. Sometimes I think, "I love this guy, but he has a family. I guess I'll be like that one day."

I get confused, because some guys tell me about their wives and children even when we are together. I've been dating my current boyfriend for six years. He's married. Sometimes I feel bad, but I just keep busy with my girlfriend when he's busy with his family. I do this for a few days, and then I go back to him.

I first met my current boyfriend on a Saturday. I was at a bus stop and he was there. He saw me talking to someone else who was very obviously gay, and then he came up to both of us and said hello, asked what we were doing. We talked a bit, then he said to me, "You are so handsome!"

The following Monday I saw him again. He said hi, and asked me out for lunch. I said no, but I gave him my number and took his. When he called me after that I told him I was at work, and if he wanted to find me he should call over the weekend. I finally met up with him one day in town and we just talked. We did that for about a year, just meeting up for coffee and lunches. He would flirt and I would ignore him, even though I thought he was a good man. He used to give me many gifts. He'd see things in a shop and buy them for me. He moved to Nairobi for a year and we talked on the phone a lot. I'd meet up with him if I ever had errands there. He came back to [illegible] the year after and left his family in Nairobi.

Before he came back, he told me, "When I come back there, I'll stay at your place."

I said, "No, you're coming for work, so your workplace will take care of you."

He said, "No. I'm looking for a friend that I can stay with, so I'm coming to you."

I said no for about a month, and then I thought back to what a good man he was, and the good things he had done for me. I thought he would have to spend too much money on hotels before he settled. I decided to let him come to my house. He lived with me for two months. When he got his own house after that, his family left Nairobi and came to live with him.

It hurts me when he talks about missing his family, but there's also an advantage in dating him. When I have sex with him, he always uses protection. These unmarried men just want to have sex without a condom. Also, I can ask him many things that I don't know. He gives me advice on how to approach women, and how to talk to them. Age is also a thing I consider. I don't want to date another twenty-something year old, because I don't think he would be mature enough. My preferred age is someone who is thirty and older. Someone who has been around a little longer than I have. My boyfriend is forty-one, and I'm twenty-six.

I've been with my girlfriend for just over two years. She's twenty-five now. Let's call her Alice. I met her at the church we both go to. My aunt was ill, and Alice heard about it at church. She came up to me and asked me if she could take me to visit her in the hospital. I thought that was kind. I said, "OK, let's go."

We went to visit her in a big group, then we had tea together at a café nearby. Because it was the first day we had ever spent time together, I figured Alice would just be a friend, or another companion at church. We talked on the phone a little after that. She asked me, "Do you like singing?"

I said, "Of course."

She got me into the church choir. She then went to for school, finished her studies and returned. The same aunt who was ill then passed away. Alice really took care of me during that time. She comes from a well-off family, and she gave me a car for running funeral errands. I realized what a good person she was. We kept talking and seeing each other as friends. I never went out with her at night, because all my nights were for my boyfriend.

I would tease her on the phone, and tell her I wanted to have sex with her. She then said she wanted to know how serious I was. I asked her why she didn't think I was serious at that time, when she knew I thought she was wife material. She said, "I know you men. You like lying to people."

So I told her, "It's OK. Take your time to decide."

Once she went to Nairobi, and then came back from that journey late at night. She called and asked me, "Where are you?"

I said, "I'm home."

She said, "I'll get a taxi and come to your house."

I said, "No! Just go home!"

She said, "My father thinks I'm coming tomorrow anyway, so it's OK. I can come."

She came to my home. I welcomed her and we slept. I saw that she really wanted us to have sex, but I didn't want to have sex with her. So I told her, "You are wife material to me, and I'm not ready to use you. I'm ready to marry you. So if it's just sex, no."

She understood and we just went to sleep and she left in the morning. We started dating officially a little later. Once she left work and came to my place. Then she said she wanted to sleep, and I said it was OK. I realized she wanted to test me. Or had she heard stories about me? I decided to just force myself to have sex with her. We had that sex *ya juujuu*. Half-hearted sex. She said she was a virgin. I wore a condom and came really fast because I was so apprehensive. I was so fast I couldn't even see what I was doing. She left in the morning. I called her the next day and asked, "Can I ask you something?"

She said, "I know."

I said, "What?"

She said, "That I'm still a virgin."

I thought, "What? I didn't do anything?"

A few weeks later, we had sex properly, and that's when I realized she really had been a virgin.

She's a nice girl. She's definitely wife material. The trouble is sometimes she just comes out of the blue and asks, "I've never see you chasing after any other girls. Why?"

So I ask her, "You want me to chase after other girls and hurt you?"

Then she doesn't know what to say. There are some times when I avoid her—I won't see her for even two months and just be very busy. We'll talk on the phone and not see each other at all, even though we live in the same town. She calls and says, "Have you found a new girlfriend? Is that why you're avoiding me?"

I say, "No. I'm just busy."

But every single day, I make time to see my boyfriend. When Alice complains, I arrange to see her and we talk, and then I leave. I'm even afraid of having sex with her these days. I don't want her to get pregnant. We had a scare some time ago. I had a bad feeling after we had sex that day and asked her, "Have you used contraception? I'm not ready to be a father."

She said she was not ready to be a mother either. I said, "So do something."

She got some family planning pills and took them, and it was taken care of. I think if she had not taken anything—if she had just gone to sleep, she would have gotten pregnant for sure. I swear I would have had a child by now.

I started a savings group and let her join, and—because I love my boyfriend so much—I made the mistake of also putting him in this same savings group. I realized that was a dumb thing to do, so I decided either I had to leave, or ask my boyfriend to leave. I decided to leave, and I left both my boyfriend and my girlfriend in that group.

Sometimes the group will have parties and invite me, but I feel weird about going and I won't go. Once, Alice forced me to go for one of those gatherings. My boyfriend had come with his wife. All of us were there. I asked myself, "What am I doing here?"

When they talked to me, I was very quiet, and I was hurting very deeply inside. It was very confusing and I wanted to leave. I dropped Alice home, and my boyfriend sensed there was something wrong. He also dropped his wife home, then he called and asked me, "Where are you?"

I said, "I'm at home."

He said, "I'm coming."

When I saw him I really felt angry. I don't know if it was jealousy I felt. When I'm angry I can't even talk. I can stay a month without talking to someone if I am angry. I told him, "Right now, I can't talk to you. I feel too angry."

My boyfriend and I are from the same social group, so when I tell Alice I am with him, she never imagines anything more between us than just being close friends. She will ask, "Who are you out with?", and I say it's him.

Because he's married, she feels like that's OK. She knows his wife, too—that's another reason I can't come out to her, she might tell my boyfriend's wife. I'm very good friends with my boyfriend's wife, too. When their baby is sick I help them, and when they have needed money I have helped them out. She sees me as a really good friend of her husband. The baby is always saying he misses me.

I think my family senses that I am gay. One time, my cousin and I were sitting together and my grandmother told us, "Do you know there are some things that are forbidden in the Bible, like a man lying with his fellow men? Those things are really bad."

I really wondered why she had brought that topic up, and especially when we were all sitting together. I think they have seen some signs. Once, a gay friend bought me a present and brought it home. The house-girl picked it up and brought it to me. My grandmother saw it and asked her, "What are you carrying? Who is it from? Who is it for?"

She really wanted to know about it. I feel like she knows I'm gay. My father usually tells me, "I don't want to see you with this guy, or that guy."

I tell him, "Dad, this is my life. There are some things you can tell me, but there are some things you shouldn't."

I have a job and I take care of myself. So it's not like I rely on him. Once, I was alone with him in the house, and he became firm and asked me straight to my face, "Are you gay?"

I asked him, "What is this you are asking me?"

I also became very firm. I added, "If I'm gay, it's my life."

I don't know how he took that. These days, he leaves me alone. But sometimes he says weird things like, "You spend a lot of time in front of the mirror, eh?"

So I don't know if he knows for sure.

Two of my cousins know I am gay. I told them. Sometimes my boyfriend has hurt me, so I can tell them about it. They're girls, so I ask them, "When your men hurt you, what do you do?"

Then they give me advice. They even know my boyfriend and we have all gone out together.

I have only dated married men, so obviously I will have a family of my own one day. When I settle down, it will be with a woman, not a man. There is no way it would be possible with a man.

My boyfriend has never opened a business for me, or paid my fees, or anything. How is he going to leave his family for me? If he leaves, he will just leave me where I am. If I think I can settle down with a man, I will just confuse myself. So I will settle with a woman, like this one I am dating now. She doesn't love me for my money, and when I have a problem, she is there, and when she has a problem, I am there. If I tell her that I don't have bus fare, she sends me a taxi and we sort it out the next day. Even if I end up getting a baby, I don't want my life to be one of struggling. I want my child to have a good life, at least.

I'm very happy. I'm very comfortable with where my life is. When I look at where I was before, and where I am now, I think at least I HAVE A FUTURE NOW.

–

I AM A HUSTLER. I sell stuff like shoes, trousers, skirts, ornaments, earrings, necklaces and bracelets. I am also a lesbian, and I am currently dating. I date ladies only, that's my life. I realized I was gay in high school. I was still young, I wasn't developed and I didn't have hips. There were these girls who would say, "She looks like a boy, walks like a boy, behaves like a boy."

I didn't like spending my time with the girls. I used to walk alone. In fact that's what made my behaviour questionable, because they used to ask, "Why is she walking alone?"

Every time I'd come to the dormitory late at night, they'd ask, "Where have you been, what have you been doing?"

When the girls started spreading stories about me behaving like a boy, I was taken to the school matron for her to check if I was really a girl. The matron was distantly related to my mother and they'd always joke that I was a boy. Even so, I was even suspended from high school because they thought I was a lesbian. I went home for two weeks. I told my parents I was sent home for abnormal behaviour. I had to go before the disciplinary committee after my suspension. I made up stories and wrote them down as a confession, just so that the story would end, and I could go back to my studies. But it hurt me. My family would go to church every Sunday. We read out Bible verses, and we were very active in church. I returned to school, but I didn't want to go to church any more. I felt that God was unfair to let me go through all that.

I realized I was gay when we went on some school outings. We'd interact with boys and I realized that I wasn't interested in them. In fact when a guy approached me it really irritated me. In high school I used to get letters from other girls saying, "I like you, I like your style, I want us to be more than friends," but I was scared. I was still in high school, under pressure, under authority.

The first experience I had was immediately out of high school. I had gone to pick my final exam results. My high school was far, in ████████, and so I couldn't come back the same day. I asked a high school friend of mine if I could spend the night at her place because it was late. She was one of those who used to hit on me in high school. I thought maybe that was a high school thing and maybe the feelings had ended.

That night I spent there, we started touching and kissing. It was the first time I ever kissed a girl, and it was overwhelming. I wanted to do it more and more. We never did it again, but after that I started looking for a girlfriend.

After that night in █████, this chick kept on calling. She thought I was using her because I never got back to her. I didn't have any feelings for her, I wanted to do it again but with another person. I used to see her as a friend, and I thought it was a mistake to kiss her. Still, I thank God it happened, because it gave me that urge to look for other girls elsewhere. After that, I didn't like commitment. I find a girl, we hook up, we make out, and then that's the end of the story. We're friends. That was my life then, because I didn't know that I could have relationships with girls.

I started dating three years ago; breakups and make-ups. The first person I dated was a straight girl. It was really troubling, she was a drama queen. She was in the same high school as myself, but four years behind me. She used to know that I was a wrong number; a gay girl, you know? We met in a supermarket, she approached me and said, "Hi, do you remember me?"

I said yes. You know the way after high school someone really transforms? She was much prettier. I pretended that I was doing research for a research company so I took her number. It turned out she lived in the same area with me, not far from my place. In the mornings and evenings I'd pass by and say hello or goodnight. We started out as friends.

One day I invited her to my place for dinner. I was having many friends over. They left after dinner, leaving me alone with this girl. We told each other stories, about high school and how people used to say that I liked girls. We stayed up until 1am. I stopped those stories and I kissed her. She kissed me back. One thing led to the other. The next morning she woke up, she was upset, and she really insulted me, "You want to convert me."

I told her that I didn't force her to do anything, she agreed to do it. She started raising her voice. I didn't want my neighbours to hear, so I kept quiet. She insulted me and left. I was hurt. She said that I'd taken advantage of her because she was younger than me. She threatened to go get her boyfriend—she had a boyfriend!—and that scared me. I wanted to run away, but I decided to stay. I figured all of us were adults, and she would also be asked how she got herself into such a situation.

That morning she left, I went to town to run errands then I went back home. I found her standing at my door. I asked her, "What are you doing here?

She said, "I've come to greet you."

I asked her, "After all those insults?"

She said she was sorry, and I told her to go away. She refused. So we entered the house, there was an awkward silence, she wasn't talking to me. I was also upset, I didn't want to talk to her. We sat, not talking. Evening came, and she didn't leave. I asked her to leave and she said, "I want to sleep here."

She told me she realized that she felt confused, and she didn't want to meet her boyfriend. She was avoiding him. We slept together. We went on like this for two years. She eventually left her boyfriend. To this day that man really hates me. He found out that it was me. He even came to my house once and told me that I was trying to snatch his girlfriend away. I told him, "She is not a child, she has a mind. If she wants to stay here, let her stay here."

She told him that she didn't want to be with him anymore. He was in college, and that story spread. The story was that his girlfriend was stolen by another girl. It was really irritating to him. It would have been better if his girl was stolen by another man, rather than a woman.

So we had a relationship, but she really changed as we went along. She didn't want to see me with other ladies or friends. We'd go out to the club, she'd find me dancing with another lady and slap me. When I was with her, I was very careful. If she found me in the club with other ladies, she'd slap me or grab and pull me away so that everyone else noticed. She was abusive physically. She left me with dents. There is a time we fought and she threw whatever she could grab at me. There was a time she even had a knife. She was very violent. The violence annoyed me.

When I told her we needed to break up because we couldn't live like this anymore, she told me that I was the one that 'converted' her, and she started blackmailing me emotionally. She said that she'd call my mum and tell her I was gay. I couldn't leave her. She said only she could leave when she wanted to, but that I didn't have a right to leave her. It reached a point where

I hoped that she'd leave me, because otherwise I'd have to deal with the consequences of her telling my mum.

I fell out of love with her the minute she became violent. I fear violence. Even in college she'd cause trouble, the lecturers would notice us fighting and wonder what was going on with us. It used to raise eyebrows, and it upset me. We used to fight so much such that one day the landlord of my house came and asked what was happening. Straight people would wonder why we were fighting like that. There are fights between friends, and then there was this. After fighting we'd be indoors and still be together. So people had questions, but they didn't ask. Violence in lesbian relationships is common.

Eventually we parted ways, she finished college and went on to university. Distance broke us up. She went back to her home, and I stayed here. I finally got an opportunity to interact with other people. I hooked up with another girl. One day, my old girlfriend came and found me with this new girl. I did it intentionally, so that she would leave me. It worked, she left me.

I was afraid of relationships after that. My longest relationship after that was three months. My friends would tease me about my short relationships, saying that they were three-month contracts. It was working for me, though. No one was hurt. I'd bump into my ex-girlfriends and they were still friends with me. I continued like that until last year, when I started my current relationship which has lasted a year.

My current relationship was healthy at first. It was nice. I met someone I liked and the months flew by. But now I'm starting to consider being single again. We don't get along any more. We are incompatible. Not a day goes by where we don't fight. My current relationship is heading for the rocks.

I think this relationship lasted a while because she's pretty, she has a good heart and she doesn't have many stories. Back then I had a steady job, so girls would meet me thinking I have money so they could exploit me. When I met this lady I wasn't financially stable, but she would chip in when I had difficulties. We help each other in life, we go to town and hustle together. She wasn't a proud girl. We even went to the village together. We used to go as straight friends. We'd do village work together, then we'd stay home together. She has a vision and we can go somewhere together. We could really help each other. I hope it doesn't end.

I am hoping to get a well-paying job, and then I hope our relationship works. If it doesn't work, I'll never date again. I am weak when I fall in love. I see relationships that fail as a waste of my time. If this works, I will stay with her for the rest of my life.

My parents don't know about me. I only have a mum. Sometimes I feel like telling her but I see she'd get heart broken. My mum is a church woman. Sometimes, we hear about gays on the radio and her reaction is very negative. I wonder what she'd do if she heard her child is actually gay.

I want to get married to a woman. I'd never want to get married to a man. I want children—I like children. I imagine my partner would also have a child. I am afraid, though. What happens if one day they leave me? She says she also wants a child but not many. When we get to that subject though, the story of carrying the child scares me. What scares me is that if she gives birth, I won't have a direct relationship with the child, and then one day they might get up and leave me. I'll have helped bringing the child up, and then one day they just go. Or the child might grow up and not recognize me as their parent. I'M UNCERTAIN ABOUT IT.

–

I AM AN IT FREELANCER and a farmer. I am growing maize and wheat. I didn't see myself becoming a farmer, but it's not bad. I identify as gay. I started suspecting I was gay in primary school. I used to stare at men and think, "Wow, they're cute."

Then I started to think, "Wait, there is something going on here."

In primary school, nothing happened, but in high school I experimented. We once went drinking with my cousin when I was fourteen. He was about seventeen years old. I didn't drink a lot, just to taste; it was my first drinking experience. I got a bit tipsy, then we went back home. We were sleeping in the same room, that's when we started making out. He didn't ask me anything, he just started touching me, and I thought, "This feels nice."

We made out, and then we had sex. We woke up the next day like nothing happened. There was guilt, we didn't even speak to each other for a while. Then he left for further studies. I've never seen him since. We never got to talk about it.

High school was interesting. I used to like this girl called Amira. I think I had a crush on her. I really liked her. One day I told her that I liked her and she said, "Oh my God, but I've been thinking you're gay!"

After Amira told me that, I started wondering about it. It started adding up; from my experiences in primary school, to shagging with my cousin. I didn't pursue anything else with Amira.

After high school, I was busy. I never got time to interact with people. But now I discovered the internet. I joined a few gay dating websites and chatted with some people. At that time I wasn't into sex because I didn't know much about it, I'd had sex only once. It was difficult, I was trying to understand myself. The problem with dating online is you meet people too quickly. They really rush you. I met a couple of people, we'd make out a bit and then they'd want to go all the way. I met another guy in a bar. We ordered drinks, chatted a bit, then he said, "Let me go put my bag in the room, do you want to come with me?"

I said sure, and shortly after the guy was all over me, and we made out. After a while, he wanted to have sex. I said, "No. We have just met, I am not comfortable."

I told him we could have sex later in the night, after we went out dancing. We went out, and I left him in the club. I disappeared. I met another guy later on. At night, we made out, and then he asked if we could shag. I said, "No. After meeting you for the first time? No."

Then he said, "OK, can you blow me?"

I said, "OK, that I can do, but only that."

That was the first blow job I ever gave. I wasn't sure what I was doing. I'd watched porn, but I hadn't really done it to anyone. It felt really awkward because he was moaning loudly, but then it also felt nice because I was pleasing him.

I kept on meeting douche-bags from the internet until I decided that this internet thing wasn't working. I got into college, so I had to focus and I moved to ██████. There, I met a guy called Felix. That was an interesting night. Felix and I made out. I was new to kissing, so I warned him, "I'm not a pro, so don't judge me."

He tried finger-fucking me, and I said, "We can't do that here."

He got pissed off when I said that. He wanted us to fuck but I wasn't comfortable. Anyway, he let me go, and we kept on talking after that. Every Thursday I'd go to his place. It was a routine. I used to feel like a princess. He'd pick me up from the college hostel, and he'd make dinner for me. It was a nice experience, but we never decided that we're dating. I asked him, "Are we dating, or are we fuck-mates?", and he always avoided the question.

It was random, but it was always sexual. We used to talk but not a lot. I think it was two weeks after meeting him that I gave into him sexually. It was awkward, but interesting.

The first gay party I went for was in Nairobi. That day I felt free. It was scary and amazing at the same time. I entered this place and saw only men. Men hitting on each other, men kissing, men in drag. It was so interesting, I thought I was in another world. I'd never seen anything like it in ██████. It was pretty intense, it was cool.

I started developing feelings for Felix, but then I saw he was not really interested in a relationship. The first time he told me that he loved me was when he was drunk. If I developed feelings for him and it wasn't reciprocated what was I supposed to do?

University was a totally different experience. During Orientation Week, these girls were standing in front of us. They turned and looked at me, then they whispered, "This is a gay man."

I wondered how they knew. I went undercover completely. My gay life in university was dead. I was scared. Our university was a Christian university with crazy rules. If they found out you were gay, they would call your name during chapel sessions and pray for you. I wasn't ready to go down that road. I stayed undercover for all of 1st Year.

In 2nd Year, some guy asked me if I was gay. A short guy, not really cute.

"Why are you asking me?" I asked.

He said, "I just want to know."

So I told him yes. A little while later he knocked on my room. I asked him what he wanted, and he stepped in and kissed me. I was shocked! In my hostel room! I didn't want that drama. I literally chased him away. He kept asking me whether I wanted to kiss again, and I said no.

A few days later, he came to my room at around 10:50pm. The university had a curfew, if you were not in your hostel by 11pm, you were required to sleep wherever you were. He came to chat. Petty chat. Small talk. I told him, "Time is up, you should be in your hostel."

He said, "Let me go say hi to my friend, I am coming back."

He went, and by the time he came back it was past 11pm. He said, "I have to sleep here, I can't go anywhere at this time."

I didn't have a roommate at the time, so the other bed was empty. I said, "Fine, you can use the extra bed."

He agreed. Later he said, "Let's watch a movie." So, movie time. He put on some porn and I thought to myself, "*Heh! Leo amewaka moto.*" Today, he's on fire.

I pushed him away, I don't like watching porn. Then he said, "OK, then let's make out," and I said OK.

We made out. He wasn't forceful. He wasn't really pushing for anything, but I was there freaking out about the school management and about getting busted. Eventually, he slept in the other bed. Before he left in the morning he said, "We should try this another day, book a hotel in ██████."

Little by little I started having gay friends in my university. I started coming out, but very slowly. A friend of mine once asked, "What's your deal? You hang around pretty women, but I've never heard you dating them."

I told her, "Oh no, I'm gay."

She said, "No way! You're lying."

She never believes that story, even now. I started coming out. I joined a music group, which distracted me because I'd go for lots of practice. Then I ran for student office in my second or third year. When I did, rumours started going around. Luckily I wasn't summoned, it was just rumours. I was in the same school with my sister, so one day she asked, "Have you heard the rumours about you?"

I told her they were just rumours. One of the guys in my music group was a devout Christian. He asked me, "There are these rumours I've heard about you, are they true?"

I said no, and I brushed it off. In the evening he went to my sister and told her, "Your brother is gay, we should kneel down and pray for him."

My sister came and told me about it later. Eventually, I didn't get the seat I was vying for. That rumour probably had a lot to do with it.

I met another guy on another website when I finished university. We kinda dated, we weren't in a relationship. We went on dates to get to know each other. He was working in ,and he'd come over to my town for meetings on Mondays and Tuesdays and we'd meet then. It turned into a relationship kinda thing. I gave in after four or five months. It was pretty awesome. We dated for two months. After a while, meeting him started getting hard, because he'd travel to far places like . At times we'd meet after a month. I sat down and thought, "This isn't a relationship. It is a sexual thing."

Every time we'd meet, we'd get excited and have sex. I wanted something better than this. So I told him we could be friends and just chill out. We broke up in a nice way.

A few months later, I went for a house party. There were not many people there, about ten guys. This guy walked in, he was very pretty. I thought, "Wow, you're the only man in this room."

He came over to me and we chatted. When it was time to leave, he came to me and said, "Can I kiss you goodbye?"

I was impressed. I thought, "This one is interesting."

He pinned me on the wall and kissed me. It was very nice; soft, interesting. We really made out, it was very intense. I finally left, but we'd exchanged numbers. I got a call at around 2pm the next day. It was him.

"I'm at 's house. Come over, we talk."

We got to know each other a little bit, then it turned into sex. The sex was so good. The sex was amazing. We had lunch and then we went for a drink. At around 8pm we went back to

█████'s house and ended up having more sex. I thought it was too much and I left. The next day, he called me and said he was around the neighbourhood, he wanted to meet. So we met and had a conversation. I got to know him slowly. He'd come to see me every day after work and check up on me.

I was impressed. This was a different person, not like the guys I had met online. After a week I felt a bit starved. I wanted to see him everyday, lie on his chest. He kept coming over, and we'd talk about his family, his issues with his wife, his kids. Yes, he was married. I helped him with the problems he was having. They say you feel better when you talk to someone. I was there for him. Later on, he decided to separate with his wife. He was really gay. He never had relations with the wife.

We kept meeting, and shagging once in a while. After a few weeks, he said he was falling in love with me and asked if we could try out having a relationship. I agreed. We dated for a year. It was amazing. I never knew I could love a man that much. It was really cool. It wasn't sexual as such, we'd have sex once in a while. He was there for me. It was a friendship-based relationship.

Eventually, we had to break up. My best friend—let's call him Arnold—kept reminding him that he was still married. Arnold would ask him, "Where is your wife right now? What does she think of what you're doing?"

It was hurtful. Arnold even told me that he had heard a story that my boyfriend was cheating on me. I asked, "Do you have any proof?"

He didn't have any proof, "I overheard it in the club when I was drinking. You should ask him."

After a while, Arnold and I drifted apart, and I became closer to my boyfriend. I felt bad about it, but I didn't care—and we were still living in the same house with Arnold. My boyfriend couldn't come over because Arnold would make faces at him. After a few months of this, my boyfriend said, "Let's take a break and end this."

I understood. You know when somebody decides, there's not much you can do. He cried and told me how much he loves me. I felt bad. It was really depressing. I felt depressed the whole month. I told him to decide. We went out for a drink after that and slept at his place. I woke up the next day in his bed, and we didn't shag. We made breakfast. I asked him if he was serious about breaking up and he said, "Let's stay how we are."

I said, "No. Let's end this now."

We broke up. I was so pissed off with Arnold, "You are the reason I can't have a boyfriend. Are you jealous, did you want me for yourself?"

We fought, and Arnold and I AREN'T FRIENDS ANY MORE.

–

I IDENTIFY AS BISEXUAL. I had an idea about this when I was in Standard 4. I was playing outside with my classmates who were boys, and then it started raining. We got wet, and then my friend said, "Let's remove our clothes!"

So we did. It was nice, because the drops were cool and it had been a very hot day. We continued playing, and then we found ourselves standing under a roof where the water was coming down like a shower, and we just started kissing. Afterwards we went into the house because it had gotten cold, and to warm up we entered a bed. I can't really remember what happened next, but I think we had some fun.

In Standard 7, I had sex with a girl and it was awkward. She was much older than I was—she was in Form Four. I am the one who approached her. I don't know how I convinced her. Neither of us ever talked about what we did ever again. She's now married, and I even attended her wedding.

In high school I had to keep a low profile so that I could concentrate on my academics. Most of the time I had crushes on men, even though I didn't do anything about them. I didn't have any sexual experiences in high school—with girls or boys—even though I was in a mixed school. After high school, I had a group of four friends that I had met in church. They used to come over to keep me company from time to time when I had to babysit my sister's children. They also liked children. I used to wonder, "Why do these guys love children they way I do? Are we the same?"

One day I was at the beach and I met some Italian tourists who wanted African t-shirts with animals on them. You know, rhinos, lions and such. We talked for a while and they told me they were gay. I came back and told my friends, "I met these guys who are gay and they are so free! They are just socializing and walking with each other and there is no problem!"

My friends looked at one another then asked me, "Are you surprised about that?"

That evening, I did a lot of thinking.

First thing the next morning I gathered some guts, went straight to my friends and told them, "I think you guys are gay."

They said, "Yes, we are. But we've always wondered if you are."

With that statement, I was free to tell them that I wasn't sure if I was totally into men, or if I was into women as well. They said, "You will find out."

So we hung out on the beach, and one of the Italian guys came back. He approached me, we went out and I really had a good time. That was the first time I realized that I could hang out with a man like that and feel loved.

It turned out that he actually had to remain in Kenya to run a resort. We began a relationship, and it lasted six months. We only broke up because I had to go and join college. We kept talking for about two months, and then things just got quiet after that.

Somebody once told me that if a guy confuses me, it means I'm in love. There is only one time I genuinely felt confused, and that was when I was with this Italian guy. I was really, properly confused. He used to do things I found irrelevant, but interesting. He would pull out chairs for me and open car doors. I'm not used to that kind of treatment. I really had to try to accept it. But I loved being around him. It took me very long to forget him—and I don't think I have really ever fully forgotten him. I still have his contacts, but I don't want to know where he is because if I do, I will go for him. That was my first, and longest relationship with a man.

When I joined college, I was kinda lonely, and looking for friends on Facebook to be able to hang out with. This guy texted me that he was from my home town, had just arrived in college and didn't have a place to sleep. I asked him, "What do you have in mind?"

He said, "I just need a place to sleep, and tomorrow I will look for my own home."

I thought, "This person is just like me, let me help him."

He came, and we had a good time hanging out. When we went to bed, we had sex. After that we had a relationship for two months, but I realized I was not committed and he wanted something more than what I felt I could give. We decided to remain good friends. We became best friends.

With time, he found another guy. We continued hanging out, but we didn't sleep together again. One day, he was helping me clean my house. While we were doing that, he took some shirtless photos of me. Later on, he showed his boyfriend those photos. That boyfriend then decided to approach me. I had never met him, so I didn't know this was my best friend's boyfriend. He flirted with me and I was interested. We started dating after a while.

Eventually, I realized the truth and I knew I had to stop it. I called both of them to my house. I really wanted to discuss it openly and retain the friendship. Everyone explained himself, and we realized that this guy was far more in love with me than he was with my best friend. I was more interested in keeping my best friend, but it couldn't work. We had to sacrifice everything. All the friendships and relationships between us broke up. We each deleted everyone else's number and contacts, and all of us moved house. None of us knew where everyone else went, and I have never seen any of them since.

I miss my best friend so, so much. We used to share a lot, but there was no way it would have worked. My best friend was really in love with this guy, and this guy was really in love with me. It would have been a challenge to maintain the friendship.

It was such a hard time for me. I even locked myself in the house for almost a whole week. One of my friends told me I needed to start thinking about moving on. After some time I thought, "Maybe I'm not gay."

So I decided to get born-again. I tried these godly things. I had talked to this guy who I considered my mentor. I told him what I was going through and he told me I should give being a born-again Christian a try. I really tried, but it just didn't work. I think I wanted to get deep into the church to help me get over losing both my best friend and my potential boyfriend. I decided then that I was going to move on.

One day I went swimming, and I bumped into a very cute boy who was in the School of Engineering. To this day, I am in a relationship with him. We've been dating for a while now. We did some mushy, soft things for Valentine's day this year.

Two people in my life will die of a stroke if I tell them I am gay—my parents. I dare not tell them. I want to get married at some point, and I have been thinking about whether I want to marry a man or a woman. I think I am sure I want to spend my life with a man. I love children and I want two kids, who I intend to get by using a surrogate mother.

Living in [redacted] is tough! When I'm in school, I have to act masculine lest people start judging me—which isn't easy! It's like being in a play! Every day of my life is like being in a drama. I think the people here are a little meaner than in [redacted] where I grew up. The LGBT community here are not really out, so it's also not easy to find friends to share the things you'd like to be able to share. You're constantly surrounded by straight guys who are always talking about football, and how which player did what, stuff like that which is very boring. You can't try out certain outfits and fashions. You have to act masculine and wear things you don't like. I would really like to wear FASHION! I'd love to be a bit free to buy things that people won't judge me for wearing.

I've never really been in a relationship with a woman, since Standard 7. So many women have had crushes on me. Some even come to spend nights in my house, but I find touching them awkward. I'd get into a relationship with one, though, if I ever want to cover my ass. If I found a lesbian who wanted a child, it might be easier. Then we'd be able to keep our boundaries, so I can date men and she can date women. I would introduce her to my family, and we could even walk down an aisle and get married. These things are challenging, though, with the new marriage laws and how tough divorce is regarding THE DIVISIONS OF PROPERTY.

–

I IDENTIFY AS GAY. Back at school, I couldn't define what it was exactly, but I knew I was attracted to guys. I sometimes thought, "Goodness, I want to see that guy naked."

The times we went to shower, I would lose concentration. I thought there was something wrong with me then. I started to realize I was gay about three years ago. I was an active member in our church youth group, and one day we went for an overnight thanksgiving service. Around 3am—when it was done—there was this youth pastor who told me, "It's too late in the night for you to go back home. How about we go back to my place, spend the night there, and you can go back home in the morning?"

I agreed, because going back home was a little tricky. The area I lived in was not safe. So I went with him. We had a drink and went to sleep in the same bed. About an hour later, I started feeling his hands all over me, and I thought, "This is weird."

I didn't expect that of him because he was a pastor and I understood him to be straight—and so was I. He continued and I asked, "Dude, what are you doing?"

I thought he was dreaming and thought I was his girlfriend. I wanted to wake him up in the hope that the moment he realized I was a guy, he would stop. But his hands went further down, and I said, "Excuse me? Hello? I'm a guy!"

He said, "I know."

I was shocked, confused. I asked, "What do you mean, you know?"

He said, "I know. This happens."

I said, "I'm going home this very minute." I checked my watch, and it was 4:30am.

He said, "Take it easy, relax. It won't happen again," and he stopped.

But the moment he started touching me, I had become erect. It had somehow been quite exciting, even while it was confusing. I wasn't sure what I was feeling. I didn't want him to touch me, but I wanted him to at the same time. So we slept, and woke up in the morning. The guilt and shame were difficult to stand, imagining the things he was trying to do. I went home.

Years later, I joined campus. In my first year, I had a close friend who was really nice to me. After evening classes we'd go for coffee together. He used to be in campus housing, and I went to his room a lot. He never showed any interest in me, or in boys. One evening, we decided to have a drink. I really don't like alcohol. There's a thing it does where you feel all weak. We drank and got sleepy. My friend undressed and we went to bed. In bed, the same thing started happening. His hands were all over me, like the pastor. I thought, "This isn't happening again!"

I asked him, "What are you doing?"

I couldn't understand what was happening. He was so straight looking, and it was so difficult to imagine that he was queer. So I decided in the moment, "Why not try this thing out?"

I'd been feeling attracted to guys anyway, and this one was good looking. That night we made out, and I was really excited. He gave me a blow job. Then it got to the part I was really dreading; penetration. That was a fight. I couldn't withstand the presence of a dick around my ass. I couldn't. But he was really easy. So we started and I was kind of resisting but in my head I thought, "Just try it out."

While we were making out, he tried fingering me with a lubricated finger. I had never tried that and I wasn't prepared for it. After a while, I became easy. He said, "If you relax you won't feel much pain."

I really tried to relax, and we had sex, but it wasn't comfortable.

Then I asked him, "Why don't I try and fuck you also?"

He said, "No, I'm a top."

I said, "What is that?"

"I only fuck. I can't be fucked."

So I asked, "Why can't you be fucked? You have an ass, just like I do."

I had to ask, because I really wanted to feel how he had felt. He explained, "I can wank you. But I can't do anything else."

So I felt used. In the morning, I could feel the discomfort. I'd been a little drunk when we fucked, so I didn't have that much pain in the night. Looking back, I know we should have taken it much slower. Also, that guy was loaded! He was 'blessed', if you know what I mean. We should have used more lubrication.

I was going all the way back home where I lived with my relatives, and I was wondering how I could even explain the kind of pain I was feeling to someone. I wondered if I should go to a hospital, but I really wondered what I would say to the doctor. I decided to take some painkillers, and I got better. I didn't want to talk to him after that. He tried calling me, but I didn't want to talk to him. I would see him in campus and when I saw him coming I would duck and go the other way. I would just see him and remember the pain.

Two weeks later, I decided to start answering his calls and replying his texts. We met up, and he said, "I'm really sorry if you felt like I hurt you."

I told him that I felt used. I said, "Why didn't you allow me to shag you? Why didn't you give me the chance to feel you?"

He said, "The way these things work, there are different roles."

He explained the whole top-bottom thing—which I thought was silly—but we became easy and continued talking, but we were not as tight as we were before. A month and a half or so later, I found myself wanting to have sex again. The experience had been a nice one, so why not have it again? This time I knew how to make it painless. So I started looking for him, sending texts like, "Hey! Hello! Are you in the room?"

He replied, "Yeah, I'm in my room!"

It was around 7 in the evening.

"Can I come over?" I asked.

He replied, "This is really unlike you. You're calling and asking to come over?"

But he agreed, "OK, come over."

That night, he actually allowed me to shag him. I had gone prepared to get shagged, and I knew he was a top, he couldn't take dick. Whatever. I don't think he can ever admit he let me fuck him, because he's such a top. He's a MAN, the ones who can rip you apart. He shagged me first, and it was amazing this time, and then I asked, "Can you wank me?"

But instead he asked, "You want to try and fuck me? You can try, even though I have never done it."

I said, “You want to try it? My pleasure.”

And I really did it. I felt like I wanted to punish him for what he had done to me the first time. I felt so exalted. I got a whole new image of this sex thing, that it can be reciprocal. I really thought that was nice. I felt such joy, and the moment I screwed him I couldn’t compare it to shagging a chick. This was way sweeter. We’re both men, and we’re shagging each other? I couldn’t take the joy, it was immense.

Later, he asked if I could date him. I thought, “Date? That can never happen. We are guys!”

But he asked me, “Why not? We enjoy hanging out, and I care about you very much.”

I couldn’t believe guys could date, but we tried it and it was wonderful. He had a girlfriend, by the way. I also had a girlfriend at that point. I still have one, even now. So he said, “Don’t worry about my girlfriend. She is a chick, and you’re a guy.”

We dated for a couple of months, and then he left the country. We’re still friends, even though he moved on with life. We’re still very close now. He’s seeing a guy, and he lives in [redacted]. I don’t think I can forget him. He comes to visit every now and then and we hang out. I really respect him also, because the guys who can change roles are few. Also, people who know you are a virgin sometimes take advantage of you, and once you shag the poor boy, that’s it; hit and run. But he was different.

I have preferences, even if I am a versatile—and I prefer topping. It’s what I really enjoy. Dating another versatile guy would be best, because I feel different things at different times. Sometimes I want to shag someone, and sometimes I want to be shagged by someone. If it was only one way, I wouldn’t be faithful. I would go out there looking for the thing I want, because I’d still have that urge. I wouldn’t mind dating a bottom, but not an exclusive top. *Hiyo kulimwa sitaki.* I don’t want to be ravaged like that. No. It’s too much work. I wouldn’t be able to handle it.

Now, my girlfriend. I started seeing her when I was in Form Two, and we’re still together. A while back, I thought to myself, “This is too much. I am living a double life.”

I was finding most of my attention going to men. I thought about telling her about my sexual orientation. It was a battle in me. She worships the ground I walk on. She's really into me. We've known each other from high school, when we were fifteen or sixteen. That's someone you should really respect, not just love. Do I love her? That's relative. I think I do. I feel attached to her, in the sense that I wouldn't want her away from me. I'd be jealous if she started seeing another guy. I'm not sexually attracted to her, though. We just make out, and that's it. I've never had sex with her. Actually, she's a virgin, and I know she is, because I've tried to penetrate her and couldn't; she was in a lot of pain. I told her, "I don't want to hurt you—let's just wait for the right time."

Since then we've just been waiting. Actually, she used to see me with guys a lot. She would come to my place to visit me and find me usually with a guy. I would tell the guys, "Act straight! This is my girlfriend!", and they would man up.

I think she would raise her eyebrows a little, but she has never asked me about it. I knew she had an idea that there was something between me and men.

I never feel attraction to other women, ever. But I really love beautiful women. I'm just so gay. I want their presence around me. Not lesbians, though. Straight women. I don't want sex with them. I even walk into clubs and women come to me and we dance. I don't want sex, but I love their company. Women would come to me—and you usually know which women have romantic interest. I don't know whether this is a fault, or a weakness—I don't know what it is, but that's me. I don't know the destiny of my sexual orientation. I don't know if I would want to marry a woman, or stay with men. Maybe I could turn straight. I don't know what I feel. I think I am naïve about how this ends. But I want my girlfriend to stick around so that later on in life I can marry her.

I spoke with a couple of my friends about telling her, and they said, "Let her off the hook. Tell her who you are. If she really loves you, she'll accept you."

They meant she would be able to continue dating me while knowing I was gay, and honestly I didn't like that. I wanted to let her know so that I could free her. I called her for a cup of coffee in town, and I said, "There's something I want to tell you, and it's very important."

I looked at her sitting there and thought how much I didn't want to hurt her, but I really wanted to let her know. So I said, "I really love you, and you know that. We've come far together, and I think there are some things you need to know about me."

And then I started crying. I couldn't imagine breaking her heart. I continued, "You know what? I'm attracted to guys. It's something I have been fighting, but it's part of who I am."

I held her hands and cried on that table, until people around were wondering what was happening. I added, "I really respect you, and I just wanted you to know. Now you can decide if you think we can continue dating. I want us to. I want you to be with me, though this is who I am."

She was looking at me straight in the eye. I told her, "Say something, please?"

She said, "OK."

She didn't react, or question me about it at all. I thought she would be all over the place. She's the kind of girl who will just say that it's easy, and then not talk about it again. She even paid my bus fare after. I'm sure she'd always known. Women are very sensitive, and it's a stereotype but—probably she knew. She said, "I love you so much."

We hugged, we even kissed. Gosh.

My girlfriend and I have never talked about it again. But about four months later, she started changing. She wasn't as affectionate as she used to be. She didn't make the calls she used to make. We still talk, even though we're not as close. I suspect if she is asked whether I am her boyfriend, she wouldn't say yes. She could be seeing someone else, and that idea makes me jealous. We didn't really break up. We're in a very uncertain place now. I've tried talking to her and asked, "Is this silence because of what I told you?"

She said, "No, not at all."

But you know women. They can fake it.

By the way, I'm a singer. I sing in church, and I'm the leader of the worship team. At times I feel like I'm not doing the right thing. I really love singing, and it's the church I want to sing in, not the club. I do karaoke and all that, but it's the church I want to sing in. When I'm in church, I tend to forget everything, and it doesn't change anything for me. When I'm in church, I focus on church.

This year, I'm thinking of releasing a gospel song, and I have this confidence that it will sell. I just feel it. But I've been hanging out with queer people, and I can see it coming; the moment questions about my sexual orientation will be raised in the media. How am I supposed to answer questions like that? I don't want my life to be public. I don't think I want to face the truth in that way, but I am thinking about it.

I'm not out to my family at all, but I think they suspect I am gay. On Facebook I had two accounts, but I deleted the queer one some time ago because I thought my family were stalking me. Nobody has been in a position to confront me. I don't think I will ever tell them.

I don't know how all this shit will go, but I also want to have a family—with children of my own. I think I would want to raise them with a woman, because of the society we live in. I think I'm still in that cocoon, and I really don't want to get out. What if I get out and people begin asking questions? I don't think I'm quite prepared for that. I think raising my children with a woman would be the easiest thing, the expected thing, the socially accepted thing on all counts, even though raising them with a man would suit me best. There is another option that could work, and I'm not sure, but I have seen people do it. Gays marry lesbians. OK, not really marrying, but you know what I mean. And then everyone figures out their sex lives. But the challenge I have is that I don't want to lose my girlfriend, and I'M REALLY FIGHTING THAT.

–

I AM A LESBIAN. I realized this when I was around sixteen, because I used to have feelings for girls, and would kiss them. My first kiss was with a friend. We had gone out to a club, and after going to the loo—I don't know, maybe we were drunk—I started touching her, and started kissing her. She responded, as much as she says she was straight. Some people really don't know another world exists, that a woman can love another woman.

After that kiss we went home. When we met up again the following day, she was a little afraid to talk but I told her she hadn't done anything wrong. I told her I didn't have a crush on her, that she was my friend and I wasn't interested in dating her. I was in high school then, and if you were found to be a lesbian you would be expelled, so one had to be very quiet about these things. Nobody there knew I was a lesbian. I kept to myself a lot.

I met my first real girlfriend in college. We were at a club, and she came out to me. She said if we hooked up it would be good. We dated, but not for very long—just three months. She was bisexual, and I didn't want to share her with a man, so we broke up.

I met the woman I'm with now the year after. We've been together for three years. I also met her in the club. We flirted, and she asked me out and I agreed. I liked her, it's just that I hadn't told her how I felt about her. She confessed her feelings for me, and I thought we could get along, rhyme, help each other out. I've even met her family, but to avoid giving her mother a heart attack, we say we are just friends.

I'm a femme. Being a femme is being girlish, for me. Everything I do is very feminine. I really wonder about butch lesbians, sometimes. So many of them are all about what they can and cannot wear. I hear them saying, "I can't wear long earrings."

I think that as much as they are butches they are still women. Many of them also like making all the decisions, and I always say, "No, we can help each other."

I guess they think being butch is being the 'man of the house'. I can also be butch if I want, but I identify as a femme. Not a butch.

I have a friend who really used to fight with her girlfriend, until they had to break up. I can't handle that kind of thing in a relationship. But things happen like this: two girls go out, and since people don't know they are lesbians, straight men approach the more feminine girl; the femme. So the butch partners get jealous and it leads to all kinds of fights. My friend was so angry at guys hitting on her girlfriend that she tried to stab her girlfriend right there. I told her, "You guys are going to kill each other one day. You need to break up and give each other space!"

I don't like fighting. When I am talking to my girlfriend I ask her to understand some things. Even if I go to the club and a straight man approaches me, at the end of the day it's her I am with. You can really love each other but no one can withstand being beaten every day.

My sisters know I am gay. I told them, because they would always ask me where my boyfriend was. They're older and they understand. They said it was OK. We have a single mother and she's getting older, so I won't ever tell her because I don't want to give her a heart attack.

I go to church, and I ask myself many questions. Even the other day when Binyavanga came out, people were forwarding us many messages telling us to read the Bible, read Romans chapter this or that verse. I know all of those verses, but I don't think I am wrong. It's not my fault that I'm not attracted to men. Even if a man touches me, I can't stand it. I would need to force myself to go through with it. Imagine if he actually fell in love with me? He's the one who would get hurt. I don't think being gay is bad. I'm happy with my life.

I'm a business-lady. I don't like having to rely on other people. If you have hands and legs and can walk, then you can do a job. So do it! All these people who say they don't have jobs and they can do something—I really wonder. I started my business with capital of just 5,000 shillings, and I got back 10,000. I save more, get more, sell more, and that is how it goes. That is life.

I am planning to have a child with my girlfriend. She's insecure about it, so I think we have to keep talking about it. She feels like if I have a child, there will be no connection between her and the baby because the baby isn't really hers. I keep telling her it wouldn't work like that, but she's against it. Also, she doesn't want a child of her own. So we have a lot of conflict. She also can't imagine me sleeping with a man to get the baby. I also think it would be weird. This isn't like other countries abroad where you can have the sperm put into you. I'm also not sure how I would get pregnant, without having to have sex with a man.

I think we should make homosexuality legal, because this hiding business is tiring. Some people have progressed, but we still live with a lot of fear and worry. I wish this was Nairobi. This town is so small. There are some clubs you can't enter if you're a lesbian or gay, and they tell you they can't serve you. Isn't the money the same? If I give you my money and you serve me, will you become a lesbian? One of my friends slapped a waiter once.

"I can't serve lesbians," he had said.

We were so angry. She said, "You're very stupid."

She slapped him, and we left. People should stop caring about these things. I don't understand those people who see lesbians on the street and make them their business. It's really strange. I think God needs to help society.

Sometimes I think it's not as hard in Nairobi—maybe people there aren't so shocked to see lesbians. But here? A taxi driver I know called me once and said, "Where are you?"

I said I was in town doing errands. He said, "Please come and see me, there is something I urgently want to discuss with you."

I really wondered what was wrong. It was strange. I only look for him when I need a cab, and we don't talk much other than that. I didn't look for him that day. I bumped into him a few days later. He's a much older man. He had the balls to ask me, "I heard… you… are done by… women."

I said, "What? What are you telling me?"

He said, "You're in relationships with women?"

I asked, "What bullshit nonsense is this you have called me all the way here to tell me?"

He added, "I… can allow you to sleep with me so you can prove you're not a lesbian."

It's total madness. This is a man who is a father with children! I said, "You want me to sleep with you to prove I am not a lesbian? Go, and know now that I'm a lesbian. What will you do to me?"

He said, "So you sleep with girls?"

I said, "Yeah, so?"

He left, and he didn't say anything else to me. I've never used his cab again.

That's why I say this town is just too small. People like talking about others. If I could move, I would have moved by now. Am I interfering with people's lives by being who I am? No. Can't we all just move on? Anyway, we just walk here and we don't care.

What are they going to do? I just pray that one day they don't come to burn us in our homes.

People think such strange things. They don't understand how we have sex and they think we must use dildos and so many people say that dildos are bad. But you don't have to use a dildo to have sex, you know? Even if you try to explain that to straight people, they don't understand how you can't.

But even straight people have issues. I went to a party with a straight friend of mine. There were very rowdy guys there, and she disappeared in the crowd. After a while, she called me and asked me to take a video of her and her boyfriend having sex. Jesus! I was so shocked my phone almost fell! I don't know what they wanted to do with the video, and why they thought I'd be OK with being there to take it. I really fear such things.

She also sleeps with a lot of men, and has sex with them without condoms. The men she sleeps with are married ones—she says she doesn't like younger men. I told her she'll get AIDS one day if today it's this guy, tomorrow it's this other one—IT CAN BE DANGEROUS FOR HER.

–

I'M GAY. I always knew that I was attracted to boys. When I was in primary school, in Standard 4 or 5, I was attracted to my best friend. He was cute and brown and very neat. We spent a lot of time together because his family were friends of ours. We went to the same schools growing up. I thought he was attractive, but the thought of me being gay hadn't occurred to me.

I went to a high school in ████████. In my first week there, I met this cute guy—his name was Kevin. We started talking and became friends. We decided to become desk-mates. I knew he was gay because he was so feminine. He was very religious, and he became an altar boy in the school. I told him I was gay, but he was in denial and he said he was not. But he also said he had nothing against gay people. That was in the first term of Form One. We used to talk about being gay. I used to ask him, "If I kissed you, what would you do?"

He'd say, "Nothing."

That was my green light.

Once, we were in class and the lights went out. I took the opportunity to kiss him. We made out, but we didn't talk about it afterwards. Later, he would come to my bed at night, and we'd share the bed and talk, and then he would go back to his bed. Soon we started making out and wanking; nothing much. After a while, we had to start talking about what we were doing. I'm not a very religious person, myself, but he was very religious; Catholic. He used to say it was a sin and that he didn't know why we had to keep on sinning. I don't believe in that blah-blah-blah. Once you're dead, you're dead. No singing. It's either you are lucky or unlucky. So I used to tell him, "People are fucking in the church, and doing all kinds of things."

I don't like the church, it's just full of hypocrisy. He didn't care about all that. He said he liked me, so we just went on. At some point everyone in school knew I was gay, but I was never bullied, and it didn't bother me that they knew. Even now, everyone knows apart from my parents. My sisters, my neighbours, my friends? Everyone knows.

My relationship with this guy went on till the end of the year, and then we had sex. We didn't decide to—it just happened. We were together till high school ended and for a year later. There were times we would have sex with other guys in the school, but we always came back to each other. We didn't do it behind each other's backs. We were busted making out with each other once; not sex, just kissing. We had skipped class and this prefect found us. He reported us to the teacher on duty, who referred us to the Guidance and Counselling Department. There, they asked me who I wanted to call. I called my sister. It was the second time she was being called for something like this, so she was used to it. His sister also came. My parents never came to school—they only came when I was admitted.

The counsellor met us separately, and then together, and then we met the parish priest. The priest told us what we were doing was a sin, that it was against creation—the usual stuff people associate with homosexuality. He told us to go and pray so that we wouldn't fall into temptation. A lot of blah that wasn't relevant. My boyfriend wanted to change. I would tell him that all of it was just hypocrisy. I told him, "If I'm going to change, maybe I'll become asexual, since I can't find anything interesting in women."

Even if I am walking in town and I see a beautiful woman, I can't look at her twice because I'm not interested at all. If it is a guy, I can look. I was almost ran over by a car once because I was checking out a guy. I was crossing the road and this hot guy walked by, and I was just carried away. He was tall, slim, and very cute.

So my Catholic boyfriend used to say that he was going to change. But he never did. Whenever I told him I wanted him, he was always there. In the morning he would say he was straight, and tell me he didn't want anything to do with gay people, "If you are talking to me, talk about constructive things. Don't call me any love names, don't do any love stuff."

I used to call him 'dear'. He would say, "Don't call me that, call me by my name."

But in the evening he would be calling me 'dear', and he was the one who would come to my bed.

After high school, he stayed in ████████ and I lived in ████████, and eventually we got tired of the distance. We used to meet every weekend. He would come to my sister's house in Nairobi, or I would go to his house. My sister knows I'm gay, even though we don't talk about it. She seemed OK with me meeting boys, and them staying over in her house. Sometimes I would even go on dates with her.

Eventually, our relationship ended. We still talk, though. And he's still gay.

I'm not certain about the existence of God, or about any spiritual things. People believe what they want to believe. I wish people could just live their lives the way they want, and there is luck or no luck. You wouldn't have to blame anyone for your misfortune—people blame the devil for everything, talking about the work of the devil. I don't believe that. Either you are lucky or you mess up, or you are a good or bad person.

My family and I are not that close. I don't talk to my dad, and not much to most of my sisters. We're fucked up, because we're my dad's second family. He had married before he met my mum. My mum was also married before that. I'm the only child my dad has had with my mum. I have four sisters from my mother's previous marriage. My dad also has other kids. It's all just complicated—I have stepsisters and a stepmother. I'm also the only son on both sides. I've never met anyone from my father's side of the family. If he died, I wouldn't know where to go. Even now, we don't talk. I've never even addressed him as 'Dad'. At some point we used to live together, but even then we didn't talk much. I moved out his house when I was in Form Two. I haven't lived with him since. When I moved out he told me, "You won't get employed, and you won't do anything with your life."

When I meet him, I can tell he's disappointed that I turned out OK. I think he is disappointed in himself. My life is moving on as usual, but he expected to find me in the newspaper shot dead, or turned into a thug, or having done something bad; but I'm OK.

I know I'm going to marry a man. I don't know if I could stand a woman. However nice the wedding was, I might just wake up one morning after ten years and tell her to leave my house. I can't get married to make people happy, because how many married men are out there fucking men in secret, and they're still married? I don't like that hypocrisy. So I just want to find a nice guy and have two kids. Maybe each of us can have our own biological children, or adopt. Either way would be fine. My mother will be very disappointed when she finds out, BUT TOO BAD FOR HER.

–

I AM A LESBIAN. I realized this when I was in high school. I had gone out with a family friend, and when we came back she undressed in front of me. I realised then that I really liked looking at nude women. I knew I wanted to be with her. She was my first kiss, too. She kissed me after I had seen her undress at our home. It felt really nice.

She became my girlfriend and this was my first relationship. We were together for two years, then I fell in love with someone else. It was a bit challenging. We fought with my girlfriend a lot, but I was more attracted to the new girl than I was to my girlfriend. Eventually, we drifted apart with my first girlfriend. We rented a house together with my new girlfriend and she became my house-mate.

One day, my family had a family meeting and I invited my girlfriend to come with me. I wanted to tell my family about us. My mother found us kissing in my bedroom before I got a chance to tell them. She stood at the door, surprised, then she closed the door. She did not talk to me for a week. We left together with my girlfriend then my mother called me a week later.

She asked me what she had seen. I wanted to cool her down. I told her that I had a crush on that girl. My mother wondered how I could have a crush on a girl. She told my dad the story, and he called me for a meeting. He beat me. He even broke my arm. He said that I should never have a crush on someone of the same sex unless I was bewitched. I kept on telling him that that is the person I loved, that it was my choice. But he said that I was young and there was nothing I knew about life. I found a way to get out of the house and left.

My dad then called my girlfriend's parents and that is when all hell broke loose. It was a nightmare. My parents called the police to look for me so that I could be imprisoned. We were beaten like thieves. My girlfriend's brother kicked me in the spine. I had a spine injury, and to this day I still have a problem with my spine. But I am still with my girlfriend. We have been together for seven years. My girlfriend has a son, who is now nine years old.

Our families eventually stopped fighting us, I think they just ignore us now. We usually visit our parents together. When there is a family function, we attend together. Her dad died and he used to like me. My mother likes my girlfriend but my girlfriend's mother can't stand me. I don't care about that any more.

Our relationship has had its ups and downs. There are times my girlfriend annoys me so I will go and find someone else to be with. I have done this on three different occasions. It has caused heart breaks. At times when I have gone out with someone else she will refuse to open the door for me and it is usually during the wee hours of the morning. We can have periods where we don't talk to each other, but then the child unites us. He will ask why we are not talking to each other.

Sometimes I think I am dangerous to myself. I am really hot tempered. Once we were at a club and some man stepped on my girlfriend. It was war. The man did not believe that I was fighting so much for a girl. When I decide to hit someone, I use whatever I lay my hands on. I fight with my girlfriend sometimes. She slaps me but I don't feel bad about it. I really try not to get worked up. When we shout at one another, our son disappears to his room. In our relationship, we slap each other. Last year I found her kissing some other girl and I hit her so hard that she fainted. But I have never done that again. It almost became a police case. She forgave me but I haven't forgotten.

My mother had to take me for therapy. A *matatu* tout once walked up to me and said that I liked dating girls. I hit him so hard on the neck, I almost killed him. At that point my mother said that I should visit a doctor. I left therapy after two sessions. I didn't find the sessions worth my time. In fact, the sessions made me angry; I thought that the therapist was wasting my time.

Raising our son together has been tough. He thinks that we are very close friends. He knows that he cannot have two mothers because a child comes from the womb. We tell him that we are good friends who live together and that she is his mother and I am his guardian. When I took him to school, he told them that I was his 'dad'. Other pupils would ask why his dad was female and he would say that his dad was a man, that he does not have breasts. As he grew up we had to stop kissing in front of him. To this day, other children keep telling him that he has no dad. We think he needs a father figure to look up to. Luckily, I have four brothers and my girlfriend has a brother too.

There was a day he asked who a lesbian is. His mother said a lesbian was a sick person, I just laughed. He asked me why I was laughing at a sick person. We realized that his understanding of issues is opening up. He is being taught out there that two ladies or two men cannot live together.

We do our best to provide. We have been discussing about getting another child. I want to have a baby, it is good to have someone who will carry on your lineage. It would be me who would bear the child but that is challenging. I am 29 and I long for a baby whenever I see babies. Our son keeps on telling me that he wants a brother, and that I am the one who should bring the baby. I wouldn't want to sleep with a man. Artificial insemination is expensive, but I have a donor already. I also have a friend who is a doctor and is WILLING TO DO IT FOR ME.

–

I AM TRANSGENDER. I was born a woman but I have always felt like I am a man. It's not about what is between my thighs, but what is in my mind. I think like a man and I want to be a man. I knew this at the beginning of my adolescence. My body was changing, and my feelings developed exclusively for women. I would also dress like a man when I was a teenager, and I'd play male dominant sports. I did not feel like being a woman.

In primary school, I was so curious about other girls. In role-playing games—*Baba na Mama*—I always played the father role. I had many girlfriends in primary school, and I would be suspended often. In high school it was even worse because I was suspended in my first week of school. I enrolled on Thursday, and I was suspended on Friday. Our head girl was light-skinned, pretty and was very Christian; born-again. I was so attracted to her, and I don't know what I told her, but *aliingia box*. She fell for me. I didn't even have breasts. It seems she liked me too.

The other Form Four girls were so angry that I had hooked up with the head girl. One of them said, "*Huyo ni dame wangu.*" That's my girl.

They broke into my locker. I found some kerosene and matchsticks and retaliated by setting their lockers on fire. I was suspended for two weeks for arson. I had to come back to school with my sister to meet the teachers. My sister asked me why I had been suspended, I cheated her that the teachers just didn't like me. By the time we got to the school, my sister was so angry—she really shouted at the teachers because she believed me. The teachers let me back in.

In Form Three, I was expelled for good. I had to stay at home, and so I never finished high school. That was a tight situation. My mother wanted me to get with a man so she could have a grandchild. She went out and found a man who was a family friend, then forced me to have sex with him. I got pregnant. My best friend advised me to get an abortion. I said to myself, "Even if I am trans, trans people also have babies."

So I gave birth to a baby girl. She is now six years old. She is a beautiful baby, a good girl. But she never calls me mum. She calls me Otieno. We live with my mother and sisters and brothers. Life is hard, but a man must try *[laughs]*!

Once I dated a female police officer. I wasn't really into her, but she was crazy about me. I got bored with her after a while and told her I was leaving her. She said, *"Ukiniacha, nitakuua."* If you leave me, I will kill you.

I said, "You can't kill me. I'm the one who will beat you."

She sent one of her fellow female officers to arrest me. The officer arrested me for loitering. I asked her, "What is loitering? Have I robbed anyone? Or raped someone? Or beaten someone?"

The officer told me to stop asking questions and explain myself in court.

I said, "I'm not going anywhere."

She started beating me, and I ran away. She followed me, and I beat her seriously. Other policemen came to her rescue. I had to stop beating her, because they came with guns. They really beat me and arrested me. I stayed in the cell for two days, and it's only my fellow queers who rescued me from the prison.

I don't date lesbians. I actually date straight women, because I'm a man. I'm very lethal; I'm very good at seduction. I've been dating my current girlfriend for a while now. She's straight. I first noticed her in the neighbourhood for over a year. I wanted to know where she lived and what she was about. One day, there was a funeral happening in our neighbourhood. There were many visitors, and that night I saw her walking with one of them who I also knew. His name was Brian. I bumped into him later on and I told him, "Brian, that girl you were walking with? I'm really attracted to her. Please tell her how much I like her."

That very night, Brian went and told her what I had said. She really laughed. The next morning, I visited her. Now that she had heard that I was attracted to her, she was very flirty with me. She was wearing hot pants. I just watched her and smiled. We sat together, and talked. That evening, she gave me a peck on my cheek. She asked me, "*Sasa tutakua tunaifanya aje?*" How are we going to be doing *it*?

I replied, "Don't be worried. You'll be very happy. You're in capable hands."

I visited her the next day and found her lying on her bed. She kissed me, and a whole lot more! I had been single for a long time after my girlfriend passed away last year. There were many girls who were interested in me, but I was a little shy. We spent the whole day and the whole night together, and she was very happy. That's how we began. I know we love each other. We're planning on living together, but I have to see if my mother will allow it. My mother knows about us and she's very tough. She asks, "What are the two of you doing?"

I tell her, "Mum, leave my life alone. If you see me with a girl, just love her the way I do."

Life is hard, still. I'm a hustler, a businessman. I sell clothes, but there's not much market, so I have to hustle. I can even do construction work. I really enjoy such work. Any job that a man can do. In fact, I compete with them.

I want to surprise my girlfriend's mum by giving her dowry for her daughter. I'm serious. My girlfriend has already accepted it. We want a child of our own. I have my daughter, and my girlfriend has three of her own. So we'll be a big family with five children. My girlfriend is good, and caring. Very nice, but she's very strict. She won't let me talk to any other women. Even a cousin or a neighbour. I'm only allowed to talk to other men. *[laughs]*.

I would like to make a physical transition. Even if my mother refuses completely to accept it, I am ready, and I've come to accept myself. When I first met my girlfriend, I was bound like a boy. She must have thought I was a boy. But binding has a side-effect. I'm asthmatic, so it makes walking and breathing a problem. When I wear a binder, I can wear a vest and walk around the estate. But that enrages my mother. She asks me, "What are you doing?"

Sometimes I make a fake dick using a bundle of cloth. Having a bulge under my boxers makes me happy. I have met some transgender people who have transitioned from being men to women.

They told me that a transition from female to male is a longer process. There is no organ transition for a female-to-male transition, like there is for a male-to-female transition. The hormones to change the breasts also cause cancer, and people transitioning from female-to-male sometimes die of the cancer before they can complete the transition. So, with my binder and strap on, I'M OK FOR NOW.

–

I AM GAY, and I am also a sex worker. In high school—when I was about seventeen years old—I realized that I was strongly attracted to men. Whenever we went to the showers, I always had strong urges to touch other guys' private parts. I found a group of guys who were gay too, and we would always meet up at night in the hostels. That's where we would make out and jerk each other off, and that's where I met my first boyfriend.

I was very hesitant to have sex with him, but he was extremely convincing and persistent. I decided to have sex with him just to make him happy. The first time he fucked me, I was in a lot of pain. Yet five days later I asked him to do it again, because I had somehow enjoyed it. It became a thing; we slept together a lot.

When I left high school, I knew I was into guys. I'd had enough experiences up until then to know I enjoyed being with a man, I had accepted it. But I didn't know where to find gay men! Luckily one time, I was walking around and I spotted a bunch of guys bathing naked in the sea. I found a spot some distance from where they were, and I sat and watched them. One of them then signalled for me to go closer. I went over cautiously and started speaking to him. He led me to a secluded spot where we touched each other, made out and exchanged numbers. He was the first guy I met after high school, and he's the one who slowly gave me the numbers of other gay men in █████. That's how I started meeting the other members in the community. It was much better than having to walk around looking for guys.

At a point in 2002, my friends—who were sex workers—made me feel like I was being foolish and naïve. I was going around giving it up for free, yet I was jobless and struggling. They explained to me that I could sell sex for money. Most of the times,

I was always the one being courted by men, so I saw the sense in commercializing sex.

I've been working as a sex worker for thirteen years now, I've built myself a house in █████, and I built it with the money I made from sex work, so I'm grateful for that. Mobile phones and the Internet—especially Facebook and Whatsapp—have really changed sex work. I've travelled throughout the country for sex work purely because of the Internet and mobile phones. Internet and phones really help, because then I can negotiate well in advance and it's then very clear what the client is getting and for how much. If the pay isn't worth it, you just hang up or you don't reply the message. It's very simple, unlike having to negotiate on the streets.

It's not always about the money though. Sometimes I want to have sex with someone because I'm attracted to them. We have some community get-togethers or meetings, sometimes you meet a guy and you're attracted to each other, you exchange numbers and hook up later. That's not about money, it's more about attraction.

The price of sex varies depending on the activity and the client. If you want me to bottom, it will cost you more than if you want me to top. Also, I'll look at how you're dressed and that'll help determine the price. To bottom, sometimes I'll charge up to 5,000 shillings, but to top I charge as little as 500 shillings. In fact, if the client is hot I can even top him for free, but he'd have to cater for my transport costs.

Sex work is difficult though; the county government and cops are always harassing us. At the moment, one of the areas we usually operate in has become quite bad, so we're operating on the down low. We're also always getting STIs. I've gotten them so many times, it's how I got HIV.

I've been in many relationships, too. Whenever I'm financially stable; I always have a live-in boyfriend. It's like an unofficial marriage. I met my first boyfriend in 2008. I invited him to live with me, but it ended really badly. He stole from me. I came back one evening and found the house almost empty. I've been robbed many times by boyfriends; the relationships just never end well. I'm no better though, I used to date a club manager from █████, and he used to wake up at around 6am to go and do the end-of-day accounting in the club. One morning, he left me to go to the club as usual, and I woke up and took about 50,000 shillings in cash, his phones, clothes, his shoes and a woofer, and I left. So it happens, it's almost expected. Even with clients, there's a lot of blackmail and theft.

I've also been blackmailed before, but nowadays I'm used to it. I'm not afraid anymore. If you threaten to go to the cops, I tell you to go! If you say you'll publish my photos, I tell you to go ahead, they've been published before. I'm not afraid. I'm wiser now, no one can blackmail me or steal from me. I know how to deal with criminals, because the society thinks I am one.

I've blackmailed some people also, there was this one guy who was a pastor, and he was double-dealing me. I met him through a friend—you know us sex workers meet new people mostly via referrals. My friend told me, "I have a pastor who has a huge dick and he likes to fuck."

So he was given my number and he called me, and that's how we started. He was very discreet, this guy. He was very careful to make sure no one in his neighbourhood knew what was going on between us. He needed to be respected by his church congregation. Whenever I'd go to his house, he would ask me to dress formally, in a nice shirt and pants so as not to raise eyebrows. We had a sort of relationship going on, then suddenly he started being very flaky; he wasn't paying my rent anymore, and he wasn't giving me money like he used to. Whenever I'd go to his place, he'd pretend he wasn't there. He wouldn't return my calls. That went on for about two months.

I thought, "This guy always like 'fresh meat'. He licks mine for a few days then he wants to go out and find a new one to lick."

That's what he was doing, and I could see it. So one day I showed up at his house, dressed very inappropriately. I showed up in a crop top, purse and a wig; he thought I had lost it. He ushered me in very quickly before anyone could see me. I was very polite and I spent the night and we fucked a lot. When morning came, I said to him, "I can see that our love is slowly fading, so before it completely fades, I need you to pay up for all the times you've fucked me."

I threatened to walk outside naked and start shouting his business for everyone to hear. I told him I would go to the cops and tell them, "He called me and told me he would fuck me for 10,000 shillings and now he's refusing to pay me!"

One good thing is that we didn't use a condom when we had sex that night, so in the morning I told him, "Your sperm is still inside me, I'll use it as an exhibit when I go to the cops."

He started cajoling me and giving me money. He used to give me between 500 to 1,000 shillings, but on that day he gave me 15,000 plus his phone. He gave me the cash while crying. I agreed to leave, but as I was leaving, I told him, "If I hear about this from anyone, I'll come back for your TV."

To this day we still see each other. I'm pretty sure he thinks I'm mad.

I used to date a woman back in 2001, and I gave her two kids. I keep wondering if I should go back. The thing that keeps holding me back is my status, she's negative and I'm positive, so I'm not too sure how that would work. I still talk to her though, and I cater for the kids' fees and all that. And I also built them the house they live in.

All the years I've worked as a sex worker, no client has ever told me their status. Some clients want bareback sex, so I usually have to gauge the situation. If he looks healthy and he wants me to top him, that's fine, I know the risk of infection is lower if you're topping someone, however, if I'm bottoming, he has to wear a condom because I can't afford to get an STI at this point. It's not HIV I'm afraid of—I already have it—it's the other small STIs that are a pain in the ass.

I have no religion. I find the church a waste of time. Many of my clients are 'godly' men who are supposed to show others the way. Some even preach against homosexuality, then come to me to get fucked. Anyway, maybe when I stop all of this, I'll go to church, BUT FOR NOW, NO.

–

I AM A LESBIAN. When I was in Form Two, I got a desk-mate who was a girl. She used to hold my hand every time I slept in class so that I wouldn't sleep. Holding hands led to feelings and emotions and she became my first real girlfriend. We didn't have any physical involvement, but we used to hold hands and cuddle a lot. Finally, we fell out because a lot of boys used to hit on her. I used to feel really bad about it and it reached a point where she became violent about it.

She asked me, "Why are you being so jealous all the time?"

Then she slapped me and stopped being my desk-mate.

The next year, when I was in Form Three, I met another girl. She was in Form One, and she had just joined our school. She was the daughter of the Deputy Principal and she had been assigned a bed in Cube 3. The members of Cube 3 were a bad lot, and they thought the Deputy Principal had brought her daughter to spy on them. They threw out her things when she tried to move in. I told them they couldn't do that, and offered to take her into my cube instead.

She used to sleep on the bunk on top of mine. I was very talkative in school, always telling stories. One day she told me, "*Ai, wewe hunyamazangi*. You need to keep quiet sometimes." You never shut up.

I really didn't like her because of that statement, she was the only person who ever told me that. But over time, we talked and became very close. Before she went home for the holidays, she wrote a note for me and left it at the gate. The note said, "I already miss you. This is my number, you can call me after tuition."

So I started calling her, and we would talk and talk and talk. We continued talking as friends, then I realized I had feelings for her. One day I sent her a note that explained that I felt like something was going on between us. I drew two boxes on the note, one marked 'yes', and another marked 'no'. I asked her to check 'yes' if she felt it too. She checked yes.

One day, while we were in the room, I kissed her on the lips and walked away. I stayed away from my room for the rest of the day and did not come back to the room until after lights-out. I came back in the dark, undressed and got into bed. She got out from her bed, came down and she kissed me, and then she said, "You didn't even give me a chance to kiss you back."

That went on and on and on, till almost 3am in the morning. Kissing her was so good. I remember that when I was younger, some boy had kissed me, and it was really yuck. I think there was just too much spit—yuck! Anyway, this was my first relationship with a girl and the first time I ever did anything with a girl. We didn't have sex until way later. The next year.

We used to chat a lot on Facebook, because she never had her own phone. She used to use her mother's computer to log in to Facebook. One day, she left her Facebook profile logged in, and her brother found all our messages and took the laptop straight to her mother. There was a big fuss, and we decided that I should I let her study. We weren't even living close to each other, anyway. I lived in ████████ while she lived with her mother in ████████. We just left each other like that. I've never talked to her since.

After high school, rumours about my sexuality had begun. A lot of people used to talk about me and I really hated that, so I got a boyfriend. We dated for about four months, and in that entire time I only kissed him four times, and I had to be drunk each time. To this day, he reminds me of that story. He's still my friend. He broke up with me when he found out that I was gay. He said, "I cannot continue to stay with you and I know you're not happy."

That's how we broke up. I genuinely cared for him. I genuinely enjoyed our time together, playing pool, learning to play guitar together, all that stuff. He used to come to my office to help out with work. But when it got to the physical part of our relationship, I just wasn't there. He said we could be friends. We're buddies even now. Then—because I was still confused—I got into a relationship with a married woman. She was my mum's friend, and she used to run a clothes shop. My mum used to shop there.

They even used to exchange cars with my mum and go shopping to the same places, so I used to be their go-between, sent with messages and things to and fro, "Take her this outfit, I think she'll like it."

I used to sit down with this lady sometimes after I'd done all those errands, and we'd just talk and talk and talk and talk. One day she told me—she knew I was gay from when I was in Form Three—how she used to have a girlfriend herself. She told me the whole story, the name of the girlfriend, and their history, and then we somehow just ended up kissing.

We started having an affair. We'd hook up in the back office of her shop, or in her car. I think I fell for her completely. My heart was in there. She would keep reminding me, "You know we shouldn't be doing this. You can't expect me to do this and that for you. Remember, I'm married."

I found out she had other girlfriends, so I wasn't the only one. Broken and crushed as I was, I managed to walk away from that whole situation.

Then I got my second girlfriend. I'm not sure how I ended up with her. I never imagined myself with her. In fact, I never thought she was pretty. She used to followed me around, volunteering to help me with my work, just being around. She followed me for almost three months and then finally I agreed to date her. My relationship with her was actually the most dramatic relationship ever. I have lots of scars from fighting with her. She even bit off part of my ear.

We started normally. We were so happy. But I'd heard stories about her. This was one reason why I didn't want to have a relationship with her. People said she used to sleep around with older men for money. Also, her ex-girlfriend used to come to our office and fight with her a lot, so she seemed like a dramatic person. Anyway, I told her I'd heard all kinds of stories about her, and she said, "You're not giving me a chance, you need to find out who I am for yourself."

I told her if we were going to be together, she'd have to stop going out so much. She used to go out clubbing Monday to Monday, and she was the kind of girl who could go out at night with 10 shillings in her pocket and come back with 2,000 the next day. So you can imagine what happened in the middle. I told her, "You need to be honest with me about where you are, and what you're doing."

People used to warn me about her, but our relationship started out fine. After about a month dating her, her best friend told me, "You need to realize that you're suffocating her. You need to give her space."

Soon after that, I got really, really drunk one night, and I messed up with that same best friend. We went home together and had sex—then she confessed to my girlfriend. My girlfriend was really pissed off. The tables turned. Now she was the one saying I needed to play by her rules. Because I was feeling guilty, I was ready to give it a try.

That's when she started going out again. A lot. I started hearing stories about her having sex with men even in cars outside clubs. I got really pissed off. Once, we got really drunk in the club and I saw her touching some guy. I felt really, really bad. I felt like she was disrespecting me openly. I didn't care if she did these things when I was not there. When we went home—I was really drunk—I remember slapping her. Twice.

The second time we had an argument was a week after we moved in together. At this point in time, I was in my third year in University. When we were living together, someone used to come to the gate to pick her up, and then she'd come back at 2 or 3 in the morning. I had to open the gate for her whenever she'd come back in the wee hours. At that point, I needed to go to class during the day. Staying up till late waiting for her was interfering with my studies.

To punish her, I decided to give her the same treatment. I went out with a friend and stayed out till 10pm. When I got to the house, she said, "This is the time you're coming back home?"

I said, "You come later than this every day. Are you the only one allowed to have fun?"

She said, "OK. I'm also going out."

I asked, "Where are you going? Why can't you stay home today?"

She said, "I'm not even listening to you right now."

She went upstairs and got dressed. As she was leaving, I said, "Seriously, let's talk about this."

She turned around and grabbed my lips, literally. She put her nails on my lips and then pulled them and said, "Just shut up."

She didn't come home that night. The next day, I woke up and went to school. One of her friends called me and said they had just dropped my girlfriend home. Then she said, "By the way, yesterday these guys had a threesome."

I asked, “Who?”

She said, “Your chick, another chick and some guy.”

I called my girlfriend and asked her about that.

She said, “I’m sorry, I didn’t mean to do it. I was drunk.”

I told her I was coming home to take all my stuff and leave.

When I came to the house at lunchtime, she said, “Don’t go. Let’s just talk about it. I didn’t mean it.”

I said, “You can’t do things like that.”

She said, “I’m sorry. You know you had pissed me off.”

So we talked about it and everything was OK for about a week. After that, there were many incidents, and so much drama between us. Now she started using slaps, scratches on the face, sometimes she would strangle me. She even threw dishes at me some other time. I never hit her back, because the first time I slapped her, I felt really bad about it. I never beat her again. Our relationship was ups and downs.

The last time she beat me, I was admitted to hospital, I had to go for re-constructive surgery on my face. My nose had actually split. It was bad. The scar is still visible now. She had bitten me with her teeth. She banged my foot on the door. I have a bad foot, because when I was younger, I was hit by a bike. She banged that foot using the door of a car.

I had to be admitted in thc hospital. I was out of school for a month. Still after that, I didn’t leave her. I forgave her for everything. My mum wanted to have her arrested. I kept protecting her. After I left hospital, I insisted that my mother drop the charges. We stopped living together, and I moved into the university hostel.

She moved back to her parents’ house for a while. She called me later, and told me that the whole situation was my fault, that I need to realize that I’m the one who started it, and that I deserved what I got. I believed her. I am the one who slapped her first. She wasn’t this angry person, I’m the one who made her angry. So I used to blame myself. Now she’s married to some guy, and she has a daughter. She’s happy now. I don’t talk to her at all. That’s a part of my life I don’t want to revisit.

I didn’t want to be in a relationship after that. I met another girl after that, and we dated for a while. She used to ask me for money, so I would send her money. She would ask for things, I used to give her everything, because she was so good to me. After three months, the girl said, "By the way, I was just experimenting, so you just go away now."

I asked her, "How do you just use someone like that?"

I was so shocked.

I said, "You can't just say after three months that you were experimenting."

But she insisted, "Seriously, leave me alone."

That really crushed me. I felt really bad about it. After a couple of months of being alone and sad, I decided to move on. I was completely healing. I was feeling better about myself. My grades were looking good. I was going to be fine. So I started juggling girls, because I was not willing to commit.

Girl Number 1 didn't know about Girl Number 2, but Number 2 knew about Number 1. Number 3 knew about Number 2 and Number 1, but not about Number 4. Number 2 was in Nairobi, Number 3 was in ██████. Number 4 was here once in a while. Why not?

But then Number 3 became very demanding. She wanted to become Number 1. So she contacted Number 1 on Facebook, and told her everything. So that just blew up in my face. That was the end of that. I stopped juggling.

After that, I met a beautiful girl. She was so beautiful, the prettiest girl that I've ever had. I felt like she was everything I needed. She's very responsible, very mature, and she's not impulsive. We've been together for seven months so far. We started dating because we used to talk a lot. I made sure to talk to her every morning, all the time; texting her to find out how she was. I realized she has very many friends, but none of them ask her how she is. Most of them usually tell her about their problems, and that was my starting point.

She told me a lot of things that she wouldn't tell anyone else about her personal life. And she told me that it was weird how she felt like she can really talk to me. And then just like that, we had an epic kiss-out at the club. She remembers all the details even now. I don't. It's a bit vague for me, but she remembers. That's how we got to be a couple. But she didn't even say yes to me after the kiss. We didn't even have sex until after our relationship was completely official. She'd tell me, "I don't want to hurt you, I don't want you to hurt me. Let's wait and see."

I'd tell her, "Let's be friends."

She'd say, "No, let's not define it. Why are you in a hurry?"

She's my anchor, because I'm that person who is constantly moving and doing things, and she tells me, "Chill out for two seconds. Let's just calm down."

So I CALM DOWN.

–

I IDENTIFY AS QUEER. Queer to me is an undefined space. My earliest memory of thinking of myself as queer was in Standard 8. We had this awesome teacher who sat us down and talked to us about sex. She told us, "Be careful. When you go to high school, there are girls who will try to seduce you, and that's how you get introduced to 'lesbianism'."

For some reason, in my head I thought, "Oh! That's who I am."

High school turned out to be quiet. I had a relationship with another girl until I was in Form Two, but we ended it. In Form Three I was made a captain. The head girl had this harebrained idea for us prefects to go round the school looking for queer people hiding in various areas around the school during entertainment.

We found some suspects, and some of them were expelled, but very few of them were actually queer. If people saw you spending a lot of time with another girl, they'd label you queer. I didn't date anybody when I was a captain. I think I just closed up after my first relationship ended. I closed up completely. I finished high school and went to university, and still I didn't date anyone at all.

I tried dating some boy, though. It was very annoying. He asked me out, and I thought he was kinda cute; nice and chubby. He was a nice person, and he always had *mahamris*[22] for me—I love them! Then he started asking for sex. It was very easy to tell

---

22. A Swahili bun, usually made with coconut milk and cardamom.

him no, because I could remind him that we were both Christians, and good Christians abstain until marriage. He kept asking and it was annoying. So I got bored.

I told him, "I don't think this is working, let's just end this. It doesn't make sense. You're not happy, and you're not making me happy."

So that was that.

My family has a clue about me being a lesbian. When I was in Standard 8, my parents found a letter I had written to another girl, so they sat me down with the entire family and asked me, "Are you a lesbian?"

I said yes.

I didn't think it was a big deal. I mean, people talk to boys, so why can't I talk to girls? I was quite naïve. They sat me down and lectured me all the way till 1am. After that, they told me to write a letter saying that I was no longer a lesbian. I decided to write about how we had just learned about sexuality in school, and saying I was a lesbian sounded like an interesting thing to say. I added that I was sorry for my over-imaginative mind. That ended there, and we've never talked about it since, but I know it will come up again. I think my mum knows, because she met my ex-girlfriend several times and they'd talk a lot. Once I left home, and was supposed to return in two days but wasn't able to. When I finally came back, my mum told me, "My friends were warning me that you might have ran away with a man. I told them, 'No, my daughter is probably with one of her girlfriends.'"

It's OK. I think she knows.

My relationship with faith wavered for a long time, I was very confused. On one hand I was being myself, on the other hand there are all these things the church says. I was kicked out of church because I was queer. I was a member of the church dance group, and they found out I was gay, so they planned this whole intervention because they felt like they should not be 'unequally yoked with sinners', and all that.[23]

---

23. 2 Corinthians Chapter 6, verse 14: Do not be yoked together with unbelievers. For what do righteousness and wickedness have in common? Or what fellowship can light have with darkness?

The bottom line of the intervention was, "If you're going to be queer, you can't be a part of this group."

Leaving was hard, because that group was like my family. The guy who started the group asked me to join and be his assistant. I told him, "OK, but I have so many issues."

He said, "That doesn't really matter. God doesn't care about those issues. You can dance, and you are responsible. You will figure out the rest as you get to know God."

And that's what I did until we got to that point where the other members started pointing fingers and saying 'we cannot be unequally yoked'. I said to myself, "OK. The family has changed, it has become something else."

So I left. I'm still in church now, I've gotten to a point where I can relate with God for myself and find my peace with God. Being kicked out gave me a lot of strength and peace, because now I really don't care what people say or do. My relationship with God is very personal, it doesn't involve you. I stopped worrying about church and acceptance. I do what I can do at church, when they need help I go and help out, but that's it.

It took me a long time to get to a level of accepting myself. A level where I moved from thinking that there is something wrong with me—something missing; all these things that people say about us. I don't think it's any easier being a lesbian in Kenya than before. I think it was probably easier long ago because there wasn't so much of a fuss around it. You could just be who you are. Long ago, you'd see some lady dress in a way that wasn't very feminine, and people would say, "She's a tomboy. That's how she is."

It didn't make a difference. It's harder now. There are spaces where we can be free like that, but we have to create those spaces. Usually those spaces are far away from the general society and community. So what happens WHEN WE MEET THE COMMUNITY?

—

I IDENTIFY AS GAY. I remember fooling around as a child, with neighbours, cousins and stuff like that. But then everyone was fooling around. I don't think much of that because I also fooled around with girls. It was around that age when kids discover their genitals. As a teenager, I suspected I was gay, but refused to acknowledge it. I just found myself staring at men more, and in a way that I wasn't looking at women.

After joining high school, the other students tried to get me to take on a sexual identity and I absolutely refused to. I absolutely refused. People would ask me if I was gay, and I just wouldn't answer. For seven years I didn't respond. I felt like I wasn't ready to be that person. I was going through so many other things at the time, that I felt that I didn't have the strength to deal with it. I decided to hold it off to a time when I was ready, which was when I finished school.

Childhood was different. I had to deal with a lot of things. I had to deal with a lot of death. I had to deal with losing a lot of people. It isolated me. One of the things I'd always hear when I was nine or ten is that I didn't act my age. It was because of having to deal with so much. I wanted to be so many things. The first thing I wanted to be was a flight attendant. The first time I travelled, I was going to London with my aunt. I was absolutely fascinated with the flight attendants. Fascinated to the point that I became obsessed. I memorized the Kenya Airways in-flight announcements. I'd practice it with my voice, and do it every evening. After that, I wanted to be a dancer. I started dancing and I really liked it. Then I wanted to become a chef. I told my parents and they laughed. And then I wanted to become a lawyer. That stuck for quite a while, then I had a journalist phase, then the last thing I wanted to do was become a psychologist.

Primary school was different. I've always been very effeminate. I don't know if it's because I'm gay, or because I was brought up by six women. It's something that I've always been. Kids pointed that out in primary school. I remember sometime in late primary was the first time that someone called me gay. I thought, "What the hell does that even mean?"

I think I looked it up in a dictionary. I looked for 'gay' and then I saw homosexual. I tried to look up 'homosexual' and I couldn't for the life of me understand what it meant. It was something like men having sex with men and I thought, "I'm not having sex with men. I'm a boy, not a man."

High school was absolutely shit. I hated high school, even though I'm glad that I went through what I went through in high school. It made me develop a really thick skin. I remember joining high school and on the first day—kids are vicious—I could tell that people were looking at each other to ask, "What's his deal?"

In about a week, the name calling had started. It got to a point where if I was able to make it through a day without being a called faggot or homo or *shoga*, that was a good day. I kept to myself, but I had a few friends. I had this friend who I made in the first year but he left. The first year was only tolerable because he was there. He was gay and he told me. We were thirteen years old, but he was solid and he knew he was gay without a doubt. He gave me my first muscle magazine. I tried to refuse it, but he said, "Take it. I don't care what you do with it, but just take it."

He left after a year, and then high school became very lonely. The bullying increased. I kept to myself. I remember my parents paid for me to have school lunch from the cafeteria, but after the first semester I went back home and told my parents that I didn't want to eat from the cafeteria because the food was bad, and I'd prefer if they gave me money. The truth is that I could never sit at the cafeteria. I would get my food and sit at a table, and everyone at that table would stand up and leave. I learned to eat behind the wall, or eat in class, or eat at the car park. I'd find a place where there was no one and eat there.

It was the same thing in the school bus. Despite the fact that I was in secondary school, I would sit in the front with all the kids from primary school. I remember once the bus was full, and the only seat was somewhere in the middle of the bus. I went there and the guy sitting there put both his feet up on the chair. I ended up standing. The teachers knew I was being bullied—because they could hear it and sometimes they could see it—but they chose not to address it.

The school prefects didn't help either. In fact, some of them were the worst. Once I had gone for a school trip to the Coast, we went to the beach to play sports and we were divided into teams. Of course the last person to be selected was me, and the team I was sent to had those school prefects. As I was walking to join the team, one of them walked up to me and said, "Don't bring any of your gay shit here."

I remember I stopped, looked at him and walked back to the hotel. I went to my room and slept. Same with the guys who played rugby. They used to slam doors in my face. High school wasn't the best experience but it taught me a lot.

Religion is something I always struggle with, because of my background. My family hasn't been the most religious, because my mum and dad were from different religious denominations. I spent my childhood going to the temple, which I got used to and kinda liked. I wanted to join the youth club at the temple, and I remember the last day I went to the temple. It was meal time in the temple, and one of the guys who was serving all us kids food asked the other guy who was serving, "Have you served this black kid any food?"

They didn't know I could understand Punjabi. For me that was it. That was the last time I ever went to the temple, and I said I'd never go back again. I never did. I started going to church, because I wanted to go to church. It was good. I joined the youth group and I was very active. The church story ended in a similar fashion, though. The last time I went to church, I was in high school. It was a regular Sunday, and I remember all the church teachers liked me. One day, they were discussing homosexuality, and at some point they were talking about homosexual people, and I remember someone in the back of the room shouted, "Like him!", and pointed at me.

I froze. The teacher just continued speaking, like it didn't happen. I waited until the class ended, and then I left. I never went back since.

I still pray, though. I believe that there is a higher being, and I acknowledge them. I don't believe in going to a church, mosque or temple.

I don't do any drugs or tobacco, which is something people find odd, but I've recently started drinking one or two cocktails. The reason I stay away from drugs and tobacco is that I lost my father to drugs, and the men in my family have struggled with alcohol, and that's what I watched growing up. I swore that I'd never ever do drugs and that I'd never drink alcohol.

My first kiss was horrible. It was absolutely horrible. I knew it didn't feel right. I remember the guy was nibbling my lower lip, and I was thinking, "No, no, no! This isn't what I had in mind."

In the same year, I met a whole bunch of really, really bad kissers. Maybe I did my time, because I haven't met any bad kissers since. I remember my first good kiss, it was quite something, I got dizzy. I felt warm, I felt heat rush through my body.

I am as out as I need to be. My family is really small. My mum and dad passed away, and I have one brother and sister. I told my brother and sister I was gay in my final year of school when I accepted it. I just started telling the people who are close to me who I felt needed to know. When I sat down with my brother and told him, he burst out laughing.

I am close with my sister. Becoming close with my brother was a long process—one that took almost seventeen years—because I absolutely hated my brother. There was a point at which something in him just changed, and it was right before I told him. I remember at some point having decided that my brother would never know what was going on in my life, at least not from me. Then somehow, we got to a point where we got close, and that's the reason I came out to him. I'm close to both of them now.

If family is people you let in no matter what, then I don't have family. I guess I have a group of friends I'm close to. I'm also close to my brother, sister, and my dad's sisters.

My best queer moment was when I made queer friends, because then I knew that I wasn't alone. I met people who I had more in common with than just my sexuality.

Every day queer life has its challenges. One of the worst things is living in fear, and being insecure, not knowing if you're walking down the street and see a group of people coming towards you. You don't feel safe. Sometimes you don't feel safe because it's a big group of people, but then sometimes you don't feel safe because you know you're gay, and you wonder if they can see it.

I am in a steady relationship with myself. I've always been in a relationship with myself because I grew up alone. I was very alone, and alone is the safest place to be. I am most comfortable when I am alone.

After my first relationship ended, I thought that it would be easier to get into the next relationship, but it's the opposite that happened, it's getting harder. I don't know at what point I'll be ready for a relationship again. My ex is trying to be my friend but I don't want it. He wants us to get back together, and he's been trying to get us back together for the past four years, but no. I wouldn't mind us being friends, I've tried it with him several times but then, after two or three months he asks if we can get back together, and I say no. Then we go back to square one, where he calls and I don't pick up the phone. It is tiresome.

Happiness to me is such a strange thing. I feel like for me to be truly happy, I need to confront everything that happened in my past and deal with it. That's something I've started doing, but there is still a lot I need to do. I have moments when I'm happy, but other than that I still feel that I'm on my journey towards happiness. Hopefully, in ten years I'll be alive and well.

It would be nice if I will have met someone I can settle down with. Someone that I like. We'd live together. I don't want children, and dogs and cats are needy. Maybe we'll have a fish that's fed ONCE A DAY.

–

I'M A LESBIAN, but I prefer the term homosexual, because it hits you. It grounds you—where you are, and what you are. When people ask if you're a lesbian, they don't really understand sexuality, they don't get the spiritual and emotional contexts.

So, I am a homosexual, and above all I am a Christian. My sexuality and spirituality don't have to balance out on a scale—they are different. I'm out to the people who matter to me. My parents and family know, although not all my sisters like it. My colleagues know. My pastor knows because I am part of the praise and worship team, and I spread the gospel in different schools. I am a homosexual and I am very proud of myself.

My first experience was with a girl called Agnes. I don't know if she is alive today. My parents said we were too close. I was so girly, but Agnes wasn't. She never missed my birthday parties. We shared dresses and dolls. We shared a lot, and of course we were also cheeky together. But dolls were our main interest—the hair, and the make-up. With Agnes we role-played as a family. My closeness with Agnes made my parents especially cautious. They made sure to separate us, in school and in the neighbourhood. I became aware that I should not hold hands with her, or be too close to her. Agnes made me know who I am and what I was.

My father worked outside the country a lot in the 90s and so my mother raised us. Between the ages of eight and fifteen, I was policed. My mother was very strict. Whenever I was alone with a girl, she would intervene and pull me away. She shuttled me between school and home, and I never really had a life.

I never dated all through high school. My best friend was one of the first people to point out my strangeness. She had noticed my fondness for talking about boys' fashion and hanging out almost exclusively with other girls. I have to admit, I always found it odd and offensive when boys approached girls. When a man approaches me, it repulses me so much. I don't know why. I also never had any crushes on our male teachers unlike most of my peers. I told my best friend that I didn't know what was wrong with me, but whatever it was, it was huge.

There was a girl in my high school called Anita. She was friendly and free and straight. She had a boyfriend, and I didn't like him. I met Anita in a strange way. I hated the school I was in and convinced my father to transfer me. News spread around the school that I was leaving, and Anita passed me a note in class that read, "I want to talk to you."

We met in the fields during a break where she declared her fondness for me. She wanted to be my best friend, although I got the feeling she wanted more than that. My father always told me, "If you can't be an African woman, be an African man."

I was raised to respect the needs of a woman. I did my best to respect Anita's wish to be my best friend. For some reason, I didn't speak to Anita for the remainder of the term, three months. But I sent her a bouquet of flowers and chocolates during Valentine's Day under a fake name. In my boarding school, they made an announcement whenever students got mail or a special delivery. Anita immediately knew the flowers were from me. She cried—she was too emotional. I think she was bisexual, but I never asked. When we opened for the next term I gave her an ultimatum: to be my girlfriend or to stop being friends. Anita asked for time to think it over.

That term, I snapped at a teacher and was given a suspension. My parents were called in, and the principal revealed that I was also under scrutiny for allegedly being a lesbian. I was asked to reveal who I was in a relationship with. I refused to tell them, and left the school. Anita had a very hard time after I left. It was tough to leave. I left some of my things on her bed because she had no idea that I was leaving. We met a couple of years later, but we could not revive our relationship.

In my next school, I was not really interested in anyone but somehow the story about what happened in my old school surfaced. Girls—especially lesbians—in the new school started sending me love notes. I was notorious for being open about sex in conversations. Once, in biology class, we were being taught about intercourse. The teacher was harping on and on about the benefits of heterosexual intercourse and it irked me. I interrupted him, saying that sex is beautiful between two women because they understand each other. My classmates gasped. My deskmate pinched me. The teacher responded by saying that it is not right for persons of the same sex to engage in any intercourse.

After high school, I met a girl called Chloe. She was an American soldier based in Iraq during the war. We met in a military base camp when I went to visit my cousin who was in the military. Chloe and I dated for four years, and nobody knew about us. Only my niece knew about Chloe. It was a long distance relationship, and it was at the height of Don't Ask Don't Tell, so I never sent her anything incriminating. You know they always screened the letters. We arranged to see each other in Mombasa or Nairobi whenever she was on a break. But she was always away. It never worked out for us because she chose her career over me. I told her, "If you leave, I won't wait for you."

She left. It broke my heart.

Then she went MIA. I got a call one day saying that Chloe was missing in action and presumed dead. I remember being in a restaurant in town when the call came, and I just started crying. Chloe had indicated that I was her next of kin and so they sent me the flag and her letters through the US Embassy in Nairobi. I stayed in denial for about three weeks. It was A VERY HARD TIME FOR ME.

–

I AM A LESBIAN, a sex worker activist and mother of three children. I am an orphan. I am also a street-child activist because I was as a former street-child. To be honest I don't know where I was born. I just found myself in Nairobi. My mother was a stripper in Mombasa. My grandparents took me away from her when I was a year old and raised me.

By the time I was seven years old, I knew I was different. I loved wearing boys' clothes. Any chance I would get to dress like a boy, I would take it. I even used to take other people's boy clothes from the washing line and wear them. My nickname was *wanja kihii* [derogatory nickname for tomboys].

My grandmother noticed that I was different and derogatorily claimed that I was switched at birth. My skin tone was darker than most of my other family members, so she claimed that I was a Luo. This really hurt me. I ran away to the expansive Kangemi market in Nairobi. I was only seven years old, but I survived through the cold nights. I later moved into the city after meeting a bunch of other street children. We slept in the streets until we were pushed out by the City Council to a children's home in ███████.

Life there was tough—getting food was difficult, and so I decided to return to my grandmother's house. My grandmother refused to let me back in, but one of the neighbours took me in. She convinced me to join primary school to learn how to read and write. I went to primary school up to Standard 3. The husband of the lady who took me in was not fond of me. He did not like the fact that I dressed and acted like a boy. He claimed I was cursed. I ran away again to the streets of Nairobi. I have passed through many children's homes and hostels.

By the time I was fifteen, my body started changing. I could no longer pass as a boy in the streets because my breasts were developing and I begun to have periods. I went by the name Joe.

The fear of being raped or beaten became more acute with every passing day.

There was a girl who would always bring me food and water from the supermarket in downtown Nairobi. She was very kind to me. At that time in Nairobi, it was not uncommon for street children to threaten to smear faeces on passers-by. I would always defend the girls when the street kids threatened them. That's how I came to know her.

One day she took me on a boat ride at Uhuru Park in Nairobi. I can still remember what she was wearing. She was in a miniskirt. She was very sexy! We got to talking and I revealed to her my attraction to girls. She told me that I was what is called a lesbian. I had never heard of the term before. It was all very confusing. She revealed to me that she was bisexual—and that she had a boyfriend.

She put me up in a lodging for a couple of days as she convinced her parents to take me in. I was afraid of rooms so I ran away again and returned to what I was used to; the streets. It didn't take long before I was raped by several boys and I got pregnant.

The girl's parents had by then accepted me into their home. I revealed to her that I was raped and that I was pregnant. She loved me even more. I was tested for HIV, and the results were negative. I gave birth to a baby boy.

A few months later she became pregnant through her boyfriend. We continued to live together, and she gave birth to a son. A few years later, she became pregnant again. I don't know how it happened but it was not planned. Sadly, she died in a car accident a few years later. I took custody of all three children. I take care of everything. My eldest is thirteen years old. Lesbian sex work does not pay well. It is also very infrequent; I get a client maybe twice a month.

I can't have sex with men. I loathe the idea of it.

I am not afraid of what people say. Where were they when I was raising myself? I don't owe any explanation to anyone. I'll wear my trousers everywhere.

I respect the women who engage in sex work. Most of them do it so they can take care of their children. Their children are in primary school and even in university. They want their children to be in better places.

Church is in my heart because I am aware that I would not be alive today without God's grace. Discrimination by Christians will not stop me from praising him. Even as a queer, I will be there to praise the Lord. I have given birth and I am raising children on this earth. My favourite story in the Bible is the one where Jesus drank from the water pot of a woman accused of being a prostitute. Jesus did not care whether she was a prostitute or whether she was HIV positive. God sees us for who we are. He sees what is good in me. He is up there telling his angels that there are things that I am doing that are better than what the Christians who are pointing fingers are doing. There is no big sin or small sin before the eyes of God. Being a homosexual is irrelevant to him.

The other day I was listening to the radio and they were reporting on some accounts of bestiality which seem to be on the rise around the country. At the end of the report, they included the story of two men getting married abroad. It angers me that the society takes bestiality, paedophilia and homosexuality as one thing. I would be the first person to beat up a paedophile. Homosexuals are not paedophiles. Paedophiles are demons. It's straight men who rape little girls and old women. It is straight men who sleep with animals! Gay people know themselves and what they want sexually.

I would like the Kenyan mainstream media to do their homework on LGBTI issues in Kenya. They just settle for false stories that demonize us in the public eye. The general public misunderstands the gay community because of such crazy stories. The media in Kenya sensationalize things and work against us WITH THEIR LAZY REPORTING.

—

I REALLY ENJOYED MY FIRST KISS. I still remember it now. Even now, I can't make love to someone if there's no kiss. My first kiss made me think, "Ai! This kiss thing is very sweet!"

He was a mixed-race boy who was a neighbour. They were rich, I lived in the slum behind their house. Our mothers knew each other, and his mother suggested that I should live with them and assist her with her farm work. This was before anyone knew I was gay.

His mother would leave us alone in the house, and he would come and watch me shower. I was a slum kid, so I really used to enjoy taking a shower with water from the shower. The first time he came, I was so scared. I was so attracted to him. He came into the shower and kissed me so intensely, and we had sex.

That became our habit. Without kissing, I don't feel love. I fell in love with him. His mother started to suspect that something was going on between us. She noticed that her son didn't want to do anything without me there. She thought of me as a *shamba* boy [farm boy], a servant, so she couldn't stand seeing me interact with her son so closely.

She chased me away, and I was devastated. I couldn't see him again. I used to hang around outside their house just hoping to see him as he left or came back from school. Every morning, every evening. I really loved him, and I was never allowed to see him again. His mother had him go to a school far away.

After that, the rumours that I was gay spread in my town. Every time I'd walk on the streets, I'd hear people saying, "*Shoga yule.*" He's a fag.

"*Msenge yule.*"

That used to bother me so much. I didn't feel safe. I ran away from that town and came to ████████. I started hustling for a while, trading sex for money. I lived with my small sister during that period. She had a female house-help, and we slept in the same room. I stayed with her for a year, and—of course—nothing happened between me and the house-help. I was not interested at all. My sister started insulting me.

"*Kwani wewe ni mwanaume gani?*" What kind of man are you?

She'd say such bad things, and I wondered why she was saying such ugly things.

"*Wewe ni shoga?*" Are you a fag?

We used to fight about it so much. Once, I slapped her so hard. How could she disrespect me so much and I was working so hard on the streets so that we'd have food to eat? After one of those fights, the house-help and I had sex. I moved out, but a few weeks later my mother called me to tell me that the house-help was one month pregnant. I tried to deny it, and my mother—who was very sick—said, "No. Don't refuse this. Come back, accept it and marry her."

I came back home, and my mother died soon after that. Because of what my mother said, I got married to this girl. We lived together for three years, but life got very hard and I had to move to ████ to find work. I wish I could live with her and my child. Even if I'm gay, I want to live with her. She doesn't know I'm gay, unless she's heard about it. Once, I had a fight with some guy and he came home to look for me in my house. He knocked on the door and asked my wife, "*Yule shoga yuko wapi?*" Where's that fag?

My wife is very clever, she told him, "*Kila siku unakuja hapa, nawapakulia mnakula, leo hii amekuwa ni 'gay' kwako? Sindio? Lakini mimi, ni babake huyu mtoto. Mimi sijui hiyo ambayo unaniambia.*" Every day you come here with him and you eat together, but today he's gay, huh? For me, he's the father of my child. I don't know what you're talking about.

When I came back home, I found she was so annoyed. I asked her, "What's wrong?"

She asked me, "*Wewe kazi gani hio unafanya?*" What work is that you've doing?

I asked her, "'*Kazi gani'? Kwani wewe miaka hii yote unajua ni kazi gani mimi nilikuwa nafanya? Kama utasikiza watu, wewe wasikize. Unaweza niacha.*" 'What work'? All these years, you've never known what work I do? If you're going to listen to gossip, go ahead. You can leave me.

She said, "*Mimi siwezi kukuacha. Wewe ni babake mtoto wangu. Kama ni ushoga ni wewe na yeye huko nje. Hapa mimi sijui.*" I can't leave you. You're the father of my child. If it's homosexuality, that's between him and you out there. In here, I don't know it.

And it ended there. My son is now eight years old.

I was really crazy those days, by the way. I used to wear dresses and makeup. I didn't give a fuck. Now you can't really tell. Those days *[laughs]*...danger! I tried sex work for a while. I used to stand on my corner on the street, looking for money. Even the other girls didn't fuck with me. They knew that was my corner. It was my space, and I used to stand there for three, four hours. '*No Maneno*', they used to call me.

I'd stand there just wishing. I'd say, "*Mungu! Nisaidie! Nipatie hata mtu anitoe kwenye hii barabara! Nitoke hapa!*" God! Help me! Give me someone who will get me out of here!

Every night, I'd stand there wishing I wouldn't have to stand there one more night.

One night, I went out clubbing with my friend in all my outrageous drag. The next morning, I had a fight with my friend and he refused to drop me home. I had to walk—the way I was dressed! People shouted at me all the way home.

"*Shoga! Mamako!*" Fag! Your momma!

They threw things at me, they insulted me. I just kept walking, and I didn't even look at them. That's what saved me. I just kept walking. From that day, I changed everything. I got home and I threw away all my dresses and makeup, and I gave away all the good ones. I changed the way I look since then.

I've accepted myself now. You know, once you accept yourself, you can live freely. I couldn't stand being called '*shoga*' years ago, that's why I ran away. But I love men. Even if you put a woman here, I can't be interested in her.

Since I accepted myself—that I love my fellow men—I respect myself, and even when people gossip about me, I don't care. I let them speak and I continue with my work. I've worked very hard to get the little respect I have now. I earned it. I worked hard to create relationships with people, even the ones who used TO GOSSIP ABOUT ME.

–

WHEN I FINISHED HIGH SCHOOL, I was seventeen. I couldn't join college because I needed to have an ID to join college, and I could only get an ID when I turned eighteen. So I had a year to spend at home, just waiting. Life was weird, just killing time. When I was in school, my brothers used to give me pocket money. Now that I was out, there was no more pocket money.

I was so restless for six months. One day, a friend of mine—she knew I was a randy guy—told me, "I met a lady in a pub last night. She's here on holiday, and she's desperate for a young guy who can fuck her properly. Someone who can stay with her for a while."

"How old is she?"

"About forty."

That was too much for me. "Forty years? It won't work. She could be my mother."

But my friend convinced me. I agreed to meet this lady. At 11pm that night, I met her in a famous pub in town. She was pretty. She didn't look forty. You'd think she was in her thirties. Thirty-four or five. Her ass? Excellent.

So I sat down with this lady. We had a few drinks, smoked a little. She even bought dinner. After that she said she wanted us to drive down to Mombasa for the weekend. I told her I couldn't, that my family would wonder where I had gone. One night out was OK, but more than that and my brothers would get worried.

"OK. Let's get a room here just for tonight."

I was nervous, because I'd never been with a woman so much older than me. We went to the room, and she told me to take a shower. I came out of the bathroom in my vest and towel, and she was naked. I was shy at first.

"Don't be afraid. Just come."

She took my towel away, and she went to the bathroom with it. I dived into the bed. She showered and came back to the bed.

"I want us to do business."

"What kind of business?"

"I want to be with you for two months. How much do you charge per night?"

"If you give me 2,000 that's fine."

"Wow. 2,000? Are you sure?"

"Yes."

"I can't pay you that. I'll give you 3,000."

I thought, "This is the place to be! A whole extra thousand!"

We slept together that night. The next morning she told me, "I'm giving you five hours. Find something to tell your family, and we can go to my place."

I went home and told my brothers that I'd found a short contract in Mombasa for two months.

"What deal is that?"

"I don't know all the details, but when I get there I'll tell you."

So they let me go. I went back to the lady, and we drove to her place. There was a maid there waiting for us. She was hot, too. I wasn't used to that. She was calling me 'Daddy' because I was the man of the house, yet she was older than me too. I managed, somehow. I stayed there for the entire two months, and she paid me as promised. I was very happy. She paid me in cash, and I had never held such money in my hands. She added an extra 5,000.

I went straight home because I was so nervous about carrying all that money. 185,000 shillings. I thought someone would rob me. I got home and gave my mother all the money. She was so shocked.

"Where did you get all this money? Have you stolen it?"

"I got a deal with a white guy, I did the work and he paid me. I don't know what to do with this money."

"OK. As long as it's genuine, give it to me. I'll keep it for you."

She kept it in the bank for about two weeks, then one day she told me, "I asked your brothers and we've decided we should buy you a motorbike so you can run a *bodaboda*[1] [motorbike taxi] until you go to school."

I refused. I didn't like that work. I told them they could buy the bike, but they'd have to hire someone to drive it. So they did.

After six months, the lady called me back. We worked out a new deal. Instead of paying me directly, she paid my tuition and accommodation fees for two years, and would give me pocket money every now and then. So I enrolled at a college to study finance. Now, I had to explain that somehow to my family.

"Mum, that white guy has come back. This time, he's told me to go to school and he'll pay my school fees in exchange for my work. So, I'm going to college. I'll be done in three years."

"What? Are you sure?"

"Yes!"

They didn't believe me. My brothers came to the college to see me and—sure enough—there I was, studying.

"Can't we meet this white guy of yours?"

"He's not around. He's in Germany now."

So there I was, stress-free. I stayed with her for three months, then she travelled again. She'd send pocket money every month.

And so I finished college, and now I'm working in a bank. I know people say sex work always ends badly, but I turned out OK. I think I am a sex-work success story *[laughs]*.

Whenever she wasn't around, I continued having other clients. One of those was a man. I met him in a pub. I was alone, and I was looking for a client. My clients until then were usually old women. He walked in and asked me, "Can I sit here?"

I didn't mind. We talked a bit and I understood what he wanted from me. I told him, "I'm not here for fun. This is my work."

"What kind of work is that?"

"This is my base, and I usually meet women here. But... If you have 3,000, I can do it for you."

He said he didn't have that amount, "What about 1,500 for a night?"

"I'm not that cheap, *bana* [man]."

"How about for two rounds?"

I said OK. "Two rounds, you give me my cash and I go."

We had a few drinks, and then left to book a room in a lodging. We fucked, he paid me and I left. Afterwards, I had many questions. A man like me? How did I do it? I had never had sex with a man. Was I drunk?

I met this guy again after a while, in the same pub. I had a date that evening, but he said, "I don't want to take too much of your time. I liked your game. Can we have another two rounds?"

Meeting him again made me remember how it had felt the first time. It felt different. It was sweeter, tighter, and it didn't take me long to cum. It didn't take long like it would with a woman, which was actually good for my business. It meant that I could do my shots much quicker and get another client. Sometimes my female clients were so watery, and it would take so long to finish one shot with them that I'd be too tired to take another client after that. After that, I started having a few male clients.

I continued with this business for two years, and then I finished college. After that I thought, "I'm done with school, I can get something else to do for money. Fucking is not a business any more."

Some of my old clients still call me sometimes, but these days I only do it because I want to, not for the money. I must say that fucking men diminished my appetite for women. I find it tiresome with women. Women automatically lubricate when they're having sex, and sometimes it's too much. You enter and it takes forever. Finding a woman with a pussy as tight as a man's ass—or an ass in general—is very difficult. There are some women with tight pussies, but it's very hard to find. I've been in this sector for two years. I know. I've been searching.

I'm not going to stop having sex with men. I'm used to it now. If you put a woman and a man side by side, I'd be more interested in fucking the man. Will I ever settle down? I've been thinking about that, and my answer is 50-50. I want to raise my own kids, and I know a man can never give me kids.

I'm thinking of getting married. The fact that I have sex with men is still underground. None of my family members know about it. Even my best friends don't know. So—to remove their doubts, and because I want kids—I have to get married. But my wife has to know about it. Any woman who refuses me to be who I am will have to sort herself out. I don't see myself stopping this. If she can't accept me, I don't think we'll live together well because I'll have to lie to her and go find myself a man. So I don't want to have to lie about it. SIMPLE.

–

I identify as femme. What that means to me, is that I can date anyone, and that no one can notice that I'm the member of LGBT family by the way I dress. I date studs, not stems or femmes.[24]

I first realized my identity when I was about 12. At first, I didn't know what I was feeling. I had a friend who already knew a lot about queerness, and she used to talk to me a lot. I realized I had feelings for her, so we started to date in secret. It was hard to tell anyone else, "This is now me."

---

24. Stud and butch are both used to identify masculine women. A stem is a woman that either alternates between femme and masculine or exists somewhere in the middle.

I still wasn't sure at that time, even though I used to date her. I knew I felt different and whenever a straight boy touched me I wasn't comfortable, but when she touched me I was OK with it.

Eventually, everyone in school discovered that she was queer, and she started having trouble at school. People were saying bad things about her, and it got to a point that they even included me in those stories. I felt terrible, because everywhere I would go, everyone I knew, my friends: people were talking about it. I felt bad and I told her that we should stop seeing one another. Completely stop, even being friends. It was a total break up, but because she loved me for real, she didn't agree. Instead, she tried to kill herself, by jumping in front of a car. She broke her leg. When I heard that, I went to see her and we got back together. This was my first girlfriend. We stayed together for a while. She was my first and I didn't have other options and I stayed loyal, but she had many other girlfriends, so I ended up disappointed. She hurt me.

At that time, people around my neighbourhood learned about the two of us. When I realized they were gossiping about us, I felt bad and worried how my mother would feel if she heard. I was scared. So I distanced myself from friends. I started being isolated, because of what I was feeling inside. I didn't have anyone to talk to. Each and every person I knew was straight, all of my friends were straight, and it's very hard to tell a straight person what you're going through. So I just stayed like that: alone.

I finished primary school and joined high school. I continued being alone. In my second year, I transferred to a new school, and in that school, there were many lesbians. I got myself one again, and I dated her. She was two years ahead of me, and we were not hiding. We were caught by our teachers and they announced that the two of us were lesbians during the school parade. They called my mum and my girlfriend's mother, and we all had to go to the Headmistress' office. The teachers and our parents talked about it and told us to stop but it was difficult. It's not like I decided to become like this, I was born this way.

Everyone in school was talking about it. Each and every teacher coming to class would talk about it. I was rejected at school. Even my mum rejected me, she said I'm not her daughter, that she couldn't have given birth to a child like me, and that I was a disgrace. She said she felt like killing me. She was so disappointed, she even cried.

At the beginning of the next term, my mum took me to school and left me at the school gate at about 6pm. She took a motorbike home. I stood at that gate feeling desperate. I was all alone with my things; my mattress, my uniform, my box[25]. I didn't want to go back to school and I felt bad going back home, because my mum had rejected me. So I just stood at the gate and cried, thinking, "If this is what it means to be myself, then what is the meaning of being alive?"

I also took a motorbike and went back home and I put my things away. My mother still wasn't speaking to me, and even my own brother did not want to talk to me. My brother and my mother were the only ones who knew why I had been expelled, but after I left school everyone knew. My school mates came home and spread the story all over our estate, so everyone knew the reason I had been expelled.

So I ran away from home. I told my friend everything that was happening with me, and she offered to introduce me to a woman I could stay with until my mum cooled down. At the time I didn't think my mum would cool down, I thought I was going to go forever. I went to stay with this woman, and I told her that my mum had chased me away from home and I couldn't go back. I switched off my phone.

I lived with that stranger for about a month, not going to school, not talking to anyone. Later, someone sent me a message on Facebook, "*U-lesbian umekufikisha wapi?*" Where has being a lesbian taken you?

I deactivated my account, because I didn't want to fight with anyone. Everyone was talking about me and I had no one to talk to. I was all alone and I would cry. I kept crying and crying. Eventually I went home to talk to my mum. I promised her I would change. But I never did: instead, it got worse. She told me, "I cannot tell you what to do, and what not to do. You're a grown up. Use your brain. If this is what you want, *siwezi kukufunga*

---

25. Inexpensive metal trunk used by boarding students.

nikakuweke kwa mfuko. But *nataka ujue kitu moja*, I'm not happy about it." I can't lock you up and put you in my pocket. But I want you to know one thing, I'm not happy about it.

There was this policewoman in our estate and she was a lesbian. We became friends. We would spend time together and I would tell her what I was going through. She would encourage me to talk to my mum and tell her about my feelings. But I would tell her, "I cannot confront my mother right now because I'm not done with school. I think I would stress her too much. So I'll just remain quiet and try to convince her that I'll change."

That police officer was transferred because of her sexuality. The other officers found out because she was dating a stud, and they are easy to spot. I left home again, and I followed that police woman and she agreed to let me stay with her. She had been transferred to ██████. I went to live there and my mother never bothered to call me or ask me where I am.

She told my brother that I had left again, and he called me, yelling, "How can you do that? How can you become a lesbian? What a shame!"

I told my brother that I cannot force myself to be something I am not. That feeling is inside me and I cannot lie to him that I can date a man. I once tried to date a man, but we broke up because I wouldn't let him kiss me or anything. My brother told me, "You're not my sister. Don't ever say that you have a brother, just forget about me."

And I told him, "If you can disown me because of my feelings, then it is OK."

After a while I went back home. I had been expelled in the middle of my third year and I needed to finish school. I promised my mother once again that I would change and she accepted that. I went back to school, but eventually the rumours followed me. I don't know how the rumours got to that school, but I was called by the Principal. She told me, "We cannot encourage lesbianism in this school."

She said I couldn't be allowed to stay in that school and corrupt the other girls. By this time I was in my final year and I had already registered for exams, but I was expelled anyway. When I got home my mother said, "*Nimechoka na wewe. Siwezi kakupe-*

leka shule ingine. Hakuna kitu nitakusaidia, hakuna kitu nitakufanyia. Kaa tuu vile unataka." I'm tired of you. I won't take you to another school. I won't help you with anything, and I won't do anything for you. Stay as you like.

I studied from home, and when exam time came I went to the school and did my papers. My straight "friends" started avoiding me. They would talk about me, and ignored my texts or phone calls. One of them sent me a text saying, "*Mimi siwezi ongea na mtu mwenye ni lesbian. Hio ni mashetani. Uko illuminati.* I cannot talk to you." I can't talk to a lesbian. That is devilish. You're a part of the Illuminati.

I didn't get mad, because I realized they were being ignorant. I finished my exams and came back home. My mum still didn't want anything to do with me, she wouldn't even pay for computer classes.

I had an aunt—unfortunately she has passed away—who was my mum's cousin and lived in Nairobi. I went to live with her. One day she looked at my phone and found out that I am a lesbian. For three days she didn't say anything, then one day she said, "I heard this thing from your brother, and I saw it for myself on your phone. So it is true?"

I didn't know what to do. I felt like I didn't want to deny it anymore, so I said, "It is true."

I was worried because everyone else who found out had walked out on me, but she talked to me and said if I ever had any problems I should tell her, because she was OK with it. Once more I felt like I had someone, a friend to talk to, someone who understood me. She said, "Anytime you feel like talking, just call me or share it with me. I'm your aunt. I know these things, and you're not the first lesbian I have met. I have a friend who is like you."

She introduced me to that friend and we became friends. Now I had no desire to go back home. I lived with this aunt until the day she passed away, one year ago. I had lived with her for three years. She understood me. I could even introduce a woman I was dating to her and she was OK with it. I could even meet a stud in her house and she was OK with it. I would tell her, "Aunt, I want to go to a party."

She would ask, "A party for your people?"

I would tell her yes, and she would only tell me to take care. She would always allow me to go. I would tell her when I got to the party and when I got back home, she would even tease me, "How was the party? Did you get a crush?"

She wanted to hear my stories. That is how I came out. I felt so comfortable with her, I could even tell her about my crushes, she would ask me how a certain stud was treating me. I felt like I had a mother, a friend, a brother, a family and everything to me. When she passed I felt like I was back to square one.

I had to go back to my mum's. When I arrived, I told her I wouldn't disturb her, as long as she let me live in peace. She told me, "I have tried. I have really tried as hard as I can, trying to get you back to normal, but it's impossible."

She also told me that they don't have "that blood" where she's from, and that it's probably from my father. At least, right now she doesn't talk about it, and we are OK. THE CONFLICT IS OVER FOR NOW.

–

I'M 31 AND I IDENTIFY AS TRANS. I knew I was trans from around the age of 6. I just knew. I've never really enjoyed masculine activities and behaviours; I was always drawn to more feminine ways. I've always been close to women, all my life.

I'm a cook. I don't work in a restaurant, instead I cook in people's homes when they have events, and I've been doing that for 16 years now. One of the things that's difficult about cooking is sometimes when I cook—especially if it's for Muslims—they say, "Oh, that person is an abomination, we can't and will not eat his food!"

This means I have to cook in hiding, so that no one can see who has cooked the food.

I didn't go to high school. I had always been drawn to the kitchen, I would spend a lot of time watching my mother cook, I've always been her favourite. My mother was also a cook, she would sometimes make up to 100 kilos of food in a day! So I decided to follow in her footsteps.

My family kicked me out when they started noticing that I was different, and that was the point when I fully committed to my gender expression, I was free. I started growing out my hair, wearing makeup, earrings: I changed how I dressed. After a while, the local Muslim community started saying that I had somehow become worse after being kicked out of home, so they called for a meeting to discuss me going back home so that I wouldn't 'lose my way'. I refused to go back.

I kept on living and doing my thing, but a time came when I wasn't doing so well financially. At that point, my father had passed away, and I knew what inheritance I was entitled to, because my father owned land and properties. So I went to the Chief Kadhi and reported that my family had kicked me out and I wanted what was owed to me.[26] The Kadhi asked me for the list of things I felt I was owed, and I listed to him all of my late father's assets. He then gave me a letter to take home to my brothers and mother. My mum was on my side on this issue. When I took the letter home, they hadn't seen me for a period of about nine months: my hair was so long, I had on earrings and my face was BEAT! When they saw me all they kept saying was, "This is not our brother," and I told them, "You are not my brothers either."

When we went to court to settle the inheritance issue, the Kadhi suggested that we sell all the property, then I could be given my share of the money, which was what I wanted. My mother instead suggested that we rent out the properties then we could all share the earnings, which we agreed to. My mother then pulled me aside and told me, "There's no need for court proceedings, let's go home and we can sort it out."

I had to cut my hair when I moved back home. I'm still staying at home till today, but my brothers and I don't talk to each other. Would you believe me if I told you that we haven't spoken to one another in the last 14 years yet we live in the same house? During Ramadhan, we'll break fast together. During Eid, we'll celebrate together, and if someone visits our home, they wouldn't be able to tell that there was any conflict, because we're good at

---

26. Kadhi courts or Kadhi's courts are a court system in Kenya that enforce limited rights of inheritance, family, and succession for Muslims.

performing togetherness, but the second they leave, we go back to the usual silence.

I still go to the mosque. I usually pray on Fridays. During Ramadhan, I never miss prayers. My brother is actually an *Imam*[27], but I have never gone to his mosque. I feel like I would undermine him if I did, because then what authority would he have to say anything? I suppose if you look at it from a religious perspective, he has a point, however, it's my life and I SHOULD BE LEFT TO LIVE IT AS I PLEASE.

–

I'VE KNOWN I WAS TRANS from my earliest memories. I remember being confused about being a boy who loved girl things and a girl whose physique didn't seem feminine. I felt trapped there. At the age of 7, I was an extremely girlish-boy. I was always playing with girls, and I wanted to wear feminine clothes. So in short, I knew I was a misfit, that's the word I like to use.

I used to feel that my world and my soul were at ease whenever I wore feminine clothes. Whenever I would play the part of a female in school plays, I would feel relaxed and comfortable. This is who I wanted to be. I was not impersonating anyone. My classmates used to say to me, "You are so good at impersonating women," but no.

No, no, no. I was just being myself.

Growing up was hectic. We had a strict dad, and he would always say, "Boys are not supposed to do this."

Over and over again, my mum would tell him, "When he grows up, he'll definitely know himself. He'll definitely take his place. *Hizo vitu zitaisha*." Those things will end.

I think it was her way of consoling herself, telling herself, "I know what my son will be like in future, so I don't want to allow his father to start making trouble, because I know the world that my son will go into WILL BE A HARSH ONE."

–

27. An Islamic leadership position, most commonly used as the title of a worship leader of a mosque and Muslim community among Sunni Muslims.

When I was a young boy, my mother sent me to the village to be raised by my step-mother. There, I was sexually abused by one of her brothers. I tried to tell my step-mother that this was going on, and she didn't believe me. She said, "I don't believe this thing can happen in this house."

No one was to help me. From that day on, I denied them and I refused them. I told them, "I don't think you people are my family," and I eventually left them.

Since then, my Dad has passed away, my Mum has passed away. So many of them have died, I have never attended their funerals. Three years ago, my step-mother said, "You need to come home, there is a portion of this land that was saved for you. You need to build your own house on that land."

My heart has never opened. When I remember what happened to me, I have a wound in my heart. People ask me why I avoid my family, and I tell them, "If you knew what happened to me there, you wouldn't ask me that question."

Lately, though, I can feel the spirit of my people calling me. They tell me no, home is home. Come back.

–

CHILDHOOD AND FIRST TIMES

Someone tried to seduce me on my first day in Form One. He was the Head Boy. I was very bemused by the whole thing, because here was this guy with a very hair-tonic'd afro.

The afro died in 1979, and in 1984 the world had gone the opposite direction to great extremes. We were now coming to the curly-kit and the box-cut. The word 'afro' had disappeared from the Universe, and people who had afros had all been killed—just picked up and thrown in the river and they all died—because surely they could not have an afro! So, to a thirteen year old boy who had older cousins and uncles who were trying to insist on the idea of an afro, this was making me physically sick, it made me want to go to hospital.

So this guy with an afro and a bounce comes to my mother as I arrived in the school. I was terrified, because this was a boy's high school and I had come with a nice car. A CEO car, with your mother who is very, very, very brown and foreign looking with hair like a Somali. And I was sitting in the back with my metal box, just looking like a beating was waiting for me, and I knew it. So this guy sauntered to the car and I saw red.

"Oh! Look at that nice, young man!" my mother said.

And I just wanted to run.

"My name is Charles [redacted], and I'm the Head Boy in this school, and we're here to protect and serve, blah, blah…and your son will be taken care of. Bye!"

So my mother left me there with my cakes, peanut butter, jam and orange juice in my box, and I was negotiating 5,000 things in my mind as I was following Charles. I was given 3 bars of soap, a blanket, a spoon and a mug, and he took me to my dorm. When he entered the dorm with me following behind—a softie like me—I could see everyone peering in the corridor.

He said, "If you have any problem, come and see me. Come and see me for cocoa in my study before supper", and then he left.

"This is great!" I thought.

Yes, this is very good. I now have protection from the Head Boy. I sat there smugly, waiting for supper until a Form Two came along and said, "Aha! So you think you're…", and I got a slap, a few head-butts and a beating, and then I was sent out to get water for a Form Two who wanted to brush his teeth.

After supper, I went to the Form Four studies and said, "I'm looking for the Head Boy's cubicle."

I got into his study and he was there. He showed me his photo album. "This is me playing volleyball…"

He made cocoa, a quarter loaf of bread with margarine and said, "Do you want some peanuts?" then quickly countered with, "Oh, you can't have peanuts, because they're a stimulant!" then he giggled.

I wondered how a peanut could be a stimulant, but I didn't ask. I just sat there. So we drank the cocoa, and he told me how he became the Head Boy. As he was talking, his hand touched my thigh. I was very uncomfortable, but I thought to myself, "You've seen the way men in rural areas hold hands, they touch each other. Just because you didn't do that in primary school doesn't mean it's not done here. This is a good person."

But then the hand kept moving up, and it entered into my shorts. I said to myself, "OK, it's not that I think he's not a good person, it's that I can't sit here any more. It's me who can't do this. I can't do this!"

So, I ran for the door. He met me at the door, grabbed me very hard and whispered in a very harsh voice, "You can't tell anybody!"

Until that point, I'd thought it was me who had a problem. I thought it was me who was too shy, and not integrating into high school life, but when he said that, that's when I realized, "Oooooh!"

On my way to prep that night, I passed through the urinal. While I'm taking a piss I studied the graffiti on the urinal walls, and there was a penis and a hole drawn on the wall. Next to it was scrawled, "CHARLES ██████ IS A HOMOSEXUAL!"

And I thought, "Oho!"

I got to class and whispered fiercely to my best friend—who was a Mummy's boy like me: "A HOMOSEXUAL! THE HEAD BOY IS A HOMOSEXUAL, AND HE TRIED TO HOMOSEX ME!"

We got out of the class, and he made me tell him the whole story. I had made up my mind that I was going to leave the school —from that day on, every time I'd tell anyone that story and mention that Charles had offered me peanuts, people would gasp, "Stimulant!"

I hadn't unpacked yet, so I planned to just pick up a few things from my box, I knew where the exit was, and I was going to leave. I was going to find a phone booth, call home and say, "There's a homosexual chasing me, and I can't do it."

At 11pm, my best friend came to the dorm with two guys. They found my bed and whispered, "Get out."

We got out and went to a study within the house. Inside was the Deputy Prefect. My best friend told me, "Tell him."

I told the Deputy Prefect the whole story—they gasped at the stimulant. When I was done, he said, "This is what we're going to do. The next time he calls you, don't go. Pretend everything is OK but come to me."

A few weeks later, the Deputy Prefect informed me that there was a case against Charles, and I was a witness. After prep, I was called for the meeting, and that was the first time I heard what homosexuality was. There were other people there, giving evidence:

"He slept with me in the volleyball court."

"He made me a prefect."

"He used to buy me masala chips."

My head was malfunctioning. There were four prefects there who had been 'promoted' by Charles. We were in that room until 3 in the morning. I wasn't traumatized, sorry to say—I wish I was—I was riveted. I was so impressed by the drama in these people's lives. I didn't have fucking drama! I'd never kissed anyone, and people are just screwing around me.

After everyone was done, we were sent away and the prefects went to see the Headmaster. The next morning, the School Chaplain—a short, aggressive guy who loved talking about sex all the time because he was the Chaplain and he could get away with anything—stood up at assembly:

"We have been having an epidemic of homosexuality. Blah, blah, blah… Charles ██████ has been expelled from this school and is demoted as Head Boy. Because he has registered for the final exams, he has to come back and complete them. But I urge you boys to be VIGILANT!"

After that, Charles became a whole different thing to me. In my head, I was thinking Charles was evil and he was fucking people in the volleyball court, but he came back after two weeks to do his exams, and I found the ensuing drama very hard to deal with.

He used to stay in his study because he wasn't allowed to stay in the dorm. He'd walk to the dining room and people would just spit on him. He didn't talk to a single person, and he sat it out. I used to see that guy walking. He never used to turn back, he'd put his head up and walk.

I wanted to say hi, and I couldn't say hi. I just felt shit about the whole thing. He finished his exams, and he passed and went to University.

Years later, I saw him coming out of a bus and I thought, "This is your chance. Just say hello to him. This is your chance."

I had never connected Charles with sexual feelings at all, but I just didn't like the humiliation. There's something I wanted to tell him, but I didn't know what I wanted to tell him. But he left, and I DIDN'T SAY HELLO.

–

MY FRIEND AND I were the two most effeminate boys in the class. Kids would bully us because we couldn't play soccer, we didn't run fast enough, our school bags were too bright, we couldn't lift as many things, we were too clean, too neat, too organized! Even when being bullied, we were not expected to cry. Which is insane, right? It was crazy. We got used to being bullied. We knew how to minimize the damage from being beaten up—hiding your face so there wouldn't be bruises. If it was the taunting, we knew not to respond at all. We waited for it to just end, because we knew we were going home at the end of the day and the bullying was not going to FOLLOW US THERE.

–

I HAD MY FIRST GAY EXPERIENCE when I was about thirteen years old. It was with an older boy from the neighbourhood, his name was Dan. When I was young, I was much 'queen-ier' than I am now. Dan was one of those boys who would look after me in the neighbourhood. When other boys wanted to harass me, he would come to my rescue. So we became friends and then we started watching movies together.

The movies evolved from Cynthia Rothrock movies, which I hated! Some actress from the 90s. She was the female Van Damme, and I'm telling you Cynthia Rothrock was a lesbian!

We evolved from those movies to more intimate things, and then from that to full-on porn. I had never had an orgasm, and he said he could show me how to. So he masturbated me, and then he masturbated himself. And later I did it to him.

It happened a couple of times, and then it just stopped. In retrospect, I think he felt like what we were doing was wrong. He started avoiding me, and a year later my family moved out and we never SAW EACH OTHER AGAIN.

–

MY FRIEND AND I were the gayest boys in our very small school—not openly gay in a sexual way, though. Somehow, it became a position of influence. It was actually an advantage to be gay. We got the whole school to watch Spanish soap operas—even the senior students. Whatever movie or DVD the entertainment prefect brought was watched after the soap was done. Boys love soaps—it's just that hard mentality that keeps them away. We also got people to listen to pop and rock—we were not here for ragga or anything like that. We made the whole school listen to 'The Emancipation Of Mimi'[1] over and over WHEN THAT ALBUM CAME OUT.

–

I REALIZED I WAS GAY in high school, although even earlier in primary school I had noticed I didn't have feelings for boys. But I fought it, tried resisting it and I constantly asked myself what was wrong with me for being attracted to girls. So I didn't want to act on it even though I felt as if I couldn't help but have those feelings.

1. Tenth studio album by American singer-songwriter Mariah Carey.

While in high school, I had a crush on a friend of mine. At the time I didn't know anything about being a lesbian or being gay and it felt to me as though I had a disorder. The school was very strict and I thought I was the only one who had these types of feelings so I couldn't open up about it. I really liked her and I had to live with the fact that I could not tell her how I felt.

It wasn't all bad though, I had friends I was really close to and we would pass notes to each other in class. I don't know whether they were love notes or not, but it was fun all the same. Those were awesome times. But there was this one time the principal called an assembly and said there were lesbian cliques in the school. She asked the prefects to compile a list of names of the girls involved and I happened to be on the list. I think the only reason I was on that list is because I had a friend who I was really close to and we spent a lot of time together, so I guess people figured we were lesbians.

Then I was implicated by five more girls. I remember the principal asked me, "What do girls see in you?"

It was a hurtful thing to say, and I didn't take kindly to that. There were a lot of consequences to being labelled a lesbian, I was the Deputy Head Girl but I got demoted after that. We were all asked to bring our parents to school the next term because of it, and so when I went home I made sure I told my parents, but I gave them a different story. I denied the whole thing. I remember telling my dad how absurd the accusations were and pointed to the fact I had a boyfriend as proof. At the time, I felt it would have been better to go through all these things for something I had actually done. I was being punished because of a rumour, I wished I had acted on my feelings and was getting punished for that instead.

I really liked that friend of mine though. I felt she liked me too but I was never sure. We were both afraid of saying it, at least that's how I felt. So we used to express our feelings in writing, we would exchange notes saying how much we cared for each other and how we would always be there for each other. She would tell me how much she loved me. It's normal for girls to say 'I love you' to each other. So I would say it back, but it meant more to me when I said it, because I knew I felt it for real. She finished school before me, I was really sad about it and I never saw her again.

After high school, I dated a man because I didn't want to accept I was gay. I didn't like it, I was not into him and I felt I couldn't go on living a lie. I didn't want to cheat on him. So I ended things between us. I began reading up about being a lesbian on the internet and I found there were people who were like me and that it's normal to be like this. I began accepting myself AND THE SITUATION RELUCTANTLY.

–

I WAS REALLY GOOD in some subjects at school, so I was tutoring kids in classes below and above me and even my own classmates. It reached a point where I used to take the class if the teacher wasn't in for a particular session. My fellow students even preferred it when I taught. That's where I had my first fling with this guy in my class. He was a sportsman—basketball and football especially—and he was really good. I used to tutor him in Geography at night after preps, and that's how I got to know that there was more to these jocks than just sports.

He was really funny and charming. We were studying one night in an empty class, and then talking, and I was just overcome with emotions and hormones and everything—I turned and just kissed him, right on the lips. Then I pulled back in shock because I couldn't believe what I had just done, preparing myself for the beating of my life. Then he pulled me towards him and kissed me for a really long time.

Once the lights went out suddenly in class during preps. The class was full and he used to sit on the other side of the class. So it got really dark, and he came across the class through the rows of kids to kiss me there and then. IT WAS SO FUCKING ROMANTIC.

–

MY EARLIEST MEMORY of being attracted to a boy is when I realized I had a crush on our class prefect. We were in Standard 4. I also used to collect pictures of men, hide them inside my geometrical set and look at them when I was alone. I didn't know how to go about it, it felt strange. I did not understand how or why I was attracted to men.

I got my first kiss in Standard 6, from the school Head Boy. I think he was in love with me, at the time I didn't know whether he was gay or not but I knew he was attracted to me, he always protected me. When school was out he would tell me not to go home immediately, as he wanted to see me or talk to me and it was on one such occasion, at around 7 in the evening that he kissed me.

At first I was scared, but later on I liked it. And we continued making out on different occasions, then we moved on to touching later. He was in Standard 7 at the time, this continued till he finished primary school and carried on all through his high school education, till he went to university. I NEVER SAW HIM AGAIN AFTER THAT.

–

WHEN I WAS ELEVEN OR TWELVE, all the guys were getting really excited about girls. I got pretty excited about girls, but not that much. It wasn't that exciting.

The girls were interested in the guys, and those guys were interested in those girls, and I wasn't part of that equation. At the time, I thought that it was because I was fat. I was a fat kid.

The first guy who hit on me—let's call him Chris—walked up to me and grabbed my nuts. He was the sort of guy who all the girls liked, and all the boys, too. They used to follow him around. I used to avoid him. I was scared of him because he was big and rough. The school used to show us movies every Saturday evening, and one such evening people were milling around waiting for the movie to begin.

Chris walked up to me and just grabbed my nuts! I looked around, because there were guys all around us, wondering—are you guys seeing this guy grabbing my nuts, and you guys call me gay? Everyone acted like it hadn't happened, except Chris' friend who was standing next to him. He started saying, "Oh, my God! You guys are gay, you guys are gay!" and he was running around, laughing and Chris chased him.

I just stood there, stunned. I wanted to talk to him about what he'd just done. I wasn't angry, I wanted to see where he was going with that idea. We talked about it a little, and found out that we both wanted to do something. We left the hall where the movie was showing, and made out.

Initially, I didn't like it. I liked the fact that we were making out, but I didn't like the guy I was making out with. The words that popped into my head when I think about it are 'hot and gluey'. I used to have some regrets about that incident, but over time it has acquired more value to me.

The first guy I hit on was in my class—let's call him Frank. We didn't get along. One day we were running into a class, and he was taking forever to get through the door. I grabbed his ass and pushed him. It wasn't deliberate, but then I became aware of him in a way that I hadn't been aware of him before.

Later on, I grabbed his nuts as well. I'd been taught how to do this. I didn't do it in public, I did it in the chapel. We were being chased around by prefects, and we ended up at the back of the chapel. I grabbed his nuts, and after some initial resistance, he let me do it. He felt me up as well. Then the 9 o'clock bell rang, and he ran off.

He avoided coming to class for a week after that, which was quite a feat—since this was a boarding school. After he started coming back to class, there was some initial tension between us. One day, we went to the school hall. It was a huge hall, and there was a backstage area where—if you closed the curtains—you had a space in which you could do things.

There was a lot of conflict in his mind about what had happened in the chapel. I reminded him that he had felt me up, too. "You let me touch you," I told him. I started to leave, but then he stopped me and tried to kiss me, and I let him. We made out for some time, and it was really nice. It wasn't 'HOT AND GLUEY'.

–

ONCE, WHEN I WAS STILL IN PRIMARY SCHOOL, my father found me plaiting a doll's hair and beat me up saying I should stop acting feminine. I love cooking and my dad didn't want me to be in the kitchen. Back in high school I used to get bullied because people thought I was too feminine. My friends were forcing me to act a certain way, and getting annoyed that I really couldn't act the way they wanted, which was the way society prefers men to act. At first, I wanted to be trans, because I couldn't see myself ever being masculine enought, but then I realized that it isn't compulsory that I give myself a gender. I don't have to. Also, my family expects me to have a child in the future and if I transition, it won't happen. So that's how I decided to remain who I am and REFUSE TO BE IDENTIFIED WITH ANY GENDER.

–

WHEN I WAS YOUNG, I used to go through these seasons when I felt like I was not a human being. I felt like all the kids around me arrived knowing what they were supposed to do with themselves, and I didn't understand how they knew, who told them, where they met. My sister was younger than me, but she knew! At that age when children know how to whistle, she knew how to whistle! And I didn't know.

I'd watch everyone and think, "These human beings are strange people."

I had that feeling as a child, and I have it now. It was the same thing with sex, or sexuality. I may have been five or six years old, and there were these guys I used to fantasize about, and I used to feel like: if that person just comes and takes me, I'll go. I'll go with that guy, and I don't understand why. It was a very strong feeling, and it was not sexual. It was just a feeling of weakness around somebody. That person just makes you feel weak and powerless, so you'd be extremely shy and awkward and not know what to do with all that information.

Somehow, at five years old, I knew that that was a problem, and I knew that I have to be dedicated to hiding it. I didn't know what a homosexual was until Form One. When you're a kid who's queer like me, you can read what's not kosher. You know what the crowd can't accept, and you know that very well, and you're always reading the crowds. If you're able to keep this thing extremely secret and fine, EVERYTHING WILL BE FINE.

–

My FIRST KISS was with a man, and I hated it. I didn't feel anything and I thought it was supposed to be like in the movies, where the girl's leg pops up during the kiss, but I felt nothing.

The first time I kissed a girl I was a little drunk, which gave me the courage to do it. I kissed her first and she kissed me back. The next day I dreaded seeing her, I thought she would feel like I had taken advantage of her. Eventually we ended up sitting next to each other and not talking. Not saying a word. So she texted me and asked me whether it really happened the previous night or it was a dream. I was afraid but I had to tell her how I felt, and it turned out she felt the same way and she liked me too. Fear had stopped us both.

The first time I fell in love was wonderful. It felt awesome; I had found what I was missing. You feel like you always want to be around this person, you can't get enough of each other. It's a beautiful feeling. The best thing in the world is loving someone who loves you back. Before, I had people in my life who loved me, but I didn't love them back. It was the first time the feeling went both ways. I had found someone who I shared the same feeling with, it was nice.

The happiest moment of my gay life was falling in love and finding someone who felt the same way I did. I never felt like this with a man. It wasn't until I understood myself that I let go; NOW I'M HAPPY.

–

I CAME ACROSS my first gay magazine when I was fourteen. Some man used to sell it just outside a supermarket. I saw the cover and wondered why does that magazine had a half-naked guy on the cover? I must investigate. I flipped through it and realized it was a magazine for homosexuals, and I must read it, I must have it.

I told that man to keep it for me, I'd come back for it the next day. And I did. It was 100 bob. I went through it and this was my first time to realize that there were gay people and lesbians out there, and I'm not the only one.

I was in a boys' school and I was effeminate, and I suffered for that. For being this girly boy. "Why can't you be manly like the other boys?"

My school-work really suffered. My relationship with teachers, which affected my relationship with my parents because they were constantly being called to school about my conduct.

I had to pick and choose. Do I sit here and stay in the bloodshed, or do I go to my happy place? For me, my happy place was away from school. It was in books, it was in magazines, it was on TV. I was addicted to TCM. It was my solace. Lots of Sidney Sheldon, John Grisham. Jackie Collins was my friend. I'd get through a book in a day, I don't do that any more.

It was a better world to be at than real life. It was the most tumultuous time of my life, and I was forced to grow up really quick—especially from an emotional and spiritual point of view. Not so much in a physical sense, because I was really tiny. But my spirit and my emotions and my mental state were forced TO GROW UP FAST.

–

I'M GAY. I noticed that when I was in my early years in primary. I found myself not doing the things that normal boys were doing. I was kind of different. The kind of games I was interested in were different. I remember at some point, some of the students wanted to find out whether I'm a boy or a girl. They told me I walk and talk like a girl. I don't know how I used to walk, or how they wanted me to walk.

The first time I got intimate with a guy was after high school; we had gone for a neighbour's burial ceremony. There was a guy there. I don't know how he noticed me, he just walked up and started a conversation. When he first kissed me, I was so nervous, I didn't even feel it. I couldn't believe I was kissing a man. I thought everyone would know what I did. When I got home, I went straight to bed, I couldn't have dinner with my family, I FELT SO GUILTY.

–

When I was in primary school in Standard 8 and I had this ultra-masculine male teacher who used to teach us mathematics. He had a deep voice, he was very aggressive, and he would carry his personality around overwhelming everyone. One day, he came to my desk to mark my paper, I think he came to point out a mistake or something. Then something happened, I had a pair of dividers in my hand and his hand was on the desk. I fidgeted and I just stabbed his hand. I stabbed him so deep, he really bled. I think it was a reflex action. He got really angry, he swelled up like a big, black cloud and I HAD AN ORGASM RIGHT THERE!

I loved high school. In high school being gay wasn't an identity yet. It was me and my thing. My weird little thing that I did when there was a blackout. I would meet these other boys, and together we would enter into this naughty space. It was a boy thing.

I think when you give it the language and the definitions, it loses its flavour and that's why I hated the idea of being called gay. I don't know how to express it, but yeah. I like it when it is not defined, it becomes something that you just do.

When I was in Form One, I was very shy and effeminate. Extremely effeminate. They used to call me '*manzi wa Form One*' [the Form One girl]. I had a classmate called Omanga. I would always tease him; tapping his thighs and groping him, making naughty jokes. Surprisingly, he was OK with it and he didn't mind it at all.

He asked if I wanted to touch him, and I touched him every so often. He touched me also. He had many girlfriends, and for him, what we were doing was never 'this is who I am'. For us, it was just messing around, not really caring or playing to definitions. We always walked away from this, back to normal life. I liked it because it was naughty and uncomplicated. When you start to give this thing a language, it becomes complicated and intense.

Later, in Form Four, there was this guy who used to play basketball. I would go into a craze and turn dim every time I met him. He was a guy's guy; masculine, muscles, six-pack and everything. He was also a very kind gentleman and a fine face. I remember I was always unable to talk to him without my heart racing. One day I was walking behind him, and he just turned and said hi! I was holding my keys, and my voice went away. I lost my coordination and flung my bunch of keys at him. They hit him hard on the head and he really laughed. He laughed and laughed at me. I used to panic every time I spoke to him. I really used to think about him.

In the weekend outside school, when I would see him on a street, I would look for an escape to avoid meeting him. One time I could not find an escape, I met him, he said hello and I just burst into tears and started to cry. I really don't know how I got over this guy. I am kinda over him now. He is a great guy. We keep in touch and he has become a good friend. But I HAVE SINCE MOVED ON FROM THAT STATE.

–

I HAD A PAINFUL CHILDHOOD; I was always insulted by the other boys because I think they noticed I was different. I didn't play sports with them, I rarely socialized with them, I always hung out with girls. So I feared going to high school. And it was the worst period of my life; I was always insulted by the male students. It was a mixed school. I hated that period. They would ask to see me naked when I went to the bathroom to check and see if I was really a man.

Then I went to boarding school and I didn't feel safe because the boys knew I was different. They used to say, "*Tumepata kadame sasa.*" We've found ourselves a girl now.

They would bother me a lot, especially at night. They tried forcing themselves on me, they denied me my privacy. I feared they were going to rape me, so I decided to go to day school. This was different because even though I felt safe I still got ridiculed for not engaging in 'masculine' things. So to avoid it all, I stayed away from the boys. Even though I liked learning, I ENDED UP HATING GOING TO SCHOOL.

–

MY HIGH SCHOOL was very easy to sneak out of. It had no gates. There were rules about getting permission slips, but in truth, if you were a nice, shiny boy with no pimples you could get out. If I walked to the entrance on a Thursday afternoon and bumped into a teacher and said, "I have no classes, and I'm just going to the library," no one would ask.

I used to go to the ████ Library. Things have changed now—those days, libraries used to order books. Even hardcover ones from abroad. I used to go there, browse through and pick some books, buy chips on the way back and go back to school.

On this particular day, I didn't stop at the usual fish and chips shop, I decided to get some roast meat near the bus stop. It was 3pm and there was nobody in this joint. It was just me and this guy wearing a white overall with no shirt inside it. He had a big smile, and he was very beautiful. For the first time in a long time, I was very, very uncomfortable inside that place and I didn't understand why.

I tried to read my novel—the one thing I know in the Universe is that when I'm inside my novel, everything else becomes vague—but I felt like he was hovering. I could hear him saying things, and the stereo becoming louder and louder. I ordered a little meat and I was sitting there. He asked me if I wanted a beer. I said no, and ordered a Fanta with a straw.

He had a drum on a fire, and he was boiling something in that drum. My memory gets weird here. It seemed like he was putting his arm into the oil and coming up with something that looked like granules. I don't know what it was. What I remember is that he was performing it. He was trying to get my attention because I was not concentrating, and when he put his hand into the oil I freaked out and stood up. He put his hand into it again and again. I was next to death. I ate my meat and went back to school, and the next day I went back to the library for twenty minutes and went back to that place. For weeks, I used up all my pocket money, just going there to watch his performances. He was beautiful; muscular, and he knew that he was hot. He just knew.

I knew that he was asking me something and I was refusing to answer, but I kept going back, and I never answer. I knew that for sure. Years later, I went back to look for that bar, looking for that guy. I can see him even now, I can even draw him. We never had a conversation at all, never. But I felt like he'd told me, "Anything here is game."

Once he told me he lived upstairs. I could have done anything. All he needed to do—the fucker—was tell me, "*Twende.*" Let's go.

–

There was this guy I kind of had a thing with, and one night I refused to give him a hand-job. In retaliation, the next day he went and told everyone that I was queer. Then everyone in school refused to talk to me. It was so bad. During the holiday after that term, I met this girl and we became friends. When we went back to school she started sending me letters. In high school the letters are presented in class, and so everyone was wondering who was writing to me. My desk-mate asked to read the letter, and then told everyone that I had a girlfriend, and everyone started talking to me again.

Then one day the guy who started the rumours walked up to me and asked to stand in front of me one day in the lunchtime queue. He unzipped my fly and started jerking me off in the lunchtime queue. No one could see what we were doing, even though it was in public. I zipped up quickly, and he went to be with his friends, and I went to sit with mine.

–

When I was about eleven, I had started to develop sexual feelings, but I didn't know what they were until one day, when I was watching a TV show with my older brother. There was some show with two guys, a girl and a pizza place or something. That episode that day had a gay guy in the show. I kept hearing the word 'gay', but I didn't know what it was. So I asked my brother what the word 'gay' meant. He very nonchalantly said, "That's when a man likes another man. Like, he's attracted to another man."

The instant he said it I thought, "Oh! So that's what I am then?"

That's when it dawned on me and made sense to me. I guess when you're a child you don't really question it too much until there's suddenly a terminology for it. The same instant that I knew that I was gay, I knew that it needed to be a secret because I started to notice people's attitudes and reactions towards it. I was an effeminate child growing up, and I was always reprimanded about it. Now, I wonder if being effeminate as a child and being gay as an adult are connected somehow. I'm not a hundred percent sure.

I remember the first person that I ever told this secret was my best friend Frank. I had never imagined that I would ever tell anybody this 'secret' that I needed to live with for the rest of my life. I think being secretive about a part of you tends to make you a very isolated and introverted person. At least, I felt that's what it did for me. It made me instantly very introverted because I never really felt I could share with anybody who I really was. I was constantly acting on a daily basis and that MADE ME FEEL VERY ALIENATED.

–

THE FIRST FOUR YEARS of primary school were quite difficult. My classmates started to zone in on how different I was and then that became a constant issue, on a daily basis. I was bullied quite intensely for the first four years of my life in primary school. That was between ages seven and ten. I had to be transferred from that first school, because I started to develop ulcers when I was ten years old. It was so bad that kids would call my house and tell me, "Wait until you get to school, we're going to kick your ass," and that was before I even got to school.

The bullying escalated to being physical. I have a scar on my forehead from a time when I was walking to my desk and I was tripped by another student. I fell and happened to land forehead-first into the corner of a desk. My forehead split open and blood was gushing out. It wasn't a happy time for me, and it caused me a lot of anxiety which I think I still carry today.

Young kids can be so evil to each other. There was a group of four kids who specifically used to really bully me. They made every single day of my primary school life hell. One day, as I was having lunch, they came into the canteen—I used to go and eat lunch later than everybody else so I could avoid being bullied.

They came in and found me sitting there, and they dragged me into the bathroom. The leader of that gang started peeing in the urinal and made the other guys bring me over to him. He made me drink his urine. I must have been eight years old, and I was so scared of what they would do to me if I didn't do it. Even now, when I think about it my heart starts racing because I remember how terrified I was. They all burst out laughing as they watched me do it. People don't really realize what kind of traumatizing things could be happening to their kids at that age. There's a lot of fucked up things that can happen to kids and I think people need to be aware of that.

Over time, I realized that I needed to eradicate the procedure where I'd meet people and become friends with them and—by not telling them I'm gay from the get-go—I have this secret that I need to tell them at some point, and I'd worry about their reactions. So I started introducing myself with, "Hello, my name is ████████, I'm this tall and I'm also gay."

Then, it wasn't an issue any more because they'd know from the start, so they were either going to get to know me knowing that, or we were not going to spend time around each other. With that realization came the knowledge that even dealing with bullies was much easier if I'd say, "Yes I'm gay, and yes you can have comments but I don't care. You can all go fuck yourselves."

At first, my high school classmates couldn't believe my gay friends and I were open about it, but it worked. I think that took a lot of the power from the bullies because we could sit at the back of the bus and just shout, "Fuck it!"

The word had no more power. We were able to say, "Yes I am gay, would you like to have a conversation about it?"

We sort of had fun with it then at that point. I remember I loved my sociology classes—especially when we were studying gender—because I was able to talk about my sexuality in a classroom and discuss it very openly with our lecturer, which I felt was very empowering. That definitely helped me really grow in that ability to identify myself in a healthy way. To do that at that age made me feel very lucky. If you're able to stand up to a bully and you don't let them rule your life with fear, you open up a whole different set of interactions and you're able to then brush things off your shoulder and move on. You're able to focus on the relationships that you should be growing rather than constantly being freaked out by all THE NEGATIVE RELATIONSHIPS AROUND YOU.

–

MY FIRST KISS was also my most memorable. I was in high school, and I was so into this one guy who was Mr. Popular. He was super-smart, good at sports and was dating one of the prettiest girls in school. We ended up becoming friends because we were all part of the same clique. I had told the girl that he was dating at that time that I had a huge crush on him. Once, while he was drunk, he told his girlfriend that he wouldn't mind kissing me. He told his girlfriend that. She came and told me what he said, and decided to hatch a plan to get us to kiss. A few months later, we were having a party at a friend's house, and a group of about five or six of us decided to play 'spin the bottle'. His girlfriend spun the bottle and it landed on him, and she dared him to kiss me. She said, "You guys have to kiss for fifteen seconds!"

So we leaned in and started to kiss, and it was really nice. Everyone started counting down and when they got to zero we kept on going and we kept on making out and it was so insane. I was a million miles away from my body but in my body at the same time. I remember feeling dizzy when we finally stopped. He stood up and we both couldn't believe that happened. After that, we went back to being friends. I do remember him saying that I was one of HIS TOP THREE KISSES EVER.

–

I FOUND OUT I WAS GAY when I was twelve. I used to enjoy playing with girls, and I used to really like men. I'm still like that now. My mum owns rental houses. Our caretaker's son was the same age as me, but he was a little more mature. I used to be fat when I was young, and he used to enjoy poking me. He'd corner me in his house, and touch me all over, then he'd let me go.

One evening—when no one was home—we came back home and he locked me in his room as usual. I thought it was the usual thing, that he'd touch me and let me go. But this time it was different; he applied saliva on his dick and fucked me. Three days later, we did it again. We kept on doing this until one day my grandmother caught us. She telephoned my mother and told her, "Your son is gay."

My mother moved me out of that compound and brought me here, but I ACTUALLY BECAME NAUGHTIER HERE *[laughs]*.

–

I KNEW I WAS GAY as early as six or seven, but I first acted on it when I was twenty-two years. I never had sex until I was twenty-two. I knew that I was gay, but I never actualized it. I knew how you could have sex with women, but I knew that wasn't who I was. I knew I was attracted to men but I never knew what you could do with that man once you got him. There was even a man I loved, but I didn't know exactly what I wanted with him.

I grew up in Western Kenya, and I never heard anyone talk about homosexuality, although I knew that homosexuality existed. So I thought something was really wrong with me. When I was sixteen I came to know of an elderly guy who used to bathe at the river—it was a stream where we used to swim, and men used to bathe there in the evening. This guy would go there in the morning. Many young boys knew that he would come at that time, and he would come with a lot of coins. If you showed him your ass, he would throw you fifty cents. That was the perspective I had of homosexuals.

In the village they would use that guy to scare young children. If you cried as a child, you were told that they would call that old guy to come and eat you up. He was viewed as a mad man. That for me was totally a struggle, because I knew I would grow up to be like him—a mad man—and that is not what I wanted. So all my life I never shared my feelings. I lived with this struggle. I kept wondering; what will happen if my parents knew about it? What will happen if my friends know? I grew up a very introverted person. I never played childhood games. I never had childhood friends. I never played with boys, because I was afraid that I was different. I didn't want the other kids to know my fears. I secretly planned to commit suicide because I didn't want to grow up to be different—because the only picture on my mind was of this 'mad man'.

Three times I tried to take my life, but it never worked. All this time, I had never had sex. When I was twenty-two, I went to live in ████████. I worked as a shoe-shiner on the streets there. I met a guy there on the streets. He was very manly and smart. I think he noticed that I was attracted to him. I discovered he was also very friendly and secretive. This made me comfortable with him. We became friends, and I told him what was happening to me. He told me that was very difficult, but he offered to introduce me to someone who could help. He had a friend who was an apostle.

Around 7.30pm when I had closed my stand, he took me to a café. The owner there was very nice to us and offered us food. He told me to come back at 9pm. So I went home and came back at 9pm—this time on my own. When I got there, the café owner closed the cafe, and asked me to join him in a room within the café. It was strange because I did not know what to do. Inside the room, he switched off the lights and he started to touch me. He told me what to do and where to touch. That was my first time.

I didn't like him, though. He was not my type of guy. To make it worse, my friend who had introduced me said that the café owner was an apostle. I got very disappointed. For me it was a very difficult time because I was looking up to God for deliverance. A man of God would have helped me out but it was my first time and he was a man of God. It really broke my heart. He kept looking for me after that, but I avoided. He would sit at my stall waiting for me, but I would find a way to leave. He finally realized I was not interested in him, so he introduced me to another religious person—apparently a musician.

I liked this second guy. He was very talkative, and he knew how to make me happy. Even when I was at his house, he was not in a hurry to have sex with me. So I liked him because he was taking things step by step. He invited me over to his house. The first night we did not have sex, but we did on the second night. He was a nice guy, so we dated until I turned twenty-five. Then I moved to Mombasa.

We drifted apart, and then I met another guy at the beach when I was twenty-six. It was 10am and I had gone swimming, then it started to rain. The beach was deserted. I took shelter from the rain under some trees, and a white guy joined me. I had never interacted with a white guy before, and I didn't know what to say. I didn't know what to say but the look in his eyes showed that he wanted me to say something.

I said hello and asked him, "Where do you stay?"

He said, "Shanzu. I am here for a short while. I'm German."

I had come out from the water and my body was wet. My pants were clinging to my body, and he could see the whole of me. He asked whether he could touch me. I was nervous, but I let him because we were alone on the beach. He realized I was nervous and he asked whether I would like to meet some other time. We agreed to meet at the same place, same time the next day. We met the next day, and he took me to his apartment and we had sex. I was with him for many years UNTIL I MET MY CURRENT BOYFRIEND.

–

HIGH SCHOOL WAS TOUGH for me. I've never been one to wear skirts or wear my hair long. No one gave me the memo that I need to change myself to fit in. Baggy pants, sneakers and a hoodie; that was me. When I went to high school, everyone said, "There's that chick who is a lesbian."

I was judged without even being asked. No one even bothered to ask me about me. They made up their mind. I played basketball, I danced, I looked like a boy, therefore I had to be a lesbian. I couldn't trust the other girls. I'd talk to them and they'd tell the other girls what I had said. I stopped talking to people and I started writing. Then I met a girl, and I liked her and she liked me back. She was in the Christian Union, and we started talking, and it was great.

Somewhere along the way, I felt comfortable enough to kiss her, and then I freaked the fuck out. I remember we were in the computer lab, and she was trying to get her project done. I sat next to her, put my hand on her chin and drew her in. I kissed her. I'm a romantic little fucker. I kissed her and the moment I moved away from her and I saw the look on her face. I thought, "I really enjoyed that... What the fuck did I JUST DO, OH GOD I'M GOING TO HELL!"

So I freaked out, and I ran out. After that things were weird between us. I never really got her back. We kinda drifted, then she left. We used to go to the same church, and I'd see her and she'd see me, and...it's wasn't worth it. I'll never talk to her. There's a day she called me and said, "I really like you and I want to see your face," and I quoted an Usher song to her: 'Let It Burn'. I thought I was cool, but I was just being an idiot. Let it burn? What the fuck? She got married to some guy, and now I don't know where she is.

The second time I liked a girl was a year later. I fell hard for this girl who was in my year. She was cute and smart. I was seventeen. One day I told her, "You and I need to talk."

So I sat her down and told her that I had feelings for her. I said, "I don't know how this will work, and I don't expect you to have feelings for me, but I needed to tell you."

She told me to get the fuck out, so I left. We didn't talk until after we finished high school. Now we flirt. Ten years down the line, we're flirting. She's had a child and NOW she wants to be experimental with her sexuality.

There are many girls I was in high school with who would gossip about me being gay, and now years later they find me on Facebook, and all of a sudden I have become fun and interesting to them. A few of them apologized for how they treated me in high school. Don't apologize to me, unless you plan on taking us back to that point in time WHEN IT MATTERED.

–

IDENTITY

I ALWAYS SAY I was raised as my father's son. I was the first-born, and I have brothers who follow me, but I was always my father's son. So even exploring femininity has always been a push and pull for me because I was also raised to be a mother and a wife. I remember when I was little we would be outside planting, and I hated it so much. It was such a chore. My dad was inside reading the newspaper and I just wanted to be a man so that I could do what I wanted. African women are raised from childhood to belong to a man and to children. Nothing in between. We can't belong to ourselves, and when we try, we're told we're being selfish. Also they will call you a 'girl' for as long as you do not belong to a man, and say you are not a woman until you belong to a man. Men are—apparently—the only ones who can give women legitimacy as a human being. We cannot be human without someone. My mother has been a widow for twenty years and she told me how at church she's in some groups, and sometimes they forget she's a widow. And that it was difficult at first. There are heteronormative privileges everywhere that you have to contend with. It's jarring in so many ways.

They still call me a girl because I have not been married, but I have felt I have been married. My significant relationships have been a union. They have been marriages for me. So when I am called a girl because I haven't had a husband, it really pisses me off.

The many people who give me unsolicited advice have been telling me to have a child because it will do wonders for me and will be that amazing thing that will make me rise up every day and fight the battle. There is another idea that you cannot be complete without a child of your own. The way for me to be legitimate as a woman without a husband, they say, is to have a child. That's the way they measure it. But most of our parents came from large families, so maybe that is where that comes from. The idea that you are responsible for yourself and are deliberate in your own happiness is the epitome of selfishness. How dare you just want to do it for you? You are only important when you are responsible for someone else. I went to see a doctor with pain from my fibroids and he asked me if I had children. I said no. He asked me why I didn't have children. Didn't I think I should have a child? He really insisted. It was a horrible consultation. Horrible, horrible. I went home in tears.

I think a lot of this pain from my fibroids is because of having to be here, having to explore this space in a woman's body, having to internalise all this shit from everywhere, and having to be silent and mute and not take ownership of my happiness. So even though I started having fibroids a long time ago, I decided not to have surgery because I wanted to understand what was happening to my body. I was fine for a while, and then suddenly the pain became unbearable again. I thought, "Something isn't right. I am not in balance. I am responding to this societal shit. I'm not practising self-love on a consistent basis, and that's why my body IS DOING WHAT IT'S DOING."

–

I AM A HOMOSEXUAL MAN. I like to say that I am a homosexual, because it's a word that people feel others shouldn't say.

"Oh my God, you're degrading yourself."

"You shouldn't say it with so much pride."

"You shouldn't say it in the open."

But it is what it is. I am a bloody homosexual, and I love it. People shouldn't tell me how to use what I am, and who I am and how I should say it.

The scariest thing is when you say it among homosexuals, and they react like that. That is the most tragic thing; that homosexuals are the most SCARED OF IT THEMSELVES.

–

WHILE I WAS GROWING UP, I was a boy and that was OK. But then I hit puberty and—ugh—boobs and things appeared, and I had to be a girl, because that's what I was. There was no pressure to be a girl, we were just kids who were let to be whatever we wanted to be. How I dressed was decided by my mum. She didn't want me to look like a boy, because everyone was calling me a boy. Where I come from, people refer to you as 'son-of', or 'daughter-of' your mum or your dad. People used to call me 'son-of' and it didn't sit well with my mum. She really tried to make me girlish.

I remember back in primary school, we would go to Sunday school, and we had these plays; competitions with other churches. I never played female roles. They never let me. Sunday school was for everyone—boys and girls—but the teachers would give me the male roles. Our teacher was my mum's friend and my mum would ask her, "*Mbona huyu anapewa roles za kijana tu?*" Why does this one always get male roles?

My teacher would reply, "She does those ones better."

All these people from my neighborhood still call me 'son-of' to date. I was home in April this year, and the lady that we've grown up around—a family friend, an old grandma—still tells me, "You know you are your mother's son? You're supposed to be the man of that house."

I've been told such things all my life and it was never a problem, but my mum didn't like it. I was having a conversation with her recently— now she can talk, because she's not as angry as she was back then—and she was telling me how much she used to hate it when people referred to me as a boy. She would beat me for being a boy. She wanted me to be her daughter. When someone called me 'son-of' she would say, "No, no, no! This is a girl!' and people would say, "Oh! But she looks like a boy..."

Being called a boy wasn't happening so much in school, because there I had to wear a dress and the boys were wearing shorts. When I hit puberty—and it was early for me—I was about 11, and things started to become difficult. At age 11 the change was still happening slowly, so I didn't have issues, I was still playing games with the boys like I used to, but then I got to an age where things had to change.

I didn't know what to expect at puberty. We were taught what to expect, so I knew they were going to come, but I hoped that maybe they would skip me. I would sleep and pray that the change wouldn't happen, but it happened anyway, because I wasn't in control of it. I just ignored the changes until I couldn't.

Boobs. Periods. You can't ignore them.

So, now I'm a girl, and I have to be like girls. I was in a girls' school and there was pressure to be a girl. I used to really try to be like a girl. I literally used to practice walking like a girl, it was that bad. I would see the other girls at school and I would think, "I want to be like that girl, I want to be a girl like that."

I would observe what they did, and I would go back home, and I would try to do those things. I would buy myself lip balm and lipstick and do my nails and then tell my mum that I wanted to do my hair, but I hated the way it looked and when it was time to go back to school, I'd say, "No, I want to shave."

So, we'd go back to the beginning.

Even with all that practice—and me thinking I was getting better at it—people would still say to me that I looked like a guy who was trying to be a girl. I would go to school and shave my head and people would say, " You look like Kanye West, without the beard."

I would protest, "No! Can't you see my face? I have lip balm!" I would actually go for the shiny lip balm, not the neutral one. The really shiny, sparkly one. "I'm a girl, can't you see?"

It was a hard time.

Once, while I was in Form Two, a friend of mine told me she thought that I should choose my gender. She told me that I looked confused about my gender and that I should choose. I was 14 at the time. I asked, "Do I have an option? Is there another option? Is this something I choose or it's just there?"

I had no idea. I knew there was no way out. This is how it is and this is how it's going to be. The teachers at my school didn't say anything. You see, in high school if you're masculine, they assume you're a lesbian, so it's not a discussion they want to have. There were some perceptive people who said, "Your problem is not being a lesbian. We know lesbians, and your struggle is different."

I had thought all my struggling was internal, I didn't know that people could see it. That made me feel so vulnerable, so I closed up. It was so bad. I got really mad because I felt like I was doing so much to be a girl—in fact I was doing more than what the other girls were doing. That's when I chose not to focus on my gender because it was really problematic for me; I chose to focus on having a girlfriend, because at least my attraction to girls was definite, it wasn't something I had to identify or anything.

Being attracted to women has never been complicated to me. It was only when I was in high school that I came to realize that it was considered wrong for a woman to be attracted to other women. I had always thought everyone felt the same way. I thought all girls love girls and that at some point as I grew older I'd start to love men, so it never bothered me. One time, I was talking with my girl friends and one of the girls asked, "Do you guys ever get attracted to girls?"

I said, "Isn't that normal?"

The girls disagreed and told me, "No, you're also supposed to be attracted to boys!"

I thought, "Maybe I'm just late. I think it will come."

It never came.

I went to high school and there were all these beautiful girls, and I would just tell them, "Oh, you look so pretty!"

I didn't know that I was being problematic, and people actually have a problem with that. I used to have girl friends; but as soon as I got close to them, they would stop talking to me. Then I realized that people were saying that I made inappropriate comments about girls. We had a really cool chaplain in our school, and I went for counselling. During the last part of my sessions, I asked her what she thinks about gay people. She told me she didn't have a problem with them, that she thought it was natural. She said the only thing she wouldn't do is marry them in the church where she was the priest. From that point I've never had a problem with being gay. That conversation made me feel like there's no problem with me.

In the process of dating, I would date a woman and they would start saying to me, "But you're not a girl. Not really," and then we would break up because I got offended at such comments. One woman I dated when I was in university told me, "I don't feel comfortable calling you 'she', but I also don't want to call you 'he' because you really try to be a girl."

So she started calling me 'her-him'. We didn't know 'they' was a pronoun. The whole time we dated she never referred to me as 'she', she just mixed pronouns like that. 'Her-him'. It was nice dating her, because then there was one person who understood me.

At around that time I was accepted for an internship at ████████. My co-workers also didn't have a problem. I used to dress very masculine. I was presenting myself as masculine, not male. It never bothered me if someone mistook me for a boy. At first glance most people saw me as a boy—particularly if I didn't talk, because I have a very feminine voice. So things were very nice, and I was very comfortable. During this period, I identified as genderfluid.

After a while, I broke up with this girl and started dating someone else who was also struggling with gender. This person knew about the trans experience, they used to identify as trans at that time. They were able to tell me things and guide me through what I was going through. They would tell me things, and give me information that helped make me feel OK about the things I felt.

For instance, if I told them I didn't want to go outside because I felt my boobs were too big, they wouldn't brush me off by saying something like, "Just put on a sports bra and you'll be fine."

You know? They would instead say, "If you don't want to go outside it's OK, I'll go get whatever you want."

They made me feel OK about not being the girl that I was trying to be, because I was still trying to be a girl. They told me "You don't have to be a girl just because you're female."

I realized I wasn't actually comfortable being feminine, even as a temporary state. It used to give me a lot of anxiety and discomfort. It made me anxious and I was always justifying myself. If you met me with my hair done, I felt like I had to explain to you why my hair was done. I realized when I'm not trying to be feminine I'M JUST COOL. COMFORTABLE.

–

I'VE ALWAYS SAID that I'm going to live life as both sexes. When I was younger, I thought I'd grow up and do a sex change, but then I grew up and didn't want it anymore. I can strike that balance. I can be a man and a woman.

Bethsheba is my inner woman. She's a powerhouse. She's my source of wisdom—because she's such an old woman. She's my strength in a lot of ways. She's endured this world and has learned a lot, all her lessons have strengthened her. She likes powerful men, perhaps because she has a better understanding of what she can do with them. She's my softer side, and my vicious side.

She's very many different sorts of women; a glamourpuss, she loves her couture, she just lives for her couture. Sometimes she seems like the one who sets the path for my boy side. I understand that I'm still a man, but there's the Bethsheba side. She's a home-maker. She's such a fucking home-maker. For her, everything starts from home.

I've always been very much in touch with the idea of Bethsheba and I want her to come to life. I want to see her manifest. I can feel her in my mind, and I can feel her in my spirit. This woman that I am, THIS ALTER EGO OF MINE.

–

I AM GAY. I don't like the sound of it, it doesn't speak of me, because being gay is tied to a certain lifestyle, a certain way of being and expressing yourself, like having an interest in interior decoration. That's not the way it is, but that's how the lifestyle is portrayed. The gay lifestyle is only tolerated in the Nairobi metropolitan region. It is very urban and peri-urban. It exists in only those urban spaces.

Over time I have began accepting being gay as part of who I am. I realize that I get frustrated when I try to force myself into the accepted heteronormative identity. I am my father's son and mother's child.

There are so many things, so many layers, so many emotions that eat you up as you grow up and try to wrap your mind around this concept of being gay. It's such a blanket description. I don't like the one size fits all LGBT framework. We are completely DIFFERENT PEOPLE FROM DIFFERENT REALITIES.

–

I USED TO BE GAY but I am bisexual AT THE MOMENT.

–

I'M GAY, A HOMOSEXUAL; QUEER. I'm liking the word queer a lot these days. I never used to like it, but I like it now. I didn't like any of those words, but as I've been out more and more to myself and my friends, I'm less bothered. It's not an issue.

I've always heard the word queer; queer theory, queer studies. That used to drive me nuts for years. And then—all of a sudden—last week, I thought. "That's the word. That's a fucking word."

I have no shame saying I'm gay, I'm homosexual. Bend over, or whatever you want to call it. I like the word 'queer'. My maths teacher used to say, "Are you queer?"—before it was a word for homosexuality. It was a mildly colonial word. You can't be shaped right. You can't fit in. You refuse to follow the program, and you can't understand why. Now I realize that all the books I used to read when I was a kid with eccentric professor characters who lived alone; queer. People who make new things; queer. James Baldwin; queer.

I suppose—before the gay liberation language—'queer' was a way for people to know exactly what you were and accept you. They needed to continue to love you, which I like. It's a bigger word than gay, a bigger word than lesbian. You cannot categorize what it is, and it's not just about sex. I like that word.

It's not about being rebellious. It's that you can't stop yourself from spending time making those new things. Sometimes you think there's something wrong with you for thinking that those new things are important; your curiosity, your imagination—and there's just this sense that it's not wrong. The landscape is different to you, so in Form Two, you will start smoking, because that is what Form 2s do in Kenya; rebellion. In Form Three, what happens? Form 3s are fairly responsible. No one knows what Form 3s do. Then Form 4s disappear. They sometimes miss classes and they're studying very hard for their exam. But Form 2s are just allowed to be loose.

In my time, you'd go to campus where you were given money by the Government to go absolutely crazy, and your parents would go to church and pretend to worry about you but really not care because they were having orgies when they were in campus, and you are having orgies because you're in campus, and then by 3rd Year you'll get married and then finish school and become a lawyer. You'll then join a church and become a responsible citizen by the time you are thirty.

So everyone continues with their temporary madness, but slowly everyone falls into place. Marketing. Law. Mathematics. Muthaiga. Then there's the 30% who get lost.

"What happened to Peter?"

"I don't know. Last I heard he was a conductor."

Committed suicide. Disappeared, and they're never coming back to Kenya. They gave up their dream of doing maths, and now they're doing something very mundane so they don't have to dream. Now they're doing something very, very, very safe. It's not about money.

Then there are the other queers who never left home. In their forties, but they never left home. But they also stopped dreaming.

My issue isn't with those who are becoming accountants, it's that you can't have a country full of people who don't make new things. Our system is made for people who obediently follow rules and make good employees. Initially, all our schools were making good employees by destroying every non-dutiful African; expulsion, suspension, church-ness. All this because there was an actual overt policy in the 50s that the New Independence was coming, and they needed to start pushing young Africans—not to become big things—but to become clerks.

Alliance High School was not built to make big leaders. Nor was Mang'u High School. It was built to make good clerks. Independence messed that plan, but the sensibility is still the same. Alliance people don't start banks. River Road guys start banks. It's people who are not in that system who start new things. So for me, River Road is queer. It is where things exist within A BIGGER SPECTRUM OF POSSIBILITY.

–

I WAS ONCE BISEXUAL, but for the last six months I'VE BEEN GAY.

–

I WAS BORN A BOY, and I still use the name I have always used, except I did shorten it, two or three years ago. I have not yet changed any of my official documents. I really am dreading the process of changing names. Ugh. I hate paper work. I've gotten to a point where I'm like, whatever. Luckily, my name isn't so feminine, especially the way I've shortened it, and my second name is not feminine, so people usually can't tell that my name refers to a man or a woman. If I found someone who could do the paper work for me, I'd do it! What's stopping me is the hassle, the follow-up and also the way people feel like you have to have transitioned first before you change your documents.

Transitioning needs a lot of money, and I don't have that kind of money. You need to pay for surgeries and hormones. Surgeries cost more than two hundred thousand, and that's just breast surgery. The others are crazy, like if I want to have my uterus removed, it could probably cost me close to a million shillings. Then there's the hormones, and the entire process of the psychologist review. You have to see a psychologist for a long time, then find a doctor who can prescribe you the hormones and the surgery; all that is money. The hormones are costly and you have to take them regularly. It's completely dependent on money. If I get money right now, I'm doing it.

I don't have a healthcare provider at the moment, but I know where I can get everything once I'm ready. I know what the process looks like, I know what to expect. I know some people who have transitioned. Not here in [redacted]; online, and in Nairobi. First I would want the top surgery, because my boobs make me very dysphoric. Most days I don't even leave the house because I feel like people are going to see my boobs and start calling me Madam. So that's the first thing I would do.

What else makes me feel dysphoric? My ass, you know. And my voice. It's just sick. I'll do everything to pass as a boy, and then I talk and the person I'm talking to realizes, "Oh, it's a girl."

Once I was seated in the back of a matatu by myself, and there were other people seated ahead of me, near the conductor. I asked aloud to alight at a stage, and the conductor turned to look behind at us. He could not match the voice he had heard to the person he was seeing seated at the back, so he just passed my stop.

I said, "No! I asked you to stop, why aren't you stopping?"

He looked so surprised and said, "I thought I heard a lady tell us to stop, but when I looked behind I didn't see her."

What else makes me dysphoric? Periods surprise me every time. Every freakin' time, I'm always surprised. I was talking to a friend about my periods—she is cis-gender and heterosexual—and she told me, "I think you need to find a permanent way to be done with periods."

I have many friends who tell me to go on family planning pills. They're not trans, they're not even queer, but they know about my struggles and they always advise me, "You can try family planning pills."[1]

I don't know how that works. I've been saying I'll try it but I don't know how. I'm working on getting binders[2]. I don't know where to get them locally. They're certainly not here in ████. So I have a friend bringing them to me from abroad. Until then, I buy clothes that feel comfortable.

I had an incident this week at the supermarket. I was going to the supermarket, and usually I get checked by the male guard.[3] On days when I look or feel very feminine, I usually just go to the ladies' queue, but I've had instances where both guards refuse to check me. Sometimes they are confused, and while they are trying to decide who should search me, I walk past them.

This time I went to the lady guard and she told me, "No, I am not checking men."

I said, "I'm not a man," but she sent me to the male guard.

The male guard said, "No, this one is female, I'm not checking women."

It was bad. They wouldn't let me in to the supermarket, because they couldn't check me. I told them if they weren't going to decide who was checking me, I would just go in. So I went in and

---

1. Self-prescribed hormones, testosterone esters and/or androgen-blocking drugs are sometimes used by transgender people in place of proper hormone replacement therapy—usually because it's the only option available to them

2. Breast binding is the act of flattening breasts by the use of constrictive materials. Common binding materials include cloth strips, elastic or non-elastic bandages, purpose-built undergarments and layered shirts.

3. Following multiple terror attacks, entry into shopping malls, offices, houses of worship and other public buildings in Kenya is generally preceeded by metal-detector security checks by male and female guards (for male and female visitors) at every public entrance.

did my shopping, but as I was coming out of the building, they saw me and apologized. I wasn't sure what they were apologizing for, and they also weren't sure what they were apologizing for, because the lady was still insisting that I was a guy.

A few days later, I went to the same supermarket. I walked to the middle, figuring that I'd go to the side of whichever of the guards grabbed me first. The male guard started to search me, but he was a bit too touchy. Usually they just run the metal-detector wand over you, right? This guard was touching me a lot. I don't know, maybe that's what they do for men. They don't touch ladies that much. I started feeling uncomfortable, so I said "Whoa, hey dude…" and walked in.

They were shocked and I felt very uncomfortable while shopping. When I was coming out, all the guards at the entry and the exit were looking at me. I think they had talked about me while I was shopping. They tried talking to me, so they could hear my voice. I didn't answer, I just walked away. I'm never going back there. It's where I usually shop, and I'll just have to find another place. That's what I do. If I get uncomfortable in a space, I move.

–

My brother is married, and I am the next in line to marry. Since my brother married outside our tribe, there is an expectation from my uncles that I should marry a Kalenjin woman. I have tried dating ladies, and they ended up being my closest friends. We would share the most intimate details of our lives, but I could not bring that sexual angle in, it couldn't work. I would love women from the inside. They were just in sync with me.

With men it was different, I would think—he is really hot or cute. It was very frustrating because I did not know how to turn this fascination with guys into a relationship. Here I was very close with women, but very platonic. Not sexual in any way.

I kept thinking that one day I could just kill this other part of myself by thinking of having sex with women. I tried to get sexual films and watching straight porn. My mind would just get overworked imagining doing that to a woman, it felt so wrong. My internal battles were very vicious.

I would instead imagine being with a perfect guy, having a perfect life. I didn't resist it. It was easy on my mind—this is just what I am. My whole body and spirit just flowed with it. One day, I think I was just sleeping, I just decided to make this my personal thing to define my sexual lifestyle. Forget my uncles and everybody else.

I want to be in that constant flow of things, where there is no resistance. I don't want to go up the waterfalls. I am just going with it. Then I could focus on other things; my talents and everything else. To BREATHE AND LET GO!

–

I WAS BORN A MAN, but inside I know I am a woman. I am not attracted to women, so I say I am gay. But I always wonder whether I am OK with being a gay man, and whether I really am gay, or maybe I am a straight woman inside a man's body. Whenever I say that I am gay, there is a part of me that thinks otherwise. Sometimes I refer to myself as transgender. If I became transgender, I wonder what would happen to the people I love. If being myself will affect people around me, why should I be me? That is my biggest challenge. I don't like being selfish.

My mother knows I am a man, even though I know I am not. If I was to transition to being myself, it would affect her, the people she interacts with, and the extended family to which she belongs. I am the last born, and I am her only friend. She separated with my dad and then we became so attached to each other. I know that she has a feeling that I am gay, and so she advises me.

She told me that gay people don't care; they have sex with anyone. They don't care whether the man they're sleeping with could be having a family, or whether they would be home breakers. I have seen gay people and been with them, and I know not all gay people are the same. I told my mother that gay people are not self-centred, they are cautious and are mindful of how the society views them.

I know that if I become a transgender, I will hurt people. I have been spotted in town with my gay friends and word has got to my mother. My siblings have also heard about it. I would have to go very far away to become a transgender and this is not something I am ready to do. I don't want to be far from my family. I want to be closer to my mother. I don't want to be selfish. I always think of other people.

This is a message to the LGBT community. People think negatively about us. Some—like my mother—say that gay people don't care. As the LGBT community we should respect ourselves. We should be who we truly are, but our actions should not affect people. Whatever you do, think of others first. Even though society has not embraced us, let us not give them more reasons to discriminate against us. Let us respect the institution of marriage by not having sex with married men. By doing so, you can break someone's home and the children in that marriage would suffer. I was raised by a single mother and I wouldn't want gay people TO BE SEEN AS HOME BREAKERS.

–

HERE IN ██████, people are not that focused. The gay people here are all about looks, drinking, having a good time, and tomorrow will sort itself out. But we're not birds. We're going to need to settle.

I'm at my most comfortable being called a stem. I'm everywhere—I can be someone's femme, just as long as we're both women, you know? But titles can really interfere with some girls' psychology. One girl once told me, "Starting today, I'm the one giving orders. If I say cook, you're the one cooking."

I said, "You can't talk like that—we have to negotiate and agree."

Many of the butch girls I have dated treated me like I was their slave!

"These are my socks, they are dirty, go and sort them out."

"Come home now, because I have said so."

If I refused to go, she would come over and shout at me, and I'd remain composed, because I like peace. I would leave her to make noise until she calmed herself down.

There was a time my mother became suspicious about my relationships with this girl because of how all-over-me this chick was. I even had to tell my mother to say I wasn't in when the girl came over. My mother would ask why I didn't want to meet her, and I would say I was busy.

These labels—the way I see them—they cause problems. Butches feel they are the man of the house. No. Even the idea of masculinity, I don't want. Don't bring me those patriarchies here. I don't want them. Let's all just be women. So in every relationship I am in—I always say, "We're both women, let's just be happy like that with each other."

If someone tries to oppress me, I'll not stand for it. In the house, I like things to be really clean, and I like to share duties. I used to share duties with my ex, because we were both really busy. We would each do our part.

–

I want a family. I'd like kids. In this Kenya right now, I'd have to marry a woman. I can't marry a man, unless Kenya changes, and I really love the guy. I doubt it. My grandmother would die of shock. I pray it never happens, I hate being in shit. It is stressful living a double life. People think highly of me. I sit in church, in the youth committee.

I am busy, trying to work at a young age. While guys are partying and having fun, I'm having all kinds of other responsibilities such as committees. This grown-up stuff. Then I have things to hide inside me, a beast I don't want to let out, because I'll disappoint people. I am concerned about what people think of me, because I'm high up. I'm that guy who cares about what people think. I've survived this far by doing that, so I've adapted.

My relationship with the church and God is complicated. In church they bombard gays, and I'm sitting in the committee wondering why I'm going through this, wondering why I was created this way, and whether it's a phase that will finish or if it'll stay permanent. It scares me. I take each day as it comes, waiting to see if one day it will disappear, like magic.

I'd love it to disappear so I can be normal. Being normal means going to school, finishing college and graduating, getting a wife, getting kids, dying old. Meeting new gay friends in ████ who are so at peace with who they are actually makes me think twice about it. Some guys are so comfortable, they go out with another guy to the club and make out.

This is a small town, you'll be seen somewhere and stories will spread. Meeting these people who are comfortable with who they are is making me think twice about my life, because they don't have all this stress that I have.

In a place like Amsterdam, I'd let myself go. Anywhere where nobody knows me, I'd go spoil myself, TO UNLEASH WHATEVER I AM HIDING.

–

I'M GAY, but I'd like to get married. Of course, to a woman. I will marry at some point because I'm in this Africa so I must marry. Especially in my family, I must marry. Even if it's just for me to have kids, that's OK with me. I see myself getting married at around twenty-six, so I have SEVEN YEARS TO GO.

–

THERE'S A PERCEPTION that there's a certain way that trans people should look, and I really don't like it. People police you, you know? People say, "Today you did your hair, this is so feminine, you're not trans."

"Those shoes look so girly."

Just because they have a pink flower. What? It's exhausting and it's annoying. We are all individuals, inasmuch as we want to tell a collective story, everyone is different. That expectation that people are supposed to look a certain way; like if you're a man, you're supposed to walk in a certain way, talk in a certain way, dress and do your hair in a certain way, I find it problematic. I don't like conforming. Even in my trans-ness, I don't have intentions of being exactly like a cisgender man.

I want to retain that trans prefix. I want it to stay. I want someone else who is struggling with gender to see that it's normal. When you transition and pass off as a cis man or woman, and you don't talk about it to anyone, and people don't know you're trans—which is OK, people don't need to know you're trans—but then the people who are struggling with gender and transitioning will continue to struggle because they can't see people like them, you know?

People expect that now because you said you are trans, or because you transitioned successfully, that you shouldn't ever express doubt or fear, you know? But the whole process of accepting yourself and transitioning was through doubt and asking questions. Those questions may never stop. I feel like we should acknowledge that even 'successful trans people' still have those questions, and that QUESTIONING DOESN'T TAKE AWAY FROM YOUR IDENTITY.

–

I THINK IT'S HARD for me to get a job because of the way I look. I did Mechanics in school. When I got out, I got a job at a shop that sells phones. I was qualified but when I got there, they told me, "You have to dress like a real woman. You have to behave LIKE A REAL WOMAN."

–

IT REALLY TROUBLES ME how very little we learn to explore pleasure. You can't close your eyes as you're eating ice-cream. Do you know what I mean? People would look at you funny. You can't just stop and enjoy a meal, or gaze into someone's eyes. You can only perform around pleasure in certain ways, in certain contexts. I've always liked pleasure. Always. If I try to intellectualise it, maybe it's that whole Freudian thing, learning about the world through our senses. I'm very tactile. Seeing. Hearing. I love the senses. But with age, I find that they are just really a starting point, a building block to explore realms outside the senses, like dreams.

I'm now having a deep appreciation for how I experience the earth. I feel incredibly orgasmic when I'm planting spinach. It's meditative. I never thought I'd be one of those people who would be excited to be with cows and pigs, picking herbs, doing all that, but I am! There's a stillness with it. I don't know what it is. I don't need as many words to express myself when I'm in that space.

I think my appreciation of the earth is part of coming into my own as I grow older, and the idea that a woman's sense of self is in the earth and in trees. We have very internal worlds. I see my own stirrings in the ocean, in the sun, in the rain and in the soil. It enables me to touch the part of me that is the Eros. There is an essay by Audre Lorde that talks about the use of the erotic[4], and people usually think sex, but no. It is the creative impetus that brings forth, expressed from the inner, expressed outwardly, in pleasure, IN DELICIOUS THINGS.

–

I WOULD LOVE to get married to a man one day. Even if I was to come back in another life, I'D STILL WANT TO BE GAY.

–

I USED TO BE RELIGIOUS when I was younger, and I would fight with my feelings. I even used to date a man to keep my sexuality undercover. I dated him for almost four years. I struggled with fighting the feelings I had for women. When I was with him and when I was with a chick, I'd feel totally different. I didn't like being with him. I started avoiding him. Even in the club I didn't want to dance with him, I'd want to dance with the ladies. He'd say, "I realize you don't want to dance with me, just with ladies."

Later, I told him I didn't feel for him anymore, but I gave him other reasons. I saw that this fake relationship was not working. Years later, he told me that I should have just told him I was gay. I told him it would have hurt him. When I was dating him, I'd meet girls WHEN HE WAS AWAY.

–

I IDENTIFY AS STRAIGHT right now. I don't really know what's happening right now, so I call myself straight. I am not completely out there. I think I am confused, I'm NOT YET SURE WHAT'S HAPPENING.

–

4. From Audre Lorde's 'Uses of the Erotic: The Erotic as Power'. Published January 1st, 2000.

The question of identity is weird for me, I identify as queer. It is not only a term which speaks to my sexuality—which is gay—but it also refers to a certain set of political identifications that my gayness means that are ethically and politically affiliated to certain kinds of politics.

I think the earliest moment in which I was aware of a kind of non-normative gender representation—I don't know if I can say that there was anything sexual about it then, but these are the ways in which we are read as queer people—was when I was nine years old. I was in class, and I sat cross-legged on my desk during break-time. Someone said that I was 'sitting like a girl', and in that moment I was very uncomfortable. I also had this idea that this was going to be something which was going to bring me a lot of conflict, because the person who said that was saying it in a policing kind of way. I got the sense that I was male and I had broke some kind of gender rule, that you shouldn't sit with your legs crossed like that.

That same year, a friend of mine sent me a note—he was very pretty then, and he's still very pretty now—that said, "Would you like to be my BF?"

I sent the note back, asking, "Do you mean best friend, or boyfriend?"

He replied with, "Could it be both?"

I felt scared and happy about it. I was very comfortable with what this meant for me, but I was very aware that this was going to have negative consequences as I went on. I don't think I ever replied to that note. It was during class time, and I was staring outside. It's a tragedy of my life, that the feeling of comfort comes just before the feeling of wild insecurity about what the things I get into might actually mean. If it were the other way round, I would have probably replied to the note.

Growing up, I definitely didn't play with boys. I didn't play sports which required us to form groups of men and exclude women. I had a lot of friendships with women, and the realization I had was that my issue was really not about sexual orientation, but this sense that you're out of place. The sense that at any one moment you cannot fully associate with boys in any meaningful sense, and that you also can't interact with girls because you're not a girl. You're not physically a girl.

I think that's a way in which our society is framed or formed, that what girls do and what boys do are two distinctive things that shouldn't overlap or intersect, and if you catch yourself in that overlap or intersect, then you're a deviant, who is breaking the rules, and who should be disciplined. That was my realization, I don't think my realization was on account of a sexual orientation. I actually started thinking about the sexual aspects of it when I was in high school, and not immediately.

I remember when I went to high school, I knew it was going to be a very difficult place for me to be in, because I was an adolescent, and I now had an inkling that I didn't like girls, and I was going to this space where I was going to be policed.

Claiming the label queer has taken some time, it has been a very arduous and painful process, because I have lived with some kind of denial for pretty much most of my life, and it's a good thing that I'm young and out now. For a substantial amount of time, I was in denial. I was deeply religious, and I was trying to relate with God.

"Please don't make me queer, please make this a passing thing."

I think when I was in high school, I was teased a lot. I was gender non-conforming. When I was seventeen years old I met this guy in school who never shied away from claiming a non-normative—or what people would call a 'deviant'—sexuality for himself. He's been my friend ever since. He taught me how to approach my sexual orientation differently from the way I taught myself, or differently from what I expected to happen.

I had this notion in my mind that God was testing my patience. I felt like I wasn't patient enough, and had fallen into temptation of the worst kind.

"God won't listen to my prayers now."

My first kiss was with this guy in high school. He used to come to my room and leave his mobile phones and electronic stuff in my room, because I used to be a very obedient child, so no one ever assumed that I would hide things for less obedient students. So one day—I remember it was a really nice day, a Wednesday—I left my class and went back to my room. This guy came to me and said, "You told the teachers that I'm hiding things in your room?"

He wanted to beat me up, saying he was going to break my arms and legs because I had snitched on him. I begged him not to beat me up, and told him the teachers must have found out from someone else. He left me alone, but he said, "I'm going to wake you up in the middle of the night and I'm going to beat you up and no one will hear."

I went to sleep. He came back thirty minutes later and apologized, but by then I was very indifferent. I told him, "Fuck you. You made me feel very bad, and made me feel very guilty."

And that's when he kissed me. I was like, "Whoa! That was amazing."

I didn't expect it. After that there was a whole period of soul searching, and then after that we had sex. It was very good, and it was an eye-opener for me. After that I thought, "There's no going back now. I've done the deed as it were."

After that there was utter release and also despair at my prospects of changing my sexuality. He was expelled from our school after a few months later for other reasons. There was a school strike, and he told me, "I'm going to be expelled anyway, so I'm going to break shit up before they do."

He was a bad boy and I was nuts. It was very exciting. I don't know where he is now. I looked for him on Facebook, but I didn't find him.

After I left high school, I made a decision to accept my 'gayness', so I read a lot about my sexual orientation and discovered new insights. I came into knowledge that in some cultures and communities, homosexuality wasn't something that was looked down upon, and wasn't something that was reacted to by means of violence. I discovered that our notions about sexual orientation, and the foundational stability of heterosexuality were actually very false. Over a period of time, I've cultivated what I'd describe as radical queer politics, which orient me to identify myself as queer to this day.

Accepting my sexuality was utter release, and it was amazing. Now I could follow the boys I wanted to follow. Now I could tease. Now I didn't feel this overwhelming sense of guilt and fear, that there was repercussions for who I was. In the same way that bad boy told me he was 'going to be expelled anyway', now I too could break shit up.

After leaving high school, I knew there existed some kind of queer community out there, and from what I'd seen and read about queer communities abroad, I had an inkling in my mind that people who identified as gay could meet and form a kind of organization and community. I had more time to spend in social networks now that I was out of school, and I had a sense of how the gay community organized—from reading blogs, online forums and dating sites—and so I tried to make contact with some of the gay activists.

I reached out to the activists due to some conception about what queer community was. In my mind I thought this is how liberal society forms. I assumed that the activists were the obvious leaders of this queer community that was somehow corralled around LGBT rights. That turned out to be a false view. If there is something to be said about my interaction with activists and my interactions with queer people who are not activists, it's that the two groups don't overlap, they are sometimes very disparate groups. I approached them thinking that this was a big community. But when I became more and more invested in social media, I found that there was actually something much larger going on. People were meeting one another for all kinds of things such as SEX, DATING AND FRIENDSHIP.

–

I THINK THE WHOLE THING about women being soft-spoken has to do with us as women wanting to be seen and not heard. You try to be as invisible as you can. I think women are made to feel incredibly invisible. I've had lovers who have told me in the middle of sex, "Oh my God, what is that you have done?"

I tell them, "That's just regular shit!"

They say, "Not really, no!"

I am becoming a lot more vocal because I realise that if I am not, then I WILL GET DROWNED.

–

The moment when I felt at my most powerful as a queer person was when I decided that I was not a person who was afraid, and that I actually have a deep well of courage and resilience within me—and I know that sounds like the smuggest shit ever, because courage is very muscular and very individualistic, at least in the way that it is presented. I decided for myself that the fact that I'm out and the fact that I say all these things and the fact that I stick to my guns and the fact that I will respond whenever someone says something which is widely homophobic was my power. I think that was a defining moment in my life.

I've never actually physically fought anyone. I've never actually made the decision to confront someone and beat them up. If there's any kind of violence that I perpetrate, it's not physical violence, it's perhaps certain kinds of ideological, even verbal kinds of abuse. I used to think, "You're such a fucking coward because you never fight anyone."

I survived years of teasing and bullying, years of people telling me that I'm wrong and sinful and perverse. I strongly feel that's charted my way as a person who is fearless in certain situations, not all of them. I think sometimes our existence is marked in a very profound and meaningful way by fear.

–

An excerpt of a conversation between two lesbians:

Kate: I like being a wife. I don't mind. I'll wash, and clean and do everything you want.

Faith: But why? We can hire someone to do it.

Kate: But I like being a wife.

Faith: You want to be a housewife? I don't think I'd want that. How about getting someone to help out?

Kate: I wouldn't mind, but not every day. Otherwise, what is the work of a wife?

Faith: But what if we're both wives? There's no husband there.

Kate: I hear the heteros split roles 70–30.

Faith: But I think times are changing. Lesbians do 50–50. We can't be on the same level as heteros. I don't like it, because it will be like you are second to me. I don't think I want you to stay in the house and just work there. You don't have to just stay in the house. You can go out and get other things done. Doesn't everyone have their own responsibility in the relationship?

Kate: Yes. I suppose we can give each other different tasks. So is it 50–50 for lesbians or we are 70–30 as well?

Faith: I wouldn't do that. I'm a woman just like you. 50–50 is what works. I can't be the only one who does laundry. Can't you also do laundry?

Kate: Look—OK. You can wash clothes, but not every day. You said 50–50, and that is what that means. It's daily. When I cook *ugali*[5], you cook the greens. If I make the *chapati*, you make the stew, yes sweetie *[laughs]*?

Faith: But what if I want to wash the dishes?

Kate: That's not 50–50.

Faith: Why?

Kate: In 50–50 you split everything equally. If I wash the dishes Monday and Tuesday, then you wash them Wednesday and Thursday.

Faith: But what if I wash the dishes when you are completely done with cooking?

---

5. Staple dish made of corn meal.

Kate: That's not 50–50.

Faith: But what if I can't cook?

Kate: You can learn.

Faith: That would take me ten years.

Kate: In ten years I want to be financially stable with my own family. Just one child. And I want to give my family—my nuclear family—the very best It can. That's all. My biggest challenge will be HOW I am going to have that child. I don't want to adopt a child, I want my own. But how to find a surrogate to carry the child for me?

Faith: Your wife can also carry the baby. She might even want to. Wait, you don't want to carry your baby yourself?

Kate: Fuck, no!

Faith: I wouldn't have a surrogate do it. Or my partner, for that matter. I don't want to end up in a situation with my partner where we fight then she says she's going to go with our child because she's the one who carried it. So my greatest challenge will be making sure that my relationship is real and I will stay with her forever.

Kate: Forever-ever?

Faith: I'm a lover, and I'm a keeper. So I can. I think we're the first generation to show society what gay couples living together looks like. It won't be easy, and we don't have a history of gay people doing that. Even now, when you live together with another woman, there is so much speculation from the neighbours. So after staying with another woman for ten years, you can't keep telling people that she is your room-mate, or your sister.

Kate: And me, as a tommy, I also have the issue of: what am I going to be wearing in ten years?

Faith: That's true.

Kate: And what will my job be? Let's say I am employed by the UN and have a child—what will I fill in under 'spouse'? There are so many issues coming. I think the only thing I can pray for is that that all this stuff will be sorted out by the time I get to that point.

Faith: By the time we turn 30, there will be so many challenges. If just going out on the street now is a problem—with the way we look—what about ten years down the line when we're older women?

Kate: We're the generation that is pushing these things. The ones before us didn't take the steps we are taking of living together. Many of them are single. Or they are deep in the closet. Or they are getting married so that people don't know, to save face in society. Or saying they are bi.

Faith: I'm lucky for now, because nobody is demanding that I bring a man home. My mother actually looks out for my relationships. When a woman visits me, my mother really looks her over, and she comes into the room suddenly to look at us when we are asleep. Then the next day she tells me quietly, "That one? I don't think so."

Kate: She's choosing someone good for you.

Faith: But I still think she is just waiting for me to bring a boy home.

Kate: Do you think we'll be lesbians forever?

Faith: Definitely. I'd rather stay alone, if anything.

Kate: I ask a lot of questions like that. The lesbians I have known... some of them said they will change. There's a lot of pressure from families and all that.

Faith: One thing I know, it's the femmes who are traitors.

Kate: Yes! You see these couples that are two butches together are the ones who stay together for long. It's very hard to get these feminine girls. Many of these femme girls are experimenting.

Faith: And then we forget that lesbians can get all these STDs; HPV, HIV, all of them. But we are so ignorant and we don't realize you can catch these diseases from being with a woman. People think they can't get sick, but we can't joke with these issues. Many people are sick.

Kate: There is also that perception that men are the ones who are players, but these femmes are all prostitutes. They're crazy! Femmes! The femmes these days have rights!

Faith: But these days there are diseases.

Kate: It's just that you are comparing now to those days a long time ago.

Faith: No, it's because I'm married now *[laughs]*.

Faith: Now my eyes are open. I don't think I am where I was a few years ago. I've changed, I have grown, I have matured.

Kate: Yes *[laughs]*, you're becoming like me now.

Faith: Yes, THINGS CAN'T STAY THE WAY THEY'VE ALWAYS BEEN.

–

I IDENTIFY AS SOMEONE WHO LIKES SEX. I love pleasure. If you had asked me three or four years back I would have said I was a lesbian. But now I find that pleasure for me is not just limited to the context of a woman, or a man—I have become broader. The labels were good for me to understand myself, but the more I delve into life, I realise how these labels of sexual identification don't express the broadness of what it is to be a human being. I may chose a partner, or partners, OR NONE.

–

EVERY NOW AND THEN I get into a 'me against the world' thing. I feel like I have to be strong. Sometimes it's emotional strength, and sometimes it's physical strength. I have to act as a bodyguard for every part of my self, my mind, my body, my heart, and it works. I see that on the streets. I'm walking with my hoodie and my headphones on and I look like 'don't fuck with me'. And that helps me survive, but it doesn't allow my femininity to move.

I don't want to just survive, I want to thrive. As hardened as I have become, I also desire to be soft and relaxed and fluid. I'm not sure how that will continuously be expressed as I move forward in the world. Ultimately for me, this life is about being whole and experiencing wholeness. Not to negate one part over the other. Feeling safe to be your whole, complete self, and to celebrate that. WE CAN'T KEEP SHOWING UP IN PARTS.

–

I'VE NEVER REALLY—even to my friends—said I'm gay. Saying it still makes me think about it and sometimes I feel like you shouldn't have to think twice when you say it. You shouldn't be thinking in the back of your mind, "Oh my God, I just said that." Every time I have to talk about my sexuality, I feel like I have to look around.

Sometimes I think, "I'm not meant to be here."

When I say here, I mean Kenya. Because why am I in this environment that is so hostile? It affects my state of mind, it affects my self esteem, it affects how I look at people. I feel like I'm automatically defensive around straight people, because I assume they're automatically against my being gay. There's only so many places we can go and just be gay.

My family doesn't understand it. My sisters don't understand it. And I think that's one of the things that troubles me most, because even my siblings ask me questions like, "Do you have to be like that? Can't you change? Why are you DOING THIS TO MUM?"

–

WHEN I ACCEPTED that I was gay, I did have that whole 'sexual awakening' phase, where all I wanted to do was just fuck. I didn't care with who, I didn't care about what or when or where, it was just like thirst. I just wanted to get as much sex as I possibly could. It didn't fucking matter if it was good sex or bad sex, as long as I was having it. That didn't last really long. I found out early that I'm picky, which is a good thing because there's that stereotype about homosexuals being promiscuous.

People think we can fuck anyone, and that's a problem. They don't think there's a struggle behind that. My mother believes that all homosexuals do it for money, and that they're sexually depraved, and that they're animals. At least, for men. She's never really talked to me about lesbians. She only knows one lesbian; Ellen DeGeneres. My mother used to love The Ellen DeGeneres Show. She'd watch it every day until she found out and she said, "We are not watching that woman in my house."

She said something the other day, "You know Ellen might look at one of my daughters and say 'I really want that one for my second wife'." I can't blame her for thinking that. She sees homosexuals as these promiscuous, loose people. She never sees the struggle. She never sees the constant battle between what you're told is right, and WHAT YOU FEEL IS RIGHT.

–

I HAVE MAKEUP AND DRESSES and shoes, high-heeled ones. I have handbags, I have everything. The problem is that I cannot go out dressed like that. I CAN ONLY WEAR THEM INDOORS.

–

I'M NOT KEEN ON HAVING gender reassignment surgery. I had a friend who was trans like me, and she had a wealthy man who was taking care of her. He even built her a house. Then she went to London for work and had the surgery, and when she came back here and was in bed with her guy, he saw her vagina and said, "I liked you the way you were before," and he left her.

It's also a very long process from what I hear so I'm not interested. I've never taken hormones, I've never felt the need to, physically, I already look feminine, so I DON'T NEED THEM.

–

I USED TO HAVE LONG, BEAUTIFUL HAIR. All the way to my shoulders. I had grown it for almost eight years: going to the salon every two weeks, braiding, washing, retouch. I cut it all on the day when I escaped a dangerous situation. I was staying with a gay friend who was living with his white boyfriend, and there was an angry mob from the mosque who had known that we were living in that house. On this day, after their service, they gathered and came to break the gate of the house down. We climbed the back wall and were helped to escape to a safehouse in Nairobi. I cut my hair after that experience. I felt like a completely different person without my hair, but now I'm used to it.

We have had to change ourselves so much. I used to have long nails, I used to make my hair in my house, and I would leave my house and people would ask me, "Why are you doing this?"

I'd tell them, "This is my life. Just leave me the way you see me."

We did a lot of training amongst ourselves so that we could exist in this place and avoid getting into violent situations. So that we could live our lives and be able to walk anywhere without attracting attention: look "normal". Cut your long hair. Dress normal. Walk normal. In exchange for some respect.

–

I WAS 'MY FATHER'S DAUGHTER'. I spent so much time with him; maybe I became him. I love like him. I'm not big on gifts, but I will take care of my woman. I will protect her, I will make sure I'm there for her.

That whole debate about whether people are born gay or not; I don't know. When I was two years old, I wasn't busy trying to get into someone else's pants! I was trying to figure out which

LEGO goes on top of which. You're told as a girl that you need to play with Barbie dolls. You know what I did with my Barbie dolls? I used to pull their heads off and BURY THEM IN THE FARM.

–

FOR ME, DONNING MEN'S ATTIRE IS A STEP BACKWARDS. Why should I take myself backwards? I have struggled. I've faced a lot of difficulties, I've fought battles, wars—emotionally and psychologically. I do not want to revisit that place. I'm only focusing on my future, and in my future I want to live peacefully with my inner and outer selves. That's what gives me motivation. For me to live peacefully as a woman, these are the things I need to do and accomplish.

At the moment, where I live, there aren't any safe places for expressing myself through clothing. There are parties held by LGBTI friends and some places in Nairobi at night, where I can dress as I feel appropriate or comfortable. But where I live? No.

Luckily, fashion is a bit more fluid now. That's a plus for me. I can decide to wear sweatpants and a baggy t-shirt. Men and women are allowed to do that these days! But if I want to wear certain things—in particular, dresses, hot pants—it would have to be in a safe environment. My favorite outfit would be sleeveless floral mini-dresses. Ball gowns. Heels, heels, heels!

–

I DON'T WANT TO USE OVER-THE-COUNTER HORMONES because I don't know what the side effects are. My body reacts to minute, tiny things. I'm saving up some money to have a psychiatric evaluation. After that, I can proceed to the hormones. That is my major goal. I want someone to prescribe them to me and to do a proper follow-up. I know someone who is using over-the-counter hormones. They are really great, but I don't want to play around with those. I don't know how that combination will react on my body.

Health services are way costly, and due to the low population of ITGNC people, especially trans people who want to transition, the cost is way too high. Many people go the over-the-counter route. At least, with my physique, if you're standing behind me, you will definitely think I'm a girl. Even when I wear hipsters and other tight clothing. With the exception of these things (points to genitals) that I want to permanently remove, my body favors me a lot.

Some trans people who are on hormones say that the rest of us aren't complete. They brag and say," This is what true femininity looks like."

But for me, the true essence of a woman is knowing who you are as a woman. You don't need anyone's permission and you don't need anyone's approval. Some people will say, "You are not a true transgender woman," but I know myself.

THE ANSWER IS ALWAYS YOURSELF.

–

SOCIETY AND THE FUTURE

I CONSIDER MYSELF a man of traditional means—I would like to have children and a man. I want a man, not a husband. Maybe a partner, not a husband. The term 'husband' is a part of honouring patriarchy—putting men above women and excluding homosexuals. I want to have children. I don't know how that would happen. I want a child of my body and not an adopted one.

I would like to go home with my man to my grandmother who does not live in the city and hardly knows English and does not know what gay means. I would like for her to have a language—I think that language exists but maybe got lost—for her to understand, for her to know that this is my partner who I will share my life with. For her to love it and accept it. I don't want to run away from my family and extended family just because I am gay. My future family life should seamlessly fit with my life and the people I have grown up with.

I don't want to run away. I don't want to have to find a new family. I want to be able to celebrate the love I have for my man in community with my people who are not tainted with gay politics. Let us just give it our language.

If faced with prejudice. I would defend myself. I would like it to be about me, this is my love story. I love this person. I don't love men, I love this person. I would defend my love for this person, not because he is a man but because he is my love. I don't like the dimensions that come with gay politics.

I am a writer—writing is my passion. I want to find that language that can accurately define it, because nobody really knows what it is. I am sure that it is more than being attracted to a man. Or needing to marry a man.

We need to define it accurately so that everyone can find peace. Even the homophobic people can then see and find peace. I have been exploring how to find an opportunity to love and to be loved outside the spaces where people think that love can be found. I feel much more at peace. I no longer have to be defensive because I am not trying to win an argument. I want to live my life, being happy and sharing intimacy with another person. I will be happy when I finally know that this boy loves me as much as I love him. I would be fulfilled, I would be intact. Now I know how to get to happiness; before I was lost and confused. I am on my way to being happy.

I didn't know how to validate myself and honor myself first. I used to look at my life and the perspective of the expectations of the society and the gay rights movement—and I would exclude myself. Now I know that I am more than what the movement or the society expects. I am more than both. This is me.

When I started to see myself, I became selfish. The good type of selfish. There will always be gay people and there will always be homophobic people. I don't have to exist in that binary of right and wrong. I want to be just happy. I have a right TO BE HAPPY.

–

I'M PLANNING TO VENTURE into the music industry. I want to sing and talk about our issues here—these LGBT ones, and it will really be a fight with the government and with church, but music is a part of my life. I also want to be in an activist organization—but even the activists sometimes don't have focus, and they waste a lot of time just sitting and talking, rather than doing more.

I want two kids, a girl and a boy. I can have my own, or adopted; any will do. I also want to settle with a woman, and I am really sure about that. My current girlfriend has a baby, and I really want to have a kid, but thinking about childbirth makes me feel depressed. But maybe it's worth it. As long as you know you are not bringing this child into the world to face troubles, YOU CAN TRY.

–

I HATE IT when I talk about the things I want to do in future, and people ask me, "Is that compatible with a family?"

Fuck that. Who told you I want to start a family? I hate the way our society feels like we need to be standardized. What happened to diversity? Why do you want us to be standardized, do we look like we're made in China? Even the people in China are not standardized. Why as a human race should we have to standardize one another and expect standardization from each other?

Those are the same people who find out you're gay and ask stupid questions like, "You're gay? Is it because you don't want children? You don't want a family?"

Or, they ask, "Have you ever tried being with a woman?"

Some people want us to laugh the same way, cry the same way, get married the same way, wearing the same colours. It's so boring! What is wrong with people? I suppose they find safety in this standardization. There is security in these norms, but they shouldn't expect that everyone seeks the same security. You might find security in your norms, but I don't find security in your norms. I find security in my freedoms. The things that make me happy are not the same things that make you happy.

My mother really sold herself short with my father. In the past I used to really blame my father, then I came to realize that my mother was a fully grown woman who made choices, and she chose that because it made sense to her. She'd always let him come back when he wanted, and let him do whatever the fuck he wanted, and because she allowed herself to be treated that way, we were treated that way. I don't want to be that sort of woman.

I want to build a good business. I want to be successful in business; film and fashion. I see myself doing a lot of philanthropic work. I want to have a say in this society as a gay person, to build a name for myself. You know, *jina ni kila kitu.* Reputation is everything.

This entire marriage thing works for other people, but I don't see it for myself. I see men for myself, but *wanaume ni kazi mingi pia.* Men are hard work, too. It could work as long as it's the sort of relationship that enables me to do other things I'm doing. I don't want those relationships for *tuketi tupendane.* Let's sit around being in love. Be your own person, and have your own drive. I see men in my life, but without them holding me back.

I see great men in my future. *Hatutaki mwanaume tu hivi hivi.* We don't want no-good men. You want to wield power through such things. If you're with a man with power, naturally you get some of it and it helps in establishing yourself and your own power. THAT'S A PLUS.

–

I'VE LIVED IN ELDORET FOR FOUR YEARS NOW. It is a nice place; open-minded and welcoming to queer people. People don't really mind. They might say bad things about it, but they won't attack you. A few years back, it was really harsh. There were some guys who were attacked, but nowadays people mind their own business. However, you still have to be careful in the clubs. If you are a man and you start dancing like a woman they'll chase you. Also, there were some lesbians who were raped some time back. I think it's really hard for the females because straight men are usually obsessed with them and they can do weird stuff.

Our governor is not welcoming to gay people. He said openly that queer people have no place in his county. He hasn't done anything legislative, he just makes statements. I think it might have been for political reasons because it was said during an election period. People did not respond positively to it. We feared they would, BUT THEY IGNORED IT.

–

THE MOMENT YOU REALIZE you're a homosexual and the world isn't going to make room for you, you realize you're going to have to earn many things; to claim many things. As a child, you think you're going to finish school, get a good job, become rich, then you realize *hapa kuna ushoga, strategy lazima ibadilike*. There is homosexuality here. My strategy has to change. Especially if like me, you can't hide it. There's no closet to go back into. I guess it'd be much easier if I was straight-acting and straight-looking, but I'm not.

Realizing I was gay changed my belief system completely. You start looking at your place in the world. You start feeling the responsibility of finding us a better place; claiming us a better place. In the past, I only used to think of myself, my husband and kids. Now, I think about future gay people, and what they'll come into this world to find. There are people who shut up when anti-gay conversations happen around them, so that no one will know you're gay. When I hear such conversations around me, I DO SOMETHING ABOUT IT.

–

THE SCENE IN [redacted]? It depends. Some people are very, very supportive while some are very opposed to us. It's 50–50. I know places where I can go and I'm totally safe. They know I'm gay and they are very OK with me. And I know of a place I'll go and they'll say, "LET'S KILL THIS DUDE."

–

THE IMAMS IN THIS AREA HAVE CHANGED. They don't act like they used to a few years ago. There are certain Islamic programs on radio, and a while back we used to hear the imams come on air and say bad things about gay people. They used to talk about the "bad behaviors of the gay people", how we behave like women, how we are spoiling the young men in the area. Every morning, the debate had to include homosexuality, and people would call to say, "If you see someone like that, burn them!"

You'd hear such debate and be afraid to even leave your home. But now, from what I've heard recently, this talk has lessened. They have other things to talk about now. This is because we began meeting these imams as a group, inviting them to our meetings. For the past three or four years, we have been having regular meetings with the village elders—men and women—in this area, imams, pastors so that they can engage with us and get used to being around us.

Just the other day, we were celebrating our 10-year anniversary as a self-help group, and the religious leader of our area is the one who opened the event. He said he didn't want any photos taken, but he was there with us. Because of this sensitization, at least these days, even when we're out on the streets, the atmosphere is much better. Long ago, someone like me, dressed the way I am? I would have been attacked and beaten. They'd look at me and know that I am a man who has sex with men.

We began this sensitization about three or four years ago, when news broke out about a gay wedding that happened in 2005. That story brought a lot of problems here, there was a lot of violence. We would invite these leaders to our space, and we would tell them, "Look at us. You might hate us now because we are other people's children, but you don't know who you will give birth to in your home tomorrow. We exist, some of us are Muslims" (because there was a time they didn't even allow gay people into the mosque), "we need to pray to God just like you, we need to access health facilities and Government services just like you."

We made them meet everyone: lesbians, gay men, transgender people; explained the difference. They used to think we were all one thing, they didn't know. Some of them even looked into their own families and found queer people in their own homes. *Kumbe kwetu pia yuko? Kumbe nilikua namchukia yule, kumbe ata dada yangu alizaanga?* You mean this is also in my own home? You mean I was hating those people yet my daughter gave birth to one like them?

These days we even sit with the police. We sit at one table and talk, and exchange ideas. Now they know, "these people exist". Now you can go to the police station, and they welcome you and listen to what you have to say, because now they have been educated. It's still difficult every now and then, when new people get transferred to the area and they get shocked at this atmosphere.

There are also hospitals that cater to us now. Whether you are lesbian, gay, transgender, whatever. You can get your hormones and treatment without discrimination. All this because of training and meeting people face to face. It took a long time, but EVENTUALLY THEY STARTED TO CHANGE.

–

I WANT A GAY FAMILY. I want to marry a man. I usually tell myself that if I have to marry a lady, I'll have to struggle to stop being gay. Living a double life is expensive. I want children, if I CAN ADOPT THEM.

–

I'M OUT TO MY SISTERS and my cousins. I don't think my parents would understand if I came out to them. I'm currently self-employed; I supply fruits and vegetables to supermarkets. I don't want children. From when I was a child I never dreamed of having children. I wouldn't want to get into a relationship and then have kids. I've never been in a relationship long enough to think about moving in together with someone. Maybe it's because I haven't met the right person yet, and I really like my space. I would want to be with my partner all the time but then the comfort of having my own space keeps me sane. I think I need to meet the right person to be entirely comfortable with living together. I need to be with a person who appreciates that I need my space and not lose myself in the relationship.

I used to go to church. The last time I went to church was when I was in Form Two. I had gone for Mass because I was raised Catholic. That's the same day I got my first Holy Communion. I'm not religious; I wouldn't go to church now.

For fun I go out. I used to drink a lot, but I stopped a month ago. I may or may not go back to drinking. I like walking, reading. I spend a lot of time with family, watch TV, I like dancing; normal things. Things that make me happy. I'm tired of the everyday weekend routine in Nairobi—go out on Friday, drink till morning kind of thing. There are so many other activities to do as opposed to drinking and being hungover the next day.

I think it's easier to be a lesbian now than how it was before. I don't know how it was before for other lesbians, but over time the general public is starting to realize that gay people are here to stay and it's not just a phase. When I came out to my friends in 2009, they took it better then I think they would have before. Being a lesbian is no longer shocking to the educated folk. I THINK IT'S GOING TO GET EASIER.

–

DO I HAVE STRAIGHT FRIENDS? Yes, I have had straight friends. The problem with them is that once they come to know about you, they distance themselves a bit. Maybe they are afraid that when they are seen with you their image will be affected, or people will start asking, "Why is he associating with that person? WHY ARE THEY WALKING TOGETHER?"

–

IN MY FOURTH YEAR of University, I took the International Human Rights Course, which was led by a prominent law professor. We had a huge debate on the rights of homosexuals. He said he found it illogical because men cannot procreate. I found his arguments very silly, because there are a lot of heterosexual couples who cannot or do not or choose not to procreate, yet they have rights.

The rights were not attached to persons because they were biologically productive to society. There are many other ways to be productive in society. I challenged him, and that was good for my ego. He is a big-shot professor, seen on national TV and radio and known in human rights circles, and I stood up to him and told him, “No, sir. I disagree respectfully.”

For me, it came from a profound inner belief, perhaps based on my lived experience. Sometimes people call me to ask me questions. Children as young as eighteen call me and say, “I’m from a single parent family, my mother has found out that I’m gay, and she’s not willing to pay my school fees any more. What will I do?”

I don’t have any answers most of the time. We’ve noticed that most of these kids end up on the street as sex workers. There’s a huge number of these kids who are now HIV-positive, and they’re spreading it like nonsense, even to bisexual men in heterosexual couples.

My conscience is disturbed when I hear four lesbians died in this country last year. Two committed suicide. Such stories gore my soul. I connect with people who give in to defeat, give in to fear because they are different. That difference is so small, yet so profound to your being that it affects the way you live, the person you become.

There are talented people who want to become musicians, but they will never do that because they know that at some point, their sex life will become a scandal and they will lose everything. There are people who want to run for political office, but they can’t do it because of ‘sexual respectability’ and how that is associated with access to power and resources in this bloody country.

I know that what’s ailing this society is deep and wide, but it’s informed by a law that states that two men are not allowed to express love. This law excuses the violence that we see, the killings that we see. The firings, the dismissals, the prejudice, the eviction from rental houses, the exclusion from family. That injures people’s dignity, and people are not able to realize their dreams because they feel less than human.

I want people to know that it's not shameful to love another man. It is not shameful for men to hold hands. It is not shameful to be called a homosexual. I am a homosexual, and very proud of that, and I AM A KENYAN.

–

THERE'S A DRESS I've been wanting to design forever. It's the most bespoke and artistic thing ever. The workmanship of this dress is just the best. It's the kind of dress that would take quite an amount of time to make. It's a floor-length ball gown with a long, long, long, long train. It's green. I'm currently loving green because for me green represents fertility. The dress is green because it shows that something has been born; this was fertile ground, and something has been born out of it, something grand.

It's a heavy dress; I like heavy embroidery and a weighty couture gown. The train is long—have I mentioned how long that train is? It's very long! I want it to be the kind of train that takes corners. It's the kind of train that has security people with walkie-talkies manning it. The dress has been embroidered by some of the finest stones; diamond embroidery and ruby embroidery. It's back-less, and my back is cut up with scarification cuts.

It might have sleeves. The sleeves keep coming and going in my head, depending on how I'm feeling. I don't know why they keep coming and going. And ooh, yes! It has to be one of those constricting dresses—one of those dresses that make you feel like you can't breathe and you're going to pass out. It's made of heavy fabric. None of those embroidered sheers we're seeing now. It's like a woollen, embroidered fabric. I've never drawn the dress. I should, shouldn't I? Hmm.

When I'm wearing it, my hair is in an up-do. Bethsheba likes her up-dos. All this wild hair I have now is for my man side. Bethsheba was a name from the Bible. She was Solomon's mother. The wise king should also have a wise mother, and THAT IS BETHSHEBA.

–

WE ARE STARTING TO FORM A LOCAL COMMUNITY for trans people. I never used to be a member of local LGBT groups, and when I finally joined, there were no trans people in there. I remember I didn't quite feel comfortable in the LBQ forums where I would be invited. I felt like there was no space for me, so I stopped attending their events until they started creating spaces specifically for trans people. Now I have a place to talk to people about gender. People are having these conversations and we have a support group.

Luckily, I've always been around people who accepted me. What's interesting is they are not even queer. They are just people who are open, they're people who read about things. I'll talk to them about something, like how I am hating having periods.

The next thing they tell me, "Hey, I was reading up about the periods, and there are actually options you can explore..."

These are the same people I tell, "I think I'm transgender. You guys should start calling me 'he'," and that's it.

There's no "Why do you think you're transgender?"

It's not the same with LGBT people. They are so transphobic. They have a sense of entitlement. People think you should explain to them why you think you're transgender. It's annoying. I don't explain. You go figure it out if you want to. Because my friends don't ask me. If I told them today, "Maybe I'm not actually trans," they'll just walk with me through that process. THEY'RE NOT ASKING ME TO JUSTIFY ANYTHING.

–

I WANT TO DATE a fat-ish person. Because I'm slim, just bones. I don't want someone with whom we'll hurt each other. Someone soft, LIKE A LADY.

–

I WANT TO MARRY a man. A lot of queer people are against marriage, perhaps because of how heterosexist and patriarchal it is. But we all know that marriage affords you legal and social recognition. I want to have tax relief from KRA[1] for my partner and I. I want my partner to be able to decide where my property goes when I die. I want to be able to visit my partner in hospital.

1. Kenya's tax and revenue collection authority.

I don't want to injure the esteem of my children because I am hiding in a come-we-stay arrangement with my partner. I want them to know that Daddy and Daddy, or Mummy and Mummy are equal to the Daddy and Mummy of their classmates.

It's not just the social benefits I want, but the legal recognition that puts you among the universe of equals in your society. It's not really about my philosophy of marriage. It's what it signifies to a society that for a long time has excluded those who are different. I want to celebrate my love in public, and have witnesses as I swear before God and man that I shall be his partner till I die, FOR BETTER OR WORSE.

–

LIVING WITH A MAN is awesome, nice, interesting. You get to know the person better and you become good friends. We used to fight a lot in the beginning. Like if we went to the club, I wouldn't let him talk to a dude. Just like that. Until I grew up, I think. We understand each other now. We know each other better. We are best friends, we are lovers.

I'd like to get married to a man. I wish it were legal, we'd be married already. I definitely want kids. Three, because I come from a family of two and it's boring. I never talk to my sister, she's young, and we rarely meet.

My relationship with God and spirituality has not changed since I found out I was gay. I believe in God but I never go to church. I never have. We pray TOGETHER WITH MY BOYFRIEND.

–

I WANT TO LIVE in a farmhouse. I am a farmer, I love vegetables and I like rearing chicken and goats and sheep. I want to tend to those, while I raise my children and teach and serve my country. I'd like to work with the Government SOMEDAY.

–

I AM LOOKING FORWARD to the days when sexuality is understood and we don't have to worry about where to run to when *Maulidi*[1] comes. I look forward to the day when LGBT people will just be like any other person living in the society. I am openly gay, and I get death threats often. It's been two weeks since I received death notes. I think this is because people misunderstand my role as a counsellor. They think I recruit boys.

People say Mombasa is liberal, but I don't agree. When it comes to sexuality, people are still hostile. I have learnt that sodomy was historically used as way of degrading slaves. It was a power tactic to finish the pride of the slave. A man penetrated like that was finished as a man, but the one who penetrated him was seen as a true man. That idea remains, and so gay men who are tops are not seen as being really gay. Gay men who are bottoms receive all the insults.

Also, anti-gay violence is different depending on the religion of the accused. When we are attacked and there is an Oluoch and an Abdalla among the accused, Abdalla will be treated differently [because he is Muslim] and Oluoch will be treated much worse. People here also think that homosexuals are rich. So they want to have sex with us BECAUSE THEY WANT SOME MONEY.

–

I LOVE KIDS—being around them—but I don't want kids. Maybe I'll have one kid, so that I can leave a specimen of myself, and so that my mum and dad CAN KEEP QUIET.

–

I'M A HAIRDRESSER, but I do sex work on the side. Hairdressing is what I do during the day, and for rent and food. My sex work is for clothes and all those other things. I really enjoy sex work.

My clients are mostly Kenyan men; Muslims, Christians. Clients choose different sex workers for different reasons; maybe because you're smart, or maybe you give good service. Some clients want special services. You wouldn't imagine *[laughs]*...

I usually meet them in the club. Sometimes we fuck right there, sometimes we go to guest-houses and fuck there, sometimes I take them home if I really like them. The fees depend on the client. Sometimes they pay you upfront, and sometimes you can ask for 2,000 shillings and they complain. "*Elfu mbili nikulipe wewe? Siwezi, afadhali niende kwa bibi yangu!*" 2,000 for you? No way, I'D RATHER GO TO MY WIFE!

–

IN THE FUTURE, I want to get married to a woman. This is Africa, I have to be realistic. So even though I know getting married will not be easy for me, and being with a woman will not be easy for me, I will still go through it. I have to start a family; it is what is expected of me. My parents are very traditional, I FEEL OBLIGATED.

–

I WAS MARRIED ONCE. I was married, and then my man left me. Now I don't want to get married any more. Some guy told my cousin, "I see you with a beautiful, slim guy. I want him."

My cousin came and told me, "There's an Arab guy who says he wants to meet you."

I agreed to meet him. That evening, the guy picked me up in his car. He took me to a big hotel that's usually for tourists. We drank a little, chewed some *miraa*[2]. Then he asked me, "Do you know why I called you here?"

I said no.

"I sent your cousin to tell you that I wanted to meet you. I want you."

"You want me? You want me now, or do you want to become one of my regulars?"

"I don't want to play with you. My wife is away in the Middle East. I live with my two kids but I travel all the time. If you agree, I'd like you to come and live with us and take care of my kids."

"How many years have you been married?"

"Two years."

I said OK. The next day, he picked me up and took me to meet his mother. He told her, "This is the one I've chosen to take care of the children."

---

2. Also known as khat, a stimulant drug derived from a shrub that is native to East Africa and southern Arabia.

He left us alone, so I sat down with her. His mother could tell I was gay. She asked me, "How do you know my son?"

I explained how we had met and what he had said to me. She said, "*Sawa. Kwa sababu amejitolea mwenyewe na amekuleta na mimi nimekukubali, hakuna shida. Wewe keti. Ile siku mkisinyana, mtaachana wenyewe.*" OK. Because he's chosen you and brought you here, I have accepted you, there's no problem. Sit down. The day you fight, you'll deal with it yourselves.

And that's how we stayed, I was really free. He was the first-born, and I was treated like his wife. His wife came back and we met. We really fought. She fought with her husband too, "*Wewe watomba mashoga? Mimi sitaki!*" You fuck fags? I won't have it!

I told him, "*Ni mimi nilikuja nikakutongoza? Si ulinitongoza mwenyewe? Ongea na bibi yako, mwambie mimi sivuti waume. Ulikuja mwenyewe. Mwambie akirudia tena kunitukana tutapelekana polisi. Kama kutukana akutukane wewe.*" Is it me who seduced you? Aren't you the one who seduced me? Talk to your wife, tell her I don't lure men. You came to me. Tell her if she continues insulting me, we'll go to the police. If she wants to insult anyone, let her insult you.

She stopped insulting me from that day, but whenever we'd meet we didn't say much to each other.

His mother said, "*Haina shida usumbuane na huyu. Mimi bado nakupenda. Alipoondoka yeye, umenifanyia kazi kubwa sana hapa.*" Don't mind her. I still love you. Since she left, you've done so much work for me.

She gave me some money and told me to rent a house for myself. She said, "*Tafuta mvulana mwengine, lakini ukitaka chochote, wewe njoo.*" Find another boy, but if you need anything, come to me.

I moved out and she continued to pay my rent in my new house. I was still free to visit them, to sleep over, to cook—whatever I wanted. His mother would be very happy to see me. After a while I thought to myself, "I have my own job, why should I let an old woman pay for me?"

We're still friends, but we don't have sex any more. I caught him with another gay boy, AND I LEFT HIM.

–

What I mostly wish for is that one day, a person of my sexuality will have the freedom to walk down the street without being insulted or having a stone thrown at them. I want to walk into a restaurant with my partner and have no one stare when we kiss.

–

I'd see boys mistreating girls and ask myself, "These same struggling boys I was with in school are the ones who are suddenly in charge of the world?"

I was not here for that. I have mild seeds of heterophobia—if there's anything like that—and ask myself why the boys got to do everything. My friends who are girls are really strong. They were the cleverest in the class, the wittiest, they were really beautiful. I'm very pro-girl. I don't know what is beyond equality, but I am for it. Girls are smarter, faster, stronger, funnier and better in most ways, and these straight boys are still the ones in charge? Fuck that.

–

Blood isn't always thicker than water. I'm seeing gay people forming stronger bonds amongst themselves than they have with their families. Friends are becoming the new family.

–

I don't think we as Kenyans have dealt with our identity as people, and of course that includes our sex. We're still pretending to be Christians, with that fucking statistic of being 70% Christian. There's nothing 70% Christian about all the unsafe sex that is going on in this country. And that's not just the gays—because us gays are always labelled as being promiscuous. But even the straights are having a lot of unsafe sex; with other people's wives and husbands, relatives, strangers, while drunk, in cars. Even the kids are busy having sex when they're thirteen, fourteen, in school, with house-helps. But when the sun rises, everyone goes back to pretending that they're respectable, and everyone goes back to judging 'others'. The gays, the single mothers, the perverts. But there's no 'other' when it comes to sex. It's the same thing for everyone, that uncontrollable force that makes logic go out of the window.

Sex scares me, honestly. And I'm not the only one. Which is why I find that blanket assumption that all gays are promiscuous ridiculous. Sex is powerful, sex overrides all our barriers. I haven't been able to have sex with anyone for a long time. I'm always too worried about whether I really trust the person I'm about to have sex with. I don't believe there is a such a thing as 'casual sex'. There's nothing casual about that connection with another human being. I think it's deeply spiritual, and so I don't just throw it around.

I don't trust Kenyans with our weird attitudes to sex. There are a lot of men and women who are walking around with STIs, and either they don't know, or they're scared to get tested, or they're embarrassed to be seen going into a VCT[1] because they're married and people will wonder why a married man needs to go to VCT if he's faithful.

"*Niliona nani akienda VCT. Kwani bibi yake anamcheza?*" I saw so-and-so visiting VCT. Is his wife cheating on him?

I'm always shocked at how casual people are about not having condoms on them. Kenyans are ashamed to even be seen standing next to the condom stand at Nakumatt, because people stare at you. People giggle like children because someone is buying condoms. How will people practice safe sex if buying condoms is shameful? And then everyone is shocked that HIV infection rates are high. And among married people, who are the silliest of them all. Do you know how many straight people are using the withdrawal method as contraception? It's ridiculous, and straight men are enjoying doing it—despite remembering being in taught in school that it's not a reliable contraception method—mostly because they see it in porn. I don't understand straight people.

People are funny, in that sense. Once they get into sex mode, they stop thinking. It's like their brains switch off until they have their orgasm, and then all the logic comes back when it's too late.

That's when you hear a straight man saying, "Oh God! What have we done?" because he's suddenly remembered he's 'straight', but a few minutes before, he was deep inside you and kissing you passionately and telling you how good it feels.

"Oh my God! It's better than pussy."

That's happened to me many times. I get into situations where I'm making out with a straight guy, and once you cross that threshold where they realize that kissing another man doesn't feel different from kissing a woman, their brains just switch off. Sex mode. The next thing you know, you're wiping yourselves after the orgasms. I usually lie there and watch what they do after. It's very funny. Some guys dress up quickly and run away, or run to the shower immediately—like they feel dirty. Then there are the others who just lie there surprised, and wondering what they just did means.

"So am I gay now, because I enjoyed that?"

No, you're just a guy who enjoyed having sex with another man. Don't complicate the issue. Straight guys are funny.

I think one sad side-effect of this Kenyan moral pretentiousness, is that Kenyans are also having very bad sex. You can't imagine how many straight guys are so surprised at how good a proper blow job feels. Not that half-ass Christian blow jobs that Kenyan women are giving. I suck straight guys off—just a simple blow job, nothing fancy, *hata sijatumia pilipili* [I haven't even used chilli]—and so many of them are so shocked at the sensations and they whisper, "*Wallahi, sijawahi nyonywa hivo.*" My God, I've never been sucked like that.

And I ask them, "*Bibi yako hajui kazi yake?*" Doesn't your wife know her job?

Of course I can suck your dick better than your wife. Because I'm not guilty about sucking your dick. I enjoy it, and I have a dick, too. I know how it works. I know exactly where to put the pressure, and exactly what to do with my tongue. Girls in this country are walking around with bad blow job techniques. I just see girls wasting their time and money buying expensive weaves and clothes to impress men and they don't know how to suck dick.

Mke mwenye kusifiwa si nywele, ni mdomo mzuri. Good hair doesn't make a good wife, a good mouth does. Sometimes I think gay men should start giving classes to our sisters who are struggling. The only other women I know who are very good at sucking dick are a few sex workers who are very good. Not all of them. Some of them just lie there and count the minutes. But there are some sex workers who know their job well. But most straight men will never have the balls to sleep with a proper prostitute who gets off getting people off, so they'll never experience proper, mind-blowing sex. They'll just stay with their Christian wives who lie in missionary position and read Bible verses after sex, or the ones who suck dick half-heartedly and rush to the bathroom to spit as soon as the guy cums. Such a turn-off.

Then straight men have all these silly attitudes to women's bodies, "I can never eat pussy. I'm straight."

And the guys who walk around thinking that because they have big dicks it means their women are automatically satisfied. That's not the way that works. Women don't get off on your size. There are men with tiny dicks who can give your wife mind-blowing orgasms because they know how to touch a woman, how to taste a woman. Men imagine that dicks are the main ingredient in sex, but if you ever watch lesbians having sex you'll realise that's not true. Lesbians have multiple orgasms all the time—no wonder they're much happier. If anyone knows how to get a woman off, it's another woman. No dick involved. I've met straight women who say they've never had an orgasm while having sex with their husbands for nine, ten years, and I tell them to just have a one-on-one with a serious lesbian. And I'm sure the husbands of such women are walking around in the city thinking they've got game. One day, your wife will meet someone who is not ashamed to use their tongue and their fingers and your wife won't believe she has wasted so many years on your five-minute nonsense.

Sex is not just stuffing your dick into a woman and pushing for five minutes. Oh my God, the number of women in this country who fake orgasms just so their husbands and drunk boyfriends can finish and get off them. Someone needs to do a survey. If women were to admit the percentage of orgasms they fake, these straight men would be so shocked. Even those ones with big dicks who go around saying, "My girlfriend loves having sex with me."

Yeah, right. She's probably thinking of what shopping she needs to do after you're done. Or she'll wait for you to leave, then take out her little lipstick vibrator and have a real orgasm. No wonder the Government makes sex toys illegal—so that women don't learn how to get orgasms without men. I'm sure it's a man who made that law.

Men also don't know their bodies. I touch men in places and their eyes go wide, "What are you doing?"

"I'm touching you. *Kwani hujawai guzwa hapa?*" Haven't you ever been touched here?

These are things most gay men who explore their bodies know. I make guys cum without even touching their dicks. Just by exploring all the other erogenous zones of men's bodies. Most men don't know where those are. And their wives know even less. If straight people spent less time feeling guilty about sex, and shaming other people, and making laws to prevent other people from having good sex, and measuring their dicks with rulers, they'd have better sex. Until then, I'll have to keep hearing, "Oh my God, your hands are better than my wife's pussy."

Of course they are. My fingers ARE NOT ASHAMED.

–

I USE THE PRONOUNS THEY AND THEM. I do ask people to use them, and some are positive about it, they just accept. Others not so much, they say I'm being stupid. I don't plan to change my name. I once tried to change my name to a feminine name, but my straight friends started bullying me, calling me a bitch. So I took it back.

How I dress depends on how I'm feeling. Sometimes I can dress in a way that is feminine, and sometimes I dress like a guy. I don't conform to a specific dress code. I can wear tights. I've never tried wearing heels, though. My favorite clothes are anything made with Ankara and African print, so I wear those.

As for my sexual orientation, part of my family has accepted me, and the rest have not. For instance, my father has not yet accepted my orientation. He has some idea that I am different, but he's not aware of the whole thing. Someone went and told him that I'm gay and he was really angry and we didn't talk for some time, and then after a while he resumed talking to me, but we never talked about *that*. My step-mum is OK with my orientation, she knows everything and we are good. My aunties know and I think they also played a part in me wanting to have children, because they told me, "No matter what you do, you must make sure to have a child."

The main reason I decided against being trans is wanting to have kids and fulfilling my parents' expectations of me. I felt like no matter what decision I make, it will affect them either way. I do want children though, it's not just for my parents. I want to have a child, from my own body. I might consider transitioning later in life, after I have a child. Right now the major issue is to conceive, TO BE A PARENT FIRST.

–

I HAVEN'T WORN baggy clothes for years. I will never wear them again. I think they are a symbol of oppression. I'm skinny. Why should I wear baggy shit? I used to be a fashion blogger, but I was also able to talk about constitutional change and level with people on whatever they needed to discuss. This is why I hate boxing people up with labels—they cultivate stereotypes and deep ignorance.

I have many straight guy friends, some of them even married. When they open their eyes and see you for who you are, and you see them for who they are, it's just such a human connection. You look at all these other things and they're so petty. That's all you need really. That's what they should be preaching in church, and in Parliament, and in schools; not all the hate. People really teach hatred. They should just change the name of some subjects in schools to 'Hate'.

Once my friends and I were coming from a club, and we stopped at a fast food place because one of us was hungry. We were standing at the counter when this group of five guys started hurling insults at us. I think they were drunk. We completely ignored them, and that annoyed them even more. Two of my friends got mad and called them out on their ignorance and told them we had just as much right to be there as they did. The watchmen were just there watching, and not doing a thing. I was really shocked and traumatized by that. Before that I had only ever read about people being harassed in public, but now it was happening to us. We walked past a few other guys standing outside the place, and I wondered if they were there waiting to beat us up. Thankfully, nothing happened. I realized that this was the real Kenya, and this is what gay people go through.

People say I am an angry child, and I agree. But I channel my anger towards good causes and for positive things. I'm not about to slit my wrists or anything—that's not going to help anyone, help my situation or help the next guy like me in 20 years. People say gay rights are the civil rights issue of our time, and they really are. There's not enough sacrifice, or examples within the gay community to take it to the next level. We don't have anyone like Rosa Parks, or Martin Luther King. I'm not really for picketing or signing petitions, but I'm ready to be an example to show people that opportunities are for everyone, and it's up to people to pull up their socks and beat this system which is forever against them. People need to do the right thing and do it well. I know how to say no to things, and I know how to say no to people. I think THAT IS WHAT HAS HELPED ME.

–

I WANT A DAUGHTER by the time I'm twenty-eight. I feel like it's part of my destiny to have children. I'm going to be unconditionally in love with her and have a fantastic relationship with her and with my brothers' kids. I really want a girl, and I even have a name picked out for her, but I wouldn't mind a boy either. I want to go to those nanny schools where they learn how to change diapers and how to wake up at 3am. My daughter will just have to be Beyoncé with a Nobel Peace Prize. Whatever she wants to do, I'll want her to be the very best worldwide at it. I want to be able to provide the best opportunities for whatever she wants to do, and I will support her, and I WILL BE THERE.

–

I THINK IT'S SO RUDE when people ask, "Are you gay?"

It's such a personal thing to ask someone, and Kenyans do that all the fucking time. It's so fucking intrusive. And it's worse when they don't have the guts to ask you to your face, so they ask your friends, "Is █████ gay? We're just curious."

My friends have their own responses when they're asked about me, and it's never 'yes'. They tell people to mind their own fucking business or ask me themselves, then they tell me who has been asking around. Kenyans are such posers. They want to be traumatized by the fact that someone is gay so that they can think, "Oh, he must have so many problems!"

It's so stupid and superficial. I don't have time to entertain people having a problem with me.

–

I've always wanted five kids. Not all of them would be mine, though. I'd adopt two. Boys or girls, it doesn't matter. Children are children. If I'm going to be a doctor, I want my partner to also be a manager or something. I've always wanted to be with someone who will be at par with me. I don't want someone who's sitting at home *na kuniomba pesa ya kiberiti.* Asking me for money for matchsticks.

I'm planning to spend the rest of my life with a woman. I wasn't very sure that it could work, but I have two friends who are lesbian and they're married. They're very successful. They have a car, they own their house, and this is very rare for lesbians. And they have a baby. A boy. Almost a year and a half now. They're doing so well, and because I've seen them, I know it's possible. Their parents have accepted them after many battles, but eventually they accepted them.

I've realized that with success comes respect. And with respect comes acceptance. When I become a doctor, that will give me some level of influence. And if after that I introduced my family to my girlfriend who has her own job and we're both stable, we don't require help from anyone, and we are supporting our mums, you think they'll not accept us? They will. If we're sending them 20–30,000 every month, *kwani watatukataa? Hawawezi.* Can they really refuse us? They can't.

Tukiwajengea nyumba, watakataa kuishi? If we build them homes, will they refuse to live in them? No. That's what I have realized. So that's my goal, in terms of family, I definitely want to keep my brother and my mother and my dad, close. But then I also want them to accept ME AND MY OWN FAMILY.

–

BEING GAY ISN'T A JOY-RIDE, my dear. My homosexuality is not something that has sunk into my parents' hearts. I am the only son and so I am such a 'disappointment' to them. They tell me, "Even though you're like that, try and have a cover plan. You can find a nice girl and marry her. COVER YOUR TRACKS."

–

EVERY TERM IN MY HIGH SCHOOL, the Christian Union girls used to come up with a list of suspected lesbians that they wanted to pray for. Fucking busy-bodies. I was always number 1 on that list, and my girlfriend was always number 2 and some people who hung out with me were lesbians by association. We told the Christian Union to keep praying if they wanted. Our Headmistress, funny enough, didn't give a shit. She told us, "So you're lesbians? You've decided to become lesbians? That's fine. Have fun. In fact, that's better than your friends, who are always hitting on boys and getting pregnant."

She was quite something, our Headmistress. I REALLY ENJOYED HIGH SCHOOL.

–

AT SOME POINT when I was in university, I realized I would have to come out to the faculty to make my academic life easier, because some things were becoming tricky. I remember telling my dean, "I'm gay, and there's nothing you can do about it. I'll write gay papers and give my gay opinions, I'll put my gay poems in the magazine—you're muzzling everyone else who is not what you want them to be. How can you have a campus that only has heterosexual people? It doesn't work like that."

The dean said, "You're just a rebel, and you'll pull everyone down with you in your rebellion."

I have to admit, I really was a kind of rebel. I used to swing on the university gates and shit. I told her, "Just because I'm a rebel doesn't mean that my sexuality is a rebellion as well."

So the dean asked me to go out for lunch with her and asked me, "OK. Tell me what you're about."

So I told her everything. Eventually, one Wednesday during the public lecture—which everyone had to attend—my dean talked about diversity for the very first time. She talked about how everyone is different, and the need to accept people for who they are. After that, there was a bit of change. It wasn't as much as I had hoped for, but it was a step IN THE RIGHT DIRECTION.

–

IN THE COURSE of my work I have to keep coming out to different people. Some of them say, "Huh? What do you mean? We have lesbians IN THIS COUNTRY?"

–

THERE ARE CHALLENGES that come with sex work. Sometimes people insult us, "*Shoga wewe! Watu wamelala, wewe wauza mkundu! Mwanaume, badala utafute kazi ufanye, umesoma, wewe kazi yako wauza mkundu?*" You fag! People are asleep, and you're selling your ass! A man like you, with your education, instead of looking for work to do, you're selling ass?

Sometimes when you want to rent a house, people tell the landlord, "*Wewe! Wakodishia yule shoga nyumba? Nyumba yako itakuja chomwa!*" You! You want to rent your house to a fag? Your house will get burnt down!

Or sometimes you want to hitch a ride on a boda boda, and people say, "*Wewe, boda! Usimpandishe huyo! Hiyo pikipiki ikifika bridge utapinduka nayo uingie kwa maji!*" Driver! Don't carry that one! Your motorbike will crash into the water when you get to the bridge *[laughs]*!

The funny thing is that our clients are never insulted. They can be seen walking with us, and they're not afraid. When I walk with my straight clients, no one can fight with him because they're afraid. They talk about it in private, "*Yule jamaa kwani yuafira masenge siku hizi?*" That guy has sex with fags these days?

But they'll keep that talk to themselves. They can't say it out loud.

"*Eh! Yuapenda sana mikundu…*" He really likes ass.

Once I was walking with one of my clients, and he argued with some of his friends about some politics. One of them said, "*Utatuambia nini? Wewe mwenyewe wafira mashoga!*" What can you tell us? You, you fuck fags!

My client said to the guy, "*Kama nafira mashoga, si ni mimi mwenyewe? Achana na mimi, napenda mkundu. Pia wewe ukitaka, njoo nikufire!*" If I'm fucking fags, isn't that's my business? Leave me alone, I like it. If you want some, I can fuck you too!

AND THEN THEY ALL LAUGHED.

–

TRAJECTORIES OF THE FUTURE are difficult, so I don't know what's in store for me in the next ten years. For me, the concept of family is very violent and patriarchal and heteronormative. I definitely don't have any desire to have kids. I love kids but, you know. So maybe in ten years, I'll be part of a growing group that's redefining WHAT FAMILY IS.

–

I'M GAY, but I had a girlfriend for a long time. Let's call her Mercy. I met Mercy in 2005 when I was in high school, and we officially started dating in 2006. I genuinely loved her. She had no pressure for us to get intimate, and she was 'church-y'. I thought she was wife material. I thought to myself, "I can love a woman and settle down with her and satisfy the society and I will still be happy."

I committed to loving her and being with her every weekend. I introduced her to my mum and my siblings. We would go hiking, and we'd have long conversations before we slept . I remember once I clocked two hours and thirty minutes on phone with her—I think that was profound. It was quite something. I had real feelings for her. The only intimacy we had was kissing, but not often; less than five times. Either she knew there was something about me, or she was genuinely waiting for marriage. Or maybe she had another boyfriend.

We broke up on my twenty-second birthday. We had lunch, and then I told her that we needed to take our relationship to the next level. I meant that we needed to start seriously and officially meeting our families and parents; the first step to getting married. She paused and looked at me and said, "No. Something is not adding up, and I don't feel like this is working."

We were in a restaurant, and she took the salt and pepper shakers and said, "Look at these two. They're very identical, but they serve different purposes. This has pepper and this has salt. I think I'm in your life like any other lady—to love and care for you—but not to be your romantic lover."

I said, "Wait, what about the four years we've been together?"

She said, "You know what? Even if we'd been together for fifteen years, I'd still walk away. I think I was in your life for a reason and for a season and it's done. I'll not meet you again, and you have to move on."

That was a wrap. That was such a blow because I didn't think it would go down that way. I sent her a message on Facebook long after, and she asked me, "Don't you think you were being unfair to me? You knew for sure what you felt in your heart, but you still insisted you wanted to go down that road with me. Don't you think it would have been messier if we didn't break up at that point?"

I NEVER MET HER AGAIN.

–

FAMILY FOR ME is people that love me, and I love them. And I choose them and they choose me. I've learned that your family has nothing to do with the people you are born into, and it is sacrilegious to say that here.

"How dare you say that I'm not your family?"

Here, we are taught that family are the people you are related to by blood, but no. Not for me. Family love you, they support you, call you out on your shit, AND THEY GUARD YOU.

–

I DEFINITELY FEEL like I have created a family out of my friends. They're the people who genuinely love you unconditionally, even though you may fight with them, or have different points of view. My closest friends are the people I have around me almost on a daily basis. I speak with them on a daily basis, and those are the people who I consider my family. It's a shame that I don't have a stronger bond with my biological family. I don't feel like they understand me. I don't feel as understood by my own biological family as I do by my friends.

My future family will be myself and a very loving man. I don't know whether we will be married, but I would like to imagine that we would be because I think I'm bit of a sucker for weddings. I'd like to have a big wedding and many dogs and animals. I do not see children in my future, at least none of my own. I have had a few friends look at me and laugh and say, "You wait and see."

My friends think that I'm going to get some sort of craving for a child, but I think I would be satisfied with my friends' children. I genuinely think that I'm too selfish to have children. I am my own top priority, which is definitely something I think is a character flaw. I'm very self involved. I spend a lot of my days thinking about myself and what I want to do, where I want to be, and who I want to talk to.

I spend a lot of time thinking about myself, and I just don't think I have the capacity to share that mental space with children. I don't think I would be happy about it. That's the joy of being single at this point, and not having to think about all these other things. You can just think about yourself, and YOU'RE ABLE TO CENTRE YOURSELF.

–

GENERALLY, I'M HAPPY. At this moment in time I can be grateful for a lot of things—I'm in a very good place. I'm healthy, and I have a lot of love around me. I finally found a career that I love. I've just come out of a very long relationship that I thought was possibly going to be for the rest of my life, but I'm in a good place about why the relationship ended and I think I'm heading in a very healthy direction to an amicable relationship with that person because I still see them in my life. So yeah, things are working out at the moment.

The moments of sadness I have are very fleeting, and they happen because I am in a country where being who I am and expressing my love is considered criminal. The fact that a majority of the population would possibly want to stone me if they had an opportunity. That makes me sad, but it's a sadness that I have to bear with everyone else that is in THE SAME SITUATION I AM IN.

–

AT SOME POINT, I wasn't in a good place in my life. I wasn't in university and I didn't have a job. I ended up living with someone who possibly wasn't the best person to live with. She was a prostitute by profession, and she used to hook up with guys and get money off them. There were a lot of drugs involved in my life at that time, which I guess helped to numb me at a time when I needed to be numb.

The problem with drugs and alcohol is that by being under their influence, you open yourself up to vulnerable or dangerous situations. We would get up on Monday, go out on Monday night, come back home on Tuesday mid-day, sleep until 6pm, wake up and go out clubbing again till Wednesday midday... It was a cycle of partying and doing lots and lots of drugs. One time I was so tired, so I stayed home to sleep and she went out clubbing. She came back home at about 6:30 in the morning with a big group of people. One of them was a bouncer from some club in town they had been at. I woke up and found him blacked out on the sofa. All those people stayed over until night. I got to bed and at about 5am, I woke up and there was somebody on top of me. I said, "Who the fuck are you and what are you doing in my bedroom?"

He said, "Relax."

And I shouted, "What the hell are you doing in my bedroom, and why are you naked?"

He suddenly got very aggressive. He pinned me down and gagged my mouth. It was very scary and I remember it was so horrible because I could hear my friends in the living room still partying but I couldn't yell because he was crushing me with his weight. I couldn't even take in a breath deep enough for me to be able to shout. Luckily, I was able to manoeuvre my way around. I kneed him in the balls and he rolled off me in pain, and I bolted the fuck out of my room.

One thing that made me really sad about that situation is that I felt like I couldn't get justice for that. I couldn't walk into a police station and say, "This man tried to rape me," because I was too scared. I didn't want to put myself in a situation where I could then be under attack, and that made me feel like I couldn't get closure from it. I remember seeing the guy weeks later in a club. He was sitting there with some women, and I remember feeling so helpless and cheated that I couldn't go to the law for protection, WHICH IS WHAT IT SHOULD BE THERE FOR.

–

I WAS SUCH A PORN ADDICT in college. Once, I went in for an accounting class, and while the teacher was teaching I was not listening. I was watching gay porn on my computer. When he was done he asked, "Does anyone have any questions?"

Just to show him I was paying attention, I said, "Yes, I do. How did you say one deletes a transaction?"

He said, "You didn't get that? OK. Anyone else who has a problem with that?"

No one else had a problem, so he said, "OK. Let me come and show you how to do it on your computer."

I'm telling you, I don't know how he walked from the front to the back where I was so quickly. The next thing, he was standing next to me and there was a clip I had paused; full-screen.

He said, "Is this what you're doing in class? That's why you cannot understand what I'm teaching?"

The good thing was the class had over sixty computers, and we were only fifteen students. The rest had sat in the front and I was at the back, so they couldn't see what he was referring to. He closed that web page, only to find twenty other similar pages I had minimized. So he would close one and find another. He closed all those pages one by one and told me, "Don't do this again, OK? Let me show you how to delete a transaction."

He showed me how to do it and he was done. No one knew what had happened, and he didn't tell the IT administrator who was in the room. I was so embarrassed, I was so freaked out, and I was so sorry. I followed him to his office and said, "Sir, I am so sorry. I am so embarrassed right now."

He said, "I know you guys. You're so curious, but don't do those things in class. Go to the cyber-cafés, OK? Apology accepted."

I stopped doing it, and HE IS MY FRIEND TO DATE.

–

I'M GAY AND I HAVE KIDS. When I was twenty-two, my friends came home with three girls. One of the three girls was very talkative. We talked a lot, and somehow ended up having sex. It was my first time with a woman. Unfortunately, she got pregnant. We told our parents, and they talked things out and agreed to take the child. After nine months, she gave birth to twins! A boy and a girl.

Many years have passed since then and I have tried my best to live with them. They visit their mother but they stay with my family. My partner Michael also has two children—a boy and a girl—but his are young. My children have stayed with us for a long time. Michael's kids have not stayed with me long enough.

It is amazing how the kids have divided our roles. We never spoke about who should be doing what when my children were growing up, but they knew how to differentiate me and Michael. He is not very feminine, but when my daughter needed her hair done she would tell Michael. When they needed school fees they would ask me. It has never been a problem for them. I decided I should tell them what was going on between Michael and I before someone else and gave them a different view. They were about twelve years, and they had always known that I am gay.

They came for a holiday and I told them, "I know you might be wondering how other families have Daddy and Mommy and you only have Daddy and Uncle. I want to tell you that Michael is not just an uncle, he is my partner."

My daughter is very intelligent so she said, "I think we know what you mean."

The boy might not say it, but I think he doesn't like it. He is not very close but we talk a lot. I know he might be struggling with the fact that his dad is a homosexual. My daughter is OK. SHE HAS SUPPORTED ME A LOT OVER THE YEARS.

–

Once I was caught in an incident in ████. The people from the community and religious leaders made a plan to get rid of gay people. They knew where we lived, and what clubs we frequented. Unluckily, I was caught. That was the worst. I was beaten so badly. They stole my phone and identity card. It had all been planned but the police came to save us. I then moved to Nairobi for three months to stay away from the attacks. I am strong now, unlike that first time. I learnt from that experience.

–

Being gay is hell here in ████. It's just that I have the strength to withstand all this stuff; stigma in hospital, stigma in the community, in the family. I have the heart for it. But some of us are not making it. Every day I hear someone's been beaten, someone's been thrown out by their family. Even yesterday, some kid was beaten so badly by his family. He's in hospital now. I've been kicked out many times, and I always go back. I say, "This is the way I am, *mtajipanga*." Deal with it.

Then they leave me alone. I'm used to it, so it seems normal. When gay people go to the hospital and the staff notice them, they start gossiping, "Look at him."

You see staff pretending to walk into the room pretending that they had come to pick up a pair of scissors, just so they can look at you and stare at you curiously. Some people ignore that, but I always insult them, "*Wewe malaya, umejileta hapa kufanya nini? Usijifanye umekuja kuchukua makasi, ni kuniona umekuja kuniangalia.*" You slut, what have you come here to do? Don't pretend you've come here to pick up those scissors, you've come to stare at me.

Then they say, "*Pole, pole! Sina ubaya!*" Sorry! I don't have any bad intentions!

"*Huna ubaya, lakini toka.*" That may be, but get out.

Then you see them rushing out without the scissors.

–

I live with my boyfriend, but nobody knows. We live as cousins. We're both not originally from here, so they can't tell that we're actually not cousins. We've been together for two years now, but we don't have any children, and we're not holding our breath because I can't give birth *[laughs]*. We want kids, though. I'm going to get a girl pregnant, and he'll get another girl pregnant, then both the kids can come home and be siblings.

He's a kind boy. Hard-working. And as gay as I am. He doesn't care what people think about us. He doesn't care what his family thinks about his relationship. I'm proud of him because of that. I've met his family, but not as his lover, as his friend. But, of course, *rumors zinafika*. Rumors reach them. They suspect he's gay, because they've never seen him with a girl.

My family knows all about me. They know because I was caught. I had a boyfriend when I was younger, but our mutual friends wanted to know what was going on between us. They spied and spied on us, and they realized that whenever we were not in school, we were in my house. What can they be doing?

So they came to my house while I was with my boyfriend and peeped through the windows. They realized we were watching gay porn. It's funny because that happened to be the first time I had ever watched gay porn. We usually used to watch straight porn. They waited until we started having sex. Unfortunately, I hadn't locked the doors. They came in.

"*Tushawapata! Msivae!*" We've already caught you! Don't wear your clothes!

They made us walk outside, naked.

"*Hatutaki mashoga huku mtaani!*" We don't want fags in this neighbourhood!

We were beaten and punished, and that story died there. They were beating us as if our gayness was something that could be beaten out of us. Since then, that boyfriend said he was straight. But just recently he started calling me, saying he wants to get back with me. I told him, "Too late. I'm married *[laughs]*."

That's how my family found out. They didn't say anything. By that time, they were tired of telling me. I have more makeup than my mother *[laughs]*. When I used to stay with my parents, my cousins would come over and wonder which bedroom was mine. "WHY IS EVERYTHING PINK *[laughs]*?"

–

My father knows that I am gay. I had a conflict with a former male partner of mine, and he went and told my father about us. My dad sat me down and asked me whether I was gay. I admitted it and told him it was true. He advised me to get married so that other people would not suspect I was gay. He said he could not stop me from doing what I wanted, but I should get married so that no one would know.

My father is a learned person and he understands me. My mother doesn't know. My mother is very harsh and too religious. If she heard I was gay, she would say that those are curses. I can never tell her.

So I married my wife, and we got a child, then I realized I was really not into women. Throughout my marriage, it was really challenging to have sex with my wife. I had to close my eyes and imagine that she was a man to get aroused. If I thought of my wife I would never rise to the occasion.

So we divorced and now I have a male partner. When I got divorced, my parents came to my house to find out what was going on. I told my father that I couldn't go on pretending, and that I had found a male partner I wanted to live with. My father decided not to tell my mother. I moved out of our home and my partner and I have been together for two years.

My ex-wife got an opportunity to go and work abroad, so she left me with our son. She visits him every now and then, and he is now nine years old. Because he is young, I have let him live with his grandmother—my mother. She treats him as her last born child, and I visit him every so often. My mother is very harsh to me—even when I come to visit him—so I don't visit him so much.

As the Kenyan law stands, I cannot marry a man. Even if I live with him in the same house, people think he is just a friend. If I married him officially, that would be a problem. I wish we could get married, though. If I was given a chance, I would marry him.

—

I WANT TO BECOME A STRIPPER; I want to go to Europe so that I can become a stripper, and I DON'T WANT TO GROW OLD.

–

I KNOW IT IS SHOCKING because I am a Muslim and I am saying things that are improper, but if gay marriage was legalized I would marry. I don't like women. I just want a man.

I am not an active Muslim, but I fast and pray. It is complicated. Some of my friends know I am gay, so they keep telling me scary things about how I will die, and that I should marry and have a family. I always promise them to change, but I know I want to be with a man. My parents have never asked me, but they are my parents so I am sure they either know or suspect I am gay.

My mother condemns homosexuality, so if she knew I would be treated differently by my family. Even when she watches news regarding gay people, she is always shouting that they should be burned. Yet she does not know that I am one of them, and I am under her roof. At one point I wanted to tell her so that she could stop talking like that, but my friends advised me against it as she suffers from high blood pressure and I would be accused OF KILLING HER.

–

FAMILY—to me—is that person that you look forward to GOING HOME TO MEET.

–

SOMETIMES THE POLICE ARREST YOU. The police know who the queer people are; they are able to tell, maybe from the way I'm talking or from the way I'm walking. So they harass me. There was a time I was even raped by two policemen. For no particular reason at all. I was on Mama Ngina Drive—it was a public holiday, and there were other people relaxing there. The police came and saw me, and arrested me. When they were taking me into custody, they asked for my ID and I gave it to them, but that didn't stop them. I got into their van, but they didn't take me to the police station. They took me somewhere and they told me, "If you don't want to be arrested, then..."

I told them, "Just arrest me, because I haven't done anything wrong," but they raped me, and then left me there on the street. I didn't report it because it was hard. You can go to talk to the police and find yourself in deeper trouble. I suppose I also didn't report it because I did not have the information that I have now. If something like that happens to me now, I know what to do. But that was some time back, I was still naïve, very green. I didn't report it because I was ignorant. I told my friends about it and they said, "*Pia sisi tumefanyiwa hivyo, we kaa tu.*" The same thing has happened to us, just leave it.

Right now, I am the one who is telling them that it is not a normal thing, and that you shouldn't accept it. *Ikikufanyikia, sema.* If it happens to you, say something. These days we say to one another, "If something like that happens to you, even if you don't report it to the police at that time, look for someone to talk to about it. THE ADVICE WILL GIVE YOU THE NEXT STEP.

–

I'VE NEVER BEEN ARRESTED, but I have spent a night at the station. There was a night we were meeting up with some trans friends who were visiting from Uganda, they were here for a conference that we were all a part of. We headed out earlier than them, so we decided to stop by a local bar for a drink. While we were having our drinks, someone called the cops, so they came and made a lame excuse about us drinking past the allowed times, and arrested only us.

Let me tell you how mad I am, when we got to the station, we were taken to the men's cell. The men in there were looking so ugly, hardened and un-moisturised: it was terrible. Anyway, we were trying to find a place to sit but everywhere we would try to sit, someone would say, "That's my place!"

So I went to the bathroom and stripped naked, put my clothes on the windowsill then filled three buckets with water. I carried them back to the cell then I kicked them into the room, so everyone had to stand up. Then I shouted, "If we have to stand, we're all standing."

The men started banging on the door and the cops came. The other inmates started shouting that we had to mop up the place, and I said to them, “Did you not say this was your place? Why should I wipe it? It’s your place, you mop it”.

We ended up being moved to the women’s cell.

–

The cops got tired of arresting me, they got so tired. Whenever they see me, they just say “Hi Malia!”

Even the new cops who come here on transfer are warned, “There’s a faggot called Malia, you’ll see her soon enough, going out at night in her heels. If she talks back at you, just leave her alone.”

I always give the cops something small from time to time. Whether it’s a soda or a beer. They haven’t arrested me since 2012. In fact when my friends are arrested; it’s usually me who goes to bail them out. I usually enter straight to the officer in charge and tell him, “You have one of my people!” and he tells the officers, “Can you release Malia’s people before she starts making a scene here! Because you know if this mad woman starts, she won’t leave!”

The cops were so tired of me by the time they stopped arresting me. I really gave them a hard time, that’s not a secret.

Did you see that time I made the news? I was caught on the streets, wearing my heels, miniskirt, makeup: I was decked out. There I was in my little skirt, walking to get a taxi to go to the club. I noticed the town was quite empty, little did I know that all my people had been rounded up. Shortly, I see a black car pulling up, so I thought it was a client. It turned out to be the police and press! They were all there, and they took my photos as the police told me to take off my wig. I was arrested and went to jail for a week, then I was arraigned in court. The judge said, “You have been found as a man in women’s clothes, and you are charged with prostituting and with the intention of deceiving your fellow men.”

I said to him, “I do not disagree, your Honor, but let me ask you something: if your body was all you had to sell to pay rent and buy food, wouldn’t you?”

He looked at me, and I saw him writing something in his notebook. I thought, “Shit! That’s probably 10 years.”

But I was actually released. They didn't even send me back to the cell, they said, "You can go now."

So I WALKED OUT OF THE COURT ROOM.

–

COMING OUT

My older brother found out I was gay by reading my journal. I used to journal a lot about my fantasies and feelings. He took my journal and read it and decided he wanted to do something about it. He told the whole world, "█████ is a homosexual," and it caused family feuds.

He'd go out and drink, come back in a drunken stupor and start yelling about it in front of my folks, "I'm not going to have a gay brother! I want you out of this house!"

And I was shouting back, "So what? Do what you're going to do!"

And my parents were asking my brother, "*Mbona unatukana ndugu yako?*" Why are you insulting your brother?

For them, it was an insult. We kept fighting about it. Our relationship was really terrible and we stopped talking. My brother never confronted me about it when he was sober. I wish he would have. He must have seen it coming. When I was younger, I used to resonate more with the female protagonists of every movie I watched on TCM. I was obsessed with Princess Diana, Grace Kelly, all these royal women. I used to relate more to the women. My brother used to see all that, and he must have seen this coming.

Whether I like it or not, he's a big influence on my life because he's the one who made me start loving art. He introduced me to basketball—and we used to watch it together. But I never watched it wanting to be a player, I used to watch basketball wanting to be *with* a player. Look at how tall these men are! Who are these men going home to? And I was a vocal child, so I used to say all these things loudly. I used to play with girls, I was just so girly, and he must have known. I guess when the reality dawned on him, he reacted differently.

I have three sisters and one brother. One of my sisters was very hateful at first, but she came round pretty fast. She saw me travelling this journey and she got to understand me. She even saw the men I slept with and she'd say, "He's interesting. He's nice."

She knows. It's not a big deal for her. Then there's my holier-than-thou sister who—to this day—I'm still trying to get to accept the reality. In recent times, I've been talking to her more about it. And she starts telling me about the Bible, about Sodom and Gomorrah and all that. To avoid arguments, I let her rant a bit and then I end the conversation. Recently I sent her a text and told her we need to sit down and talk properly about this shit. She's always trying to change me, she thinks I woke up one morning and said, "Heeeey! Let's do the gay life, try it then I'll go back to the straight life!"

Then my other sister doesn't want to talk about it. My mother discovered from other people. Neighbours. These heifers would go up to my mother and tell her, "Your child is going to be a homosexual. This is the how they behave."

Then my mother would preach to me a bit. She's a Bible person, and I'd tell her, "If the Lord has a problem with me, He'll let me know."

Once when I was drunk, I went up to my father and told him, "Listen, and listen very carefully. I know I haven't ever been the sort of son that you expected me to be, because I'm gay and I act like a woman, and I look like a woman, and it's fine. Whatever it is you think you're denying me by trying to cut me off and show me all these petty *madharaus* [spiteful actions]? Just bear in mind, I will conquer this world one sequin at a time."

I was all tear-y. I'd talk to other boys and they'd tell me what their fathers would talk to them about. My father would never tell me such things, but I'd see him doing it to other people's children. He was in a quagmire of sorts. His older son is a drunken fool, and the other one is a queen. He's torn between the two; which is the lesser evil? The drunk or the queen?

If your very own people can treat you as a lesser person, what do you think the world is going to treat you like? These are the things that made me decide I'm going to be a fighter. And I've been living my life like one since then. Gay people are underdogs, you have to aim much higher to get what the rest are getting. I WAS TAUGHT THAT AT HOME.

–

I HAVEN'T OPENLY IDENTIFIED MYSELF as trans to my mother. I like to think it goes without saying. After I get my psychiatric evaluation, then I will open up to my family or come out to them as a trans woman. I don't want to face challenges before then in my transition, especially around what my mom or dad would say. They would hurt me and they would try to bring me back. I don't want that interference.

I have three sisters, and they are very open and they embrace me the way I am, but my challenge remains the relationship between my parents and I. My dad has been extremely vocal against my being the way I am. He has opposed me very, very clearly. He is against whatever I am, to the extent of divorcing my mum. He asked her to choose him or me, but my mum is the one who carried me. She's the one who nurtured me, nursed me to health, took care of me. *Yeye hawezi kuniacha*. She can't leave me.

She told him, "We created that child together. We created that 'devilish boy' together. How can you tell me to abandon my son and follow you? I can't."

So she chose me. Because of that, I see myself as a family breaker, and it makes me think I don't want a family of my own. If a partner can force you to choose sides like that, then no. I DON'T WANT A FAMILY.

–

I THINK MY FAMILY KNOWS about me. I'm sure my mum must know something. Once, my phone had a problem and I needed to talk to some guys so she let me use her phone. I chatted with the guys but I forgot to delete the texts. My mum went through the texts, and I didn't know anything about it. My phone developed the same problem later on, and I asked her for her phone again. She said, "You can use mine, but remember to delete your messages. Not like the ones you left."

So I think she has a hint.

One day, I'll not be afraid to tell my family. My mum would be the first to know. I have an elder brother who asks me questions like WHY I'M NOT INTO LADIES.

–

I'M OUT AT WORK, and everyone seems to be OK with it—and I'm grateful for the people at work giving me room in their lives. You can't forget gratitude, and decide that it's your right to be there. I've gotten people really talking about this things at work. We even have open forums. My God, they're so intense. Sometimes people ask stupid questions, but I'd rather they do that if only to educate themselves.

I usually just walk in and people gather and ask me questions like, "Do you have a boyfriend?"

And I say, "No, I'm not so good with men."

"Why don't you have a boyfriend?"

"I haven't met the right one."

"What's sex like for gay people?" and I explain.

They ask, "What sort of man do you want?"

"Can you tell a gay man from a straight man?"

"Do gay people cum with their asses?"

Do you know how many times I've been asked that question? And they can't Google these things, they even feel ashamed to Google such things. Are they going to Google 'how gay people come with their ass'? I suppose Googling it isn't like hearing it from a gay man. These days I know to expect that one question, someone always brings it up.

I explain and that's when makes you realize there are very many misconceptions out there. People need to have these forums to put those misconceptions at rest. There are people who are not happy about those forums, but they don't say it to my face. You can always tell them apart, the people who don't want to know. They walk out, because they don't want to know. Like knowing is such a bad thing.

I don't know if someone tells people that gay people have horns running down our backs—that would have been so hot, such a nice silhouette. After a while, they see that I'm hustling just like them, I'm employed just like them, trying to climb the work ladder just like them, I have dreams and ambitions just like them—they realize we're just normal people. Then you see people starting to open their minds, and their hearts and their spirits.

The thing I love about these forums is that these people will go and have their own. You can speak to five people, and this one will go and have it with her husband, this one with his girlfriend, this one with his friends while they're drinking—so it grows. They'll be in a bar drinking at a table, and someone will try to have an anti-gay conversation, and because this person listened and understood will say, "You know these gay people are not so bad. I know a gay guy, and we were talking and he told us..."

These are not things that you're going to wake up and change in one day, it has to happen slowly. Imagine if all the gay people would do something like this. All the out ones—you know you can't rush people out of the closet. You have to give them time. Long ago, I wanted everyone out of the bloody closet. Blow up those closets! You're either in or out! Then as I grew older, I realized it doesn't work like that. People move at their own pace.

There are those who crawl while others are walking, and jumping and running—while others are flying! Everyone has their journey, and you have to respect that. Sometimes I run into gay people who shut up, then pull me aside and say, "Sweetheart. The rest of us can't live our lives like that."

And I tell them I understand; YOU DO WHAT YOU CAN.

–

I AM SORT OF OUT to my family. I think they know. It comes out in little slips in conversations. They don't have a language for it. I think my brother knows, he has never brought it up though. My mother sort of suspects I'm gay. Most times she ignores my effeminate expressions. Once I was sitting, talking with her and I made a gesture which was very girly and she said, "█████, I know you were born that way, but just try..."

My sister is married. There were numerous incidences—while she was pregnant—when she'd get worked up and would confront me, asking why I don't have a girlfriend at my age. She would threaten to go home and tell my parents that they should not expect that I will ever get a wife or children—which was a big deal. She would assign me the task of getting a girlfriend. Or she'd tell me to go away to find people who are like me and live in a location far away since people who are like me are not wanted in the society.

She would use the word 'kookie' [a gay character in a popular TV soap opera] to refer to my mannerisms. She would say these 'kookie' type of characteristics are not accepted in this society. If I don't find a separate place to live, she would expect that I find a girlfriend. It was always so urgent.

I am not very keen on the family relationships, I don't speak to them about my gay life. It is a taboo. I know so much about them.

They just vent all the time about their wives, their work and I just listen. I am very close to my mother, but I have never felt the need to tell her. I have never told my siblings, I don't think they need to know.

I think that relates to the politics of definition. Why should I feel obligated to tell anyone? Coming out is such a big obligation. It is seen as a big part of being in the movement. You are not seen as part of the movement if you do not come out, if you don't say who you are to your family. Other people don't do it. It is not necessary. Straight people don't have to tell their parents and siblings that they are heterosexuals. They just come home with their girlfriends and life goes on. They are not obligated.

I just want that. One day I come home with my boyfriend and let's move on. Let's not talk about it. IT'S NOT A NECESSARY CONVERSATION.

–

I GREW UP in a Christian family, I was raised by my grandmother and I feel like it would be a disappointment if she found out I was gay. So I would not want her to know. Right now I am out, but only to a couple of select friends. I think my dad suspects that I'm gay and he once told me he would be OK with it if I was gay, but I think it was a trap! I didn't buy it, so I didn't tell him.

No one in my family knows. I have a fake boyfriend, everyone at home knows him. They think it's the real deal and that's how I would like to keep it. I don't want my family to know.

The first person I told was a really close friend of mine. She was very supportive, it surprised me. She told me it's normal and that there are people like me. It meant a lot coming from a straight person. She told me I should learn to accept who I am, because at the time I was breaking very many hearts trying to be straight, trying to find myself.

It's weird coming out to a straight friend. There's this thing where they end up acting differently WHEN THEY FIND OUT.

–

MY MOTHER SUSPECTS I'm gay, but I really try not to give her a reason to suspect anything. My closest cousins and friends know, but her? I think it might kill her slowly. I have many girlfriends, because I really don't like being alone. When I am alone I have scary thoughts. The safest time is when I am asleep—I feel like I have left my troubles behind, JUST FOR A BIT.

–

THE FIRST PERSON I CAME OUT TO was my sister and she was OK. She told me she already knew. She sat there, and I talked and I talked. She gave me a hug and said, "You know what? You're my brother. This doesn't change my relationship with you, and I will support you. Can I meet your boyfriend?"

She met him, and she's our friend; she hangs out with us sometimes. Next, I told my brother and his fiancée. I told them, "I need you guys to know that I'm gay."

They were not very surprised. All of them had had a feeling I was gay. My brother said, "I had a feeling. You've been having parties in your house but you never invite girls."

He discussed it with his fiancée, and they said it was OK. I told them to ask me questions; anything they wanted to know. I told them, "I need you to know who I am. I don't want to pretend around you."

They asked questions, "What's your role?"

"How does sex happen?"

I explained everything I could and they were OK. They said, "Fine. This will not define our relationship with you. Only two things; don't tell mum yet and don't act like a lady around us. We would have a problem with that."

I told them, "Wait. I've been gay for so long and I've never acted like a lady."

They said, "Oh, OK. Yes. Carry on the way you are."

They thought that after I came out I'd become feminine, so they had to warn me in advance.

"If we're walking with you in town, be a gentleman. If we're going out with you, be a gentleman. Don't act like a lady."

I said, "Fine, I don't have a problem with that. I've never acted like one, have I?"

I'm not out to my folks yet. I think I will tell them one day, but in a few years' time. I know it will be a shock. I need more time to gather the confidence to have that conversation because it will not be an easy one. Several friends of mine have come out to their folks willingly or by mistake, and it has backfired on them because they didn't know how to conduct the conversation. They didn't have the strength to face their parents and discuss it. I think I probably need a bit more time, then WE WILL SIT AND TALK.

–

I LIKE THE WAY Binyavanga Wainaina came out. I think his coming out has done a lot for the gay community. But, as much as it has brought conversations in areas where people don't have the information, it has not worked for everyone. For instance, we used to have this establishment where most gay people would go to have a drink but after the Binyavanga story, the owner decided that he didn't want TO SEE GAY PEOPLE IN HIS ESTABLISHMENT.

–

WHEN I CAME OUT to my mother, she told me I was A DEVIL WORSHIPPER.

–

COMING OUT TO MY FAMILY was death and rebirth at the same time. I had dreaded having to do it almost all my life, from the moment I knew I was gay. I did everything I could to escape having to have that conversation with my family.

I always considered myself to be very close to my family, but after coming out—everything became different. I started by telling my brother. I couldn't face him, so I called him and told him I was gay. He sounded shocked, and asked me how I knew, how long I had known. Then he shocked me by saying he still loves me, and is still my brother. We're not that kind of family. We don't use the word 'love' with each other. This was the first time I'd ever heard him use that word near me, and to me. He asked to meet me about a week later, and we had a very adult conversation about it. It sounded like he'd taken the week to think about it, and speak to his wife and his pastor about it. He told me his wife said she had always known. I wasn't surprised. I always knew she had solid gaydar. She used to give me a knowing look, but never said anything.

Then I geared up to tell my parents. I read articles online: 'How to Come Out to Your Parents'. Most of these articles were written by Americans, with cute tips about asking your parents to join the local PFLAG chapter. We don't have those here. But the one thing most of the articles said was to listen. Listen to them and let them express themselves. OK. I will listen.

So I drove to my parents house one Sunday morning, telling myself that the only courage I needed was the courage to walk into the house and say, "I have something to tell you."

That's all. If I could do that, the rest would happen by force. So I walked in and told my parents. It was hell. So many tears, so much drama. My mother's face crumpled when I told her. Like I was dead or something. My father held his head in his hands and moaned like he was in pain. Because it was Sunday morning, they were going to church. So we couldn't talk for long. I guess that was my plan. I knew they'd never cancel their trip to church unless I was bleeding.

"We'll talk," they said.

And I went home, exhilarated at myself for having said the thing that I'd dreaded saying for years. A few days later, my mother asked to meet me. I sat in her car while she wept, and wept, and wept, and said all kinds of ridiculous things to me. Listen. Remember to listen, I told myself, willing myself not to interrupt her.

"I knew we shouldn't have sent you to a boarding school. I always used to tell your father, will he be OK?"

Listen. I passed her some more tissues, the ones she was holding were soggy with tears and mucus.

"It's unnatural, and you know God wouldn't allow it, because humanity would end."

Listen. The last time I saw her cry so hard was when her sister died. She was mourning me, and I'm sitting right there. Death. Rebirth.

A week later, it was my dad who called me. He wanted to talk man-to-man. Ha. We sat together outside the house and he told me to tell him everything. I told him everything. Except for the parts where I'm naked. I'm sure he was imagining worse, anyway.

"That lifestyle…" he muttered when I was done, "Why would you choose it?"

Oh God. Listen. Don't argue that you were barely four years old when they found you kissing the boy next door under the bed. It was only weeks later that I asked if I could say something. And then I lashed out at both of them for the ugly insinuations they'd made. High school? Nothing happened in high school! I never touched anyone. I studied hard and I got good grades because I didn't want to disappoint them. How dare you accuse me of being 'recruited into becoming gay' in high school? Do you imagine I was floating from one orgy to another in between classes? And how dumb do you think I am, to be recruited into anything? Don't you know me?

They were astounded. My mother said she didn't know when I became 'such an angry young man'. Hardly surprising. My relationship with my family until then was pretty much me listening to them talking about their lives and their opinions, so that they wouldn't ask me why I still haven't brought a girl home. Be inconspicuous as possible. Listen.

Later on, my brother asked me how it went. I heard myself say, "I've been cured of my love for my parents."

And it's true. I know it's a hard thing to get your head around, but I was so disappointed by how ashamed of me they were. How cowardly they were, about asking me to hide and get married nonetheless. To leave my bad, gay friends and move back home with them. To not tell anyone, be quiet.

The other day I watched a YouTube clip in which some two white kids came out to their father and recorded the whole thing. Americans. I watched it and was brought to tears when their father said, "Nothing changes. I still love you, and I'm still proud of you."

Oh, if only my father had said the same things. Instead, he calls to ask me if I've made any decisions about 'changing my lifestyle'.

I no longer feel connected to them. My family are now a group of people who I have known for a long time, but I am not connected to. My friends are my family now. When I'm in trouble,

I scroll past my parents' names on my phone and call my friends instead.

Free of the burden of being their good son. It doesn't matter how good I try to be now, whether or not I show up to help them, I am irretrievably flawed, and there's a kind of freedom that comes with that—the freedom of not having some ideal to live up to. I died, and was reborn as a new person. They died to me, too, AND IT'S FINE.

–

MY FAMILY DOESN'T KNOW I'm gay. I'd like them to find out for themselves, because my mother has problems—she's got high blood pressure and my dad really adores me. I'm the first-born, the breadwinner—they look up to me. I wouldn't want to break the bond we have in the family. If they find out, it's OK, but I won't be the one to go and tell them and start problems. If they ask me, I'LL BE OPEN ABOUT IT.

–

WE ARE SIX KIDS. I'm the fifth one. My family found out about me when I got suspended. My mum said, "What? Is this a curse or what?"

She was mad at me. I have an elder sister who understands me. She explained everything to them and from there, THINGS HAVE NOT BEEN BAD.

–

IF I COULD CHANGE anything in my life, it would be coming out to my family when I was young. Then I wouldn't have to get married and live a life full of secrets. If I came out now after all this time it would hurt them. Maybe I was born too early; nowadays younger gay people seem to have an easier time being gay than we did back in the day, and I always tell them. When I realized I was gay I didn't know how to go about it, where do I find gay men? Nowadays the younger generation has the internet, access to dating sites and chat rooms. I wish I was born in this generation; I would be totally gay, not bisexual, and I WOULD HAVE COME OUT TO MY FAMILY ALREADY.

–

My family knows I'm gay. My mother, my father and a few of my aunts know. I told them about two years ago. Having them not know was eating me up. One night it hit me. I keep my family at arm's length. I don't have that strong connection that I want to have with them, because I don't have that freedom of expression. That night, I wondered about the things that were hindering me from having that connection with them. So it dawned on me that I had never had this conversation with them.

Maybe I live in the dream world, but I always wanted to be able to call my mum and tell her that I have a crush on this guy, and tell her how it's going. I want to call my dad and be able to tell him what I am struggling with in my current relationship. Maybe I was just naïve. It was late in the evening and I had this burning urge—it was around 11pm—so I texted my mother. The next day, I sent my dad an email because he was far away at the time. It took my mother two days to respond to the message. She told me that she had had a conversation with one of my aunts—whenever my mum has a crisis she runs to her sisters. She talked to her sisters—I'm not sure what they talked about—and the response was that a mother can only love a child. I wasn't satisfied with that, so I forced the conversation.

I brought it up again, and she said that she does not believe that people are gay, that people have preferences. She believes that the way the world is going, people will start marrying animals. So she told me to wait. When she was telling me this, we were sitting in the car and I could see she was about to cry. I don't know what it was, I think it was rage. Then I discovered there is the mother I imagine I have, and there is the mother I actually have.

My dad called me and he said, "Thank you."

He said he had got my email and he said that at the time he didn't have airtime so he called to say thank you. I will just sit with that 'thank you'. I think they had known before because I would always have boys come over for sleepovers and have them stay the week. We would spend the entire day in my bedroom.

Someone must have figured it out. But they have never changed THE WAY THEY TREAT ME.

–

I WAS IN UNIVERSITY with a bunch of people who were deeply closeted, and I would only meet them at queer socials or out clubbing. I would ask myself why they had to hide so much when people already knew they were gay. Why couldn't they just accept it, acknowledge and slay? It's pretty easy after that, and you deal with the hurdles as they come, but first you have to accept yourself and embrace it. I'm definitely not the Martin Luther King [Junior] of gays, but I can say I know myself—all my late blooming has paid off, and I'm currently helping a couple of other people come to terms WITH THEIR SEXUALITY.

–

MY YOUNGER BROTHER dragged me out of the closet. He asked me when I was going to tell everyone the truth. He said he thought I was really sexually frustrated—because he thinks I'm too uptight—and that even in my world, I must not be getting any.

I know my parents know I'm gay. My mother sometimes asks, "Why have you never brought your girlfriend home to meet us?" and I just remain silent.

Are they really entertaining the thought that I will come out to them, so that they can actualize their trauma and engage in denial? I came out to my friends, and that was it. Everyone else can Nancy Drew it. It doesn't matter, at all. There is no formula for these things. It's not some superficial shit for your Facebook update. Check what it is that you have brought out.

There's a big ass difference between coming out and exposing yourself. All you've done is just remove the make-up and the masks. People have this idea that the red carpet will roll and they will be on Real Housewives of Atlanta, but it's not like that. They need to come out to add value to themselves, and change those around them, and influence others in a positive way to see homosexuality as something of value to humanity. Coming out is transformation, especially IN THIS DAY AND AGE.

–

MY FAMILY KNOWS that I'm gay. I didn't tell them. It just worked out that they knew. I had a conversation with my mother about it. She raised the topic one evening, at my sister's wedding. We were in a bar. My father was sitting on the far side of the table talking to his friend, and I was on the other side bonding with my mother. My mother said, "I have reached menopause already, and I cannot have any other children, so I'll just be grateful for what I already have. If you can manage, I'd like some grandchildren."

I thought that was nice of her. It was A LOVELY CONVERSATION.

–

MY COMING OUT STORY is really weird. My mum was told that I'm a lesbian by gossips. I had gone out clubbing one night, and my girlfriend and I made out in the club. I was in university at the time, so some of my fellow students saw that. The story spread in school, and people were looking for me to ask me about it. I couldn't deal with that, so the next morning I went home. I found my mum at 6am, leaning on the kitchen counter. She had a glass of wine. I remember this image so well.

Her opening statement was, "So this is why you liked watching 'The L Word'?[1]"

She thought that that series was where I'd learned to be a lesbian. I said, "Mum, I need to go to school because I have class at 7:30."

She repeated, "So this is why you liked watching 'The L Word'? I thought about coming to your bed and stabbing you, but I imagined I'm the one who's going to have to bury you. You're the devil himself."

---

1. American/Canadian television drama series portraying the lives of a group of lesbian, bisexual, straight and transgender people.

She beat me—my mum used to beat me—and then she left me locked in the house. After a while, she told me to pack and leave her house. While I was packing, she came back and said, "No. You're not going anywhere. Stay here. You're a disgrace. I'm going to lock you in here."

I told her, "You don't know me, you haven't raised me."

I wasn't raised by my parents. I stayed with my grandparents in *ushago*. In the country. It was such a village. I started living with my mum when I was in Form One.

I said, "You can't come into my life and start dictating things."

She said, "You can't talk to me like that."

End of discussion. My parents wanted to do damage control, because my parents are well known in ███████. They wanted to do damage control to save their name from being destroyed. *Tuanzie hapo*. Let's start there.

They told everyone that I was seeing a therapist, and that those rumours were from the enemies of the family. So I was forced to see a therapist. I only went for one session, which was not helpful. The therapist was a Christian therapist, so the answer to everything was Jesus. I stopped going after that first session. Also, nobody in my family was actually interested in the therapy. They were too busy trying to save themselves. Nobody asked me if I was happy, nobody ever asked me if I even went to the next therapy session. They only wanted to say that I went for therapy. They wanted to be able to say that. So I didn't go on with the therapy and no one ever talked about it after that.

I don't live at home. I'm staying in the university hostel. Once in a while, my mother says something like, "You really embarrass me sometimes. Those things you do in the clubs..."

What things? The 'things' I do at the clubs is just hanging out with my fellow gay people. Anyway, somehow my mother really likes my current girlfriend. They know each other, but I don't think she knows we're together. She really, really likes her. She's even offered her a job once she's done with school. That's how it is with my mum.

I do have siblings. I'm the first born. My brother knows I'm gay. Most of my cousins know I'm gay. They're OK with it, except one of them who told me she's not. She told me she feels like this whole issue is messed up, and that people are trying to impose things on themselves that are not there. She told me, "You should just be straight and continue with life. What's wrong with you?"

She confessed to me later that she had a relationship with her best friend while she was in primary school. She had a sexual relationship with two girls, actually. I think she just felt guilty, because for her it was about sex. It wasn't really emotional. So I guess that's why she feels like the rest of us are having unnecessary struggles just for sex. I love women, it's not just sex. Now she's seeing men. She's very promiscuous with men, and SHE'S ONLY IN FORM THREE.

–

HERE IN [redacted], the very public coming out of Binyavanga Wainaina caught people by surprise. Some people said, "You mean these things happen?"

"This guy has been paid, he's lying."

"He studied in South Africa, those are habits he learned there."

In the library at my college, students were obsessed with the story whenever it ran in the daily newspapers. People would converge on a table and read the story together. Most people were saying, "No, this is not possible. He is an African!"

I would tell them, "He's only saying what he is."

"No, that is madness! Maybe he's sick…"

I didn't know what to tell them, so I said, "If it's really a sickness, let's handle it like a sickness. Let's give him space. We have doctors in this country, let people research and find out what this gay sickness is. Once they come up with a medicine, then HE CAN BE HEALED."

–

I AM OUT, even though I don't believe anyone needs to be out about anything. I think it's your choice to decide who to come out to and under what circumstances. I also feel you should be accountable to certain people with the information that you choose to diverge or withhold. I'm out to pretty much anyone who may ask, but I still maintain discretion. When it comes to family, I had lots of books about sexual orientation which I display publicly on my bookshelves.

My family found out I was gay on their own, and it's never been raised as an issue. There were always threats that it was going to be raised in a formal way, but it has never happened. I know my brother doesn't think homosexuality is a sin or a choice or a problem or something that needs to be responded to in a violent way. I know my parents are very religious, and I wouldn't speculate on how they'd react if I ever came out in any meaningful way about my sexual orientation. It's not an encounter I desire, especially at this point where I'm materially dependent ON MY PARENTS.

–

EVENTUALLY I'LL HAVE TO come out again to my parents because the first time it happened, it was just accidental. I was seeing a guy then. We had just come from going out and we decided to go to my place because it was too late for him to go home. In the morning, we had breakfast with my mum and dad then the two of us left. When I got home in the evening my mum said, "I need to see you in your room."

There was something about the tone of her voice. It wasn't really stern, it was just…something. I could tell it wasn't going to be a good conversation but I didn't know what the subject was. I was very sure it wasn't about the guy I was seeing because when we were at home in the morning we were both being very straight-acting; suppressing our body language, no physical contact. But I suppose the body language of two people who are seeing each other or who are in love is easy to spot. I think parents can tell, especially your mum who knows you best.

So I went to my room and she came over then she said, "I'm going to ask you a question and I want you to be very honest with me. Don't lie. Are you a gay?"

'A gay'. I couldn't believe I got that from my mum. 'A gay'.

Anyway, I looked at her and asked her, "What are you talking about?"

I made sure to give her my best 'how dare you ask me that question?' disgusted look, and I asked her, "Mum how could you think that? No!"

She told me, "I'm going to ask you again, are you what you call a homosexual?"

I said, "No, I'm not."

Then she says, "You better tell me the truth because I don't want to hear anything from anyone. So you better tell me now."

So I just realized *hapa nimeshikwa*. I've been busted. So you know what, I might as well just get over with it. It was just me and my mum—my dad wasn't there. My heart started beating, I was sweating, and I started crying.

She looked at me and she asked me, "Answer my question."

I told her, "Yeah. I am."

Then, it's like all the tough skin she had just left and she just broke down. Now both of us were crying and I was thinking, 'This is just a mess.'

You know, my mum could have got high blood pressure or had a heart attack and I was not having that. My mum is extremely religious, as is I think almost 90% of homes in this country, so when she gave me the whole Bible story she told me, "It's a sin. It's an abomination. It's in the Bible, it's wrong. It's un-African. For how long have you had this?"

I was so tempted to be rude, but I said, "For as long as I can remember."

Then she says, "Where did I go wrong? Did I not give you what you wanted? Is this why you haven't been talking to me for the past year?"

For the past year or so, I'd really pulled away from my mum because I was already seeing how this would end so I just started staying away.

Then she asked, "Who else knows?"

So I told her my sisters kind of knew.

Then she looked at me and asked, "Do your friends know?"

And I said, "Yes, most of my friends know."

And she asked, "And they accept it?"

And I said, "Yeah, they don't have a problem. That's not the basis of our friendship."

So now she asks, "So I'm the last one to find out?"

And I said, "Pretty much."

So then she started crying again and said, "I can't believe you couldn't just come and talk to me. Why didn't you tell me?"

Then I said, "Well, you know I can't just come up to you and say 'Mum, I'm gay.' This is not the movies. I couldn't do it. I'm sorry, I couldn't. You see how you're reacting now? This is what I didn't want."

Then she weeps and cries and cries because she feels like she's been left out of my life. That she lost me somewhere down the road.

So then I said, "Mum, don't worry."

And she asks, "Why do you chose to be like that?"

And I say, "No, I didn't chose it. I can't just chose to be something that is so hard to be here. I'm not in it for the thrill."

And she says, "So why are you doing it?"

And I say, "Mum you don't choose. Contrary to what your people and your Bible people tell you… It's not logical."

Then my mum goes on to say, "Don't tell anyone else."

We're a respected family in church. We're one of those families that other families look up to in church. We're good kids. People look at my mum and my dad and say, "Wow, you've raised your kids so well. You've taken them to school and now they're helping you do all sorts of stuff. You guys are sorted, you guys are good."

My two sisters are married, so my aunties are on my case with, "You're the next one."

Life is such a script and that's why I find myself pulling away from even my extended family because the only people I feel I owe an explanation to are my parents. Relatives are so nosy, so into your business, so sometimes I feel like I'm pulling away from the others and quite frankly I don't mind doing it.

What I've come to realize is that, yes, your parents know you because they raised you, but the people who really know you and your ratchet-ness are your close friends. People who get you. Your relatives won't get you, your family won't get you, they'll get you because you're theirs, they know you for your outer shell. But then your good friends really know who you are, they've been with you through shit because you can't tell your parents everything. We're still a closed society, so as much as your parents may say, "You can talk to me," that's not how things work.

So my mum said, "Don't tell anyone."

And the next question—which I was kind of expecting, "Are you willing to change?"

I didn't want to crush her hopes, so I just said, "I can try."

She asked me, "Do you want to see a counsellor? Do you want to see a pastor? Do you want to see one of your aunties?"

I told her I could try, but I wasn't going to see no pastor and I'm not seeing no therapist.

Then I told her, "I'm sorry, mum. I'm sorry if I've disappointed you. This doesn't mean that I'm not going to be successful in life."

She was worried, she was saying, "You know it's not accepted. What are people going to do to you out there? You could get in trouble."

And I said, "I'm sorry if I've disappointed you, but then it's not my doing. I didn't do this to hurt you."

She came over to my side—because we were sitting on opposite sides—and told me, "You know what, at the end of the day, we will fight this together and you're my son and I'm so proud of you and whatever way you decide to go I'll be there for you because I'm your mum."

And that finished me. I just broke and wept and wept.

And she said, "Don't worry about anyone. This is between you and me and we'll fight this together, leave other people out of this."

That was the first time since I was eight or nine, that she tucked me in bed, prayed with me and stayed there until I slept. I also remember, in the morning, she made me breakfast. She was so… As much as she didn't approve of it, she was all 'my son is vulnerable, I have to protect him'. Since then, we don't talk about it, but my mum and I are very close. It's like she feels like she has to be there for me, she feels like she needs to be there to protect me but WE JUST DON'T TALK ABOUT IT.

–

I CAME OUT to my sister when we were watching 'The Tyra Banks Show'. This one gay guy came on, and my sister said, "I don't know why people judge gay men. They're just living their lives and it's not affecting anyone."

I froze, and my heart started pounding and I told her, "Do you know I'm actually gay?"

She turned and looked at me for about five seconds, and then she said, "I kinda knew, but I just wanted you to tell me yourself."

Awkward silence for about ten minutes, still watching 'Tyra'. Then she asked, "So, do you have a boyfriend right now?"

I said, "It's too much already! It look me so long just to tell you this—ASK ME AGAIN IN LIKE, FIVE DAYS!"

–

THE ONLY PERSON that I actually came out to officially in my family was my mother. I'd never felt very close to my siblings or my father—it might have something to do with my being gay and the fact that I felt different—but we never had a bond growing up. I came out to my mother because at that point, I felt like I should only come out to people whose not-knowing was affecting our relationship.

I am very close to my mother, and I felt that my not telling her was dishonest. First of all, she literally dragged me out of the closet—thanks to my best friend who bumped into one of our ex-teachers and was very open about his sexuality. So this teacher went and had a conversation with my mother about it. She said, "Did you know your son's best friend is gay and very open about it, and blah, blah, blah..."

My mother thought, "Oh, OK."

She came home and sat me down on the sofa and asked, "I just wanted to ask you a question. I just heard some things about your friend, is it true that he's gay?"

I asked, "What does it matter?"

She said, "I just wanted to know. Does it affect your friendship? Does he ever try to make you do things?"

I said, "To be honest, I'm also gay and I'm the one who even helped him come out of the closet. So if you want to ask questions, let's start with that question."

And she totally flipped. She said, "This is completely unnatural, you're going through a phase and nobody in our family has ever been gay. This can't be happening!"

She totally flipped out, and I told her, "Well, it's not a phase. I don't know what else to tell you, because this is just who I am and I'm telling you what it is that I am."

Then she said, "I'll never have you living with another man and calling him your husband."

I said, "Well, if you're worried about that, I'm never planning on getting married to anybody—man or woman."

For some reason, that seemed to calm her down. Then I told her, "You know, we can act like this never happened, or we can be open about it."

She said, "No, let's definitely have it out in the open, and let's talk about it."

I wondered whether she was going to tell my father and my siblings but she didn't, and I found out six months later why she didn't tell anybody; it is because she had forgotten. She completely just blocked out the entire event from her head. Six months down the line, I came home to get dressed up for a party, and she calls me to the couch again.

She said, "I wanted to ask you a few questions. I was hearing some things about your friend."

"What kinds of things?"

"I hear that he's gay. Is this true?"

And I said, "You can't be serious. Don't you remember us having this conversation?"

She said, "No, what do you mean? We didn't have this conversation."

And I told her, "You know what, I did it once and I'm not doing this again. I'm gay. Deal. I'm going out," AND I LEFT.

–

I CAME OUT TO MY SISTER and she was very understanding. She had always been suspicious about my sex life. My girlfriend and I were together for eight years, but I couldn't talk about her to my sister. My sister and I were very close, and we would talk about her marriage. I felt guilty about revealing 80% of my life while she was 101% open about her life.

So I decided to be honest with her. One night, we were seated in the bedroom in silence. My mouth was dry. I remember opening the conversation.

"Do you know why I don't have a boyfriend?"

"I don't know, but you have many male friends," my sister replied.

"I don't have feelings for men."

She woke up from the bed.

"Since when?"

"Since Form Two."

"FORM TWO?!"

"Yes, I love women."

"*Mwathani*!" Jesus!

"I'm a lesbian."

She kept quiet for a long time—then, "I knew it. Why did you tell me – what prompted this?"

"I wanted to tell you so that I can be free. You tell me so much about your life and you never get to know the real me."

Eventually we got to the dicey questions.

"How do you do it?"

"I can't tell you. Please Google that one – I won't tell you."

"When you see a woman on the road do you like them, or love them?"

"When you see a man on the road, do you like them or love them?"

"No!"

"Exactly."

I became so free after I told her. She always tells me to take care and be sexually responsible. SHE HAS MY BACK ALL THE TIME.

–

BEING INDEPENDENT has definitely made me feel like if any of my family members ask about my sexuality, I can be upfront with them. At one point, my sister asked me, "I just wanted to ask you, are you gay?"

I said, "Yes, I am."

She said, "Oh, OK."

And then she had a few follow-up questions about roles, and whether I was the woman or the man, and I told her, "I'm not talking about that with you. That's weird. You don't need to know about my sex life the same way I don't need to know yours."

I have a cousin who is also gay, and one day he got drunk at some family event and said, "Everybody listen up! You all need to know I'm a homosexual, and it's fine and I don't care."

His brother was really accepting of it. I met him once and asked him about it. He said, "What do I do? He's my brother, and it doesn't change anything."

I asked my own brother how he felt about my being gay, and he said, "I know, and it's fine. It's not an issue, we should all just be family."

It's nice to have that kind of support, but I also realize that I don't need validation from any of them. This process was more about them coming to terms with it on their terms. The other day, some guy met me and my friends and said, "You guys are gay, right? Explain it to me, help me understand."

We were so irritated. How the hell do you ask someone to help you understand their lifestyle or who it is that they are? Gay people have to explain themselves so much that we forget that it shouldn't be our responsibility to go around explaining our sexuality to every Tom, Dick and Harry who feels that they deserve an explanation. If you want to understand what being homosexual is, go read a book, or Google it, OR FIGURE IT OUT ON YOUR OWN.

–

I'M GETTING MORE CONFIDENT by the day. I came out to my best friends. They were not OK with it. They told me, "We love you so much, but we're not OK with this. Give us time to process this."

I think they're working on it. It's been two months now and we still hang out. One of them came to visit me one Saturday afternoon. I was doing my laundry. He came, took a nap, woke up, cooked with me, then we talked and he left. So I THINK HE'S REALLY TRYING.

–

WHEN I WAS TWENTY-FOUR, I went back home for a funeral. People there already knew I was gay. They had heard rumours. My family organized a meeting after the funeral. I come from a very big family—my father has three wives. There were about fifteen people at this meeting, including my brothers, sisters and sisters-in law. My father said, "This meeting is about you."

They asked me if it was true. I figured if I said no, the process would be much longer for nothing. So I admitted and said, "It is a problem. Maybe you can help. You can let me know if there was anyone in the family who was like this."

So I threw it back to them and no one spoke. The meeting sort of ended there and so I told them, "If anyone feels my being gay is a hindrance to our relationship, I will not come near you. If any of you come to me, then I will know it is not a problem."

And for a whole year no one came to see me.

There was a funeral after that, and I went. You can imagine the disconnection that was there. It was bad. I carried food and nobody touched it. And when they prepared food for guests, they would not bring a chair or a plate for me. I stayed there for two days then went back to Mombasa. Then my sister came to see me and she said, "We understand you. We are being too hard on you. We will try to make mum and dad understand."

Later my mother came and visited me, too. That's how I knew THEY HAD ACCEPTED ME BACK IN THE FAMILY.

–

LOVE, SEX AND EVERYTHING IN BETWEEN

There was this guy who used to live in my neighbourhood. He was still in high school, and I saw him a couple of times in high school uniform, running around like he was practicing for some sports thing. I wanted to see him again, so I started timing his runs. I can be quite voyeuristic. I can watch people. I used to make time to go and watch him. And when I never saw him, I'd get sad and gloomy. I was such a romantic those days. I used to think some gentleman would come and sweep me off my feet, and we'd get married. We'd be young lovers and run and we would love each other till the day we died. He'd be good to me and we'd adopt children. I used to even have dreams about being pregnant with his children.

Then he moved out, and I didn't see him for a while. One day, on my way to school I saw him at the bus stop. And then I started keeping a look out for him at that very stop and I'd see him every now and then. At some point we even came face to face and talked a bit.

Talking to him threw me off. It made me realize a man's power. You want to be part of it. Or maybe you want to be the reason for it. When I see a man who strives for excellence, you want to be the reason for it. This man looks like something you want to keep, to be with. That conversation gave me insight into the kind of man he was. He was an excellent man. A man who knew what he wants, a man who went out and got what he wanted. And that's the sort of man you want. You want a man who strives. You don't need a man, you need a champion. He was that champion; physically, mentally. You just want that under your roof, let me tell you. In between your thighs.

Talking to him made me realize one thing: this is stupid. All these things he's doing to me. He was the kind of man who could tell me, jump. Go get me a handful of red diamonds, and I'd have gone out to get them. I don't like to be in that place. So I ended it. I needed to save my soul, where this man was concerned. It was my soul or his. I had to pick mine. I chose mine, and I ended it. It was a very strategic move on my part.

How did I end it? Let's just say I stalked the fuck out of him, and then I let him know who was stalking him. Of course, that wasn't going to end well, but that—for me—was the point. It needed to have a tragic end.

That experience was the first time I realized that no one should ever have such a hold on you. I don't care what people say about this love business. No. You need to hang on to yourself first, before you hang onto anyone else. When you feel your soul is being lost, you claim it and run with it.

I don't want to be in a place where you feel like someone is more important than you. It's stupid. No one should let themselves get there. It doesn't work for everyone. It was doing bad things to me. That vulnerability was breaking me. Being in that place where you're so vulnerable. I couldn't take it. I thought either I get out of this in one piece, or I STAY IN THIS IN PIECES.

–

I CAN'T DATE SOMEONE WHO IS TRANSPHOBIC and can't date a lesbian or a bisexual person who wants a girlfriend. My current partner identifies as GNC, and they are not transphobic. They date females and trans people. Transphobia from your partner is usually revealed in the course of the relationship. We're not talking long-term dating, we're talking two months, three months, because it's not easy to stay with someone who has internalized transphobia and isn't aware of it.

This is how it happens: you meet someone, you tell them that you're trans. They say they understand, they'll read about it and what-not. Then, as you proceed with dating, some small things start to happen, like them missing your pronouns, or they keep referring to you as a woman. Maybe when you argue, they remind you that you're a woman, and they constantly remind you about your boobs and your periods. Even things like "Why can't I see your boobs? Why can't I touch your boobs?"

You tell them "I don't feel comfortable with you doing that right now," and they tell you, "But you're my girlfriend!" and you have to remind them, "I am NOT your GIRL-friend!"

You know?

So those relationships just end. We don't stay friends. Unless they start respecting that I'm trans. I once dated another trans person, and it was way easier. They understand, they're not transphobic. Even if you annoy them they never bring your gender up as something to get back at you. THEY DON'T USE YOUR INSECURITIES OR YOUR DYSPHORIA AGAINST YOU.

–

I AM CURRENTLY DATING a bisexual who is so into women. I just try to put up with him even though it hurts. He is attracted to both men and women, but more to women. He was dating another man before he met me, but the guy cheated on him so he said he'd stop dating men. I told him I am a man of my word, and I would be faithful to him. He said he could be faithful to me, but he can never leave his women.

At the moment I am OK with him, but should I meet someone who is purely gay, I will move on. I wish he would change and stop having multiple relations with women. He has a barrage of girls around him all the time, but then he lives with me. I am not completely sure if I am the only man he is seeing. I am still in love with him. He is just the right person for me, except that I am certain that he will eventually leave me FOR A WOMAN.

–

I HAD NEVER READ anything where someone was having gay sex, I'd never read anywhere that a gay person had kissed another one, or touched another one. Gay people were just buffoons, they occurred sometimes in books; flouncing about.

I was certainly very sexually excited when I touched a girl's breasts the first time; it just didn't last. It didn't have endurance, but I was prepared for it. I had a language to build up to it, and that revelation was exciting.

With gay sex, what am I doing? What am I imagining? I knew there's something this man can do to me that must be crazy. I can't imagine what the transaction is, except *hawa watu wanaweka mboro ndani ya mkundu*. These people who put dick in the ass.

I used to download erotic gay stories a lot. For about ten years, I used to avoid all the anal stories. Anus, no. I couldn't understand. It didn't exist to me as a sexual body part at all. I liked the more romantic stories, not the porn-y stories. I didn't like gay porn at all. In fact, for the large majority of that time, I was consuming a lot of straight romantic porn, where I'd put myself in the girl's place somehow.

One thing I had learned at that point is that I have really, really sensitive skin. Women would kiss my skin and I'd shiver. I enjoyed fucking enough, I liked that idea of a penis in a hole. I was prepared for it, and it was fine with women. I liked the idea of boobs, somehow. I liked women who were very small. But the first time I kissed a man, I liked it. The first time I had a man's tongue on my skin, I liked it, and I have liked it all the time.

I tried going to the baths in London—in black neighbourhoods in the South of London. You'd get a big towel, pay 11 pounds and go and display your body, and people who like you find you, then you book a room for six pounds…I felt like giggling. I felt like all those public, gay courtship rituals seemed so fake and crazy. I had never been part of those rituals, so I wondered what I was supposed to say. I just felt silly. I was never turned on, it felt like such a meat market.

I went to gay bars, nothing. Then I happened upon a review site for male escorts where all these people would talk about various escorts and how good or bad they were, top, bottom—I didn't know what tops and bottoms were, I didn't know what I was—but I used to consume those stories. I liked the idea that I could pick a person who had this whole resumé of what they did with another person, and I know what I'm picking. The difficulty of ordering escorts is they'd say, "Call me and tell me what you want. Do you want frottage, do you want to be dominant…?"

I didn't know what those were.

Once, I went for a conference in Vancouver and I had a nice hotel room and a per diem. I called this escort called Mathieu and I told him I'd pay for an extra hour so we could meet for a drink. He was—I can't even explain—beautiful. He was like a lumberjack. A French lumberjack from the 19th century, and he was an escort. A very, very expensive escort. He was just lovely.

We got into the room afterwards, and he just kissed me. He kissed me for almost three or four hours, charged me for one hour and that was it. I didn't know that there are many people who do sex work who get off people getting off. There are a lot of people like that. For several years, all I did with men was just have them kiss me and kiss my body. Even now, it's just THE MOST BEAUTIFUL THING.

–

I'M NOT MONOGAMOUS because monogamy is just insane. It's not viable. It's just a crazy thing. I identify as poly. Consciously, since 2016. I was looking back at my dating patterns, and I realized that there was never one time that I was dating only one person. And it wasn't like I was going behind someone's back about it: the people I was dating always knew that I had someone else. It would come up in a conversation, and if someone wanted exclusivity then I would be out, because I can't promise something that I can't do.

I didn't know what polyamory was for a long time. You know the way you're told that females shouldn't be poly, that it's only men who can be polygamous? That's how we're brought up here, so it didn't cross my mind then, but right now I'm OK with it, I'm comfortable with it.

I'm poly because we all have needs, even if we don't talk about it. You interact with someone because of a need you have. I believe that you can't get everything you need in one person. It's the same thing with my friendships. I don't have one best friend who is my go-to person for all my friendship needs. I have this one person who is my friend on this level, this other person who is my friend on this other level. They're all my friends; if I need this one thing, I go to this person, if I need this other thing, then this other person is the one I go to and we relate like that.

I'm not the kind of person who can have all my friends on a table because they are very different people. They wouldn't spend time together. I'm the unifying factor. The way that I talk to one of them isn't the way I relate with the other person. If I brought them all together, everyone would see the way I am with the others and ask me, "Is that you? Is that really you?"

I realized I used to go to spaces with more than one friend and then one of them would be staring at me the whole time saying, "No, that's not you. That's not what you usually do."

But this other person would know that side of me. So, I realized that even with romantic relationships, it works out that way.

–

I HAVE NEVER really been in a relationship. I have never met a guy who could get into the space where I want to be in. I have never met someone who would give me what I want. I have met some guys, though most of them are not into me or they are straight. I have a thing for straight men, I sometimes imagine they would be the perfect guys. The guys I meet tend to rush me. They make it so quick, first day we meet and talk, we text in the evening, the next day we go out for dinner and the next time we meet with friends, they introduce me as their boyfriend. It irritates me because we have only met five times.

Many guys are into dominance, just sit there and be pretty. They want to introduce you to their friends as their new catch. It is very difficult to find someone with whom you can find balance. It could just be a guy thing. Let him be a guy, let you be a guy. I have not had a relationship where someone has not tried to dominate me—sexually, financially and whatnot. I have never found someone who has met me as an equal.

I met this straight guy; I love him and he supports me. He is a perfect gentleman. I have told him I am gay. He does shopping for me, cares for me, motivates me and empowers me without expecting anything in return. I am just myself with him. I am not defensive with him. I also met another man; I enjoy his company but I cannot tell him because he will become weird. I like it easy. For me it has to be easy, YOU CANNOT PUSH ME.

–

I HAVE A THING for men with power. I know it as my truth, and I know I'm always in pursuit of men with power, in power, for power. I like men to have some sort of power. Men are a lot of work, they're not easy work. Even if you think you can tame them, you tame them with fire and tears. Someone said men should love you more than you love them. That way they meet you halfway.

That way, while you're working on your business in your stilettos, no one wants to fuck with you. Because they know you're a bad bitch, and your man is also unstoppable. That idea of making sure he loves you more than you love him is kinda fucked up. It's about making sure he has more to lose than you do. I refuse to be in that position where I lose more. I know that turns this love thing into a power dynamic, but isn't that what it is? People want to believe that love is this rosy thing, but even a rose has soft petals and a thorny stem.

This love game is easier to play when you know the rules of the game. You can't be an idealist about it. Yes, love can be about two people just wanting to be with each other, but that's rare. For most men in our society, love is about power plays. I see them do it to women. For an effeminate man like me, they want to do the same thing. They act like you ought to have been expecting them in your life. Let me tell you, I've had situations where men are literally dictating what I should wear to go and meet them. Because—apparently—otherwise, I'll wear clothes that are too tight. Or I'll wear flamboyant colours, or I'll wear my hair 'too high up'.

"Don't dress the way you normally dress."

I was getting that a lot from men. I don't know what it is about being effeminate that makes men think I'm waiting for them to tell me what to do with my life, and tell me how skinny I am and want to feed me. I get that a lot. They're always telling me, "You're so thin. *Tunafaa tukupatie nyama.*" We should give you meat.

What the fuck is that? Am I your little project? This is why I'd rather be by myself sometimes, and deal with my own bullshit. What has my thin-ness got to do with you? The right man for you will see your thin-ness or your big booty as part of your beauty. That's what sets a good man apart. Wanting to change your lover is not a love thought, it's a power thought.

If people want to play these games, YOU'D BETTER BE THE BEST PLAYER.

–

IF IT WERE LEGAL IN KENYA, I would settle down with a stud, someone who can stand next to me like a man. Someone who will understand me. We could plan on how to get children, start a family, raise our kids, be OK. But that is not legal here. I still believe I will get married, though. Not to a man, to a woman. I am sure of it. But my worry is whether my mum will ever accept that marriage. And in Kenya, will the people around us accept my marriage?

God must help me to find a good job, somewhere outside Kenya, in a place where people are more accepting. Then I will settle there, and have a family. The reason that I want to leave is for security, acceptance. Only that. If it was safe here in Kenya I wouldn't want to leave.

For now, I don't know anyone abroad, and sometimes it feels like a dream that will never happen. I hope that one day I will get a connection. If that happens, I'll go. I'll start my family. That is where I will settle, and after that I can come explain it all to my mother. At that point she won't try and stop me because I WILL ALREADY HAVE A FAMILY.

–

I'VE BEEN WITH my current girlfriend for a year and three months. The longest relationship I've been in was two years, though, so we'll see. I met her at a gay party in Nairobi, and it was love at first sight. I was immediately attracted to her, just like that. When she hugged me, I just knew.

I'm a femme, *kubisa* [completely]. A femme is a woman—a lady. You dress like a lady, put on make-up—you're just a normal lady. I'm attracted to butches only. If I dated a femme, I would want to be the dominating one in that relationship. I'm really into butches, though. It's really satisfying for me. Chores are 50/50. Everyone does their part—she can't tell me that because she is the butch she won't do housework. Never, ever, ever. I'd like to have at most three kids. Just like a normal family—SUCCESSFUL, LIVING HAPPILY.

–

I MET MEN through dating sites. Most of them were married and the meets ended up being one night stands, but I always wanted more than a fling. I was looking for a man to be in a relationship with. Then I started going to parties organized for gay men, and that's where I started meeting men whom I could date.

Some relationships lasted two or three years. I knew one man in particular for fifteen years, we dated for seven years. He was married too and even though we worked and lived in different towns, we found ways to make it work and spend time together. I ended things because I caught him in the act with a friend of mine I had introduced him too. It broke my heart, I don't like being cheated on.

Right now I have been dating a man for two years; he once suggested we introduce our families to each other. I felt that was a bit weird, but he has been persistent. He wants to meet my wife and kids and he wants me to meet his wife and kids.

One time I was at an LGBT meeting, and a neighbour who was there went and told my niece who in turn told my mother. She confronted me about it, of course I denied it. She said she had been told I was the chairman, I denied that too. it got to my wife eventually, she knew I was working with an LGBT organization but she still asked me about the rumour. I told her there must have been a mistake. That's all it took, she has never asked me about it since.

I slept with a woman because she loved me. She wanted to have sex, and she initiated it but I was afraid because I knew I was attracted to men. So every time she would come over to my place I always made sure my friends were around so that nothing happened. Eventually she did get me alone in the house and the first time we had sex I was afraid I wasn't going to have an erection. It only took one time for her to get pregnant.

I think my mum always knew I was attracted to men, and she always kept my secret. We are very close and the baby came as a shock to her because she always knew I was gay.

I don't know if my wife knows that I am gay. We have never had a conversation about my sexuality, she didn't know when we met and I don't know if she knows now. She knows I have gay friends though. I would really love to know if she knows. Maybe she suspects because one time while we were walking she pointed out that I like looking at men. Of course I denied it. But I would love to know if she knows.

With time, I learnt how to accept our sex life, she satisfies me and I satisfy her sexually. At first, I would rush my performance.

Quickies. As time went by I began to learn how to be intimate with her, especially from the internet by reading articles on how to make love to a woman.

Adjusting to married life was hard, I had never spent a night with a woman in bed, I had never shared a house with a woman in that way, and it was tough at first. I LOVE MY WIFE A LOT.

–

I AM THIRTY-TWO YEARS OLD, and I identify as a lesbian. When I was younger, I tried to break my attraction to girls by getting into a relationship with a boy. There was a boy in my neighbourhood who was attractive, so I called him over and things just progressed to us having sex. He was my first sexual experience. I remember feeling nothing. I pushed him away. That was the first and last time I ever saw a dick. Now I only see a dick in movies, and I get disgusted at the thought of PUTTING A DICK INSIDE ME.

–

I REALLY HATED UNIVERSITY. I didn't fit in, and I was studying a course I hated. In my second semester there, I went into a class and—as usual—sat there, hating it, barely paying attention. And then I saw him. He was sitting a couple of rows behind me—this was an auditorium-style lecture hall, and in my memory there was a shaft of light coming from above and falling on him. Maybe my mind is making it up, or maybe there was a patch of translucent roofing above him. I don't know. Anyway, he was glowing.

I wondered what he was doing in our class. I'd never seen him before. Maybe I was in the wrong class. I thought he was the most beautiful man I'd ever seen, and I had a strong feeling that he was going to be a part of my life. That was a strange feeling, I don't think I've ever seen a stranger and felt like that about them. Turns out I was right, but not exactly how I imagined.

I kept glancing over my shoulder to look at him, and my best friend noticed. He turned to see what I was looking at, so I had to stop looking back. In the weeks that followed, this guy kept turning up to our classes. I figured he must be a new member of our class. Strange, because he'd missed a semester. He was always serious, silent. Taking notes. My best friend noticed the new guy, too.

Then I finally met him for real. I remember that day so vividly. We'd had a heavy lunch, and my friends were too sleepy to attend class. They asked me to go and take notes on their behalf. I agreed, mostly because I wanted to see the new guy again. He was there, wearing a faded yellow shirt. I can still see it so clearly. The class was boring, as usual, I can't remember what it was. When it was over, I left—heading back to my room. The new guy was behind me, I could see his yellow shirt out of the corner of my eye. The distance to my room was quite far, but he kept behind me.

What the fuck? I kept walking, taking all the turns it took to head towards my room—he was still behind me, across from me, we were weaving alongside each other across paths, corridors, buildings. And then he started coming closer. Oh, my heart. And then he skipped a little to catch up with me—Oh my God—and said, "Hey!"

I kept walking, unsure whether he was actually addressing me. "Hey!" he repeated.

I turned. Oh my God. He was talking to me.

"Hey," I said.

I can't remember what he said, my heart was beating so loud. He said he was joining our class and he had a lot of catching up to do, and he was wondering whether I could help him out with notes from the previous semester.

That was the start of a long friendship that lasted many, many years. I loved him desperately all those years, and I never once told him how I felt. One Valentine's day, I even went out and bought a card for him. My intention was to slip it under his door without saying who it was from. Then I felt silly, and I tore it up and threw it away.

Later on, he discovered I was gay, and he was OK with it, but we never had a serious conversation about it. I'd joke about it now and again, and he'd laugh with some embarrassment. I always wondered if he knew how I felt about him, because there were times he'd give me a look of such profound understanding, it made me feel naked.

He even had a couple of girlfriends, and that was a strange experience for me. It brought out all my ugly bits; my selfishness, my petty jealousies. The irony of being protective of something I didn't own wasn't lost on me. I could barely mask my contempt for the girls he dated. Too loud, too girly, too giggly, too perfume-y. What did he see in them? Did they know how lucky they were?

I once heard him describe sex between two guys as 'gross'. "That shit is gross," he said.

I caught his eye in that moment, and I don't know what I saw there. The word stayed with me. I've heard myself use it to describe my own sexuality when I'm feeling ugly. We all have those days, I guess.

In all those years, it never got easier to be around him. My breath would still catch at the idea of being alone with him. I'd still get flustered. The silences were always pregnant, with the undercurrents of unsaid things swirling around us.

In the end, I had to get away from him. I stepped out of that needy dynamic. I haven't seen him in years. We don't talk. I still love him, and I miss him sometimes. I miss the memory of him, but I'm not CONSUMED BY HIS PRESENCE ANY MORE.

–

SEX HAS A WEIRD WAY of eroding friendship. Now I'm trying to get deeper intimacy, not just sexual intimacy. I want to be in that space where I want to be…between your spaces. I'm having a lot less sex, and A LOT MORE CONVERSATION.

–

RIGHT NOW, I'M A STEM—I can be either a butch or a femme. For me, being butch is like being the guy—I treat my girlfriend like the chick, so I'd be the one dropping lines, I take her out, and do all those romantic things, pay the bills. I'm used to being a femme, so sexually it would be hard for me to be a stud only.

When I was a femme, I was the one who had things done for me. My ex used to make me feel like a girl. She was older than me. I was the quiet one, she would talk and I would do—that was what I was used to. Now I feel like I can do more in a relationship, so either of them can work for me. Right now, I can do the chores, or we can share duties—she can cook and I wash—it's not fixed that one person does everything.

My family don't know. I think I'll have to tell them at some point, because they will keep waiting for stuff to happen that I'm not planning to do. When I imagine my future family, I see myself with a partner and each of us could have a kid, hopefully a girl and a boy. I don't know how yet—we'll cross that bridge when we get to it. I'd want to make my daughter LOOK LIKE A DOLL!

–

ONE TIME I WAS WORKING in a hotel, I met a white man, a tourist. He told me he was gay and the wife knew and accepted and encouraged it. She allowed him to live his life as a gay man the way he pleased. At the time we met he was already in a relationship with another man, and I generally stay away from such situations so even though he kept asking me out I turned him down and told him to look for me if things went south with the other man.

When he did end things with him, we started going out. On and off, whenever he is around that is because he spends most of his time at home in Europe. Even though we are dating, white men are not exactly my cup of tea. I love black men. I am not into him that much and I made it clear we are just having fun. He wants us to have a relationship and I know he loves me but I can't do it. I don't want to be with a white man in that way.

The major difference though between dating a white man and a black man is how financially supportive white men are. It's like dating an ATM. Black men are not supportive in that way. He is always willing to help me out financially, I don't have to ask. He's even 'adopted' two of my kids, the youngest ones. He takes care of them financially. My wife knows about him and the financial support from him. But only as a friend of mine, nothing more. He spoils me. I can't wait for Valentine's Day when he is around—I get everything I want. But I STILL PREFER DATING BLACK MEN.

–

SINCE HIGH SCHOOL, I haven't found a person that can offer real love to me. So what I've been doing is just going to have fun with my friends. I don't trust anyone here. I once went out raving with my friend, and this guy drugged us and took us to a campus here in ████. The drug didn't affect me much, though; I could tell where I was and what was going on. He wanted to take advantage of us. My friend, whom the drug really affected, was taken advantage of. They fucked him till his rectum came out.

So I realized that this is what's happening out there so I should not trust anyone. Whenever anyone approaches me and wants to have a relationship with me, I turn them down because I don't trust people at all. I do believe I will get to a point where I trust people. Maybe one day, one time, I'll find the right partner who I'll trust with all my heart. I feel like I can trust someone loyal to me. Someone trustworthy. Someone generous, caring, loyal. He should be A GOOD AND RESPONSIBLE PERSON.

–

I'M ANDROGYNOUS. I look like a girl. All my life people have always mistaken me for a girl. I look more like a man these days, my masculinity is starting to show much more these days. A while ago, I used to be called 'madam' so many times on the street.

There was a bar called ████ we used to visit very often with my friends, because the beer was cheap, everything was so much cheaper there. One Friday after work, we went there and ordered drinks. It's a back-street bar, and that's not a gay-friendly place. Gay stuff happens, but it's hush-hush, and we're supposed to act like men. I was sitting there, sipping my drink and this man started looming around me, giving me eyes.

My friend asked me, "What does that guy want?"

I said, "Leave him alone."

He kept staring in our direction. He'd leave to refill his drink then come back and stand there with a cheeky, boyish smile.

"It's you he's looking at."

"No, it's not me."

He was slightly shorter guy than me, a really stocky guy—like a construction worker. He kept smiling at me, then he walked up to me, took out his wallet and shook it. Some coins fell out, totalling thirty shillings. He pointed at me, showed me the coins and asked me to go with him. I felt like thirty shillings were a bit on the lower side. Everyone just burst into laughter. Thirty shillings! To be the best queen I can be.

Then he stood there, waiting for a response. I had to lift my hands and tell him no. It was kinda sweet. There were other working girls in that bar, but he chose me.

My friends kept telling that story to everyone over and over again. I think my friends found it really funny because I'm that bitch who says, even though we're in the back-streets, let's carry ourselves with grace. Posture is key. They said, "You and all your posture, you're worth thirty shillings."

Everyone was laughing, and I said I'm going to look for the diamond in the rough. I just looked for that diamond, and it took weeks to find it. I remembered that he'd pulled out his pockets to show that he had nothing more. That was my diamond. I was worth his last penny. His last thirty shillings, he'd rather spend it on me than on bus fare. He'd probably walk home, but he'd be walking home happy that he got a piece of me. That was in the diamond in the rough. At least, I'm worth a man's last coin. THERE IS REDEMPTION IN THAT THOUGHT.

–

I HAVE NEVER fallen in love. I have no idea what it is. I have deep crushes but I have never been in love. I would imagine that for love there has to be reciprocation of some kind. With crushes, it's about one person being obsessed with another and the other person knows nothing about it. There is no reciprocation. I don't think THAT IS LOVE.

–

I THINK SEX is really emotional, and that's why I'm still a virgin. I'm not ready to give myself in that way—I feel like it's too much of an investment. I'm getting there very slowly, but I'm not feeling pressure. It's a strange place, being comfortable with being a gay virgin at my age—it's like being the 40 year old straight virgin in that movie! People expect you to give it up easily, and even straight guys feeling bi-curious expect you to be there for that because what's on TV is that gay guys are promiscuous. If it comes, though, it will come. Hopefully it will be someone I want to emotionally invest in, but I'm also not making it a huge deal. It's not like you've seen Jesus, or anything—IT'S JUST SEX.

–

I FEEL LIKE most gay people are kind of stumbling, because there are jabs from this side, jabs from that side, and people are refusing you, your family is refusing you, and Christians are refusing you, and you're just there, and you're lonely, there's no one to fall in love with, so when you finally get into a relationship you're confused, and if your partner beats you, you stay, because who isn't beating you? I was in a very violent relationship, and I discovered that I'm not the only lesbian who's been beaten. A lot of lesbians beat each other. It's actually a major issue. You stay, because you know YOU DON'T HAVE MANY OPTIONS.

–

I ONCE TOLD a friend of mine that I was looking for someone who would take care of me, someone who is like this, like this, like that, like that. My friend asked me, "Are you all those things, yourself?"

She had a point. Here I was, saying I want someone who is strong, someone who is stable, someone independent, someone smart, someone intelligent, yet I am not like that myself. Most of the time, we want what we are not. So I took time to figure out what I wanted, and learning to be that person myself. And then, as soon as I became stable and OK with being alone, everything just fell into place, and I feel really good about the relationship that I have now. Although it's been a couple of months, I'm really feeling good about it. I'm convinced if you figure yourself out, God will give you THE PERSON YOU REALLY NEED.

–

I GET INFATUATED A LOT. I have people in my mind who I feel are beautiful, intellectual, stimulating, maybe good in bed, people I'd like to be with, people I'd like to raise kids with—which isn't something I aim to do—but the irrationality of infatuation is amazing. You start to imagine doing things that you'd never think to do. I have fallen in love in the sense that I've been infatuated a lot of times. The first time I had sex, it wasn't with someone I ever thought I was infatuated with, even though I thought he was attractive. He had muscles.

Someone once told me that love is a demand, and that to love back is to respond to these kinds of demands and have certain demands be responded to in certain ways. Infatuation is a very one-person kind of thing—especially when you're queer—because you sit down and you think, "Should I tell this person? How will they react? What are the consequences?"

You see all these narratives piling up on one another, and sometimes people then decide that it's best not to tell someone else. I feel infatuation for queer people is sometimes very solitary. And then sometimes it comes out, and your fantasies are somehow responded to by the cosmos, and someone you're in love with ends up responding to you in the same way.

I don't know. Maybe that's what we're getting from a lot of gay cinema. Maybe people just have explosive sex, AND THEN THE LOVE DIES.

–

I'M NOT OUT TO MY FOLKS. A part of me doesn't want to disappoint them, but the other part of me thinks it's not their burden to deal with. The moment you come out to your parents, it becomes their burden too, because then they have to worry about how it reflects on them. I don't want my mother to have to worry about who is saying what about her child, and how she's going to deal with that. I would much rather bear that burden on my own because I am better equipped to handle it.

Also, my sexuality has little to do with them. I love them and I want the best for them, but my sexuality is just that; it's mine. It has nothing to do with them.

Same thing goes for my little sister and my nephew; they're both younger than I am, so I feel this need to protect them from having to deal with a gay sister or gay aunt. As much as I don't come out and say that I'm gay or lesbian, I know what I am, and I know the person that I love, and I know it is one person. I have no time for anyone else. I know what I am, and I know who I love; and for me THAT'S ALL THAT MATTERS.

–

I FALL IN LOVE ALL THE TIME. I love love! I love things and people and spaces. But my most memorable love? When I met her, I was preparing to come back to Kenya, but I met her and there was no way I could leave. I just had to pause. She was a spoken word artist, and I watched her perform one summer. Afterwards, I went up to her and I said, "Oh my God." And I don't approach girls, but this is what happens with love when it beckons. There was no way I could not. I had to speak with her. We connected, and after that I started following her and we'd visit one another. And we went on like this for two years. That love is what helped me get through my depression. It still does. We talk all the time. Skype, phone calls, all that. I miss her very much, and I miss her family, because they became mine.

Being with her was a nice way for me to experience what it is like to be black in the States, and understand race and the navigation around it. Her family welcomed me, and made fun of my name, and my African-ness, but it was done with so much love because they loved her. And whoever she loved, they loved. I wasn't just her partner, I became their family. The hardest thing about being back here is not being able to be with her nieces as they grow up. I miss cutting up stuff in the kitchen with her mum, and listening to their playful banter. All the things that make family and community what they are. It's very hard. These are things you want to do when you are younger, because when you get older you get a little set in your ways and it's challenging TRYING TO RECREATE IT ELSEWHERE.

–

One day I was in the dorm with some guy. It was raining outside, so we were stuck. Everyone else was in the dining hall watching a movie. Somehow our conversation veered to sexual things, fucking girls...and I noticed he was hard. I asked him, "Do you want me to do something about that?"

He said, "Yes."

I did.

–

I like African men. If I have to date a white man, it should just be for business reasons. I don't think there is any white person that I have ever loved. I have met many of them, though.

Once I was in a relationship but had a white guy who I was also dating. Every time I had to go and see him, I would let my then-boyfriend know that I was going to meet him. For the white guy, I was only after his money. That was the motivating factor. My boyfriend didn't mind, because he knew that he was the one I loved. I don't think that I have ever loved a white guy. I usually just lie to them in order to get what I need.

–

There's this tendency with men—gay, straight, bi, whatever—we can commit when we want to, when we find the right person, but until we do? Most men are dogs. Even me.

–

I always date men. Men with dicks. Men who identify as men. Cis-men. I don't do trans men.

I went out one night, and a man approached me. He sat next to me and started to buy me drinks. He thought I was a woman. Afterwards, we went to his place and he started trying to touch my privates, and that's where the problem started. Do you know that man became sober?

He told me, "*Mimi nimeishi Nairobi, nimejua mashoga, lakini sikuamini.* I thought you were a woman." I have lived in Nairobi, I know homosexuals, but I can't believe you!

Luckily, he didn't turn violent, he was just confused. Shocked. He asked me so many questions, "Were you born this way? I know there are gay men pretending to be women, but you're in a class of your own."

Some trans people get killed in such situations. The man can even call you a thief and call the guards. Thief! Thief! Then the guards come and arrest you and take you to the police and say, "This is a man pretending to be a woman."

They strip you naked. They take photos of you, they upload them on Facebook, share them on WhatsApp. IT'S VERY SHAMING.

–

I DIDN'T KNOW my first boyfriend was cheating on me. My friends pointed out that his excuses were weird, and so I confronted him about it. I met him when he was going to board a bus. On the way he told me that his family had just found out that he was queer, and he was dealing with it in his own way. I asked him where that left us. He started talking about his parents again, and I asked him, "Do you still love me?"

He talked about needing time. I said to him, "I asked you a question. Do you still love me?" When he talked about his parents again, I turned and walked away. Two years later, I saw him again at a party. He said, "About that day, I was actually cheating on you, and I'm sorry. Can we work things out?"

I said, "I DON'T EAT MY OWN PUKE."

–

ONE NIGHT, I WENT OUT ALONE to a club and found a nice guy dancing. I told him I liked him and offered to buy him a drink, but he said he didn't drink alcohol. I challenged him to try some, and he let me recommend him a drink. I ordered a beer for him. He had never drunk alcohol before, so he got really high. So I told him again, "I like you."

He said, "You already told me that."

I told him, "I mean sexually."

He then became violent and we started fighting. The bouncers caught us and took us out. They asked why we were fighting but none of us said anything. The bouncers told us not to come back inside. I decided to go back home. This guy said, "I don't have bus fare to go home."

I told him, "See what you have done to yourself."

He said, "What you said was very bad. Even God doesn't like those things."

I asked him, "What do you want to do?"

He said, "I want to go to another bar."

So we boarded a *matatu* and it took the route to where I lived. We never got to the bar, we went to my house instead. When he came to my house, he never left for one year and two months! I must say there is no one I loved like I loved him. He was very sincere. He told me he realized he had had all those feelings but he had never acted on them. He was very protective of me. Possessive. He would see someone looking at me flirtatiously, and he wouldn't say a word, but the next day—he was violent, a part of him that I didn't like—he would attack that person. I didn't like it because it caused so many problems. He was the type that doesn't say anything, but acts compulsively.

He had been living in my house and had introduced me to his parents. He was brought up by his mother, since his father had died when he was young. I even knew his siblings—they were very happy that we got along. His mother was happy, too. She thought we were just good friends. They told me that he had changed since we met, because he was always very difficult to get along with.

After that one year and two months, we separated after he cheated on me. It was devastating. I became very sick. My friends advised me not to take him back, even though I liked him a lot and had tolerated a lot of nonsense from him. When he came back we talked things over. I thought I could forgive him, but it was very difficult so we agreed to separate.

How we separated was so silly. We agreed that we would separate that Friday. We planned to have dinner then separate. We had dinner together, then we had an emotional crying session, then we set rules so that we wouldn't see each other at least for a year. I bumped into him some time ago on the streets, and I felt the same thing I felt for him. But I had decided I couldn't take him back. I STILL SEE HIM NOW AND THEN.

–

WHEN I FIRST MET MY BOYFRIEND, he had all those politics about tops and bottoms. He'd say, "I've never been fucked. I don't think I can. I can only top."

I'd tell him, "Then go find a woman. She's the one who will never have a dick. I'm a man, so your politics don't involve me."

So we made an agreement. Some days he fucks me, some days I fuck him—and he has to allow it. We argued and fought about it, until finally he gave in. Now he's fine with it, but he's not proud of it in public. He wants my friends to believe I'm like a woman to him. He addresses me like I'm a woman in public. It's a process—I WON'T RUSH HIM.

–

I'M TIRED OF WOMEN who think all I am is a sexual object. I've become this fantasy person. There's all these girls who watch 'The L Word' and when they see me, they really want a piece of that. It's great that you watch those type of shows, but there's very little reality in them. This is the problem especially with younger lesbians; they're so quick to embody that way of being. You find a lot of them dressing in a certain way, to look a certain type of gay, and I always tell them, "Find *you* first."

I've never been the kind of girl to wear dresses and make up and long hair—that's never been me. My sexuality didn't come with a new wardrobe for me. It didn't change the way I see myself. If your sexuality does that to you, there's a problem. If I were straight, I'd still wear the same clothes; SNEAKERS AND A T-SHIRT.

–

I CAN'T REMEMBER the first time it hit me that I like girls, but I do know for a fact that I've always been very fascinated by the female form. It's so soft and gentle. The chiselled chin and structure of a man is so harsh, so boxy. You know? But the female form is so fluid; I wonder what kind of day God was having WHEN HE MADE IT.

–

SEX WORK

A NOTE ON THIS CHAPTER:

Sex work and the stories of sex workers are a vital part of the Stories of Our Lives lexicon. Of the queer, trans and non-binary identifying people who do sex work, some count being a sex worker as a part of their identity, their politic and their value system. Others do it as a job for earning money, without considering it as much else, in the same way that someone could also be an accountant, a nursery school teacher, a clinical officer, an NGO program manager, a chef, an artist, a kiosk owner, a social media influencer or a CEO.

The discussion around sex work must be nuanced, layered and above all respectful. Many things in this tense space are true which can seem to exist at odds. People are marginalized by any number of things, including being of minority race or religion. A lot of marginalization in this context is economic: living in poverty since birth, or changed socioeconomic status in the course of life. Sex is a valuable quantity and will always be in demand, and as such there will always be service providers who can meet these demands at all possible price points. The income from sex work does exactly the same things income from anything else would do: enable people to eat, seek healthcare, pay rent, provide for families, make investments and possibly build wealth.

We cannot discount queerness and the ways it causes families to disown their children to the mercies of this cruel world, thus limiting opportunities for education which then leave young people economically vulnerable. Many of the queer, trans and non-binary people we spoke to during Stories of Our Lives interviews told us about multiple suspensions, expulsions and other arbitrary terminations of educational opportunities especially at the secondary and tertiary levels. These qualifications are often the gateway to the few employment options there are, and the data shows that these options are not as open to queer, trans and non-binary people as they are to cis- identifying and heterosexual folk with equal qualifications.

Starting a small business requires initial and ongoing access to capital, along with proof of educational opportunities, or even guarantors to help in credit access that people may not have. We come to a place where sex work is one of very few options available for them.

This situation does not mean that people cannot also opt to offer sex work as a service even when other options exist. Continual sex work activism, academic work and changing narratives around transactional sex has shifted public conversation on this issue worldwide. Escort services offered at higher socioeconomic cadres to high net worth individuals confers upon providers multiple protections: access to full sex and reproductive healthcare options, security, legal protection through corporate mechanisms and many others. A lot of sex work can begin as survival and grow like any other small and medium size enterprise ran by a single person or a group into something much more solid and sustainable, and the agency this confers enables dignity, a stronger sense of self and societal equity.

At the same time, sex workers all over the world have been building on their strong sense of community, mainstream networks and savvy business sense to build institutions that offer diverse services. Usha Bank in Kolkata, India, started by the sex worker-ran and -led Usha Multipurpose Cooperative Society in 1995, has enabled sex workers to save and invest their earnings.[1] Started by 13 women who pooled their savings of 30,000 rupees (USD 418), the bank now turns over more than 300 million rupees annually (USD 4.1 million) enabling them to avoid having pimps, loan sharks, madams, husbands, partners and boyfriends as their only sources of income. The bank has enabled women to buy land, build homes, support aged parents, educate children and open small businesses. Supporting sex workers in countries where their legal status is precarious has to go beyond "key population" status and handing out condoms and lube once in a while. The children of sex workers are often marginalized because of their parent's work, and day/night care centres for them, as well as schools, continue to be necessary. The road to decriminalization and supportive systems for sex workers for many countries remains long.

---

1. Dhillon, A. "No longer at the mercy of the madams": India's bank for sex workers. The Guardian. 6th Dec 2017.

Sex work can be both survival and personally fulfilling, creating space for provision of services that transcend the sexual: meeting human needs for connection, intimacy, support and friendship. The internet has also increased the spaces for sex work to be done in diverse ways, even using the interpersonal distance as a way to sell cam services, voice work, ethical trade in consensually obtained images, audio and video and more. This conversation must be separated from the conversation around human trafficking, in which people are forced to provide sex services and are unable to escape these abusive, tragic and violent circumstances.

One of the Nest Collective members has long, thick curls that cascade down past her shoulders, and when we met one wonderful group of male sex workers in Mombasa, one of them touched her hair gently and said, wistfully, "I used to have hair like this." He continued to tell us that cutting his hair, stopping to wear makeup and dressing more masculine, or butch, had opened veins of respect for him in the society that hadn't existed before. As he and the other sex workers have grown older and in their ability to support themselves, they have taken up stronger positions in society. It is no longer so much about whether they were queer or even if they do sex work (and the small communities they live in know that they do), it was more about "fitting in"; proving that they were part of the society and not operating counter to it.

The intersections of all these things—respectability, agency, social integration—increase the net privileges and access people have. This is problematic if we are a society pushing for all people to have all human rights unconditionally. Queerness in and of itself can be taken to mean multiple ways of living and being, over and above sexual orientation and behavior. Queerness engages society from a different space, and for it to remain true to itself this tension must remain. Queerness isn't queer because it agrees and remains quiet. And so sex work sits in the middle of these things—offering the services and erotic care work that human beings need without acknowledging their true value, and at the same time building honest, dignified and decent livelihoods in legally grey zones. Queer, trans and non-binary sex workers also sit at this intersection of respectable queerness and the truth about what human beings need without admitting their true dependence.

There's a reason that this is said to be the oldest human profession, or the profession which determines whether a digital social network lives or dies, and even the profession that scientists will spend billions to try to integrate as seamlessly as possible into robotics and machine-work. People—queer, trans, nonbinary or otherwise—want to have sex, and they will continue to be willing to pay to have it. Whether we accept this or not, WE'LL HAVE TO FIND A WAY TO LIVE WITH IT.

–

As A SEX WORKER, you have to learn the difference between work and love. You can have a client who you meet very often. Every time he comes to your street, he doesn't take anyone else: just you. Sometimes a client tells you, "Honestly, I like you, and I don't want to see you working on the street."

And you tell them, "I am on the street because that's where I get my daily bread. I have rent to pay, I have a child in school. If you take me away from the street, what's your plan for my life?"

Sometimes they decide to take you out of the street. So you begin to bond, and he gives you money and helps you out from time to time. You think of him as your special person, "I am with him and he is with me."

Your life can change through him, as long as you show him love. And then when he wants you, all he has to do is call, "Where are you? I'm leaving work and I'm coming."

Some clients even get it for free. You like them, you fall in love. So you make your money on the side, and you give him some for free *[laughs]*. Love is equal. It's not gay, it's not woman or man. The way you love is the same way I love, even as a sex worker. Because it's the heart that loves.

Love must be shown to be seen. My lover wouldn't want to kiss me and I refuse to kiss them in return. Or touch me and I refuse to touch them as well, because I—as a sex worker—have become accustomed to "short-time". This is something else, this is love. YOU MUST LEARN TO RECEIVE IT.

–

Every time we go out, we carry with us our condoms and lubricant. Thank God for lube, long ago we used to fuck with saliva! These days, we have lubricant. Sometimes you meet a client, and when you take out your condoms they say, "*Condom? Na haina utamu...kwani kutoka lini mtu akala ndizi na maganda?*" Condom? But it isn't as sweet...since when did one eat a banana with the peel on?

So you remind them, "I don't know your history and you don't know mine."

And even as the client wears it, you check the condom for tears, and you make sure the client is using it properly. Some clients tell you afterwards that they didn't know all that about safe sex.

However, some clients still insist on bareback sex. There's a friend of mine who taught me how to use the female condom in such instances. If the client is offering good money and they want bareback sex, then before you get down to business, you excuse yourself and go to the bathroom, put on your female condom with lube and then you're good to go. You tell the client to turn off the lights and do it—they think it's bareback, but you know there's some protection.

The female condom, though, is very risky. You have to keep a hold on it during sex, otherwise if he's too big, it can go all the way in. But it's OK for a quickie, and you can wash it and use it another day.

–

We now know so much more about our health and safe sex practices these days. Long ago, you'd have things happen—like condom bursts and rape—and there wasn't enough knowledge like there is now. Now we know that if something happens, if I'm raped I know what to do within 72 hours, I know where to get PEP etc.

Now we know there's PrEP, we are better at condom negotiation even when the clients want to pay for bareback sex. And for those of us who do have HIV, there is less stigma. There are support groups, reminders for ARV. Now there is more knowledge that taking ARVs reduces the risk of transmission. These days, no one dies from AIDS. Even in the countryside, people know how to stay healthy. We use PrEP—because condoms are always bursting, and even then we still use condoms because we know there are other STIs to protect ourselves from, NOT JUST HIV.

–

THERE IS LESS VIOLENCE NOW towards sex workers. It's still there, but it's less these days. We have learned to keep one another safe. We have community security for sex workers, and most of us have phone numbers for the security team. If you get into a situation and you feel insecure—like for instance, you can get into a client's car and then once inside you find there are six people in the car, and you thought there was only one because the car had tinted windows. And you can look around and see that these men don't have good intentions. Now we know to call or text the security guy in that zone and tell them, "I'm in a client's car but I can see there are many men in the car. If there's a problem, I'll let you know."

So he remains on standby, in case of anything he can follow-up, or he can advise me, "When you get to such and such a place and you get a chance, get out of that car."

So we have a system of people in different zones, if something happens, the person in charge is around to go to the police station, provide statements, get a lawyer.

These days, if you're caught by the police, they don't write "gay" on the charge sheet. They will be more specific and say you were loitering, or you were drunk—because now they know "gay" isn't a charge. Also, these days they put you in a separate cell, not with all the other prisoners, because now they know that things could go wrong in a general cell. Some of us even have boyfriends who are police. You can find love anywhere, EVEN IN A CELL!

–

I HAD MY PERSON and we were together for four years, then his wife managed to outsmart me somehow. She found out that her husband was with me, but she never confronted me about it;

she instead came and befriended me. I had never met her before so I didn't know what she looked like. We became really good friends, she would even come and bitch about her husband to me, but at this point I still didn't know who she was and neither did I know this husband she was bitching about was my person. She used to come home to visit me quite often and she knew that over the weekends I enjoyed chewing miraa. She would always bring me some and give me some money also. She became an extremely close friend. Then one day I found out she was my *mke mwenza* (co-wife).

I didn't want her to feel like I had stolen her man, so I slowly started distancing myself from both of them. To this day, when I see that guy, HE STILL WANTS ME SO BAD.

–

SEX WORK IS QUITE SEASONAL, it keeps fluctuating, depending on the tourist seasons. Most of it happens online nowadays; we use apps. Trans sex workers are at the most risk of violence. When you're going out to meet a client and you're all dressed up, things can get tricky on the way to the client and back, so you have to make sure you have your transport sorted, whether it's a taxi or a *bajaj*[2]. Even the bajaj's are risky because sometimes they pretend they need to pick something on the way so they use a different route so that they can expose you.

It's very difficult to shame me, though, because I love dressing up as a woman, and I love to be seen. It's who I am. So if I'm walking in the streets and people start shouting insults or whatever, I never answer, I just keep walking with my head high.

Clients are so interesting, some of them want you to arrive all dressed up in your femme clothes, but some want you to have it all in a bag then get dressed in their home; I guess they don't want people to know what they're into or they want to watch you get into the clothes.

Let me tell you, I love stockings! My closet has so many! I have this one body stocking that has a big cut-out in the front

---

2. Also tuk-tuk; a three-wheeled motorbike commonly used as a cheap form of transport over short distances.

and one in the back *[laughs]*. I call it porno underwear. When I'm walking in the street, you obviously can't tell what I have underneath, partly because I still have a bit of respect for my brothers and their role in the community (they are religious leaders in the area), but I know once I reach where I'm going and undress, even a cis woman would be in shock, she'd throw her hands in the air in defeat.

For now, I'm not stale yet, I'm still hot stuff, but the time will come when younger girls will take over and I'll be a retired woman. Seeing as I'm not getting any younger, what I would love is to get a small restaurant where I can cook and serve my guests and NOT HAVE TO HIDE.

–

THE POLICE CAN REALLY BE A BOTHER sometimes. There was a time when my friend and I were going to a club, and just as we were passing the casino, a police car flashed its lights at us and drove towards us. They asked us for our IDs, my friend gave his and I gave mine. Then they said, "This isn't you! This isn't your ID! Give us your ID that shows you as you are now."

So I took off my wig and said to them, "Take a good look."

They started asking me why I was dressed like that and I told them how I was dressed had nothing to do with my ID. They let go of my friend and kept me there. After a while they called me and said, "We know what you do, so we're letting you go because we know you'll make some money tonight and later you'll come and share it with us."

They let me go and I went into the casino, where I immediately met a group of Somali guys who were visiting from London, and they just loved everything about me! They asked me to sit with them and entertain them. The moment I sat down, they ordered three crates of beer and gave me 3,000 shillings *[laughs]*. I made a lot of money that night. Do you think I went back to give those cops anything? HA! NEVER!

–

I THINK I'M APPROACHING FIFTEEN YEARS IN SEX WORK. This tattoo on my face is new. It was a bit painful, but I was so drunk when I got it. It's a star as you can see, so that when someone looks at me, the star lures him *[laughs]*. I used to like wearing miniskirts in Nairobi on Koinange Street. You would always find me in a miniskirt and a trench-coat on the street. Here at the Coast, I mostly wear jeans or tights because these hoes are crazy. They fight a lot—especially over clients—so you have to be ready to fight or run.

I just want a nice white man to marry me so that I can retire. I've met many nice guys but I was always so restless at the time—always jumping around—so no one thought I was serious. They all thought I was just a regular hoe, but now I'm ready to settle. I still want a daughter.

I was in a three-year relationship with an Italian guy called Roberto, but he passed away. He loved me with his whole heart, and he waited for me for so long, but he got tired. I was an alcoholic at the time, and I would always cause a scene whenever we went out and pull stunts on him. He just got tired. ALL HIS PROPERTY WOULD BE MINE BY NOW.

—

I HAVE TO GO TO A WITCH DOCTOR in order to attract clients. I have to. This is the Coast. It's hectic, and you can be bewitched. You can be with a client and things just crumble as you watch, and you don't understand how it happened. That's very common here. So you have to go and protect yourself and your body. A mix of things to swallow and apply, so that when you go to the club, you're the only one who stands out; you literally sparkle.

Very many people here go to witchdoctors, but they never admit it, they're very secretive about it. They'll go to the mosque or church on one day then to the witchdoctor the next day. I don't want anyone to bewitch my star, so I have to protect it. The witchdoctors don't care if you're trans or queer, you go to them, you pay them and that's that, MANY OF THEM ARE ACTUALLY MY FRIENDS.

—

I AM A TRANS SEX WORKER. Sex work is difficult when you're trans. We find it more challenging than the gay and female sex workers. They also make fun of us, "You want to be a woman, but you are not a woman. You're standing there wearing dresses and miniskirts, looking prettier than me, but at the end of the day I'm the one who's gonna make the catch. *Utampa nini mwanaume?*" What will you offer a man?

Men approach us expecting that what they see is what they are getting, but we can't put up a sign where we're standing that says, "We are women but we don't have vaginas."

How do we end up doing sex work? Many of us didn't finish school because of our nature. We had parents refusing us to go to school because they were ashamed, and didn't want us to be seen in public. Some of us are outcasts in our own families. Some of us have been disowned and kicked out by our families, and we can't be employed because of our gender. Our lives are very complicated.

Sometimes I get one client per night—that is, one client that was willing to have sex with me after finding out who I am. Many of us can only offer anal sex, but many men only want vaginal sex. Sometimes we say, "I've got my period" to try to convince them into performing anal sex, but many men are not used to anal sex with women. So it is challenging.

Sometimes they refuse to pay. You plead with them, "Pay half of what we agreed. I cannot go out like this. I've got so many debts, my landlord is coming. I went to work on an empty stomach, just give me something to eat."

Maybe he promised you 2,000 shillings, in the end he can give you 300. It is also really difficult to negotiate for condom use. A client will give me ultimatums, "I've accepted what you are, but I don't like condoms."

What will I do? I want that money so that I can go home and put food in my mouth. Maybe he's offering me 2,000, and I haven't earned anything else that day. Will I refuse? No. It's difficult. If you refuse, they leave you or they tell you, "You either take what I'm offering, or you go empty-handed."

I don't want to go empty-handed. I'LL TAKE THE MONEY.

—

I ONCE HAD A CLIENT who was a lawyer. He got me out of sex work while I was with him. He told me to change the way I dressed, that he didn't like it. I stayed with him for a while, about six years. When we parted, I was heartbroken. I stayed in the house for a month. I couldn't eat, I lost weight. He was also badly off, he drank for three months. He would even send his friends to check on me, but it was over.

While we were together, I had stopped going to clubs on my own. We would go together, and he would tell me what to wear. He changed my style. After the month of mourning our break up, I left the house determined to start again. That's when I started sex work in earnest. I wasn't afraid of anything. I did the work with one heart. And I was successful; there wasn't anyone I wanted that I couldn't seduce.

There are many straight men who are curious about gay sex, and some of them want to try these things out and see for themselves. Sometimes we meet men when they are with their girlfriends. The girlfriends point us out and sa, "That one is gay."

The next day the boyfriend will come alone, looking for me, because it's a new experience he's only heard of. He'll work hard and seduce me, so he can experience the sex for himself. Sometimes they will hear that there are a lot of us gay sex workers in Nairobi, and they will go to Nairobi to see for themselves. There are others who leave Nairobi to come to this other side of the country, saying they came all the way because THEY HAD HEARD CERTAIN THINGS.

–

I'D LOVE TO TRANSITION. Fully. If I were able, I would transition completely. When I was younger, I didn't like seeing the difference between myself and cis women, I wanted to be exactly like a woman. One time I went to a pharmacy and made some enquiries. The pharmacist asked me why I wanted to ruin myself, so I stopped talking. I had wanted a cream for increasing my curves. The pharmacist said they had them, but he didn't approve of my using them. If I transitioned, I would move to Nairobi, because here everyone is used to me being a certain way. It could give me a fresh start. I'd have the procedures and move on the very same day. If it's possible, I'D EVEN CHANGE MY NAME.

–

I DON'T WANT A FAMILY. Even if I were able to give birth, I wouldn't want kids. Maybe if I had a husband. But for now? No. You know when a sex worker has a child, it holds them back. They're not able to go work. And when you die, you leave the child in a lot of problems, because they will be harassed.

I've had several relationships, but sex work is what ended up making us part. Once I was dating this guy, and my friends wanted to break us up because while I was with him, I wasn't available to see them or to undertake sex work. My friends would call me to go out, and I would refuse to join them. My man had made me promise that I would stop doing sex work, and I did. My friends knew this, so they started telling him that I was still working behind his back. He told them he would only believe that if he saw it with his own eyes.

So one day they came up with this plan. They told him to call me and tell me he was going to Nairobi, then come to the street, because he would catch me working. At the same time, they called me and told me that my man was cheating on me with a sex worker on the street, and that if I called him, he would lie to me about being in Nairobi. So we both showed up on the street, looking to catch the other.

He saw me and I saw him. He took off his hat, and went off to drink with another sex worker. They drank until morning. After that, we started to fight, and I have a mouth on me, I really insulted him. We broke up after a while and I was hesitant to get back together with him, in case he tried to bewitch me. I'm afraid of people from Mombasa, YOU NEVER KNOW WHAT WITCHCRAFT THEY MIGHT PERFORM ON YOU.

–

THE THING WITH SEX WORKERS AND POLICE is that how they treat us varies by individual. I think it really matters how you approach and speak to them. Police officers are people too, if you are honest with them. I usually say to them, "I'm gay, and I am a sex worker, but I am not a thief."

They are surprised but they don't arrest me.

I once got into a fight on the street. I had moved to a new site, and the sex workers there started beating me up. I ran to the police and they helped me out. Another time some street kids who had seen us cat-walking nearby started pulling us from *tuk-tuks*[3], we ran into the police station. The police put us in their car and drove us out of there, TO A SAFER SPOT IN TOWN.

–

WHEN I DRESS FEMME, you really cannot tell I am trans. I go to the salon, I do my nails. Even my voice changes.

This can be a bad thing sometimes. I've seen many of my colleagues get beaten up because they went with a client to their place without telling them that they are trans. The men get angry and say, "Why didn't you tell me so I could have taken a woman?"

It's best to tell them when you are in their car, in case they might not have realized it already. If he's still into it after you tell him, then you go with him. If he isn't interested, you offer to call a friend of yours for him, and he might even give you some money. But it's best to disclose early.

I have friends who have been beaten. One was on the street, wearing a dress. They got picked up and went home with this guy, even cooked for him. He wanted to shower together, and my friend refused to undress. The man undressed them by force, and said, "Today I will kill you. Why didn't you tell me you are a man? You've drank my wine, eaten my chicken."

He carried my friend out of his house—naked—to the car and dumped them on a road side. But since they are used to working the street they weren't afraid. They just dressed up and went back to work.

Other clients like a manly man. Some will pick you up and ask if you have a different set of clothes, they want you to change. Some will find me in the club with my makeup and blouse on and give me their number and when you talk later, they ask you to go visit them BUT DRESSED LIKE A MAN.

–

3. Also bajaj; a three-wheeled motorbike commonly used as a cheap form of transport over short distances.

RELIGION AND SPIRITUALITY

I AM MUSLIM, AND I AM VERY COMMITTED, I do my normal *salahs*[1], but when it comes to entering a religious space, I'm torn. In the Islamic way of living, females and males don't intermingle in public spaces; females go this way, males the other. So I don't know whether to wear a *hijab* or a *buibui*[2] and sit on the women's side, or to wear a *kanzu*[3] and sit on the men's side. This has made me a religious introvert. I usually conduct my *salahs* at home because I'm afraid of what will happen to me in public. And my being a religious introvert has prevented me from learning a lot of religious things. There are a lot of religious platforms in public where people are educated on the religion, but I miss out on those opportunities. Where will I sit? How will I identify myself?

Islam strictly condemns my being the way I am. When I learned this, I wanted to lock myself in my house and take poison, saying, "I don't want to go to hell. If my being the way I am provokes Allah, then let me end my life."

Luckily, I came across and joined a group here that is called Young Queer Muslims where we sit together and have all our questions regarding religion and being queer answered. I thought I was cursed, but I discovered that I am not. God created you. Embrace yourself. God does not make mistakes, so WHO ARE YOU TO QUESTION YOUR BEING?

–

I AM A SPIRITUAL PERSON. I was raised Catholic, and all those verses that they recite and preach about are always present in my mind. The door will be closed and we shall be outside with the witches, dogs and homosexuals.[4] Or that bit in the creation story where the man was put to sleep and a rib was removed and now there is a woman carrying your ribs around. The message of the Bible has been inculcated in me, but it is difficult to just read the Bible and see a better message. This made me stop going to

---

1. Islamic prayer, one of the Five Pillars in the faith of Islam
2. Head coverings worn in public by some Muslim women
3. White or cream coloured robe worn by men in the African Great Lakes region. It is referred to as a tunic in English, and as the thawb in Arab countries.
4. Revelations 22:15

church. Maybe there is another way of reading the Bible. I think the Bible is more than just a punishment structure for sinners.

I could not fit in that patriarchal framework; that idea of how you should live, how to be a man, how to carry out obligations as a husband, have children. What they were selling, I wasn't buying. I stopped going to church.

Maybe there is a different way of looking at Christianity, Jesus and religion, but as at now that is very distant to me. It is so frustrating to me because I think Jesus would be an awesome person being God. I would like to know him better but I don't how to begin to know him. I wish I could find someone to help me de-construct everything I know about the Bible and give me a fresh perspective.

I feel frustrated because I consider myself a Christian, but I can't read the Bible. Right now I am reading New Age spirituality and philosophy books centred around you and how you live your life. About revering life and honouring life. It feels peaceful, but I sometimes feel that all this spirituality and philosophy... I cannot put it on a cross and crucify it to save my life. At such moments I feel like I need Jesus.

The significance of this is amazing; that someone can be nailed on a cross and die for someone else. I think that person is the perfect guy. I want him in my life. I would like to know Jesus IN A DIFFERENT WAY.

–

I DON'T REALLY GO TO CHURCH. I used to. I was even an altar boy, but my friends from church used to condemn gay people, saying gay people are sinners that are going to hell. I decided I can maintain my faith on my own. I don't have to worship God in church; I can do it anywhere, EVEN ON MY OWN.

–

THE WILL OF GOD as I know it is pure love. Everything else is silence. It's not about controlling people with a Bible. Over the past six months, we've been having Sunday conversations with other queer people who are struggling with their faith. We read the Quran, we read the Torah, we read the Rastafari Bible, we read the Christian Bible.

I see myself as a spiritual being, more than a physical being. When I love and kiss my boyfriend, when I make love to him—in that act of surrender—there is no criminality. It is a fellowship that I long for. I have found my place in the UNIVERSE OF THINGS.

–

I GO TO CHURCH. I'm even the choir mistress! I sing, and I take those people to heaven. Let them listen to me, and stay with their questions. I dress really nicely and go. I believe God is love—and you don't choose who to love, you just find yourself where you are. So I live my life, you live yours, we will find each other eventually. My heaven is on earth. The one up there is even a top-up. If I create hell for myself down here, HOW WILL I LIVE?

–

I'M VERY SPIRITUAL. I go to church. I've been a Christian Union chair-lady through primary and high school. I love anything that has to do with the church. I love it so much. Being a lesbian doesn't change that. You just love someone and it's OK. It doesn't have anything to do with HOW I RELATE WITH MY GOD.

–

BEFORE I JOINED UNIVERSITY, I became a Muslim for many reasons including the fact that while wearing a *buibui*, no-one would ask me if I am female or not. I could walk around in public without questions, and it was working, but then underneath the *buibui*, I was who I am, and I was walking the way I walk. I remember people saying, "You're a guy underneath that *buibui*, aren't you? You're pretending that you're a girl."

But it was working, in its own way. I am still a Muslim, but these days I don't wear the buibui. I'm OK being who I am without having to dress and look feminine. I never struggled with reconciling all my identities, because they have all always been there. I became a Muslim because I identified with some things I learnt about it that made sense to me. Even when I was converting to Islam, I was a lesbian, I was dating women, and for me it wasn't something to debate about. You can't tell me I cannot be a Muslim because I date women. If you think my sexuality and my spirituality are mutually exclusive, that's on you. On my side, THESE SIDES OF ME ALL CO-EXIST.

–

I WAS RAISED in the church. My grandmother was my guardian for seven years when my mother left when I was two months old. I believe God is interested in the state of your heart and nothing else. I won't even argue with people about homosexuality. I believe God is for all. If it were not for God, I would not be where I am, in spite of everything. I came from a very poor family. Now even my mother comes to my home and really admires it. I haven't even gone to anyone's college, it's just the hustle. I started out washing toilets in a hotel! But you come into my house and it is comfortable, nice chairs, all of that. I believe God is a caring God. He doesn't choose ONLY MEN THAT LOVE WOMEN.

–

I AM IN COLLEGE studying theology; it has always been my dream to be a preacher. I want to reach out to the gay community but I want an all-inclusive congregation; gay and straight. Most gay people I know don't want anything to do with religion because of the stigmatization and how the religious community judges them. So my prayer has always been to be the bridge, I always ask God to make me the one who reconciles the two. Because God loves everyone.

Even if homosexuality was decriminalized in Kenya and gay unions made legal, I still would not tell my wife and kids that I am gay. I also would not leave my wife because I love her but if the opportunity presented itself to get married to a man I would do it. I would love it, having my wife know I'm gay and knowing and accepting my husband.

I know God loves me. I know He loves me the way I am. Don't let anyone tell you as a gay person that God doesn't love you. It's religion that has something against homosexuality, NOT GOD.

–

THERE WAS CONFLICT with my religion. There was a time it was really depressing and weighed heavily on me. I thought I wasn't going to go to heaven. The conclusions from the religious community about gay people are not positive, and it affected me. It was a battle I had to fight. But I realized it's only God who can judge me, not people. We are told He knew us before we were born, that means He knew I was going to be like this but he still choose to let me and us exist. So I MADE PEACE WITH IT.

–

I AM EXTREMELY SPIRITUAL. My belief in God is very strong. There's a time when my belief wasn't strong, but I realized it was weakening because other people were making me feel like God doesn't want homosexuals. But I looked around me and I realized God is a diverse God, and people were trying to standardize Him and His creations.

Being a gay person, you really need God on your side. No one guides and protects like He does. I'd pray for guidance and see myself being delivered from messy situations. You emerge and you wonder, "If this is not God's grace, what is it?"

This gay cause needs God. He's the one who WILL GUIDE US AND PROTECT US.

–

WITH CHURCH, sometimes I feel like there's a spirit telling me that I'm doing the wrong thing and another telling me that God knows that He made me like this. I feel like I am in between. I can go to church, feel like a strong Christian then after a while something draws me back and makes me feel like, "You're pretending. You're gay."

Church has been a challenge for me so far BECAUSE OF THAT.

–

I DO GO TO CHURCH but I'm not that active. I do believe in God. According to me, I know that being gay is 'against the Bible'. So whenever I'm in church I remember, "Oh my God, I'm gay."

When I start praying and doing church stuff, IT'S LIKE I'M MOCKING GOD.

–

I THINK I'M A GOOD CHRISTIAN. I don't think being gay affects my religion. I go to church, and I don't have a problem with the church, though sometimes you hear the pastor condemning gays. In our church, we have guys in the praise and worship team who are gay—even some of the ushers are gay—then suddenly the pastor starts condemning gay people, talking about how we'll burn in hell, saying we're so immoral, so unnatural. It gets really awkward. I'm used to it though, I know in the end IT'S JUST ME AND MY GOD.

–

WHEN I WAS A SMALL KID, I was a Christian but now I'm not into any religion. My parents were Muslim and Christian, but I can't say that I'm either, though I am an upcoming gospel artist. I sing gospel music—Christian gospel—but I don't go to church. I only go to church when I HAVE A PERFORMANCE THERE.

–

I AM A RELIGIOUS PERSON, I even sing in the church choir. I love God, and I have a relationship with Him. What I believe is He made me gay for a reason. I don't question God's love for me; I know HE LOVES ME.

–

I CAN'T REMEMBER the last time I went to church but I always pray. When I wake up, before eating, before I go to sleep and every Sunday. Even if I don't go to church, I do believe. There is the issue of condemnation. Mostly in Protestant churches, you get pastors who condemn homosexuals. It hurts me. It makes me feel isolated, like I'm not like anyone else. So whenever I think about going to church, I rethink my decision and decide it's better if I stay home and pray. There is no difference between someone who goes to church and someone who stays at home praying, AS LONG AS YOU BELIEVE.

—

My favourite Bible verse is Proverbs 13:20; "walk with the wise and become wise, for a companion of fools suffers harm". It's been in my head since Christian Union. When I'm a CEO, it will be on my door. It pretty much says that the people you are always around are who you become. I don't go to church or anything, but this verse has really meant a lot. You have to surround yourself with people who are going to take you somewhere, who you're going to learn from, and teach, and you have to learn how to listen, and make people listen to you, and show courage and confidence over time.

If you see someone going wayward, tell them. Be in their shoes. If you see them struggling, be there for them however you can. Gay people need to get to that level. Beyond the politics, beyond the oppression. That community feel is what we need. It's not that I'm going to pick up your burdens—because gahdamn, I have my own!—but just know, at the end of the road is your freedom.

—

I think gay people either find glamour or the glamour finds them. I was in the Christian Union for that reason. Being in the Christian Union in a national boarding school was a big deal. I used to lead praise and worship for the whole school—and kids in high school love them some dancing, so you had to choose songs that got people stomping. The ballads, too—I used to love that song, 'Above All Power', and harmonize with whoever else was leading.

—

The prosperity gospel is a humanitarian disaster. It's actually evil, making people believe that they can beat their wives on Monday and feel forgiven by Saturday night because they gave the pastor money to build a house in the suburbs. It's not something that I can cope with and it's ridiculous that people are able to be so hypocritical. I can't deal. For me, spirituality has always been personal. I respect the belief systems of all my different friends, but when your little religious cart comes into my lane, I will push it out, because who are you?

I've never entertained religious fanaticism. They're all just Al Qaeda, without the seventy-two virgins at the end. If people refuse to think for themselves, and refuse to engage positively and challenge things to learn and grow, they will just be there attending church every Sunday. I'm not a Christian, but I can tell they're doing it wrong. I'm not a pilot but I can tell when one engine is off, because there's goddamn smoke. Their whole religion is on fire, and they've literally just created POCKETS OF HELL HERE.

–

I DON'T GO TO CHURCH nowadays. I think going to church is no longer about faith these days, it is more of a trend. Like those people who hire cars to go show off at church. Also, I don't think I would ever focus in church with all the young ladies there. I would be ogling at the girls. I would rather watch Christian programs ON TV ON SUNDAYS.

–

I WASN'T BORN A MUSLIM, but one guy convinced me to convert when I was thirteen. I changed my name and started going to the mosque. But everyone in our family is a Christian. My dad was very angry when he heard I had converted, but my mum accepted the change. In our house, if my mother is OK with something, it's fine. If my father refuses it doesn't matter, as long as mum is OK with it.

My mum is the most important person in our family. I have never imagined life without my mother. It would be so challenging. My mum can sit you down and give you advice, but my father? Never. I respect both my parents, but I love my mother. So when she said she was OK with me being Muslim, it was fine. I feel that there is no problem with the Islam religion and my sexuality. MY BOYFRIEND IS ALSO MUSLIM.

–

I THINK THE IDEA THAT QUEERNESS AND RELIGION CANNOT CO-EXIST is so wrong, because I've had the best relationship with God, and whenever I pray to God He answers my prayers. That's why I am convinced that God loves me the way I am because I know I am queer and I can talk to God, and EVERYTHING I ASK FOR, HE GIVES ME.

THE FOLLOWING IS EXCERPTED FROM A CONVERSATION BETWEEN JULIA AND MARSHA, TWO MEDICAL STUDENTS WE MET WHILE DOING THE INTERVIEW TOURS. THEY BOTH IDENTIFY AS LESBIAN.

Marsha: When I was in my first year of university, I had two very Christian room-mates who used to pray SO HARD. One of them was the Christian Union Chairperson, and the other was the Secretary. They made a rule; no secular music in the room.

Julia: They did what?

Marsha: They made a rule about what kind of music we could play in the room.

Julia: Why? As who? Didn't you have a say in the matter?

Marsha: Not really. You know how these things work. Christians can decide how the space around them works.

Julia: It's the worst.

Marsha: Then they would bring their boys from Christian Union fellowship who would hang out in the room and stay till morning, and they would make this tea in this big *sufuria*[5]. I'd come back to my room and find them sitting on my bed. I hate it when people sit where I put my head on my bed. And the worst part is they would eat popcorn and cupcakes, and the crumbs would get

5. Swahili for an aluminium saucepan.

inside my bed. So I would wonder exactly how crumbs got inside my bed.

Julia: Maybe they were blessing your bedding…

Marsha: They would play LOUD gospel music until 2 or 3 in the morning, then they'd wake up at 6am and continue praying. Most of the times I would just put on my own earphones. Gospel music is not that bad, but seriously, it gets really old. You want to listen to something else after half an hour. They really, really battered me emotionally, when they found out I was a lesbian and I had a girlfriend. On the day they found out, they told me not to go to class. They had a sit-down with me. They said, "We need to talk to you about your issue. God can revive you from this. You need to be saved. You need to accept your salvation, and accept it open-heartedly. Call this girl you have a relationship with and tell her."
I called my girlfriend and told her I didn't want her any more. My room-mates cheered…

Julia: They cheered?

Marsha: They cheered, and they prayed for me. They said that I have a demon in me, and that's the thing that I believed for a very long time. The reason I started to believe that maybe it was true, is because I did go for a mission outreach, to Tanzania, and there I watched this whole demon-removing ceremony. It was happening right in front of my face. Someone was preaching, and then she started feeling these forces, and she dropped right there and rolled on the ground. The ceremony leaders started praying for her, and she started screaming, and they started coming out from her.

Julia: The demons?

Marsha: Yes. One of them hit the bus. It was really intense. So for me, this demon stuff became really real. For me, now, it's not a theory.

Julia: I'm a Christian myself, and whenever I've come across this demon narrative, I wonder what all the people who have had demons have had in common. We're medical students, and we like evidence. And I wonder what are the aims of the demon when it possesses somebody, and I wonder if a person would have the capacity to grapple with these questions if indeed they were possessed? Would the demon be trying to keep you from an awareness that you had before? Like, in your case, you felt for yourself that maybe you were possessed, and I wonder if that would be possible if indeed you were. I have many existential questions. So I feel like it's very dangerous for this girl to walk around with all her Christian Union bullshit informing other people that they are demon-possessed, unless the Lord Himself came and talked to her and told her so-and-so has a demon. And indeed, if the Lord is who He said He is, it would be upon her not just to inform you that you are possessed—what good is that?—but to also help you to remove it, you know? I can't come and tell you that you have a demon, and then I leave you with that. What's that about? Christ never told people, "You have demons," without helping to cast them out. If we are to base this on Christ, is that the right thing?

Marsha: It wouldn't be the right thing.

Julia: In your story, I can hear that you have a very present awareness of who you are, of where you've come from, what you're trying to work towards. You're active in the process of building a healthy relationship, knowing what's healthy for you, and knowing that health means that you go slowly, accommodating your girlfriend in every possible way. I don't think that's a thing that would necessarily be different, just because you or she were a boy. You know what I mean?

Marsha: Yeah. But I wonder whether I am in love with her parts, or with her heart?

Julia: And you know the answer to that.

Marsha: I do.

Julia: I feel like gender is such a stupid reason to be in love with somebody.

Marsha: Exactly.

Julia: Like, their gender alone. For their reproductive potential, for instance, because Christians are always playing the 'the world needs women to procreate' card.

Marsha: Go out and fill the world.

Julia: As if the world will fucking procreate by itself. This is why we've all moved forward. This is why we have medical knowledge for people to have more options. Before this, the fight that we were having with the world is that contraceptives are evil, and we're not there any more.

Marsha: People used to think that contraceptives were evil?

Julia: Yes. And here we are now. People used to say, "You can't be with that girl who's not willing to have babies." And I say all of these are just systems of power.

Marsha: And they're just there to oppress people.

Julia: Exactly. I thought about it and realized that Christ was a very odd man. He was odd, because He was a thirty year old man, wasn't married, didn't have kids, was celibate—as far as the reports go—and He was uprooting married men from their homes to walk around the country with him, leading rallies and telling people they're sinners and whatever, and telling children stories, sitting with prostitutes, having His feet washed by them. He was a strange, strange man.

Marsha: Queer?

Julia: Yes. Like, He was fucking queer. Not in the sexual way, but in that way that He was so outside the boundaries that usually surround a man of His age. And I feel like for a bunch of people who claim to follow such a queer man, Christians are also very strange.

Marsha: They are.

Julia: They are queer for following a queer man, and NOT RECOGNIZING THAT QUEERNESS.

–

I WANT A LIFE where I can walk down the street and people greet me nicely. I want a life where people don't abuse me, and say nasty things about me. I want to exist peacefully, and I'm not asking for special privileges. No! I am the same person that you are. I am a child of God like anyone else. In my heart of hearts, I believe there is a place called Forward, and I'm going to reach there. I believe in God, more than anyone can imagine. I am a Muslim, A VERY DEVOTED ONE.

–

I TRIED TO THINK OF MYSELF as an extremely inquisitive person who had been viciously subdued by my teachers—possibly, my parents, but not so much—and this whole superstructure called society, so when I was in high school I started questioning my belief in God and whether it was rational. I questioned whether my belief could be explained using science, or whether it could explain itself. So I started thinking about contradiction in religious texts, and I started reading widely.

I became a secular Christian for some time, and then I tried to do a mish-mash of Christianity and Buddhism, and that didn't work. I decided that there was a lot of violence and coercion in the church, and it had been inflicted on me on several occasions, especially by teaching staff. I knew that along with violence and coercion was also an element of irrationality to do with religious belief. So I became a full-on atheist when I was seventeen years old. I'm done with this coercion. I try to see myself as having participated in religious circles on account of cultural reasons, or for the sake of fellowship and community. But that stopped making sense for me when I became aware of my sexual orientation, and what that meant in relationship with the church. So at this point, I'm an atheist.

I try not to see myself as cynically rebelling against religion and God on account of my sexual orientation. But sometimes it seems to me that that is what happened. It's fine by me, because I'm pretty sure all my life I've had a train of thought and feeling that pretty much pits my sexual orientation against God. I've always leaned towards science, the cosmos and the individual.

My parents found out that I'm an atheist a very long time ago. It wasn't a big deal, but there were all these underlying sentiments—especially on Sundays or religious holidays—and I choose not to participate in any of those. I sometimes feel like there's an underlying pain and resentment on the part of my parents on account of my lack of religious belief, AND THAT BOTHERS ME.

–

GOD KNOWS WHY HE CREATED ME. God knows why I feel the way I feel, because this is not something induced. It's not something that is passed in the air, *ama mafuta unapaka unakua shoga*. Or a lotion one applies and becomes gay.

So I don't think God made a mistake making me. It's humans who make a mistake in judging me. I believe God exists, AND THAT'S IT.

–

I GO TO CHURCH LESS OFTEN these days. At first, I really condemned myself. I'd go to church and meet my friends after the service, and they'd be saying things like, "Praise God! How was your week? How are you doing?"

I was not OK with that pretence; that smiling and huggy-huggy behaviour, and saying 'praise God'. In my heart I was asking myself, "Where am I? Am I not a sinner?" When I say 'praise

God', am I pretending? When I walk into the church and pray, am I pretending? I think I am.

That was the first conclusion I made. It was so tough. I remember I struggled so much. One day, I went for Bible Study and I could not move because the topic that day was homosexuality. I can't remember what they said because I was sweating throughout. I just sat down and leaned back. After that service I went up to the pastor and told her, "Please Pastor, we need to talk."

So we sat back and talked. I told her, "I want us to talk about what we were discussing today. First of all, I want to let you know that I am gay."

At that point, she cut me off and said, "Sorry. That must have been an uncomfortable situation for you; knowing that you are gay and the topic was being discussed. I don't know how sensitive we should have been, but we didn't know. So I am saying sorry, for any discomfort that you felt in there."

So I relaxed and she asked me, "What do you want?"

I told her, "I want to end this. I want to be a normal human being and I want to get involved in church. I don't want to pretend any more, I feel like I'm a sinner."

She said, "OK. I will bring in a youth leader who's a man and we will help you through this. I can't wait for that moment when you'll stand in front of everyone and say that you got over this habit."

After that I joined the praise and worship team, the drama team; everything. I went to church and got re-dedicated. I really believed that I could get over it, and that it was a habit. It didn't last, though.

In a Bible study class after that, one lady told us that her boyfriend was a member of a praise and worship team of a very big church in Nairobi. After conducting the service, the team would go to a house of one of the guys and watch porn. This lady said she couldn't take it. She broke up with the boyfriend and left that church.

Then in 2012, I met another lady who told me that their pastor sleeps around with small boys. Another group of friends showed me a pastor who has his own church and he's gay. I couldn't take it any more. I was convinced in my heart that there are more pretenders in the church than outside it. I had labelled myself a pretender. Every time I went to church and I looked around and thought to myself, "Wow. How many pretenders like me are here?"

I slowly moved from labelling myself a pretender to seeing that no one had any moral authority to judge me. I got to a comfortable position where I could define my own relationship with God. I pray, read the Bible, listen to sermons and sing praise and worship songs, but I'm not going back to church any time soon. I still have difficulty in that space, and I'm slowly building my spirituality again. I'm comfortable with myself and no one has THE MORAL AUTHORITY TO JUDGE ME.

–

SPIRITUALLY, I AM STILL STRUGGLING. I am a prayerful person, but I would say I am not prayerful in the manner in which a Christian or Muslim should be. My mum is from the Coast, and my Dad is from Western Kenya. At one time they were all Muslims. My father went back to Christianity and my mum remained a Muslim. I do my devotions, and I love fasting. I prefer the Christian way over the Muslim way.

Work can make you feel distant from God, so—for me—getting back to God calls for fasting. That is my personal choice. I also fast when I have a personal burden and feel that it is something I should pray about. My relation with God is like tithing; it is a passage rite. I don't go to church, but I MAKE UP FOR MY TIME AWAY FROM GOD.

–

I AM MUSLIM. I was not born a Muslim. I was brought up in a Catholic family. I converted to Islam when I came to Mombasa. Most gay people have not accepted any religion. I think it's because there is no faith that has accepted the gay community. Whenever there are attacks against gay people, the Muslims who are gay go into hiding. I don't think we are safe at all HERE IN MOMBASA.

–

I AM A CHRISTIAN, and I go to church. I believe that God exists, and I believe that no human being is perfect so I don't have to stop going to church just because people think I am imperfect. My relationship with God is good; and I always say, "Let God be my judge, not any human being."

I am actively involved in the church. I am actually in the choir and I also participate in the church plays. Many of the people at church don't know my lifestyle. I've never had a good reason to tell them about that part of me, and I also hesitate because of the experiences I have been through, losing friends and being talked about behind my back. If there is no reason to tell people, I've learned to remain silent and let them see me the way they see me. Maybe if there was a good enough reason to tell them, I would, but since we have a good relationship and they see me as just one of them—a church member—I prefer it to stay that way.

–

I WAS DEDICATED to the Lord as a child, and I grew up in the church. It was church every Sunday without fail. I was never given the chance to figure out what church and my relationship with God were supposed to be. I was just taken to church on a conveyor belt like a little soldier being manufactured for the army. You're put into the line, and you become. That's how we're raised.

And then you find out this thing about yourself, and you try to reconcile it with your faith. Organized religion brings a bad taste to my mouth, because they're so many bad things that come about from the church. The most cruel people are people who claim to be very religious. It got to a point where I started going to church not because I wanted to, but because in my mother's house you go to church. So every Sunday—to this day—I go to church.

But on most days I don't go *into* the church. I go outside and play pool with my cousins. I'm starting to have a lot of conversations with God by myself, because I feel like that's a more honest thing to do. I pray a lot more and I believe that there is someone listening to me, because little blessings have come to me now that

I'm more in tune with God. A lot of things have become a little easier.

I thank Him for the fact that I have a great family, I thank Him for the fact that I have seen love. I fell in love with someone, and that—for me—was good. It brought about many things that added blessings to my life, and that's all I can speak about.

I don't necessarily have to subscribe to the orthodox vision of what Christianity, salvation and faith are supposed to look like. I'd shoot myself if I were one of them. There's no room to question anything or anyone.

What bothers me most about Christians is this smugness about them; "We who have found the Lord are far better off than you who are out there and have not seen the glory."

You know? So I can't tell you to come to Jesus, I can only tell you about what He has done in my life. And maybe I am wrong, maybe I am believing in this person who looks down on me and doesn't see His child, He sees a sinner. Maybe when I die I'll go to hell, but all that is not for me to worry about. All I have to do is live my life properly and treat people in THE BEST WAY I CAN.

–

THE RELATIONSHIP between my sexuality and my spirituality doesn't bother me. I go to church every Sunday and Wednesday. When a car runs down, you take it to the garage. God made me, and He knows all the parts that I'm made of. When I go to church, I'm going to see my God so He can fix me and any problems I'm having. If anyone wants to gossip about me on the side, that's their problem. I don't know what they have come to do in church, I know I'VE COME TO SEE MY GOD.

–

ABOUT THE NEST COLLECTIVE:

We are a multidisciplinary arts collective living and working in Nairobi. Founded in 2012, the Nest Collective has created works in film, music, fashion, visual arts and literature such as the critically-acclaimed queer anthology film Stories of Our Lives based on the stories collected in this very book. The film has so far screened in over 80 countries and won numerous awards, regardless of a 2014 ban on its screening, sale and/or distribution in Kenya. The ban remains in effect to date.

We use an applied-research holistic methodology to create cultural bodies of work with film, fashion, literature and other media. These interventions are designed to engage audiences using multiple points of entry and reflection, thus enabling nuanced consideration, discussion and debate of the issues raised, while also advancing aesthetic and artistic value. Our work usually finds multiple platforms, spaces and audiences, including academia, other cultural practitioners, civil society, young people in urban spaces, and through numerous forms of media.

Our work—borne in Nairobi—makes strongest reference to African urban and contemporary experiences, establishing this as our primary datum for inquiry on our histories and reflections about possible futures. While our work often responds to and is aware of interconnected issues at a global scale, we primarily address Kenyan young men and women, and are excited when the work speaks to other audiences. Find out more about us and our work at WWW.THISISTHENEST.COM

www.ingramcontent.com/pod-product-compliance
Lightning Source LLC
Chambersburg PA
CBHW031143270326
41931CB00006B/130

* 9 7 8 0 9 9 6 7 0 4 8 5 4 *